1600+ Practice Questions for the GMAT®

ONLINE + BOOK

GMAT® is a registered trademark of the Graduate Management Admission Council, which neither sponsors nor endorses this product.

This publication is designed to provide accurate information in regard to the subject matter covered as of its publication date, with the understanding that knowledge and best practice constantly evolve. The publisher is not engaged in rendering medical, legal, accounting, or other professional service. If medical or legal advice or other expert assistance is required, the services of a competent professional should be sought. This publication is not intended for use in clinical practice or the delivery of medical care. To the fullest extent of the law, neither the Publisher nor the Editors assume any liability for any injury and/or damage to persons or property arising out of or related to any use of the material contained in this book.

Published by Kaplan Publishing, a division of Kaplan, Inc.
750 Third Avenue
New York, NY 10017

Printed in the United States of America

10 9 8 7 6 5 4 3 2 1

ISBN-13: 978-1-5062-0267-9

Kaplan Publishing print books are available at special quantity discounts to use for sales promotions, employee premiums, or educational purposes. For more information or to purchase books, please call the Simon & Schuster special sales department at 866-506-1949.

Table of Contents

Welcome

Congratulations on your decision to take the GMAT, and thank you for choosing Grockit for your GMAT preparation. With Grockit's online tools plus the practice in this book, you get the following resources:

- 1,600+ practice questions, with explanations for every answer
- 3 realistic full-length computer adaptive tests
- Grockit's study plan, which provides structure and support to ensure you cover all of the most important and most highly tested content on your exam. You'll get encouraging feedback and assessment on every area of the test throughout your preparation.
- Grockit's full suite of analytics, which allow you to understand the components of the GMAT that you're struggling with. You'll be able to review those questions until your weaknesses become your strengths.
- Grockit's data on your overall performance, plus insights on test timing, question difficulty, and concept frequency
- Grockit's advanced algorithm, which serves up practice targeted to your personal strike zone—questions that are not too hard, not too easy, but just right. The strike zone is where your optimal learning takes place.

To register for online access, go to grockit.tv/gmat1600.

The material in this book is up-to-date at the time of publication. However, changes in the tests or test registration process may have occurred after this book was published. Be sure to carefully read the materials you receive when you register for the test.

For the most up-to-date information about the exam, helpful tips, and more, please visit us online at **grockit.tv/home**.

Thanks for choosing Grockit, and best of luck with your studies.

Chapter 1

About the Test

About the Test

The GMAT is a standardized test that helps business schools assess the qualifications of aspiring business students. The GMAT is taken on computer at a private workstation, scheduled at your convenience in a test center near you. It's a computer-adaptive test (CAT), so you see only one question at a time. The computer selects questions of varying difficulty based on how well you are doing. You cannot skip a question, and you cannot move around within a section to check a previous answer.

The GMAT measures basic verbal, math, writing, and reasoning skills. It begins with the Analytical Writing Assessment (the AWA). You are required to complete an essay, typing it into the computer using a simple word processing program. You are given 30 minutes for this essay, during which you have to analyze the reasoning behind a given argument, explain its weaknesses or flaws, and recommend how to correct them to improve the argument. Your own personal views on the topic are not relevant.

After the AWA, you have a 30-minute section called Integrated Reasoning. This section has 12 questions, each of which may require more than one response. The questions in this section ask you to draw conclusions based on information in tables, interpret graphs, understand information presented across different layouts, and sometimes find two answers leading to a single solution.

Then you'll move on to the two 75-minute multiple-choice sections: Quantitative (Math) and Verbal. The Quantitative section—37 questions in all—contains two question types: Problem Solving and Data Sufficiency. The Verbal section, with 41 questions, has three question types: Reading Comprehension, Sentence Correction, and Critical Reasoning.

GMAT Exam Section	Questions	Time
Analytical Writing Assessment	1	30 min
Integrated Reasoning	12	30 min
Quantitative	37	75 min
Verbal	41	75 min
Total Testing Time		**3 hours, 30 minutes**

Order and Length of Sections on the GMAT

Some important things to note:

- After you complete the Integrated Reasoning section, you'll get an 8-minute break. Then, between the Quantitative and Verbal sections, you will get another 8-minute break.
- There are a few "experimental" questions scattered throughout the test. They look just like the other multiple-choice questions but won't contribute to your score.

We'll talk more about each of the question types in later chapters. For now, note the following: You'll be answering 90 multiple-choice questions in 3 hours. On average, that's 2 minutes per question, not counting the time it takes to answer multiple parts of Integrated Reasoning questions or to read the Reading Comprehension passages. Clearly, you'll have to move fast. But you can't let yourself get careless. Taking control of the GMAT means increasing the speed of your work without sacrificing accuracy.

Overall scaled scores, which are based on the Quantitative and Verbal sections, range from 200 to 800. Because the test is graded on a preset curve, the scaled score will correspond to a certain percentile. The percentile helps business school admissions officers to see where you fall in a large pool of applicants.

THE GMAT CAT EXPLAINED

The GMAT "adapts" to your performance. This means that the questions get harder or easier depending on whether you answer them correctly or not. Your score is not directly determined by how many questions you get right, but by how hard the questions you get right are.

A few basic rules make the adaptive format possible.

- You're presented with one question at a time, and you must answer it to move on to the next question.
- You can't return to previously answered questions within a section.
- You can't skip questions—or rather, the only questions that can be skipped or omitted are any questions at the end of a section that you leave unanswered.
- Within a section (Quantitative or Verbal), the questions are not grouped by topic or type. You don't, for example, finish Reading Comprehension and then move on to Sentence Correction and then to Critical Reasoning; those three question types are interspersed with one another throughout the section.

After a while, you will reach a level where most of the questions will seem difficult to you. At this point you will get roughly as many questions right as you get wrong. This is your scoring level. The computer uses your scoring level in calculating your scaled score.

GMAT SCORING

The most important score on the GMAT is the total score, which ranges from 200 to 800. This score is the GMAT result that schools look at primarily. The population of these scores follows a standard distribution: Most students score near the mean score, and more than half of all GMAT test takers score within 100 points of 560, the median score. Pulling yourself out of that cluster is an important part of distinguishing your application: The top 10 business schools accept students with an average GMAT score of 718, at almost the 94th percentile.

Percentile	Score
99%	760-800
94%	720
90%	700
78%	650
69%	620
50%	560

Some GMAT Percentiles vs. Total Scores

The total score is calculated from "scaled scores" from the Quantitative section and Verbal section. While the scaled scores haven't changed over time, the population of test takers has. Quant performance has gone up over time, and Verbal performance has gone down. While Verbal section scores still follow a fairly even distribution, Quantitative scaled scores now skew high. Schools view your percentile performance (which is the same thing as a "percent ranking") overall and on each section of the GMAT.

Quantitative		Verbal	
Percentile	**Score**	**Percentile**	**Score**
98%	51-60	99%	45-51
90%	50	97%	44
83%	49	96%	42-43
78%	48	93%	41
73%	47	90%	40
71%	46	88%	39
68%	45	84%	38
63%	44	81%	37
61%	43	79%	36

Some Percentiles vs. Scaled Scores for the Quantitative and Verbal Sections

Your overall score is about balanced performance on the two sections. Generally, you will not win on the GMAT by nailing one section and hoping your performance will overcome a deficit on the other. Since Quant and Verbal percentiles aren't obvious from the overall score, admission officers often look at them specifically.

The overall score of 200 to 800 is the most important score, since it's a balanced measure of absolute and relative performance. Next come percentiles, which admission officers often look at. The Integrated Reasoning section has its own scoring scale, independent from the 200 to 800 scale. You'll receive a score from 1 through 8, in whole-point increments.

The Analytical Writing Assessment (AWA) is scored separately from the rest of the GMAT. Unlike the total and scaled scores, AWA scores aren't available on Test Day. When you do get your score, it will take the form of a number from 1 to 6 in increments of 0.5.

Within 20 days after your test date, your official score report will be available online. Your report also includes the results of all the GMAT exams you've taken in the previous five years, including cancellations. In 2014, the testmakers added the option for students to be able to preview their unofficial scores before deciding whether to report or cancel them.

GMAT Study Tips

CREATE A STUDY PLAN

Take time to familiarize yourself with the key components of your book and online study materials. Think about how many hours you can consistently devote to GMAT study. We have found that, on average, students spend about three months preparing for the GMAT. Schedule time for study, practice, and review. One of the most frequent mistakes in approaching study is to answer questions without reviewing them thoroughly—review time is your best chance to gain points. It works best for many people to block out short, frequent periods of study time throughout the week. Check in with yourself frequently to make sure you're not falling behind your plan or forgetting about any of your resources.

LEARN AND PRACTICE

This workbook and its online practice provide many opportunities to raise your score and learn the skills you'll need on Test Day. Depending on how much time you have to study, you can approach the book chapter by chapter, or you can choose to focus your study on those question types and content areas that are most challenging for you. You will inevitably need more work in some areas than in others, but know that the more thoroughly you prepare, the better your score will be. Online quizzes give you additional test-like questions so you can put into practice the skills you are learning. Review the explanations closely.

TAKE CONTROL OF THE TEST

In addition to learning test content, you must also devote time to building the right mentality and attitude that will help you succeed on Test Day. Take time to understand and incorporate these basic principles of good test mentality:

- Be aware of the test and keep your composure even when you are struggling with a difficult question; missing one question won't ruin your score for a section.
- Build your stamina by taking as many practice tests as you can.
- Be confident; you are already well on your way to a great score!
- Stay positive; consider the GMAT an opportunity rather than an obstacle.

Chapter 2

Quantitative

Section Overview

COMPOSITION OF THE QUANTITATIVE SECTION

Slightly fewer than half of the multiple-choice questions that count toward your overall score appear in the Quantitative (math) section. You'll have 75 minutes to answer 37 Quantitative questions in two formats: Problem Solving and Data Sufficiency. These two types of questions are mingled throughout the Quantitative section, so you never know what's coming next. Here's what you can expect to see:

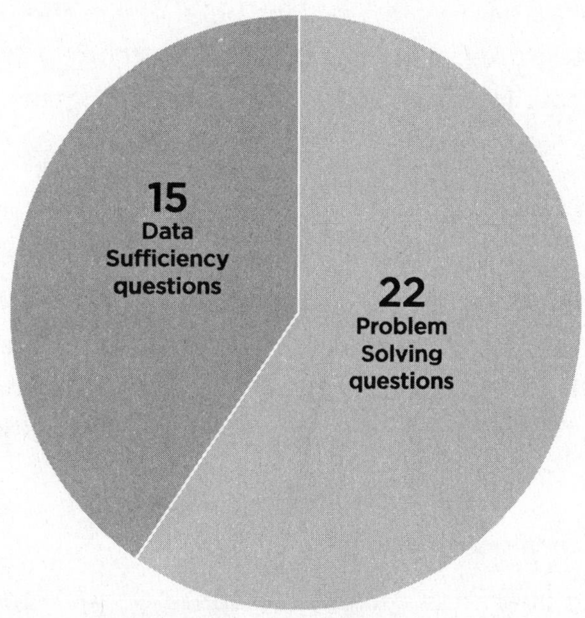

The Approximate Mix of Questions on the GMAT Quantitative Section: 22 Problem Solving Questions and 15 Data Sufficiency Questions

You may see more of one question type and fewer of the other. Don't worry. It's likely just a slight difference in the types of "experimental" questions you get.

WHAT THE QUANTITATIVE SECTION TESTS

Math Content Knowledge

The GMAT tests your basic math skills. You will have to work with concepts that you may not have used for the last few years. Even if you use math all the time, it's probably been a while since you were unable to use a calculator or computer to perform computations. Refreshing your fundamental math skills is definitely a crucial part of your prep.

The range of math topics tested on the GMAT, though, is fairly limited. As you progress in your GMAT prep, you'll see that the same concepts are tested again and again in remarkably similar ways. Areas of math content tested on the GMAT include the following: algebra, arithmetic, number properties, proportions, basic statistics, certain math formulas, and geometry. Algebra and arithmetic are the most commonly tested topics—they are tested either directly or indirectly on a majority of GMAT Quantitative questions. Geometry questions account for fewer than one-sixth of all GMAT math questions, but they can often be among the most challenging for test takers. You may benefit from thorough review and practice with these concepts. Note that you will not see trigonometry, advanced algebra, or calculus.

A large part of what makes the GMAT Quantitative section so challenging, however, is not the math content but rather how the testmakers combine the different areas of math to make questions more challenging. Very few questions test a single concept. More commonly, you will be asked to integrate multiple skills to solve a question. For instance, a question that asks you about triangles could also require you to solve a formula algebraically and apply your understanding of ratios to find the correct answer.

Pacing on the Quantitative Section

The best way to attack the computer-adaptive GMAT is to exploit the way it determines your score. Here's what you're dealing with:

- Penalties: If you run out of time at the end of the section, you receive a penalty that's about twice what you'd have received if you got all those answers wrong. And there's an extra penalty for long strings of wrong answers at the end.
- No review: There is no going back to check your work. You cannot move backward to double-check your earlier answers or skip past a question that's puzzling and return to try it again later. So if you finish early, you won't be able to use that remaining time.
- Difficulty level adjustment: Questions get harder or easier, depending on your performance.

Difficult questions raise your score more when you get them right and hurt your score less when you get them wrong. Easier questions are the opposite—getting them right helps your score less, and getting them wrong hurts your score more.

Obviously, the best of both worlds is being able to get the early questions mostly right, while taking less than two minutes per question on average so that you have a little extra time to think about those harder questions later on. To achieve that goal, you need to do three things:

1. **Know your math basics cold.** Don't waste valuable time on Test Day sweating over how to add fractions, reverse-FOIL quadratic equations, or use the rate formula. When you do math, you want to feel right at home.
2. **Look for strategic approaches.** Most GMAT problems are susceptible to multiple possible approaches. So the testmakers deliberately build in shortcuts to reward critical thinkers by allowing them to move quickly through the question, leaving them with extra time. We'll show you how to find these most efficient approaches.
3. **Practice, practice, practice.** Do lots of practice problems so that you get as familiar as possible with the GMAT's most common analytical puzzles. That way you can handle them quickly (and correctly!) when you see them on Test Day. We've got tons in the upcoming chapters.

Problem Solving

PREVIEWING PROBLEM SOLVING

On the GMAT, Problem Solving questions test math skills and an understanding of mathematical concepts from algebra, arithmetic, and geometry. Most importantly, the GMAT tests the ability to reason quantitatively. All GMAT Quantitative questions depend at least as much on logic as on math. Even if you know how to do the math, reading too quickly or jumping into the algebra without really understanding the question can lead you to the incorrect answer.

The most advanced questions rarely involve math that is much more difficult than the math used in lower-difficulty questions. Rather, the task of analyzing the problem to figure out what math to use becomes harder.

QUESTION FORMAT AND STRUCTURE

The instructions for the Problem Solving questions look like this:

> **Directions:** Solve the problems and choose the best answer.
>
> Note: Unless otherwise indicated, the figures accompanying questions have been drawn as accurately as possible and may be used as sources of information for answering the questions.
>
> All figures lie in a plane except where noted.
>
> All numbers used are real numbers.

There are about 22 Problem Solving questions on each GMAT Quantitative section. The format of the questions is simple enough: Each Problem Solving question consists of the question stem—which gives you information and defines your task—and five answer choices. To answer a question, select the choice that correctly answers the question.

The directions indicate that some diagrams on the GMAT are drawn to scale, which means that you can use them to estimate measurements and size relationships. Other diagrams are labeled "Not drawn to scale," so you can't eyeball them. In fact, when a diagram says "Not drawn to scale," working past the confusing picture is often the key to the problem.

The directions also let you know that you won't have to deal with imaginary numbers, such as $\sqrt{-1}$, and that you'll be dealing with flat figures, such as squares and circles, unless a particular question says otherwise.

Problem Solving Practice

1. All of the following could be the value of $\frac{1}{3-x}$ EXCEPT:
   - o -3
   - o 0
   - o $\frac{1}{3}$
   - o 3
   - o 5

2. Which of the following equals $\left(\frac{3}{10}\right)^4$?
   - o 0.3
   - o 0.09
   - o 0.075
   - o 0.027
   - o 0.0081

3. $$\frac{\frac{8}{1}}{6} + \frac{\frac{6}{1}}{8} =$$
   - o $\frac{12}{25}$
   - o $\frac{25}{12}$
   - o 48
   - o 96
   - o 100

4. A team is selling candy bars in order to raise money for new team uniforms. The team has a total of 120 candy bars. After one week, 75% of the bars are sold. The players then eat 40% of the remaining bars. How many candy bars are left?
   - o 6
   - o 12
   - o 18
   - o 30
   - o 90

5. A billboard measures $11\frac{1}{2}$ feet × 7 feet. If the billboard has ads covering both its sides in their entirety, what is the combined area, in square feet, of its current advertisements?
   - o 20
   - o 38.5
   - o 80.5
   - o 154
   - o 161

6. 180 is what percent of 60?
   - o 3
   - o $33\frac{1}{3}$
   - o 66
   - o 300
   - o 333

7. The ratio of 3 to $\frac{1}{4}$ is equal to the ratio of
   - o 12 to 1
   - o 7 to 1
   - o 4 to 3
   - o 3 to 4
   - o 1 to 12

8. Jack and his brother are sharing a monster piece of licorice that is 28 inches long. Since Jack is older, he's decided that his share will be 8 inches longer than his brother's. How long, in inches, is Jack's brother's piece?
   - o 8
   - o 10
   - o 13
   - o 18
   - o 20

9. Roger can eat 12 hot dogs in one minute. At this rate, how many will Roger eat in one full day if he does not fall asleep, get sick, or rest?
   - o 720
   - o 1,532
   - o 17,280
   - o 43,200
   - o 1,036,800

10. How long (in hours) will it take Steve to run *m* miles if he runs at a constant speed of *x* miles per hour?
   - o $\frac{x}{m}$
   - o $\frac{m}{x}$
   - o xm
   - o $\frac{60m}{x}$
   - o $\frac{x}{60m}$

11. Derek can read *x* pages in 5 minutes. At this rate, how long will it take him to read *p* pages?
   - o $\frac{5p}{x}$
   - o $\frac{5x}{p}$
   - o $\frac{p}{5x}$
   - o $\frac{5}{px}$
   - o $\frac{px}{5}$

12. What percent of 90 is 18?
   - o 5
   - o 16.2
   - o 20
   - o 50
   - o 500

13. Stephanie's dog gave birth to a litter of purebred chocolate and black Labrador retriever puppies. There were 3 more chocolate puppies than black ones. If there were a total of 11 puppies in the litter, how many were chocolate?

- o 3
- o 4
- o 5
- o 6
- o 7

14. At least $\frac{3}{4}$ of the soccer team's 17 members must be in good academic standing for the school to keep the team's funding. What is the greatest number of players who could be in poor academic standing while the team still has funding?

- o 13
- o 5
- o 4
- o 3
- o 2

15. If $3x > 12$ and $x - 5 < 8$, the value of x must be between

- o 3 and 4
- o 3 and 9
- o 4 and 13
- o 8 and 12
- o 13 and 36

16. The total rainfall recorded at 8 different cities in one day was 23 inches, 16 inches, 10 inches, 12 inches, 33 inches, 15 inches, 18 inches, and 23 inches. What is the median rainfall of these totals?

- o 16
- o 17
- o 18
- o 18.75
- o 23

17. How many integers n exist that satisfy the equation $11 < 3n - 1 < 17$?

- o One
- o Three
- o Five
- o Seven
- o Fourteen

18. $$(\sqrt{5} + \sqrt{5} + \sqrt{5})^2 =$$

- o 15,625
- o 45
- o $9\sqrt{5}$
- o 15
- o $3\sqrt{5}$

19. If 1 hectare equals approximately 2.5 acres, about how many hectares equal 8 acres?

- 5
- $\frac{16}{5}$
- $\frac{5}{8}$
- $\frac{5}{16}$
- $\frac{1}{5}$

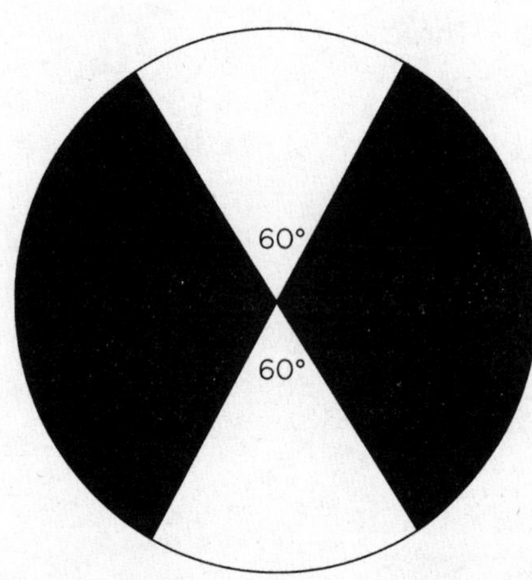

20. What fraction of the circle is shaded?

- $\frac{1}{12}$
- $\frac{3}{12}$
- $\frac{2}{3}$
- $\frac{1}{3}$
- $\frac{1}{6}$

21. Which of the following is closest to the following expression?

$$\frac{40.3 \times 0.38}{98.7}$$

- $\frac{1}{9}$
- $\frac{4}{25}$
- $\frac{2}{5}$
- $\frac{8}{25}$
- $\frac{8}{5}$

22. A display case contains x sections. Each section contains b bracelets, and each bracelet contains 12 diamonds. If no other jewelry in the case contains diamonds, how many diamonds are there in 4 display cases?

- $12bx$
- $\frac{12b}{x}$
- $48bx$
- $\frac{48b}{x}$
- $\frac{48b}{bx}$

23. If $30 < x < 40$, what is the sum of all prime values of x?

- 31
- 37
- 68
- 101
- 107

24. All of the following could be the sum of two prime numbers EXCEPT:

- o 7
- o 11
- o 18
- o 22
- o 30

25. A positive whole number has factors of 4 and 6. The number must be divisible by

I. 12
II. 24
III. 48

- o None
- o I only
- o II only
- o II and III only
- o I, II, and III

26. $\frac{43^2 + 43}{43} =$

- o 1,892
- o 1,849
- o 86
- o 44
- o 43

27. If $c = 4x + 5$ and $r = 21 - 2x$, then for what value of x does $c = r$?

- o $\frac{3}{8}$
- o $\frac{8}{3}$
- o $\frac{13}{8}$
- o 8
- o 13

28. $0.4 \times (0.4)^2 =$

- o 0.0256
- o 0.064
- o 0.16
- o 0.256
- o 0.64

29. $\sqrt{(12)(21) - (10)(18)} =$

- o $6\sqrt{7}$
- o $6\sqrt{2}$
- o $5\sqrt{3}$
- o $6\sqrt{7} - 6\sqrt{5}$
- o 36

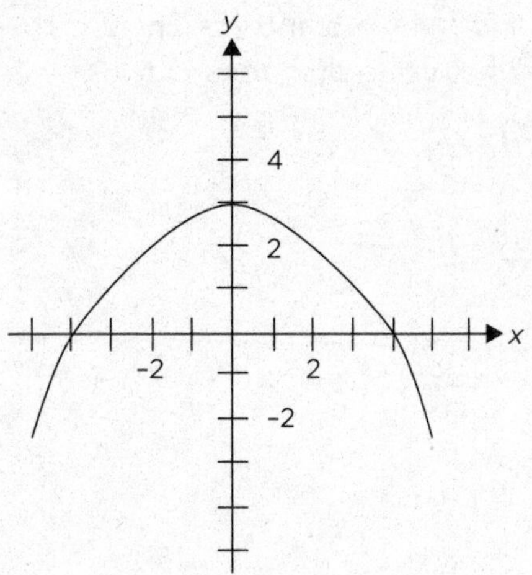

30. The graph shown is symmetrical with respect to the y-axis. When $x = 0$, $y = 3$, and when $x = -4$, $y = 0$. According to the graph, what is the value of y when $x = 4$?

   - O -1
   - O 1
   - O 0
   - O 2
   - O 3

31. When $\frac{1}{5}$ percent of 2,000 is subtracted from $\frac{1}{5}$ of 2,000, the result is

   - O 0
   - O 4
   - O 360
   - O 396
   - O 400

32. The city of Boston decided to reconstruct its major tunnels. It estimated the job would require 612 mini projects spread evenly over an 18-month plan of completion. Only 108 mini projects had been successfully completed after 6 months. At this time, the construction was behind schedule by how many projects?

   - O 34
   - O 96
   - O 198
   - O 204
   - O 504

33. $0.4 + (0.4)^2 + (0.4)^3 =$

   - O 0.48
   - O 0.624
   - O 0.64
   - O 0.84
   - O 1.2

34. Which of the following is the least positive integer that has factors of 1 through 8, inclusive?

   - O 210
   - O 420
   - O 840
   - O 2,520
   - O 10,160

35. If $\frac{11.2}{0.4+x} = 8$, then what is the value of x?

   - O -2.8
   - O 1
   - O 1.8
   - O 10.88
   - O 35

36. Last month, Jake's credit card balance increased from \$5,005 to \$5,775. At the end of the month, Jake's balance represented 77% of his credit card limit. What was the difference between Jake's limit and his balance at the beginning of the month?

- O \$725
- O \$1,495
- O \$1,725
- O \$2,495
- O \$7,500

37. Apartments on the first floor of a building are labeled 2 through 56 consecutively. What is the probability that a tenant living there will have an apartment with a tens digit of 3?

- O $\frac{9}{55}$
- O $\frac{2}{11}$
- O $\frac{5}{27}$
- O 10
- O 55

38. Three plows working at identical constant rates can clear 123 feet of snow per minute. At this rate, how much snow could 8 plows remove in 5 minutes?

- O 328
- O 984
- O 1,640
- O 16,400
- O 131,200

39. Rachel has 12 pairs of shoes. If 9 shoes are taken away, what is the greatest number of complete pairs she can have left?

- O 15
- O 9
- O 7
- O 5
- O 3

40. If one value of x in the equation $x^2 + 6x + y = 21$ (where y is a constant) is 3, what is the other value of x?

- O -9
- O -6
- O -3
- O 6
- O 9

41. Two sides of a triangle measure 2 and 9. Which of the following could be the value of its third side?

I. 7
II. 8.5
III. 11

- O II only
- O III only
- O I and II only
- O II and III only
- O I, II, and III

42. Danny went on a shopping spree. He bought h hats and x shirts. The number of shirts he bought was 15 greater than the number of hats. Which of the following expresses this relationship?

- O $h > 15x$
- O $h > x + 15$
- O $h > x - 15$
- O $h = x - 15$
- O $h = x + 15$

43. Sally writes her brother a check for $55, which represents her repayment of 20% of an earlier loan. If this is Sally's first payment on the loan, and if her brother charges her no interest, how much does she still owe him?

- O $11
- O $44
- O $220
- O $275
- O $1,100

44. After the last snowstorm, Kelly and Amanda shoveled their driveway together. If Amanda shoveled 65% of the driveway and Kelly shoveled the rest, what is the ratio of the amount of driveway Kelly shoveled to the amount Amanda shoveled?

- O 1 to 3
- O 7 to 20
- O 1 to 2
- O 7 to 13
- O 13 to 20

45. A circle is divided into four sections. If three sections constitute $\frac{1}{4}$, $\frac{2}{5}$, and $\frac{3}{10}$ of its total area, respectively, what is the fractional value of the area of the fourth section?

- O $\frac{19}{20}$
- O $\frac{16}{19}$
- O $\frac{9}{20}$
- O $\frac{1}{10}$
- O $\frac{1}{20}$

46. The average of 6, 15, and 45 is 4 less than the average of 8, 33, and

- O 25
- O 26
- O 29
- O 37
- O 41

47. Which of the following is NOT equal to an integer squared?

- O $\sqrt{16}$
- O $\sqrt{9}$
- O $\frac{27}{3}$
- O $37 - 12$
- O 49

48. If $xy = 8d^2$ and $5d = 15$, what is the value of dxy?

- 3
- 24
- 72
- 144
- 216

49. During a 24-hour day, Ron devotes all of his time to three activities: sleep, work, and leisure. The ratio of hours spent on these activities is 3:2:1, respectively. During this day, how many hours does Ron spend working?

- 12
- 10
- 8
- 6
- 4

50. A football field is 9,600 square yards. If 1,200 pounds of fertilizer are spread evenly across the entire field, how many pounds of fertilizer were spread over an area of the field totaling 3,600 square yards?

- 450
- 600
- 750
- 2,400
- 3,200

A B C D E

-3 -2 -1 0 1 2 3

51. If the figure provided is drawn to scale, which of the following points on the number line has the greatest absolute value?

- Point A
- Point B
- Point C
- Point D
- Point E

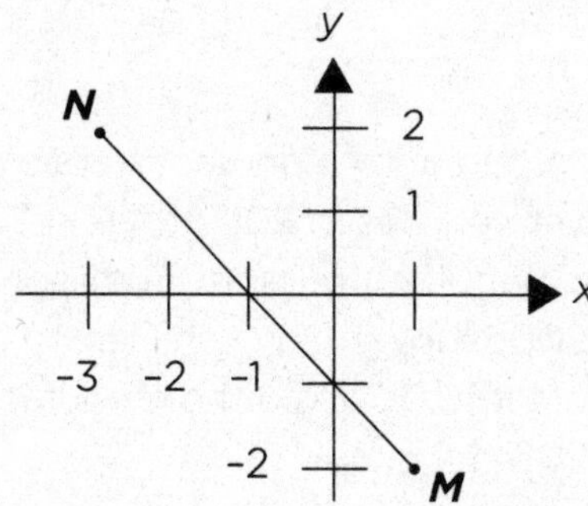

52. In the figure, the point on segment NM that is three times as far from N as it is from M is

- (-2, 1)
- (-2.5, 1.5)
- (-1, 0)
- (-0.5, -0.5)
- (0, -1)

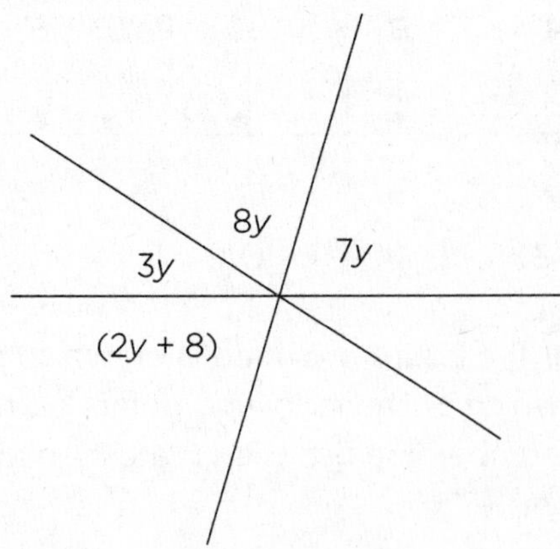

53. What is the value of y in the figure?
   - 10
   - 30
   - 31
   - 62
   - 70

54. A certain auto manufacturer sold 3% fewer vehicles in 2007 than in 2006. If the manufacturer sold 2.1 million vehicles in 2006, how many vehicles, to the nearest 10,000, did the manufacturer sell in 2007?
   - 63,000
   - 2,000,000
   - 2,030,000
   - 2,040,000
   - 2,300,000

55. X is the set of odd positive integers between 2 and 20. Y is the set of prime numbers in set X. How many numbers does set Y contain?
   - None
   - Two
   - Three
   - Five
   - Seven

56. The ratio of $2 + \sqrt{6}$ to 3 is approximately equal to which of the following ratios?
   - 2 to 1
   - 3 to 2
   - 4 to 3
   - 7 to 6
   - 13 to 12

57. A clothing store's total opening-year sales were $50,000. The total sales increased by 20% in the second year, increased by 10% in the third year, and decreased by 5% in the fourth year. What was the total amount of the store's sales (in whole dollars) in year 4?
   - $19,300
   - $62,500
   - $62,700
   - $67,500
   - $69,300

58. Mr. Jones divides his math class into equal groups of 6 or 8 depending on the day's activity. What is the least possible number of students in the class?
   - 2
   - 12
   - 14
   - 24
   - 48

59. If an investment is sold 4 months after its date of purchase, the percentage of its yield (y) can be found by using the following formula:

$$y = 300\left(\frac{D + S - P}{P}\right)$$

where P is the original purchase price of the investment, D is the 4-month dividend received, and S is the investment's selling price. If an investment is bought at a price of $550 with a dividend of $10 and is sold after 4 months for $650, what is its percent yield?

- O 0.2%
- O 15%
- O 20%
- O 30%
- O 60%

$$\begin{array}{r} p\ 3\ 6 \\ 5\ 2\ 7 \\ +\ 1\ q\ 8 \\ \hline 9\ 1\ 1 \end{array}$$

60. If p and q represent nonzero single-digit values in the correctly worked addition problem above, what is the value of $q + p$?

- O 2
- O 4
- O 6
- O 8
- O 20

61. Jacob rolls two normal playing dice. What is the probability that the product of their faces will be 6?

- O $\frac{1}{81}$
- O $\frac{1}{18}$
- O $\frac{1}{9}$
- O $\frac{5}{36}$
- O $\frac{4}{3}$

62. What value of x would yield the greatest value of the expression $381 - 231x$?

- O 250
- O 150
- O $\frac{1}{4}$
- O 0
- O -2

63. Michael can paint a spoon at a rate of 15 spoons every 3 minutes. Erika can paint at a rate of 8 spoons every 2 minutes. If the two paint simultaneously, how many minutes will it take them to paint 297 spoons?

- O 29.7
- O 33
- O 37.125
- O 59.4
- O 74.25

64. An airline charges customers 30% more than the base price for nonstop service. Frequent flyers receive a 15% discount on the total price every time they fly. If a frequent flyer books a nonstop flight with a base price of $420, how much will the ticket cost?

- $338.10
- $357.00
- $464.10
- $546.00
- $627.90

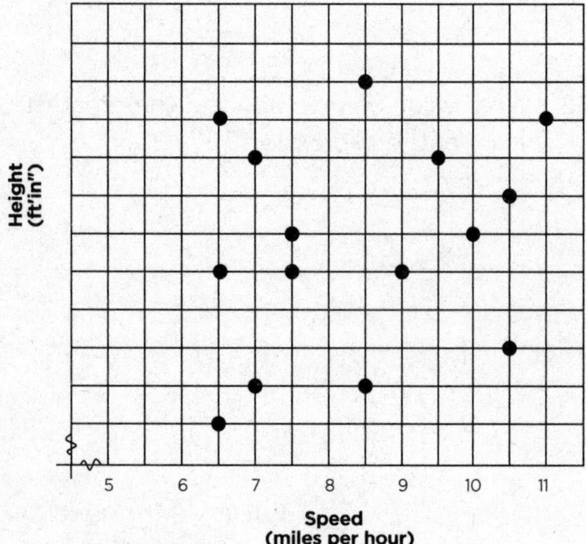

65. The points on the graph above represent the heights and average speeds of 15 male distance runners. How many of the runners are taller than 6 feet and run faster than 7 miles per hour?

- 3
- 6
- 9
- 12
- 14

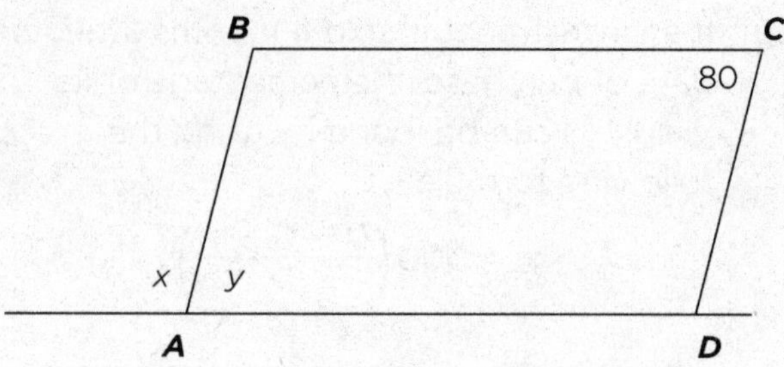

66. Which of the following is true of the parallelogram *ABCD* in the diagram?

- $4x = 5y$
- $5x = 4y$
- $y > x$
- $x = y$
- $y > 180$

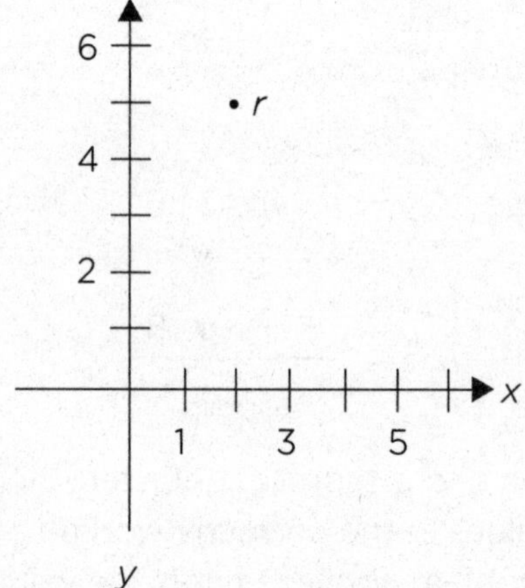

67. What are the coordinates of point *r* in the figure?

- (-2, 5)
- (-5, 2)
- (2, 5)
- (5, 2)
- (2, -5)

68. $$\frac{84 - 6\left(\frac{15}{5}\right)}{\frac{1}{3}} =$$

- O 22
- O 66
- O 134
- O 198
- O 702

69. A jet flies a distance of *m* miles in *x* minutes. At this rate, how far does it travel in *h* hours?

- O $\frac{m}{(hx)}$
- O $\frac{(mh)}{x}$
- O $\frac{(60m)}{hx}$
- O $\frac{(60mx)}{h}$
- O $\frac{(60mh)}{x}$

70. $$\frac{9.009}{3.003} =$$

- O 0.003
- O 0.03
- O 0.3
- O 3
- O 30

71. $$\frac{3}{3 + \frac{3}{4 + \frac{1}{2}}}$$

- O $\frac{2}{11}$
- O $\frac{9}{11}$
- O $\frac{8}{3}$
- O $\frac{11}{9}$
- O $\frac{11}{2}$

72. What is the greatest integer that is the sum of three different prime numbers that are less than 20?

- O 83
- O 54
- O 49
- O 41
- O 31

73. If the average of 7, 8, 11, and 14 is equal to the average of 3, 5, 15, and *x*, what is the value of *x*?

- O 11
- O 13
- O 14
- O 16
- O 17

74. In an increasing set of seven consecutive integers, the sum of the last four integers is 34. What is the sum of the first three integers in the set?

- 120
- 36
- 18
- 15
- 12

75. $\frac{1}{4} + \left[\left(\frac{2}{5} \times \frac{3}{2}\right) \div 2\right] - \frac{11}{20} =$

- $-\frac{71}{200}$
- $\frac{1}{4}$
- $\frac{11}{10}$
- $\frac{7}{5}$

76. A powder consists of nothing but sodium and potassium. If the ratio, by weight, of sodium to potassium is 3:9, how many grams of sodium are there in 288 grams of this powder?

- 72
- 96
- 144
- 192
- 216

77. Jesse and his sister Joanie work at a bakery. Jesse can package the entire day's product in 3 hours. Joanie can do it in 5 hours. If the two work together while maintaining their respective constant rates, how many hours will it take them to package the day's products?

- $\frac{8}{15}$
- $1\frac{1}{4}$
- $1\frac{7}{8}$
- 2
- 4

78. Jake's computer downloads songs at a rate of 80 songs every 2 minutes. Jane's computer downloads at half the rate of Jake's. If each computer downloads at a nonstop, constant rate, how many songs will Jane's computer download in 8 minutes?

- 640
- 320
- 160
- 80
- 40

79. A diner adds a tip of 20% to his dinner bill. If he pays a total of $90 for the bill and tip, how much less would he have paid if he had tipped 15% instead of 20%?

- $3.75
- $4.50
- $5.00
- $11.25
- $13.50

80. A worker can load one full truck in 6 hours. A second worker can load the same truck in 7 hours. If both workers load one truck simultaneously while maintaining their constant rates, approximately how long, in hours, will it take them to fill one truck?

- O 0.15
- O 0.31
- O 2.47
- O 3.23
- O 3.25

81. The data for one clinical trial of an experiment are 5, 6, 8, 13. The data for the second clinical trial of the same experiment are identical to the first set except for one additional unknown value. If the medians of both the sets are equal, what must be the value of the unknown result?

- O 5
- O 6
- O 7
- O 8
- O 9

82. A taxi driver earns a base pay of $250 a week plus 8% of the total amount of fares that exceeds $600. If the driver earns $570 in one week, what is the total amount of her combined fares for that week?

- O $4,000
- O $4,600
- O $5,125
- O $5,550
- O $7,125

83. If x and y are integers such that $x + y = 14$, which of the following could be their product?

- O -72
- O -40
- O 9
- O 21
- O 32

84. If $x < 1$, which of the following could be the value of x?

- O $3\frac{9}{25}$
- O $\frac{3}{\sqrt{3}}$
- O $1\frac{1}{4}$
- O $\frac{\sqrt{19}}{4}$
- O $\left(\frac{7}{8}\right)^2$

85. There are 12 coworkers who work on projects in teams each month. Each team is composed of 3 people, and every team is together only once before the rotation begins again. How many unique teams can be created?

- O 4
- O 12
- O 220
- O 660
- O 1,320

86. If $\frac{2x}{x+1} = x - 1$, what is the value of $x^2 - 2x - 1$?

- -1
- 0
- 1
- 2
- 3

87. An elevator at a construction site has a weight capacity of 1,720 pounds. If each worker at the site weighs at least 200 pounds, what is the maximum number of workers the elevator can hold at one time?

- 5
- 7
- 8
- 9
- 11

88. Coffee House sells beans only by the one-pound bag, and each bag contains beans from a single country. Before an open house, 65% of the bags in stock contained South American coffee. The rest of the bags contained coffee from other sources. During the open house, Coffee House served 60% of its South American coffee and 40% of the rest. What percent of its total coffee did it serve at the open house?

- 50%
- 52%
- 53%
- 54%
- 56%

89. If $x(3x + 1) = 0$ and $(4x + 1)(x + \frac{1}{3}) = 0$, what is the value of x?

- $-\frac{1}{3}$
- $-\frac{1}{4}$
- 0
- $\frac{1}{4}$
- $\frac{1}{3}$

90. On the Richter scale, which measures the total amount of energy released during an earthquake, a reading of $x - 1$ indicates one-tenth the released energy as is indicated by a reading of x. On that scale, the released energy corresponding to a reading of 9 is how many times as great as the frequency corresponding to a reading of 5?

- 40
- 50
- 10^4
- 10^5
- $10^9 - 10^5$

91. What is the greatest integer x for which $3^8 > 9^x$?

- 2
- 3
- 4
- 6
- 8

92. If x and y are positive prime numbers such that x does not equal y and the product of xy is not even, which of the following CANNOT be true?

I. $x + y = 85$.
II. $x - y$ is an even integer.
III. $\frac{x}{y}$ is an integer.

- O II only
- O I and II only
- O I and III only
- O II and III only
- O I, II, and III

93. All of the following have the same value EXCEPT:

- O $\frac{11 + 13 + 8}{4}$
- O $\frac{1}{2}(4, +, 4, +, 4, +, 4)$
- O $\frac{1}{8}+\frac{1}{8}+\frac{1}{8}+\frac{1}{8}+\frac{1}{8}+\frac{1}{8}+\frac{1}{8}+\frac{1}{8}$
- O $\frac{6}{1.5}\left(\frac{1}{2}, +, \frac{1}{2}, +, \frac{1}{2}, +, \frac{1}{2}\right)$
- O $\frac{1}{2}+\frac{8}{4}+\frac{4}{8}+\frac{48}{16}+\frac{64}{32}$

94. Certain flowers sell for $4 each when purchased separately. If a bouquet of six such flowers sells for $27, the bouquet is what percent more expensive than six individual flowers?

- O 3
- O 11.1
- O 12.5
- O 25
- O 88.9

95. If x and y are negative integers, which answer choice must be less than 0?

- O $\sqrt{\frac{x}{y}}$
- O $\frac{x^2}{y^2}$
- O $2xy$
- O $\frac{x}{y}$
- O $\frac{x}{y^2}$

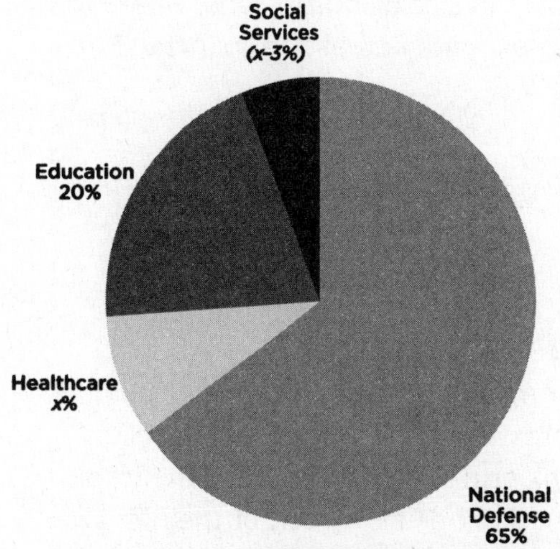

Government X's 2006 Spending

96. According to the graph, what percent of Government X's 2006 spending went toward social services?

- O 3%
- O 6%
- O 9%
- O 12%
- O 15%

97. A donut shop sells three types of donuts. If sales of donut A are 25% higher than sales of donut B, and sales of donut C are 45% lower than sales of donut B, approximately what percent of donut A's sales are donut C's sales?

- O 223%
- O 65%
- O 55%
- O 44%
- O 20%

98. The ratio of magnification of a certain lens is 9.1 to 3. If a magnified image is 36 inches in size using this lens, what is its approximate actual size, in inches?

- O 6
- O 10
- O 12
- O 14
- O 48

99. For a certain six-month period, a cookie factory sold an average of 80,000 cookies per month. The company sold 70,000 cookies in each of the first two months of that period, and 60,000 cookies in each of the next two months of that period. What was the company's average cookie sales per month for the final two months of the period?

- O 30,000
- O 70,000
- O 90,000
- O 110,000
- O 220,000

100. Allyn has t tattoos, which is half as many as Krystal and 4 times as many as Joshua. How many tattoos do the 3 of them have together?

- O t
- O $\frac{5t}{2}$
- O $\frac{11t}{2}$
- O $\frac{13t}{4}$
- O $\frac{15t}{4}$

101. A tour group of 25 people paid a total of $630 for entrance to a museum. If this price included a 5% sales tax and all the tickets cost the same amount, what was the face value of each ticket price without the sales tax?

- O $22.00
- O $23.94
- O $24.00
- O $25.20
- O $30.00

102. If it takes a tub 3 minutes to drain $\frac{5}{7}$ of its content, how much more time will it take for the tub to be empty?

- O 48 seconds
- O 1 minute, 12 seconds
- O 1 minute, 50 seconds
- O 2 minutes, 14 seconds
- O 4 minutes, 12 seconds

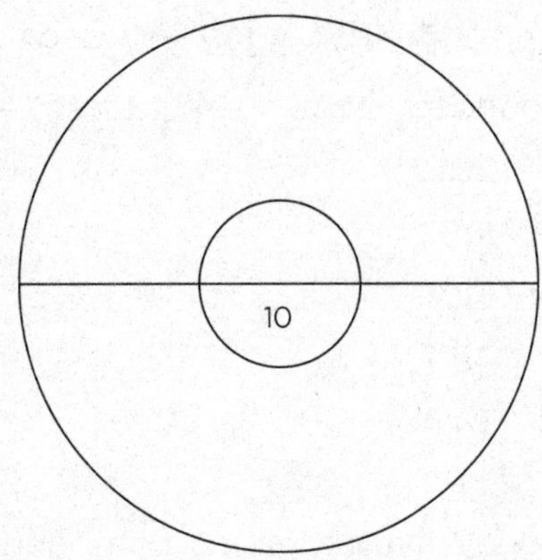

103. The figure shows a circular fountain, surrounded by a circular walkway with the same center. If the fountain has a circumference of 2π, and the walkway has a circumference of 10π, what is the area of the walkway alone?

- O 96π
- O 64π
- O 24π
- O 21π
- O 8π

104. The product of three positive integers is 70. If all of the integers are greater than 1, what is the sum of the greatest two integers?

- O 2
- O 7
- O 12
- O 14
- O 35

105. A cookie batter recipe consists of flour, sugar, and butter in a ratio of 5:3:1, respectively, by ounces. If 81 ounces of the batter is prepared, how many more ounces of flour than sugar will it contain?

- O 2
- O 9
- O 18
- O 27
- O 45

106. A dresser contains *b* blue shirts and *w* white shirts. Then 5 blue shirts are added, and 4 white shirts are taken away. If the dresser contains no other shirts and 1 shirt is chosen at random from the new selection, which of the following expressions represents the probability that a blue shirt will be picked?

- O $\frac{b}{w}$
- O $\frac{b}{(b + w)}$
- O $\frac{(b + 5)}{(b + w + 9)}$
- O $\frac{(b + 5)}{(b + w + 5)}$
- O $\frac{(b + 5)}{(b + w + 1)}$

107. If $6x - y = 24$ and $y = 2x$, what is the value of x?

- O -6
- O -3
- O 3
- O 6
- O 12

108. Ellen's dog has x times as many toys as her cat. If together the two animals have a total of t toys, which of the following expressions represents the number of toys Ellen's cat has?

- O $\frac{x}{t}$
- O $\frac{x+1}{t}$
- O $\frac{x-1}{t}$
- O $\frac{t}{x+1}$
- O $t + tx$

109. During an auction, Jerome sold 75% of the first 1,000 items he offered for sale and 30% of the remaining items offered for sale that day. If he sold 40% of the total number of items he offered for sale throughout the auction, how many items did Jerome offer for sale?

- O 750
- O 1,050
- O 1,800
- O 3,500
- O 4,500

110. If $x > 0$ and the cube root of $\frac{y}{x} = 2x$, what is the value of y in terms of x?

- O $\frac{1}{2x}$
- O $\sqrt[3]{x}$
- O $2\sqrt[3]{x}$
- O $2x^4$
- O $8x^4$

111. If $°F = \frac{9}{5}(°C) + 32$ and $°F = 94$, then $°C$ (rounded to the nearest tenth) =

- O 201.2
- O 169.2
- O 52.2
- O 48.7
- O 34.4

112. Money invested at x%, compounded annually, triples in value in approximately every $\frac{112}{x}$ years. If \$2,500 is invested at a rate of 8%, compounded annually, what will be its approximate worth in 28 years?

- O \$3,750
- O \$5,600
- O \$8,100
- O \$15,000
- O \$22,500

113. The product of 6 and a positive number x is divided by 4. The square root of this value then equals x. What is the value of x?

- O $\frac{9}{4}$
- O $\frac{3}{2}$
- O 1
- O $\frac{2}{3}$
- O $\frac{4}{9}$

114. If $x = -2$, then $\frac{x+1}{x^3 - x^2 + x} =$

- $-\frac{1}{6}$
- $-\frac{1}{14}$
- 0
- $\frac{1}{14}$
- $\frac{1}{6}$

115. The positive integer x has a factor of 16. If the square root of x is greater than 16, which of the following could equal $\frac{x}{16}$?

- 13
- 14
- 15
- 16
- 17

116. A certain photograph is 2 inches longer than it is wide. If the perimeter of the photograph measures 18 inches, what are its actual dimensions, in inches?

- 3×5
- 5×7
- $\frac{11}{2} \times \frac{7}{2}$
- $\frac{13}{2} \times \frac{11}{2}$
- 8×10

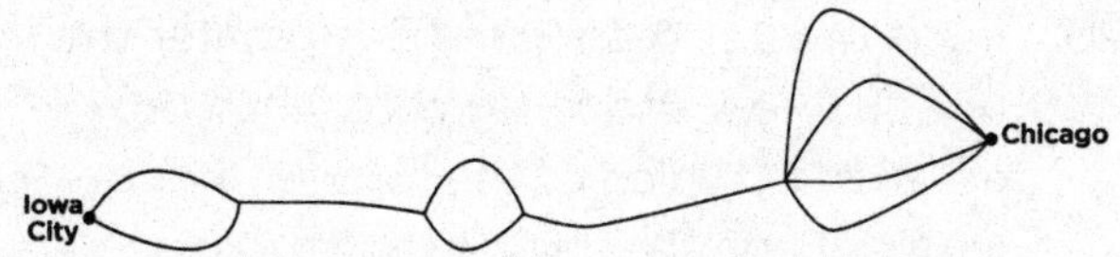

117. The diagram displays the different roads that stretch from Iowa City to Chicago. How many direct routes are there between Iowa City and Chicago if each road is used no more than once per route?

- 7
- 8
- 16
- 18
- 20

118. Shana has 56 pairs of shoes, 25% of which are sneakers. If she buys 14 more pairs and makes no other changes to her current collection, how many of the new pairs must be sneakers in order to increase the percentage of sneakers in her collection to 30%?

- 5
- 7
- 10
- 14
- 21

119. Last year, an airline flew 3.2×10^9 passenger miles. If the airline burned 200 million gallons of fuel last year, what was the airline's average fuel consumption, in passenger miles per gallon?

- 16
- 32
- 64
- 128
- 160

120. If y is greater than 9 and 3 is greater than or equal to x and x is greater than or equal to 0, which of the following CANNOT be the value of xy?

- -6
- 0
- 5
- 18
- 33

121. A car stereo system costs $366. If the tax on the purchase is greater than 3% but not more than 6%, the final cost of the system must be between

- $349 and $361
- $363 and $375
- $377 and $387
- $376 and $388
- $388 and $400

122. A loan has a variable interest rate that fluctuates between 5% and 9% of the base payment per month. If base payments remain at $250 each month and an additional monthly surcharge of 1% is added to the combined base plus interest, what would be the greatest possible payment due in any given month?

- $262.50
- $265.13
- $272.50
- $275.23
- $286.13

123. A barrel contains 40 kilograms of syrup that is 35% sugar by weight. If 10 kilograms of sugar are added to the barrel, the resulting syrup will be what percent sugar by weight?

- 17
- 28
- 37
- 48
- 60

124. A fifth-grade classroom decorates its bulletin board with a repeating border of alternating shapes. These are, in order, a triangle, square, circle, and rectangle. If the top border begins with a triangle and ends in a circle, how many total shapes could the top border contain?

- 12
- 18
- 26
- 34
- 47

125. If the digits 37 in the decimal $0.\dot{0}0037$ repeat indefinitely, what is the value of $(10^5 - 10^3)(0.00037)$?

- 0
- 0.37 repeating
- 3.7
- 10
- 37

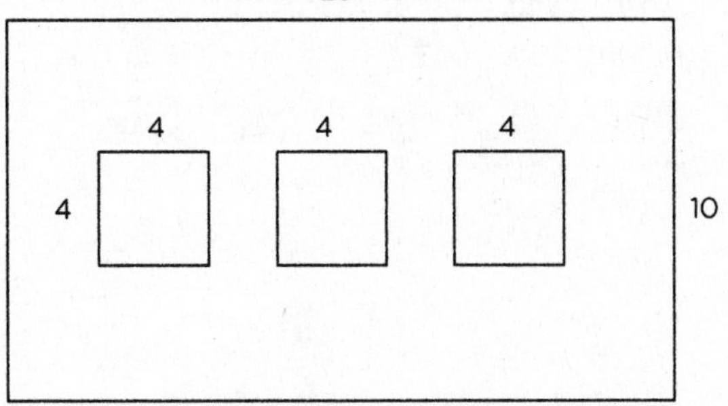

126. A rectangular sandbox contains 3 raised square playing areas, as shown. If the entire sandbox measures 20 × 10 feet and each square has a side length of 4 feet, what is the fraction of the sandbox that is not raised?

- $\frac{1}{8}$
- $\frac{6}{25}$
- $\frac{1}{2}$
- $\frac{19}{25}$
- $\frac{7}{8}$

127. Nancy is 20 years younger than Devon. If in 6 years Nancy will be $\frac{1}{3}$ Devon's age, how old will Nancy be in 2 years?

- 5
- 6
- 11
- 18
- 26

128. A wholesale club sells mulch in bulk. It bought 200 bags at a total price of d dollars. If it then sold each bag for 40% more than its original cost, how much did it charge for each bag of mulch, in terms of d?

- $\frac{7d}{1,000}$
- $\frac{20}{d}$
- $200d$
- $\frac{d + 8,000}{200}$
- $\frac{280}{d}$

129. There are a total of 19 students in Mr. Schmidt's gym class. Over the course of a badminton unit, each of the 19 students will compete exactly once against every other student in the class. How many total games of badminton will be played?

- 38
- 171
- 190
- 210
- 361

130. Let $x \triangle y = \frac{x^2}{y}$ for all positive values of x and y.

What is the value of $(6 \triangle 9) \triangle 2$?

- 2
- 4
- 8
- 14
- 27

131. A company pays contractors a rate of *a* dollars for the first hour and *b* dollars for each additional hour after the first, where $a > b$.

In a given month, a contractor worked on two different projects that lasted 2 and 4 hours, respectively. The company has the option to pay for each project individually, or to treat all hours worked during the month as one lump sum. Which arrangement would be cheaper for the company, and how much would the company save?

- Per month, with savings of $\$(a + b)$
- Per month, with savings of $\$(a - b)$
- The two options would cost an equal amount.
- Per project, with savings of $\$(a + b)$
- Per project, with savings of $\$(a - b)$

132. In the *xy*-coordinate system, if (*a*, *b*) and $(a - 4, b + k)$ are two points on the line $x = 2y + 8$, then what is the value of *k*?

- -4
- -2
- $\frac{1}{2}$
- 1
- 4

133. Let the operation _ be defined by the equation $x\_b = \frac{1}{(x + b)}$. If *x* does not equal 0 and $x\_c = \frac{1}{x}$, what does *c* equal?

- $-x$
- $\frac{1}{x}$
- 0
- 1
- x

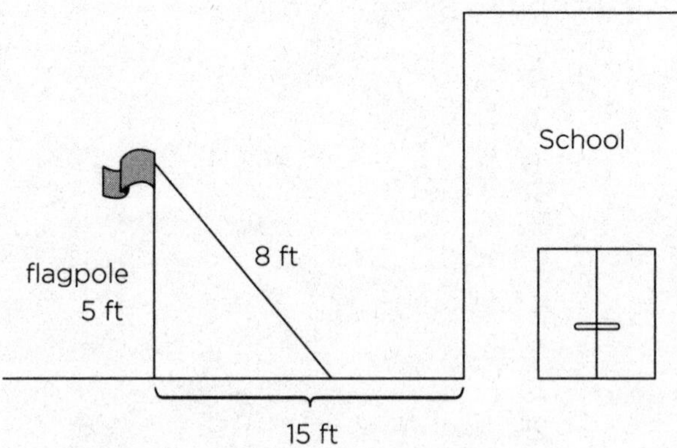

134. A flagpole stands 5 feet tall at a 90-degree angle to the ground in front of a school. The end of the shadow it casts on the ground is 8 feet from the flagpole's top. If the flagpole stands 15 feet from the school, how far is the distance from the shadow's end to the school?

- $\sqrt{39}$
- 7
- $15 - \sqrt{39}$
- $\sqrt{89}$
- 13

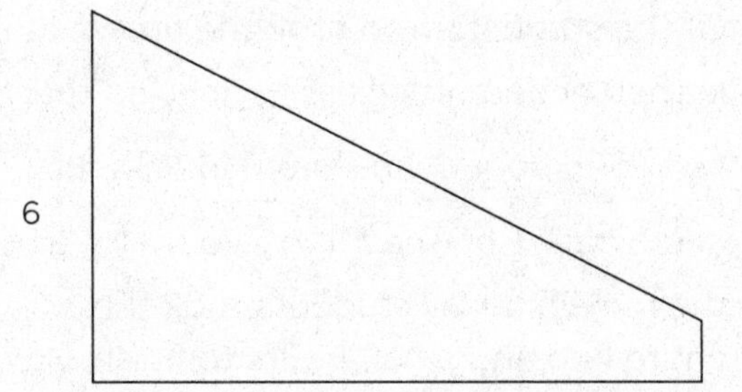

135. What is the total area of the shape shown if the distance across its top equals $\sqrt{61}$?

(Assume the sides are perpendicular to the base.)

- 6
- 15
- 18
- 21
- 36

136. If $3 + \frac{3}{x} = 4 - \frac{4}{x}$, then $x =$

- -1
- $\frac{4}{7}$
- $\frac{3}{4}$
- 4
- 7

137. During the last holiday season, for every 100,000 sets of Christmas tree lights sold, 73 were returned because of faulty bulbs. If 5 million sets of Christmas tree lights were sold, how many of these were returned because of faulty bulbs?

- 365
- 146
- 3,650
- 1,460
- 36,500

138. Twenty percent of the members of a senior class have already been accepted to a graduate school. Among the seniors who have not been accepted to a graduate school, 200 have applied but not been accepted, and 440 have not applied. How many members are there in the senior class?

- 800
- 1,000
- 1,200
- 1,400
- 1,600

139. At a certain restaurant, the ratio of the number of cooks to the number of waiters is 3 to 13. When 12 more waiters are hired, the ratio of the number of cooks to the number of waiters changes to 3 to 16. How many cooks does the restaurant have?

- 3
- 6
- 9
- 12
- 15

140. Which of the following could be the value of $x - 9$ if $(x - 2)^2 = 900$?

- O 41
- O 21
- O -37
- O -38
- O -41

141. If $9 - w^2 > 0$, which of the following describes all possible values of w?

- O $3 > w > -3$
- O $w > 3$ or $w < -3$
- O $3 > w > 0$
- O $-3 < w$
- O $3 > w$

142. A certain businessman wears only three different colors of shirt—white, blue, and gray. The probability that he will wear a blue or gray shirt on a given day is $\frac{2}{3}$. During a four-day workweek, what is the probability that the businessman will wear a white shirt at least once?

- O $\frac{16}{81}$
- O $\frac{8}{27}$
- O $\frac{2}{3}$
- O $\frac{19}{27}$
- O $\frac{65}{81}$

143. Of the students who took the final exam in their economics class, $\frac{1}{8}$ finished the test in an hour, $\frac{1}{6}$ finished it in an hour and a half, $\frac{2}{3}$ finished it in two hours, and the remaining 20 students took the entire two and a half hours to finish. How many students took the final exam?

- O 20
- O 250
- O 460
- O 480
- O 960

144. If x is increased from 98 to 99, which of the following will also increase?

I. $3x - 15$

II. $\frac{2 - 3}{x}$

III. $\frac{5}{x^2 - x}$

- O II only
- O III only
- O I and II
- O II and III
- O I, II, and III

145. A rectangular monolith is 4 miles wide, 1 mile long, and 9 miles high. If a straight line is drawn through the monolith from one point to another, what is the greatest possible distance, in miles, of that line?

o $\sqrt{17}$

o $7\sqrt{2}$

o 13

o 14

o $\sqrt{370}$

146. An audit determined that, between 1998 and 1999, a certain business increased the amount it spent on health insurance by 30%. Over the same period, the business reduced employee bonuses by 45%. If the business spent $8,700 on health insurance and $3,000 on bonuses in 1998, how much did it spend on health insurance and employee bonuses combined in 1999?

o $11,850

o $12,960

o $13,030

o $13,840

o $14,170

147. If $w \gg z = wz - 5(w + z)$ for all integers w and z, then $-5 \gg 4 =$

o −19

o −15

o −5

o 5

o 15

Sport	Number of coaches
Track	8
Tennis	5
Baseball	4

148. The table shows how many coaches work with each of the major sports teams at a school. Although no single coach works with all three teams, 3 coaches work with both the track and tennis teams, 2 coaches work with both the track and baseball teams, and 1 coach works with both the tennis and baseball teams. How many different coaches work with these three teams?

o 6

o 9

o 11

o 12

o 17

149. During a recent evaluation, X students were given a two-question test. If $\frac{1}{5}$ of the students answered the first question correctly, and, of those students, $\frac{1}{2}$ answered the second question correctly, which of the following expressions indicates the number of students who did NOT answer both questions correctly?

- $\frac{x}{10}$
- $\frac{x}{5}$
- $\frac{5x}{7}$
- $\frac{9x}{10}$
- $9x$

150. The ratio of a man's ties to the number of dress shirts he owns is 3 to 5. If the man buys 4 new ties and 4 new dress shirts, what is the new ratio of ties to dress shirts?

- $\frac{7}{12}$
- $\frac{3}{5}$
- $\frac{11}{15}$
- $\frac{7}{9}$
- The ratio cannot be determined from the information given.

Answers and explanations begin on the next page.

Answer Key

PROBLEM SOLVING PRACTICE

1. B
2. E
3. D
4. C
5. E
6. D
7. A
8. B
9. C
10. B
11. A
12. C
13. E
14. C
15. C
16. B
17. A
18. B
19. B
20. C
21. B
22. C
23. C
24. B
25. B
26. D
27. B
28. B
29. B
30. C
31. D
32. B
33. B
34. C
35. B
36. D
37. B
38. C
39. C
40. A
41. A
42. D
43. C
44. D
45. E
46. D
47. B
48. E
49. C
50. A
51. A
52. E
53. C
54. D
55. E
56. B
57. C
58. D
59. E
60. C
61. C
62. E
63. B
64. C
65. B
66. A
67. C
68. D
69. E
70. D
71. B
72. C
73. E
74. D
75. B
76. A
77. C
78. C
79. A
80. D
81. C
82. B
83. A
84. E
85. C
86. B
87. C
88. C
89. A
90. C
91. B
92. C
93. C
94. C
95. E
96. B
97. D
98. C
99. D
100. D
101. C
102. B
103. C
104. C
105. C
106. E
107. D
108. D
109. E
110. E
111. E
112. E
113. B
114. D
115. E
116. C
117. C

118.	B	**129.**	B	**140.**	C
119.	A	**130.**	C	**141.**	A
120.	A	**131.**	B	**142.**	E
121.	D	**132.**	B	**143.**	D
122.	D	**133.**	C	**144.**	C
123.	D	**134.**	C	**145.**	B
124.	E	**135.**	D	**146.**	B
125.	E	**136.**	E	**147.**	B
126.	D	**137.**	C	**148.**	C
127.	B	**138.**	A	**149.**	D
128.	A	**139.**	D	**150.**	E

Answers and Explanations

PROBLEM SOLVING PRACTICE

1. B

Remember that 1 divided by any number cannot equal 0. Even if the denominator is 0, the value of the fraction will be undefined, not 0. Therefore, the value of $\frac{1}{(3-x)}$ cannot be 0.

Answer choice (B) is correct.

Let's look at the other answer choices:

(A) This one's a bit tough, but if $x = \frac{10}{3}$, then we end up with a value of −3 for the expression $\frac{1}{(3-x)}$. Eliminate.

(C) x could easily be 0, which would make the expression $= \frac{1}{3}$. Eliminate.

(D) While it is true that if $x = 3$, we'll have an undefined fraction, the question asks for the answer that cannot be the value of $\frac{1}{(3-x)}$.

(E) This could be the value, if $x = \frac{14}{5}$.

2. E

This one just involves some quick fraction-to-decimal conversion and a bit of calculation.

Change the fraction to a decimal value to model the answer choices.

$$\begin{aligned}\left(\frac{3}{10}\right)^4 &= (0.3)^4\\ &= \left[(0.3)^2\right]^2\\ &= (0.09)^2\\ &= 0.0081\end{aligned}$$

Answer choice (E) is correct.

3. D

This one's a straightforward arithmetic problem. Remember that any whole number divided by a fraction can be multiplied by the reciprocal of that fraction:

$$\begin{aligned}\left(8\times\frac{6}{1}\right)+\left(6\times\frac{8}{1}\right) &= (8\times 6)+(6\times 8)\\ &= 48+48\\ &= 96\end{aligned}$$

Just estimating alone will help you improve your odds dramatically: 8 over a fraction less than 1 plus 6 over a fraction less than 1 is going to be at least 14, so we can eliminate (A) and (B) without any calculation.

Answer choice (D) is correct.

4. C

Cut out most of the calculation on this one by working with familiar fractions instead of decimals. You can also save time by working with what's left instead of what's missing.

First, calculate the number of bars left after the first week's sales: $75\% = \frac{3}{4}$, so we're left with $\frac{1}{4}$ of $120 = 30$ candy bars.

Next, if the players eat 40% of what's left, they'll be left with 60% of 30, or $0.6 \times 30 = 18$ candy bars left in the end.

Answer choice (C) is correct.

5. E

Let's try to make the math as painless as possible here. Remember that the area of a rectangle = width × height. The number $11\frac{1}{2}$ would be tough to work with, but since we'll need to double the area of one side anyway, just double $11\frac{1}{2}$ now and get an even 23. (Note: The total area of both sides would be 11.5 × 7 × 2, so only double one of the values—and doubling the 11.5 is the way to make your calculations easier).

Therefore, the total area of both sides of the billboard combined is 23 × 7. Making that easier again, break 23 into parts: 7(20 + 3). This is math you can do in your head: (7 × 20) + (7 × 3) = 140 + 21 = 161 ft^2.

Answer choice (E) is correct.

6. D

If you want to be technical about this one, you can use the percent conversion formula:

$$\text{Percent} = \frac{\%}{100} = \frac{\text{part}}{\text{whole}}$$

$$\text{Percent} = \frac{x}{100} = \frac{180}{60}$$

Then you could cross multiply to solve the proportion: 180 × 100 = $60x$, so 18,000 = $60x$ and x = 300.

But the considerably easier alternate solution is as follows: Observe that 3 × 60 = 180 and note that multiplying by 3 is the same as taking 300% of something. Therefore, 180 = 300% of 60.

Answer choice (D) is correct.

7. A

All this question wants us to do is simplify the ratio we're given. The ratio of 3 to $\frac{1}{4}$ is the same as $\frac{3}{\left(\frac{1}{4}\right)}$. When dividing by a fraction, multiply by its reciprocal. So $\frac{3}{\left(\frac{1}{4}\right)} = 3\times\frac{4}{1} = \frac{12}{1}$, which is just another way of saying "the ratio of 12 to 1."

Answer choice (A) is correct.

8. B

This question can be looked at either one of two ways: as a straightforward arithmetic word problem, or as a single-variable algebra word problem.

Thinking it through the arithmetic route: Jack's older, so he gets a larger piece of the licorice he shares with his little brother—8 inches longer, in fact. So let's take the 8 extra inches of licorice that Jack has off the total. Now we know that the remaining 20 inches will be shared evenly between them, so each one gets 10 inches, which means the little brother's piece is 10 inches and Jack's is 18 inches total.

If you want to be formal about things, you can translate the given information into an algebraic equation. Let x = the length of Jack's brother's piece of licorice. The question tells us Jack's piece is 8 inches longer. Therefore $x + 8$ = the length of Jack's piece. The total length of the licorice is 28 inches. So $x + x + 8 = 28$. Simplify the expression and solve for x. Combine like terms: $2x + 8 = 28$. Subtract 8 from both sides: $2x = 20$. Divide both sides by 2: $x = 10$.

Answer choice (B) is correct.

9. C

In rate problems like this one, perhaps the most useful thing you can do to avoid getting lost in the conversions is to track your units. To solve this one, you'll need to apply Roger's consistent hot dog-eating rate to a full day, beginning with a rate of 12 hot dogs per minute. You need to multiply the number of hot dogs eaten in a minute times the number of minutes in an hour times the number of hours in a day.

$$\frac{12 \text{ hot dogs}}{1 \text{ minute}} \times \frac{60 \text{ minutes}}{1 \text{ hour}} \times \frac{24 \text{ hours}}{1 \text{ day}}$$

Minutes in the numerator and denominator both reduce, as do hours in both numerator and denominator, leaving us with hot dogs in the numerator and 1 day in the denominator. Now we just have to multiply 12 × 60 × 24: 12 × 60 = 720, and 720 × 24 = 17,280.

Answer choice (C) is correct.

10. B

To solve this one, just recall the formula for speed: speed = $\frac{\text{distance}}{\text{time}}$. If you have a hard time remembering that, think about how speed is measured: in miles (*distance*) per (*over*) hour (*time*). And if speed = $\frac{\text{distance}}{\text{time}}$, then with some quick manipulation, we know that time = $\frac{\text{distance}}{\text{speed}}$. Let t equal the total time, m represent the total number of miles Steve runs (*distance*), and x represent his speed. So $t = \frac{m}{x}$.

To make this more concrete, pick numbers for m and x: Say m is 10 and x is 5, so Steve runs 10 miles at 5 miles an hour, meaning he'll take 2 hours to run that distance. Now plug your numbers into the answer choices until you find a match for 2 hours.

Answer choice (B) is correct.

11. A

Derek's reading rate (speed in $\frac{\text{pages}}{\text{minute}}$) can be expressed as $\frac{x}{5}$ pages per minute. Use this value for the formula total number of pages = rate × time. Let t equal the time in minutes it will take Derek to read p pages. So $p = \left(\frac{x}{5}\right)t$.

Solve for t: $p = \frac{xt}{5}$. Multiply both sides by $\frac{5}{x}$ to isolate t on one side of the equation: $\frac{5p}{x} = t$.

If this is too abstract for you, try picking some values that work well for x and p: $x = 10$, $p = 30$. Solve the equation with those values plugged in to find that it will take him 15 minutes to read 30 pages, then plug $x = 10$ and $p = 30$ into each answer choice until you find the one that equals 15.

Answer choice (A) is correct.

12. C

This can be rephrased as 18 = x% of 90, which is the same thing as $18 = \frac{x}{100} \times 90$.

Use the percent proportion (think literally, *per* = *over* and *cent* = *100*) to solve this problem.

$$\text{Percent} = \frac{\%}{100} = \frac{\text{part}}{\text{whole}} \ldots \frac{x}{100} = \frac{18}{90} \ldots$$

Cross multiply to solve for x: $1{,}800 = 90x$, so $x = 20$.

Answer choice (C) is correct.

13. E

To do this one using traditional algebra, translate the given information into an algebraic equation.

Let b represent the number of black puppies and c represent the number of chocolate puppies.

The litter had 3 more chocolate puppies than black, so $b + 3 = c$.

The total number of puppies in the litter was 11. Since $b + c = 11$, then $b + b + 3 = 11$.

Solve for b: $2b + 3 = 11$; $2b = 8$ and $b = 4$.

But be careful here! The value 4 is the number of *black* puppies in the litter. So 3 + 4 = 7 is the number of *chocolate* puppies.

Alternate solution: Work backward from the answer choices to see which satisfies the given information.

Answer choice (E) is correct.

14. C

We can use a shortcut and a little bit of logic to make this fraction question easier. Since 17 is a number that's not divisible by 4 (in fact, it's prime), let's think this through using 16 as our "baseline" number. If there were 16 members, at least $\frac{3}{4}$ of whom must be in good academic standing for the team to have funding, then we'd need 12 to be in good standing, and a max of 4 could be in poor standing. That's our answer, because adding the 17th person to the "poor academic standing" group would make the fraction in poor standing greater than $\frac{3}{4}$, which is unacceptable in terms of receiving funding.

If you want to work this out mathematically, $\frac{1}{4}$ of the 17-member team can be in poor standing: $17\left(\frac{1}{4}\right) = 4.25$. You cannot have a fraction of a person, so a maximum of 4 students can be in poor standing.

Answer choice (C) is correct.

15. C

This is an inequalities question. To solve this one, handle each inequality like a regular equation, but note that each one presents a limit rather than an actual value.

Solve each inequality for a limit of x.

If $3x > 12$, divide both sides by 3 to find $x > 4$.

Next, if $x - 5 < 8$, add 5 to both sides to find $x < 13$.

The value of x must be between 4 and 13.

Answer choice (C) is correct.

16. B

To approach this question, first recall the definition of the term *median*. The median of a set is the middle value in the set when the terms in that set are arranged from least to greatest. If there is an even number of terms in the set—and, therefore, two middle values—the average of the two middle terms is the median of the set.

To solve this question, let's first list the values in order from least to greatest: 10, 12, 15, 16, 18, 23, 23, 33. Since this list contains 8 numbers, we must find the average of the two middle values, 16 and 18.

The average of 16 and 18 is 17, so that's our median.

Answer choice (B) is correct.

17. A

Solve the inequality to find the values of n that satisfy the given information.

$11 < 3n - 1 < 17$

Add one to each value: $12 < 3n < 18$

Divide each side by 3: $4 < n < 6$

The question asks for all integer (whole number) values of n. n cannot equal 4 or 6. Therefore there is only one possible integer (5) that satisfies the inequality.

Answer choice (A) is correct.

18. B

This question is testing us on our knowledge of how powers and roots behave.

Simplify the expression:

$$\begin{aligned}(\sqrt{5} + \sqrt{5} + \sqrt{5})^2 &= (3(\sqrt{5}))^2 \\ &= (3^2)(\sqrt{5})^2 \\ &= 9(5) \\ &= 45\end{aligned}$$

Answer choice (B) is correct.

19. B

Whenever you have a single rate or ratio expressed in different terms—even if simply with different numbers—you should consider setting it up as a proportion. That is, set two fractions equal to one another. In this case:

$$\frac{1}{2.5} = \frac{x}{8}$$

Since the units are the same on both sides of the equation, they will cancel when you cross multiply and divide. So you can ignore them:

$$2.5x = 8$$

$$x = \frac{8}{2.5} = \frac{16}{5}$$

You could also use estimation here by asking yourself how many times 2.5 goes into 8 (a little more than 3). This would be an efficient way to eliminate all but the correct answer.

Answer choice (B) is correct.

20. C

Since there are 360 degrees in a circle, and 120 degrees are not shaded (60 + 60 = 120), then $\frac{240}{360}$ is shaded.

Divide the top and bottom of the fraction by 120 to reduce it to $\frac{2}{3}$.

Answer choice (C) is correct.

21. B

To estimate the value of the expression, round off the given values to make computations easy: $\frac{(40)(0.4)}{100} = \frac{16}{100} = \frac{4}{25}$.

When you multiply two numbers together (40 and 0.4 in this case) you can "trade" decimal places between the two factors. Whether you divide 40 by 10 or multiply 0.4 by 10, the product will be the same, 16. You might find it easier to multiply 4 by 4 than 40 by 0.4.

Answer choice (B) is correct.

22. C

Each of x sections has b bracelets, each of which contains 12 diamonds. Therefore, the total number of diamonds in 4 display cases would be $(4)(x)(b)(12) = 48bx$.

If you have trouble translating from English to algebra, consider picking numbers to replace each of the variables.

Let's say that there are 2 sections in each case and 3 bracelets in each section. That would mean 6 bracelets in each case. With 4 display cases, that's 24 bracelets altogether, each with 12 diamonds, for a total of 288 diamonds.

Now, simply plug your numbers into each answer and see which one totals 288 diamonds.

Answer choice (C) is correct.

23. C

There are two prime numbers between 30 and 40—31 and 37—and their sum is 68.

Answer choice (C) is correct.

24. B

In this EXCEPT question, we absolutely *have* to work backward from the answer choices. Test each choice using different prime numbers. If the value can be found by adding two prime numbers, *eliminate* the answer choice (this question is looking for the value that CANNOT be the sum of two prime numbers). Since we're discussing prime numbers in this question, we can work solely with positive values less than the sum in each answer choice.

(A) Since 2 + 5 = 7 and both 2 and 5 are prime, this answer choice can be eliminated.

(B) 1 + 10 (neither is prime); 2 + 9 (9 isn't prime); 3 + 8 (8 isn't prime); 4 + 7 (4 isn't prime); 5 + 6 (6 isn't prime); if we go any further, we're just duplicating what we've already seen. This can't be reduced to two prime numbers, so it is the correct choice.

(C) Since 5 + 13 = 18 and both 5 and 13 are prime, we can eliminate this one.

(D) Since 5 + 17 = 22 and both 5 and 17 are prime, we can get rid of this answer choice.

(E) Since 7 + 23 = 30 and both 7 and 23 are prime, this answer choice isn't correct.

Answer choice (B) is correct.

25. B

You don't have to take a very formal approach here. What's the smallest number you can think of that's divisible by both 4 and 6? If you don't think of 12 (the lowest common multiple, or LCM, of 4 and 6) right away, then just start counting by 6 until you get to a multiple of 4. The LCM of 4 and 6 is 12. Every larger number divisible by both 4 and 6 is divisible by the least common multiple (LCM) of 4 and 6, so 12 works here. However, since 12 is a multiple of both 4 and 6, but not divisible by either 24 or 48, the credited response must be I only.

Answer choice (B) is correct.

26. D

While you could square 43, add 43, and then divide by 43, instead of doing all that math, it's easier to think of arithmetic in algebraic terms. If you changed 43 to x, the shortcut here would probably be more apparent: $\frac{(x^2 + x)}{x}$.

Factor out the x and reduce, and you're left with $x + 1$, at which point you could plug 43 back in for x and find that the equation equals 44.

Answer choice (D) is correct.

27. B

The question states that $c = r$. So $4x + 5$ must equal $21 - 2x$. Set the expressions equal to one another and solve for the value of x:

$$4x + 5 = 21 - 2x$$
$$6x = 16$$
$$x = \frac{16}{6} = \frac{8}{3}$$

Answer choice (B) is correct.

28. B

When multiplying two numbers with the same base but different exponents, we can simply keep the base and add the exponents.

And since $0.4 = (0.4)^1$, then $(0.4)^1(0.4)^2 = (0.4)^{1+2} = (0.4)^3 = 0.064$.

Alternate solution: Solve each unit of the expression individually, then multiply:

$0.4^1 = 0.4$; $0.4^2 = 0.16$

$(0.4)(0.16) = 0.064$

Answer choice (B) is correct.

29. B

You can approach this one either of two ways. Most students will likely work out the math, which is fine . . . but it's not always the fastest way. Here, our approaches take roughly the same amount of time. Here's the straight math:

$$\sqrt{[(12)(21) - (10)(18)]} = \sqrt{252 - 180} = \sqrt{72}$$
$$\sqrt{72} = \sqrt{12 \times 6} = \sqrt{2 \times 6 \times 6} = 6\sqrt{2}$$

Fully reduced, $6\sqrt{2}$ is correct. Not too shabby. But using common factors, we might have gotten there a little bit faster. Here's how:

$$\sqrt{[(12)(21) - (10)(18)]}$$
$$= \sqrt{[(3 \times 4)(3 \times 7) - (2 \times 5)(9 \times 2)]}$$
$$= \sqrt{[(3 \times 2 \times 2)(3 \times 7) - (2 \times 5)(3 \times 3 \times 2)]}$$

Factor out the common elements:

$$\sqrt{[(3 \times 2 \times 2)(3 \times 7) - (2 \times 5)(3 \times 3 \times 2)]}$$
$$= \sqrt{(3 \times 3 \times 2 \times 2)(7 - 5)}$$

Pull the perfect squares out from under the radical sign:

$$\sqrt{(3 \times 3 \times 2 \times 2)(7 - 5)} = 3 \times 2\sqrt{(7 - 5)}$$

Final answer: $6\sqrt{2}$

Answer choice (B) is correct.

30. C

We don't even really need the parabola graph to find this answer.

Since the graph is symmetrical about the *y*-axis, for any given *x*, both *x* and *–x* have the same value for *y*. So, if $y = 0$ when *x* is –4, $y = 0$ when *x* is 4.

Answer choice (C) is correct.

31. D

Usually, when you're asked to multiply by a percent, you'll find it easiest to think of that percent as a decimal. In this case, though, since the numbers are nice and round, you might have gone a different route:

$\frac{1}{5}$ of 2,000 = 400.

1% of 2,000 is 20, so $\frac{1}{5}$% of 2,000 is $\frac{1}{5}$ of 20 = 4.

400 – 4 = 396

If you want to take the decimal approach:

$\frac{1}{5} = 0.2$ and $\frac{1}{5}\% = 0.002$

Translate the problem into a mathematical expression using these decimal equivalents:

(0.2)(2,000) – (0.002)(2,000) = 400 – 4 = 396

Answer choice (D) is correct.

32. B

The fastest way to solve this arithmetic word problem is to do some shortcut math. At 6 months, the project is $\frac{1}{3}$ into its planned timeline, and therefore it should be $\frac{1}{3}$ through the planned number of projects. One-third of 612 is 204—this is the number of projects expected to be completed at 6 months.

Since the city actually has only 108 projects done, then the reconstruction is (204 – 108), or 96 projects behind schedule.

Answer choice (B) is correct.

33. B

The best way to approach this one is through traditional math. Simplify the expression and solve:

$0.4 + (0.4)^2 + (0.4)^3 = 0.4 + 0.16 + 0.064 = 0.624$

Answer choice (B) is correct.

34. C

The question is asking us to find the lowest answer choice that is divisible by the numbers 1 through 8, inclusive. The word "inclusive" means that we'll count both the "bookends" (here, 1 and 8), so "1 through 8, inclusive" would mean that we want a number divisible by 1, 2, 3, 4, 5, 6, 7, and 8. The quickest way to solve this one is to test each answer choice, starting with the smallest.

Stop as soon as you find one that is divisible by all eight values:

210 is not divisible by 8 (since 200 is and 10 is not, or count by 8 from 200: 208, 216 . . .).

420 is not divisible by 8 (since 400 is and 20 is not, or count by 8 from 400: 408, 416, 424 . . .).

840 is divisible by 8 (since 800 and 40 each are divisible by 8). It is divisible by 7 (since 84 is a multiple of 7, and 840 is a multiple of 84).

It is divisible by 6 (because it is divisible by 2 and 3). It is divisible by 5 (because it ends in a 0). It is divisible by 4 (because it is divisible by 8). It is divisible by 3 (because the digits 8, 4, and 0 sum to 12, which is a multiple of 3). It is divisible by 2 (because it ends in an even digit, or because it is divisible by 8).

Answer choice (C) is correct.

35. B

Solve the given equation: $\frac{11.2}{(0.4 + x)} = 8$.

Multiply both sides by $(0.4 + x)$: $11.2 = 3.2 + 8x$.

Subtract 3.2 from both sides: $8 = 8x$.

Divide by 8 on both sides: $1 = x$.

Alternate solution: Plug in answer choices to see which value of x satisfies the given equation.

The correct answer choice is (B).

36. D

Use the percent proportion to find the total amount of available credit on the card.

$$\frac{\text{percent}}{100} = \frac{\text{part}}{\text{whole}}$$

$$\frac{77}{100} = \frac{5{,}775}{x}$$

Before you go any further, though, note that you won't stop at x. You want to solve for the difference between x and Jake's balance at the beginning of the month, or x - $5,005.

Cross multiply to solve for x: $577{,}500 = 77x$.

x = $7,500, which is the total amount of credit available on the card.

(If you're handy with percents, you could have gone straight to $0.77x$ = $5,775, rather than cross multiplying.)

Subtract the balance on the card at the beginning of the month from the card's total capacity to find Jake's available balance at the beginning of the month: $7,500 - $5,005 = $2,495.

The correct answer choice is (D).

37. B

First, remember that to calculate the number of apartments from 2 through 56:

56 - 2 + 1 = 55 apartments. We add 1 because we're including both endpoints in the calculation; normal subtraction only counts the distance moved from one endpoint to another on a number line, so it essentially leaves one of two endpoints out.

Next we consider the element of probability. The formula for probability is:

$$\frac{\text{number of desired outcomes}}{\text{number of possible outcome}}$$

In this scenario, there are 10 apartments that begin with a tens digit of 3 (30 - 39), so we have a total of 10 desired outcomes. We already determined that there are 55 total possibilities (55 possible apartments labeled 2 through 56), so we get $\frac{10}{55} = \frac{2}{11}$.

The correct answer choice is (B).

38. C

First, find the rate for 1 plow: $\frac{123}{3}$ = 41 feet per minute per plow. Multiply this rate by the total number of plows × total minutes:

$$41 \times 8 \times 5 = 1{,}640 \text{ feet}$$

The correct answer choice is (C).

39. C

If Rachel has 12 pairs of shoes, she has a total of (2)(12) = 24 shoes. Then 9 shoes are taken away, so she has 24 - 9 = 15 left. Now 15 shoes could represent as few as 3 pairs, plus 9 single shoes, or as many as 7 pairs plus 1 single shoe. If we want the greatest number of pairs to remain, we should assume that Rachel's remaining shoes pair up as much as possible.

Another approach: $\frac{15}{2}$ = 7.5. Therefore, Rachel can have a maximum total of 7 complete pairs of shoes left.

The correct answer choice is (C).

40. A

The fastest way to solve this quadratic equation question is to just do old fashioned math. Plug in the known value of x to find the value of y:

$$\begin{aligned} 3^2 + (6)(3) + y &= 21 \\ 9 + 18 + y &= 21 \\ 27 + y &= 21 \\ y &= -6 \end{aligned}$$

Next, plug the value of y into the original equation to find the other value of x: $x^2 + 6x - 6 = 21$, so $x^2 + 6x - 27 = 0$.

Now factor the equation to find values of x: $(x + 9)(x - 3) = 0$.

Therefore, $x = 3$ and $x = -9$.

The correct answer choice is (A).

41. A

For this Roman numeral question about triangles (geometry), you could simply try out the answer choices and eliminate those that don't work, but there's an easier approach: the *triangle inequality theorem* states that one side of a triangle must be less than the sum of its other two sides, but greater than the difference of those two sides.

In order to satisfy this law, the third side of the triangle must be greater than 7 and less than 11. Choice II (8.5) is the only length that satisfies this criterion, so we can eliminate anything that contains either Statement I or Statement III.

The correct answer choice is (A).

42. D

Translate the given information into an algebraic expression. Let's translate piece by piece:

The number of shirts (x) was (=) 15 greater than (15 + . . .) the number of hats (h).

Since h is always on the left in the answer choices, let's rearrange the equation as follows:

$$x = 15 + h \rightarrow x - 15 = h \rightarrow h = x - 15$$

The correct answer choice is (D).

43. C

You could solve algebraically: $55 = 0.2x$; $x = 275$; $0.8(275) = 220$.

However, it is much faster and easier to solve for the balance directly.

Since the $55 payment is equal to 20% of the loan, the balance is equal to 80%. Then 80% is four times 20%, so the balance is 4 × $55, or $220.

You could also have done this with fractions, using $\frac{1}{5}$ and $\frac{4}{5}$ in place of 20% and 80%.

The correct answer choice is (C).

44. D

If Amanda shoveled 65% of the driveway, then Kelly shoveled 100 - 65 = 35%. The ratio of the amount Kelly shoveled to the amount Amanda shoveled is therefore $\frac{35}{65}$, which reduces to $\frac{7}{13}$.

The correct answer choice is (D).

45. E

For this one, fight the urge to draw out the circle. This isn't really a geometry question, despite the fact that it mentions a circle. It's really just a fraction question.

Add the three known sections of the circle's area. To do so, find the lowest common denominator and add the fractions.

$$\frac{1}{4} = \frac{5}{20}; \frac{2}{5} = \frac{8}{20}; \frac{3}{10} = \frac{6}{20}$$

The total fractional value of the three sections is $\frac{19}{20}$. Therefore, the area of the fourth section must be $1 - \frac{19}{20} = \frac{1}{20}$.

You could also backsolve if this one's confusing. Look for the choice that, when added to the three given fractions, equals 1.

The correct answer choice is (E).

46. D

Here we can either do the math or work backward from the choices. The math's probably easier. First, find the average of the first three numbers:

$$\text{Average} = \frac{\text{sum of terms}}{\text{number of terms}}$$

$$\frac{(6 + 15 + 45)}{3} = \frac{66}{3} = 22$$

Next, from the given information, the average of the second set of numbers is 22 + 4 = 26. Use x in the formula to find the missing number (or you could backsolve from here, but why?):

$$\frac{(8 + 33 + x)}{3} = 26$$

$$8 + 33 + x = 78$$

$$41 + x = 78$$

$$x = 37$$

The correct answer choice is (D).

47. B

Make sure you read this question carefully. It essentially asks which answer choice contains a value that is not a perfect square. Simplify each answer, then find the one that isn't a perfect square.

The correct answer choice is (B).

48. E

First, find the value of d. You are told that $5d = 15$, so divide both sides by 5: $d = 3$.

Plug the value of d into the first equation to find the value of xy:

$$xy = 8d^2;\ xy = 8(3^2) = (8)(9) = 72$$

Plug the value of d and the value of xy into the final equation: $dxy = (3)(72) = 216$.

The correct answer choice is (E).

49. C

You can do this with or without algebra.

With algebra: Translate the given information into an algebraic equation. Use x as a common variable since the given information already provides a ratio. Make sure to note that you need the value of $2x$, not just of x.

$$3x + 2x + x = 24$$

$$6x = 24$$

$$x = 4$$

Therefore, Ron spends (2)(4) = 8 hours working.

Without algebra: Since you know that the parts given in the ratio make up the whole, you can do this by simply adding the parts.

24 hours = 3 parts + 2 parts + 1 part = 6 parts

Since the 24 is divided into 6 parts, every part in each term in the ratio must represent $\frac{24}{6} = 4$ hours, so (2 x 4) = 8 hours are devoted to work.

The correct answer choice is (C).

50. A

You could create a proportion to solve the problem:

$$\frac{\text{total fertilizer}}{\text{total field}} = \frac{\text{amount of fertilizer}}{\text{amount of field}}$$

Plug the given values into this proportion:

$$\frac{1{,}200}{9{,}600} = \frac{x}{3{,}600}$$

Simplify and cross multiply to solve for x:

$$\frac{1{,}200}{9{,}600} = \frac{1}{8} = \frac{x}{3{,}600}$$

$$8x = 3{,}600$$

$$x = 450$$

However, you really don't even need to do all that math; there are shortcuts. You may have noticed that 3,600 is just a little more than one-third of 9,600, so you'll need just a bit more than one-third of 1,200 pounds.

Only 450 fits this criterion.

The correct answer choice is (A).

51. A

Absolute value on a number line is determined by a point's distance from 0. Since point A is farthest from 0, it has the greatest absolute value.

Alternate solution: Estimate real number values for each point and determine their absolute values.

The correct answer choice is (A).

52. E

This one may look harder than it is. With a little bit of eyeballing and point notation, you can quickly calculate what you need between N and M. Don't even worry about things like the distance formula or any other formalities. Just remember that slope is $\frac{\text{rise}}{\text{run}}$, then notice that the slope here is –1: For every one move up (+1 for rise along the y-axis), there's a corresponding one move to the left (–1 for run along the x-axis). That means that wherever the line crosses two adjacent coordinate points—for instance, at (–1, 0) and (0, –1)—there is an equal diagonal "segment." We can see that there are four diagonal segments between N and M.

Which point is three times as far from N as it is from M? Find the point that is three diagonals from N and one diagonal from M: (0, –1).

The correct answer choice is (E).

53. C

To answer this geometry question, we'll need to recall some basic rules about lines and angles. The angles measuring $3y$, $8y$, and $7y$ are supplementary angles (which means that they add up to 180) because, when combined, they create a straight line. So we can solve for y: $3y + 8y + 7y = 180$; $18y = 180$; $y = 10$.

And since the angles measuring $7y$ and $2x + 8$ are vertical angles (which means that they're on opposite sides of a vertex, or intersection), they must be equal. So $7y = 2x + 8$. Plug in the value of y to solve for x: $(7)(10) = 2x + 8$; $70 = 2x + 8$; $62 = 2x$; $31 = x$.

The correct answer choice is (C).

54. D

Since the 2007 sales were 3% lower than the 2006 sales, they were 97% of the 2006 sales. Multiply the 2006 sales by 97% (0.97) to determine the 2007 sales, then round to the nearest 10,000.

$$(0.97)(2{,}100{,}000) = 2{,}037{,}000$$

Then 2,037,000 rounds to 2,040,000.

Alternatively, it might be easier simply to estimate that 3% of 2,100,000 is about 60,000 and then subtract:

$$2{,}100{,}000 - 60{,}000 = 2{,}040{,}000$$

The correct answer is choice (D).

55. E

List the values in Set X: 3, 5, 7, 9, 11, 13, 15, 19. A prime number is a number that has exactly two factors: itself and 1. In Set *X*, only the values 9 and 15 have factors other than 1 and themselves. Therefore, Set *Y* contains the numbers 3, 5, 7, 11, 13, 17, and 19. This is a total of seven values.

The correct answer choice is (E).

56. B

This may look like a very difficult question, but there's an underlying logic to it all if you stop to consider what's given in the question and answers.

The first thing to calculate is the root of 6, which we know is greater than 2 but less than 3. Try the average of the two: $2.5^2 = 6.25$ . . . that's pretty close. So let's just go with 2.5; no need to be more specific than that, since the question asks for an approximately equal value.

Adding that together, we get (2 + 2.5) to 3, or $\frac{4.5}{3}$.

Now find a few handy equivalents to that ratio:

$\frac{4.5}{3}$ is equivalent to $\frac{9}{6}$, which equals $\frac{3}{2}$.

The correct answer choice is (B).

57. C

Generally, a simple way to calculate percent change problems is as multiplication problems, rather than as addition or subtraction problems. To add x%, multiply by $\left(\frac{1+x}{100}\right)$; to subtract x%, multiply by $\left(\frac{1-x}{100}\right)$. Here's the math:

$$(50{,}000)(1.2)(1.1)(0.95)= 62{,}700$$

Because 50,000 is a nice round number, and the percent changes are easy, you could actually add and subtract with this particular example.

Year 1: 50,000

Year 2: 50,000 + 20%(50,000) = 50,000 + 10,000 = 60,000

Year 3: 60, 000 + 10%(60,000) = 60,000 + 6,000 = 66,000

Year 4: 66,000 - 5%(66,000) = 66,000 - 3,300 = 62,700

The correct answer choice is (C).

58. D

The least number of students possible is the least number that can be divided by both 6 and 8, that is, the least common multiple (LCM) of 6 and 8. You don't have to remember from middle school how to find an LCM. You could just count by 8 till you get a multiple of 6. It won't take long; 24 is the answer.

What if the question didn't lend itself to that method?

You could also work from the answers. It probably isn't necessary for numbers as simple as these, but when you're asked to find the least number that satisfies a certain condition, start with the smallest of the answer choices and work your way up. Stop as soon as you find an answer that satisfies the condition.

The correct answer choice is (D).

59. E

Lucky for us we don't need to know this formula. Let's just see what we're given first:

$$D = 10$$
$$S = 650$$
$$P = 550$$
$$y = 300 \times \frac{(D+S-P)}{P}$$

Now plug everything in and solve for *y*:

$$y = 300 \times \frac{(10 + 650 - 550)}{550}$$

$$y = 300 \times \frac{(660 - 550)}{550}$$

$$y = 300 \times \frac{110}{550}$$

$$y = 300 \times \frac{1}{5} = \frac{300}{5}$$

$$y = 60$$

The percent yield for the investment in this scenario is 60%.

The correct answer choice is (E).

60. C

To tackle this one, let's start with what we know for sure by adding up the ones column: 6 + 7 + 8 = 21, so we've obviously got to carry a 2 over to the tens column.

In the tens column we now have (carried over 2) + 3 + 2 + q = _1. Let's think this one through as its own separate addition problem. 7 + q = _1. We need to add something with a 4 in the ones column (of the new breakaway addition problem) to get a sum with a ones value of 1 (that is, a sum of 11), so q can only equal 4.

Plugging q = 4 into the original addition problem, we now see that we'll need to carry a 1 (from the sum of 11 in the tens column) over into the hundreds column. In the hundreds column, we'll now add the carried over 1 + p + 5 + 1 = 9; 7 + p = 9, so p = 2.

Now for the last step: $q + p = 4 + 2 = 6$.

The correct answer choice is (C).

61. C

Recall the formula for probability:

$$\frac{\text{the number of desired outcomes}}{\text{the number of total possible outcomes}}$$

There are 6 possible outcomes for each die independently, and when we want the probability of two events happening together (i.e., two dice), we multiply the number of possibilities for the first event and the number of possibilities for the second event. Here, since there are 6 sides to each die and two total dice, there are 6 × 6 = 36 total possible outcomes for the faces (and their corresponding products).

Of these, there are a total of 4 desired outcomes whose product would be 6 (1 and 6; 6 and 1; 2 and 3; 3 and 2). So the probability is $\frac{4}{36} = \frac{1}{9}$.

The correct answer choice is (C).

62. E

Although a form of working backward from the choices must be employed here, some number properties knowledge will serve us well here by helping us determine the traits we'll want to look for in the credited response.

The $231x$ term is being subtracted, so the smaller the x value (and negative values count here, too), the greater the value of the entire expression. The smallest value of x among the answer choices is –2.

The correct answer choice is (E).

63. B

This one looks like a more complicated combined work question, but there's a much easier way to handle this one: as a proportion. We're given both Michael and Erika's spoon-painting rates, but they're in different formats. Let's standardize them first to a per-minute rate:

$$\text{Michael} = \frac{15\text{ spoons}}{3\text{ minutes}} = \frac{5\text{ spoons}}{1\text{ minute}}$$

$$\text{Erika} = \frac{8\text{ spoons}}{2\text{ minutes}} = \frac{4\text{ spoons}}{1\text{ minute}}$$

So how many spoons can they paint together in one minute? They can paint 5 + 4 = 9 spoons/minute. Now we need to determine how long it'll take the pair to paint 297 spoons. If they're working at a rate of 9 spoons/minute:

$$\frac{9 \text{ spoons}}{1 \text{ minute}} = \frac{297 \text{ spoons}}{x \text{ minutes}}$$

Now we've got a simple proportion, and all we really need to do to solve it is divide 297 spoons by 9 spoons/minute = 33 minutes.

The correct answer choice is (B).

64. C

This is a slightly disguised multiple percent change question, and we'll just need to do some quick calculations to solve it. Here's what we're given and how it works out:

b = base price = \$420

n = fare for nonstop flights = 1.3*b* = \$546

f = frequent flyer discount = 15% off of *n* = *n* - 0.15*n* = 0.85(\$546) = \$464.10

The correct answer choice is (C).

65. B

Draw a horizontal line from the *y*-axis at the value of 6 feet. Then draw a vertical line from the *x*-axis at the value of 7 miles per hour. Count all points that lie to the right of the vertical line and above the horizontal line (but do not lie *on* either line). There are 6 points that fulfill these criteria.

The correct answer choice is (B).

66. A

In parallelograms, opposite angles are always equal, so in this case, $y = 80$.

Since *x* and *y* add to a straight line, we know $x + y = 180$.

If $y = 80$, then $x = 100$.

Which answer is true when $x = 100$ and $y = 80$? $4x = 5y$.

The correct answer choice is (A).

67. C

You can probably do this one by "eyeballing" the figure, but if not, draw a vertical line to the *x*-axis from point *r* to find $x = 2$. Draw a horizontal line to the *y*-axis from point *r*; $y = 5$. Since the point is in Quadrant I, the values for both *x* and *y* will be positive.

The correct answer choice is (C).

68. D

Following the order of operations, simplify first, then solve:

$$\frac{\left[84 - 6\left(\frac{15}{5}\right)\right]}{\left(\frac{1}{3}\right)} = \frac{(84 - 18)}{\left(\frac{1}{3}\right)} = \frac{66}{\left(\frac{1}{3}\right)}$$

When dividing by a fraction, multiply by its reciprocal: $66 \times 3 = 198$.

The correct answer choice is (D).

69. E

Since we see the same variables in both the question and each answer choice, we never have to solve for any particular variable. That means you can assign values to *m*, *x*, and *h*, picking easy numbers to work with to make light work of the math. Using the numbers of your choice for *m*, *x*, and *h*, you can solve for a value. Then, just plug the same values you chose for *m*, *x*, and *h* into the answer choices to find the only one that works.

Let's say the jet flies $m = 20$ miles in $x = 10$ minutes, and it flies for $h = 2$ hours. If it flies 20 miles in 10 minutes, then it flies 120 miles in 60 minutes, or 1 hour. Then 120 miles in 1 hour means 240 miles in 2 hours. Plug in $m = 20$, $x = 10$, and $h = 2$ into each answer and find the answer that equals 240.

The correct answer choice is (E).

70. D

Solve by dividing: $\frac{9.009}{3.003} = 3$.

Alternate solution: Multiply the answer choices by 3.003 to see which yields 9.009 as its answer.

The correct answer choice is (D).

71. B

Keep this complex fraction straight as you go, observing proper order of operations. Simplify and solve:

$$\frac{3}{3}+\left\{\frac{3}{\left(\left[4+\left[\frac{1}{2}\right]\right]\right)}\right\}=\frac{3}{3}+\left\{\frac{3}{\left(\left[\frac{8}{2}+\frac{1}{2}\right]\right)}\right\}=\frac{3}{3}+\left\{\frac{3}{\left(\left[\frac{9}{2}\right]\right)}\right\}$$

Keep simplifying:

$$\frac{3}{3}+\left\{\frac{3}{\left(\left[\frac{9}{2}\right]\right)}\right\}=\frac{3}{3}+\left\{3\times\left[\frac{2}{9}\right]\right\}$$

$$=\frac{3}{3}+\left\{\frac{6}{9}\right\}$$

$$=\frac{3}{\left(\frac{27}{9}+\frac{6}{9}\right)}$$

$$=\frac{3}{\left(\frac{33}{9}\right)}$$

$$=\frac{3}{\left(\frac{11}{3}\right)}$$

Finally, to divide by a fraction, multiply by its reciprocal:

$$\frac{3}{\left(\frac{11}{3}\right)}=\frac{3}{1}\times\frac{3}{11}=\frac{9}{11}$$

The correct answer choices is (B).

72. C

It's smart to know the first ten prime numbers cold (2, 3, 5, 7, 11, 13, 17, 19, 23, 29). To get the greatest sum, add the greatest permissible numbers. Pick the three greatest prime numbers that are less than 20: 19, 17, and 13. The sum of these is 19 + 17 + 13 = 49.

The correct answer is choice (C).

73. E

This one is an arithmetic question (average of sets of numbers), but we can think through this one a little and save some unnecessary labor.

Since we're told that the two averages are equal, and both averages are made up of four terms, we know that the sums of the two sets must also be equal. We just need to find the sum of the first set to find the value of x in the second: $7 + 8 + 11 + 14 = 40$, so $3 + 5 + 15 + x = 40$; $23 + x = 40$; $x = 17$.

The correct answer is choice (E).

74. D

There are two ways to handle this: algebra or arithmetic. First, here is the algebra most test takers will employ:

Translate the given information into an algebraic equation. Increasing consecutive integers are represented algebraically as x, $x + 1$, $x + 2$, etc.

The last four integers in an increasing set of seven consecutive integers are:

$$\begin{aligned}(x+3)+(x+4)+(x+5)+(x+6) &= 34\\ 4x+18 &= 34\\ 4x &= 16\\ x &= 4\end{aligned}$$

(If you're not sure that you've correctly solved for x, check whether the integers 4 through 10 give you the appropriate sum. They do.)

If $x = 4$, the integers in the set are 4, 5, 6, 7, 8, 9, and 10. Therefore, the sum of the first 3 integers is $4 + 5 + 6 = 15$.

But the smart test taker can do this faster, using only arithmetic. If the sum of the last four integers is 34, then the average of those four integers is $\frac{34}{4} = 8.5$. So two of the four integers in question are immediately greater than 8.5 (read: 9 and 10), and two are immediately less than 8.5 (read: 8 and 7). That list must be 7, 8, 9, and 10. So the first three in question are 6, 5, and 4. Add $6 + 5 + 4$ to get their sum, which is 15.

The correct answer choice is (D).

75. B

To make lighter work of this fraction problem, cancel out elements to simplify. Starting with the innermost portion, the 2s cancel out, so $\left(\frac{2}{5} \times \frac{3}{2}\right)$ reduces to $\frac{3}{5}$. Next, dividing by 2 is the same thing as multiplying by $\frac{1}{2}$, so let's do that to keep things simple: $\left[\frac{3}{5} \times \frac{1}{2}\right] = \left[\frac{3}{10}\right]$.

Putting what we have so far together, we've got:

$\frac{1}{4} + \frac{3}{10} - \frac{11}{20} =$

We need a common denominator, so let's use 20 (the lowest common denominator):

$\frac{5}{20} + \frac{6}{20} - \frac{11}{20} = \frac{11}{20} - \frac{11}{20} = 0$

The correct answer choice is (B).

76. A

To solve this ratio question, we must keep in mind the two different types of ratios: part-to-part (as we're given here) and part-to-whole (which we'll need to solve).

For every 3 parts sodium, the powder contains 9 parts potassium. In algebraic language, for every $3x$ parts sodium, there are $9x$ parts potassium. That's a part-to-part ratio.

So the whole, then, would have $12x$ parts, and we're told that the whole equals 288. So if $12x = 288$,

$x = \frac{288}{12} = 24$. But remember, we need $3x$: $3 \times 24 = 72$ grams of sodium.

The correct answer choice is (A).

77. C

The fastest way to solve any combined work question is to know this formula:

$\frac{A \times B}{A + B}$ = time to complete a job together, where A = time for the first person to complete the job alone and B = time for the second person to complete the job alone.

If you didn't know the formula, you could still reason through this (or any) combined work question by holding the time constant, rather than the work. In this case, that means asking how much each can package in an hour, rather than how many hours it takes each to do the job.

Jesse can package $\frac{1}{3}$ of the day's products in one hour. His sister can package $\frac{1}{5}$ of the day's products in one hour. Working together the two can package $\frac{1}{3} + \frac{1}{5} = \frac{5}{15} + \frac{3}{15} = \frac{8}{15}$ of the day's products in one hour.

You have now calculated the number of jobs per hour. But since this question asks about the hours per job, just invert your answer: $\frac{15}{8} = 1\frac{7}{8}$ hours.

Here's a good elimination tip: Since there are two people working together, they will, obviously, take less time to complete a job than would the faster person alone. Eliminate anything equal to or slower than the rate of the faster person.

The correct answer choice is (C).

78. C

Set up a proportion to solve this rate question.

Jake's computer downloads $\frac{80 \text{ songs}}{2 \text{ minutes}}$, and since Jane's computer works at half this rate, it'll take her twice as long to download the same number of songs.

So Jane's computer's rate is $\frac{40 \text{ songs}}{2 \text{ minutes}}$. Now multiply by 4 to find the number of songs downloaded in 8 minutes: 40 × 4 = 160.

Jane's computer will download 160 songs in 8 minutes.

The correct answer choice is (C).

79. A

We know that the bill plus a 20% tip was $90. Algebraically, if *b* represents the bill, then $b + 20\% \times b = 90$ or $b + 0.2b = 90$, so $1.2b = 90$. Divide each side by 1.2: $b = \$75$. And the tip, let's call it *t*, would then = $15.

Next, we're asked how much less the diner would have paid if he only paid a 15% tip. Calculate 15% of $75: $12.25. Subtract this from the original $15.00 tip to find the savings: $15 - $12.25 = $3.75.

Alternatively, we know the 20% tip was $15. Since 15% = $\frac{3}{4}$ of 20%, a 15% tip would be $\frac{3}{4}$ of $15. Quickly, then, we can determine that the diner is saving $\frac{1}{4}$ of $15 (note that $\frac{1}{4} = \frac{1}{2}$ of $\frac{1}{2}$), or $3.75.

The correct answer choice is (A).

80. D

To nail questions like this one quickly, use the combined work formula:

$\frac{AB}{(A + B)}$ = time it takes two workers to complete a project working together, where A = worker A's time to complete the project alone and B = worker B's time to complete the project alone.

Here, $A = 6$ and $B = 7$. So:

$$\frac{6 \times 7}{(6 + 7)} = \frac{42}{13} = 3\frac{3}{13}$$

Now find the closest approximation among the answer choices.

The correct answer choice is (D).

81. C

Make sure you're clear on the definition of *median* and read carefully. The median is the middle-occurring value in an ordered set; if the set contains an even number of terms, then the median is the average of the two middle-occurring values.

Since the two sets have the same median, but the first has an even number of terms—and, therefore, a median of 7 (the average of 6 and 8)—while the second has an odd number of terms (because it also contains the new value), we can determine that the new value in the second set must, in fact, be the median value of 7. Otherwise, it would alter the median of the second set.

Alternate solution: Plug the answer choices into the second data set to see which produces a median that is equivalent to the median of the first list.

The correct answer choice is (C).

82. B

You could solve this with algebra. Translate the given information into an algebraic equation where *f* represents the week's total from fares:

$570 = 250 + (0.08)(f - 600)$

Simplify: $320 = 0.08(f - 600)$

Divide each side by 0.08: $\frac{320}{0.08} = f - 600$

Multiply the top and bottom on the left side by 100 to make the math easier: $\frac{32,000}{8} = f - 600$.

Simplify: 4,000 = *f* - 600; *f* = \$4,600.

Alternatively, you could use backsolving to work backward from the answer choices. Start with (B) or (D) to minimize the number of answer choices you need to assess.

The correct answer choice is (B).

83. A

By the far easiest method for this question is to try out factors for each answer choice to see whether those factors sum to 14.

Start with (A). What are the factors of -72? Since this is a negative number, one of the factors will have to be negative and the other positive. Since the sum is 14, the positive factor will have a greater absolute value than the negative factor it is paired with to get a product of -72. Make a "factor T" and start with small negative values, working up:

-1 × 72 . . . Sum is 71. Numbers need to be closer to one another.

-2 × 36 . . . Sum is 34. Numbers still need to be closer.

-3 × 24 . . . Sum is 21. Getting closer, but not close enough.

-4 × 18 . . . Sum is 14. Correct!

Stop as soon as you find an answer that works.

The correct answer choice is (A).

84. E

Any positive proper fraction squared is another, smaller, proper fraction.

You needn't calculate, but if you want to: $\left(\frac{7}{8}\right)^2 = \frac{49}{64} < 1$.

The correct answer choice is (E).

85. C

You might want to learn the formulas for combinations and permutations, but questions employing them are rare on the GMAT—you'll probably only see one, maybe two on your test. You can also just think through a question like this using logic instead.

If we have 12 coworkers, then there are 12 possible people who can fill the first slot on each team. Once this person is placed, there are 11 remaining possible coworkers to fill the second slot in each scenario . . . which means we have 12 × 11 possible combinations of the first two people on each team. Finishing things out, there are 10 possibilities for the last slot on each team in each of those 12 × 11 possible scenarios, so multiplying it out, we have 12 × 11 × 10 = 132 × 10 = 1,320 possible unique teams . . . *if* the order of the team members mattered.

But order doesn't matter here, and this value has counted each possible team 6 times. This is because this number assumes that each of the following is a unique team: ABC, ACB, BAC, BCA, CAB, and CBA.

But here, we know those six are all the same to us, so we'll divide 1,320 by 6 to get a total of 220 unique team combinations.

If you want to learn the combinations formula, here it is: $\frac{n!}{k!(n-k)!}$, where n = number of possibilities in the total group, k = the number chosen from that group, and ! stands for "factorial"—multiply the number by every positive number smaller than itself (e.g., 3! = 3 × 2 × 1; 6! = 6 × 5 × 4 × 3 × 2 ×1).

So here we'd have:

$$\frac{12!}{3!(12-3)!} = \frac{12!}{3!(9!)}$$

$$= \frac{12 \times 11 \times 10 \times 9 \times 8 \times 7 \times 6 \times 5 \times 4 \times 3 \times 2 \times 1}{3 \times 2 \times 1(9 \times 8 \times 7 \times 6 \times 5 \times 4 \times 3 \times 2 \times 1)}$$

$$= \frac{12 \times 11 \times 10}{3 \times 2 \times 1} = \frac{1,320}{6} = 220$$

[Hint: Don't do all these calculations; instead, cancel out like terms on top and bottom to make lighter work of this step.]

The correct answer choice is (C).

86. B

This one's actually not as bad as it might look. First, cross multiply to get rid of the fraction in the initial equation:

$\frac{2x}{(x+1)} = x - 1$, so $(x + 1)(x - 1) = 2x$

Next, multiply $(x + 1)(x - 1)$ using the FOIL method [Hint: This is a classic quadratic— its a "difference of two squares," or DOTS—the same terms with a different sign in the middle, where the middle terms cancel one another out] to get $x^2 - 1 = 2x$. Now get everything on one side so we can set the equation to 0: $x^2 - 2x - 1 = 0$.

Great! Now that we're here, we see that no further labor is required. We're asked for the value of $x^2 - 2x - 1$, and we already have it: 0.

The correct answer choice is (B).

87. C

To find the maximum number of workers who can ride the elevator, assume all workers are at the minimum weight (200 lbs). Translate the given information into an algebraic expression where w represents the maximum number of workers: $\frac{1{,}720}{200} = w; w = 86$. Since a fractional value cannot be used here—you need a whole number of people—the maximum number of workers is 8.

Alternate solution: Using the answer choices, work backward using a constant weight of 200 pounds per worker. Choose the answer that comes closest to the elevator capacity (1,720) without going over.

The correct answer choice is (C).

88. C

This is just a weighted average question that sounds tricky. If a question gives you nothing but percentages in the stimulus and responses, that means that the credited response will work regardless of the whole you start with. So make up a value for the total stock. Since the problem deals with percentages, use 100 to make the math easier. Since the company had a total stock of 100 bags, 65% or 65 bags were from South America, and 35% or 35 bags were from elsewhere.

Calculate the actual amount of coffee served at the open house:

South America: 60% of 65 = (0.6)(65) = 39 bags

Other: 40% of 35 = (0.40)(35) = 14 bags

The total amount used is 39 + 14 = 53 bags. Since the total stock is 100 bags, 53 bags also represents the percentage of stock that was served, 53%.

The correct answer choice is (C).

89. A

The simplest way to solve this is to recognize that each equation gives you two values for x and that the credited response will be the value for x that is a solution to both equations.

If the product of two numbers is 0, then one or both of those numbers must be 0. So, if $x(3x + 1) = 0$, then either $(x = 0)$ or $(3x + 1) = 0$. That is, $x = 0$ or $x = -\frac{1}{3}$.

Similarly, if $(4x + 1)(x + \frac{1}{3}) = 0$, then $x = -\frac{1}{4}$ or $x = -\frac{1}{3}$.

The solution these equations share is $x = -\frac{1}{3}$.

Note that you could also work backward from the answer choices.

The correct answer choice is (A).

90. C

You'll need to begin by translating the statements that "a reading of $x - 1$ indicates one-tenth the released energy as is indicated by a reading of x."

The statement quoted above means that a reading of 3, for instance, indicates 10 times the energy as does a reading of 2 and 100 times the energy as does a reading of 1.

Lets call energy *e*. For each increase of 1 on the scale, multiply *e* by 10:

Reading of 5: e

Reading of 6: $10e$

Reading of 7: $100e$

Reading of 8: $1{,}000e$

Reading of 9: $10{,}000e$

So a reading of 9 indicates 10,000 (or 10^4) times the energy of a reading of 5.

The correct answer choice is (C).

91. B

The first thing you should know is that solving this question involves absolutely no lengthy calculations of values raised to powers, as long as you know the basic rules for calculating exponents. In this case, the rule that you can use is this:

When raising one exponent to another, leave the base as is and multiply the exponents.

So let's rewrite the inequality to make the bases equal:

$3^8 > 9^x$ becomes $3^8 > (3^2)^x$

Now apply the rule of exponents above: $3^8 > 3^{2x}$.

Thus, $8 > 2x$, and $4 > x$.

Thus, the greatest possible integer value of x is 3.

The correct answer choice is (B).

92. C

If this question was too theoretical for you, pick some numbers for x and y and try out the statements with those numbers plugged in. This question's prime for such a strategy: Odds and evens always behave in predictable patterns, and so do prime numbers.

Based on the given information, we know that x and y are positive prime integers, x cannot equal y, and the product of xy is odd (which tells us that neither can equal 2, since an even times an odd will always be even).

Begin by assessing the statement that shows up most often in the answer choices. If it does not match the requirements of the question stem, all answer choices containing that statement can be eliminated.

Statement II shows up most often in the answer choices, so assess this statement first.

Statement II: $x - y$ = an even integer.

The difference of two odd integers is even. Since x and y are both odd integers, their difference will always equal an even integer. So Statement II must be true, and any choice *containing* it should be crossed out. Eliminate answer choices (A), (B), (D), and (E).

On Test Day, you can stop at this point because you have the correct answer, choice (C).

93. C

You need to determine the values of the expressions until you find at least two with the same value and a third with a different value.

(A) is $\frac{32}{4}$, or 8.

(B) is $\left(\frac{1}{2}\right)16$, or 8.

(C) is $8\left(\frac{1}{8}\right)$, or 1. You're done.

(D) $\left(\frac{6}{1.5}\right)(2) = \frac{12}{1.5} = 8$

(E) $\frac{1}{2} + 2 + \frac{1}{2} + 3 + 2 = 8$

The correct answer choice is (C).

94. C

To handle this percent change question, first find the price of 6 flowers if they are each sold separately: $6 \times 4 = 24$.

Now calculate how much more the 6 would cost as a bouquet: $27 - 24 = 3$.

To find the percent increase, divide the increase by the original value of the individual flowers:

$\frac{3}{24} = \frac{1}{8} = 12.5\%$

The correct answer choice is (C).

95. E

To determine whether a fraction is negative, ask yourself, "Which fraction has a numerator and denominator of different signs?"

This question requires you to know that when you raise a negative number to an even power, you get a positive number. It also requires you to know the results of multiplication and division by signed numbers.

(A) is positive, since the number under the radical is positive.

(B) is positive, because it is a positive over a positive.

(C) is positive, because *xy* is a negative times a negative, which is a positive.

(D) is positive, because it is a negative over a negative.

(E) is negative, because it is negative over a positive.

The correct answer is choice (E).

96. B

This question presents a pie chart, which is a way to break down percentages that add up to 100%. Using this knowledge, we can solve for *x*:

$$\begin{aligned} 65\% + 20\% + (x-3)\% + x\% &= 100\% \\ 85 + 2x - 3 &= 100 \\ 2x - 3 &= 15 \\ 2x &= 18 \\ x &= 9 \end{aligned}$$

But we're asked to solve for the portion of spending allotted to social services, so we'll need to plug $x = 9$ into $x - 3$: $9 - 3 = 6\%$ spent on social services.

Alternate solution: Work backward using the answer choices. Choose the value that brings the sum of the pie chart's elements to 100.

The correct answer choice is (B).

97. D

Since all the information is given in terms of percentages, and all the answers are in terms of percentages, you can choose values for the unknown quantities rather than treating them algebraically. For percentages questions, it makes sense to pick 100. Since *A* and *C* are both given in terms of *B*, assume that the shop sells 100 of *B* and then express $\frac{C}{A}$ as a percentage.

$B = 100$

$A = 125$

$C = 55$

$$\frac{C}{A} = \frac{55}{125} = \frac{11}{25} = \frac{44}{100} = 44\%$$

Algebraically, it looks like this:

Let *a* represent the sales of donut A, *b* represent the sales of donut B, and *c* represent the sales of donut C:

$a = 25\%$ more than $b = 0.25b + b = 1.25b$

$c = 45\%$ less than $b = b - 0.45b = 0.55b$

Plug these values into the percent proportion $\left(\frac{\%}{100} = \frac{\text{part}}{\text{whole}}\right)$.

$$\frac{x}{100} = \frac{c}{a}$$

$$\frac{x}{100} = \frac{(0.55b)}{(1.25b)}$$

$$1.25x = (0.55)(100)$$

$$x = 44\%$$

The correct answer choice is (D).

98. C

To solve this ratio question, set up a proportion and label each element with units. Be sure to keep units consistent across ratios, but since we're asked for *approximate* size, we know we can estimate:

$$\frac{9.1\text{ magnified}}{3\text{ actual size}} \approx \frac{9\text{ magnified}}{3\text{ actual size}} = \frac{3\text{ magnified}}{1\text{ actual size}}$$

We've determined that the magnified image is about 3 times as large as the actual image, so we can then determine that a 36-inch magnification has an actual size of $\frac{36}{3} = 12$ inches.

The correct answer choice is (C).

99. D

$$\text{Average} = \frac{\text{sum of values}}{\text{number of values}}$$

Use this formula to calculate the total number of cookies sold during the six-month period.

$$80{,}000 = \frac{\text{sum}}{6}$$

$$\text{sum} = 480{,}000$$

Now calculate the actual number of cookie sales in each of the first two-month periods.

1st two months: 70,000(2) = 140,000.

2nd two months: 60,000(2) = 120,000.

Therefore, the total cookies sold in the first four months was 140,000 + 120,000 = 260,000.

Subtract this from the total for all six months (480,000) to find the number of cookies sold during the final two-month period:

480,000 − 260,000 = 220,000

Use the average formula to find the final answer: $\frac{220{,}000}{2} = 110{,}000$.

Alternatively, you could ask, "How far below the average had cookie sales fallen in the first four months?" Since the company fell behind 10,000 in each of months 1 and 2 and 20,000 in each of months 3 and 4 (that is, 60,000 total), it needs to compensate with an extra 30,000 in each of months 5 and 6.

The correct answer choice is (D).

100. D

Since you have multiple variables here, and all answers are expressed in terms of t, the easiest way to solve is to pick a number for t. Let's say Allyn has 4 tattoos, so $t = 4$.

This is half as many as Krystal has, so Krystal has 8. It's 4 times as many as Joshua has, so Joshua has 1.

So they have 4 + 8 + 1 = 13 tattoos among the three of them.

Now plug 4 in for t in the answer choices to find the answer that equals 13.

If you wish to do the problem algebraically, translate the given information into algebraic expressions:

$$A = t$$

$$K = 2A = 2t$$

$$J = \frac{A}{4} = \frac{t}{4}$$

Add the totals to calculate their combined sum.

$$t + 2t + \frac{t}{4} = 3t + \frac{t}{4} = \frac{12t}{4} + \frac{t}{4} = \frac{13t}{4}$$

The correct answer choice is (D).

101. C

The hardest aspect of this question is keeping track of the different parts. It cost a total of $630 for 25 tickets, including tax (we'll get to the tax later). So $\frac{\$630}{25}$ = $25.20 per ticket, including tax.

Next, we know that each ticket price includes 5% tax, so (the base ticket price) + (5% tax) = $25.20.

Simplify that: base ticket + 0.05(base ticket) = $25.20; 1.05(base ticket) = $25.20

Divide each side by 1.05 to get the base ticket price (price before tax): base ticket = $24.00

However, there's a simpler way: You might have noticed that 30 is 5% of 600, so you can quickly subtract $30 from the $630 total price to remove the tax and get the total face value of all tickets combined. Now divide $600 by 25 to get $24 per ticket.

The correct answer choice is (C).

102. B

If it takes 3 minutes to drain $\frac{5}{7}$ of the tub, then it will take $\frac{7}{5}$ of 3 minutes to drain the entire tub.

$\frac{7}{5} \times 3$ = 4.2 minutes, or 4 minutes, 12 seconds

4 minutes, 12 seconds - 3 minutes = 1 minute, 12 seconds

The correct answer choice is (B).

103. C

First, use the information given to determine the radii of the two circles. Then, use the radii to determine the areas. Subtract the area of the small circle (fountain only) from the area of the large circle (fountain and walkway) to determine the area of the walkway.

For each circle, we need to use circumference to find radius:

Large circle (fountain and walkway): Circumference = $2\pi r = 10\pi$.

Diameter = 10; radius = 5.

Area = $\pi r^2 = \pi(5^2)$

$\text{Area}_{\text{(large)}} = 25\pi$

Small circle (fountain only): Circumference = $2\pi r = 2\pi$.

$2\pi = 2\pi r$, so $r = 1$

Area = $\pi(1^2)$

$\text{Area}_{\text{(small)}} = \pi$

Finally, let's get to the subtraction:

Area of walkway = $25\pi - \pi = 24\pi$

The correct answer choice is (C).

104. C

At first glance, this question seems to offer very little information, but we're looking for factors of 70 (three numbers that multiply to 70), so let's use a "factor tree" to find the prime factors of 70:

$$70 = 2 \times 35 = 2 \times 5 \times 7$$

We're also told that all three of the integers are greater than 1, so they must be 2, 5, 7, and the sum of the greatest two is 5 + 7 = 12.

The correct answer choice is (C).

105. C

The cookie recipe calls for 5 parts flour, 3 parts sugar, and 1 part butter, so we've got a total of 9 parts (5 + 3 + 1 = 9). Since there is a total of 81 ounces of batter, we know that each "part" represents 9 ounces (81 ounces of batter ÷ 9 "parts" = 9 ounces per part).

Now plug that into the recipe ratio, multiplying each number in the ratio by 9 ounces to find the actual ounces of each ingredient:

5 parts flour : 3 parts sugar : 1 part butter =

45 oz flour : 27 oz sugar : 9 oz butter (to check the math, 45 + 27 + 9 = 81)

Finally, we're asked how many more ounces there are of flour in the batter than there are of sugar: 45 - 27 = 18.

The correct answer choice is (C).

106. E

Probability = # desired outcomes/ # total possible outcomes. In this case, the equation would be blue shirts/total number of shirts.

Blue shirts = $b + 5$

Total = $b + w + 5 - 4 = b + w + 1$

Therefore, $\frac{b+5}{b+w+1}$ represents the probability of choosing a blue shirt from the final configuration of the dresser.

The correct answer choice is (E).

107. D

In this question, we're given the value of y in terms of x, so all we need to do to solve for x is to plug the value of y into the first equation and solve for x: $6x - 2x = 24$; $4x = 24$; $x = 6$.

Alternatively, you could work backward from the answer choices, looking for an answer where $4x = 24$, but when the algebra is this straightforward, why would you?

The correct answer choice is (D).

108. D

Translate the given information into algebra. Begin with one variable for the number of toys the cat has and another variable for the number of toys the dog has.

Let c represent the number of toys Ellen's cat has and d represent the number of toys her dog has.

Then $d + c = t$ and $d = xc$. Therefore, by substitution, $xc + c = t$.

Factor out the c: $c(x + 1) = t$.

Divide both sides by $(x + 1)$ to solve for c: $c = \frac{t}{x+1}$.

Alternatively, you can pick some easy numbers for c and x, use them to solve for d and t, and then plug the same values into each answer choice to see which one works out to your value for c. Let's say $c = 2$ and $x = 4$. Then d must = 8 and t must = 10. Plug these values into the answer choices to find the one that works out to 2, the value (of c) that the question asked us to find.

The correct answer choice is (D).

109. E

This is just a thinly veiled systems of equations question. First, let's organize the information we have and add a variable for the one we're missing. Let's call the unknown number of remaining items (beyond the first 1,000) r.

Now, let's calculate with the info we're given:

75% × 1,000 = 750 items sold out of the first 1,000.

We're told that this 750 items plus 30% of the remaining number of items is equal to 40% of the total number of items:

$750 + (30\% \times r) = 40\% \times (1{,}000 + r)$

So $750 + 0.3r = 400 + 0.4r$

Let's get rid of the decimals by multiplying everything by 10:

$$7{,}500 + 3r = 4{,}000 + 4r$$
$$3{,}500 = r$$

Since we're asked to solve for the total number of items offered for sale, we're looking for $(1{,}000 + r)$.

1,000 + 3,500 = 4,500

The correct answer choice is (E).

110. E

Solve the given equation for the value of y in terms of x.

The cube root of $\left(\frac{y}{x}\right) = 2x$.

$$\frac{y}{x} = (2x)^3$$

$$\frac{y}{x} = 8x^3$$

$$y = (8x^3)(x)$$

$$y = 8x^4$$

The correct answer choice is (E).

111. E

To solve this, just plug the given value of °F into the equation and solve for °C:

$94 = °\ C\left(\frac{9}{5}\right) + 32$

Subtract 32 from each side:

$62 = °\ C\left(\frac{9}{5}\right)$

Multiply each side by 5 to get rid of the fraction:

$310 = 9°\ C$

Divide each side by 9 to solve for °C:

$34.44 = °C$

You might also have plugged in the values from each answer choice to see which one satisfies the given equation.

The correct answer choice is (E).

112. E

Plug the provided values into the given equation to see how often the initial $2,500 triples in value within this period.

$$\frac{112}{x} = \frac{112}{8} = 14 \text{ years}$$

The money will triple every 14 years. Therefore, the money will triple $\frac{28}{14}$ times = 2 (twice) in 28 years.

So after 14 years, the initial $2,500 investment will have grown to 3 × $2,500, or $7,500. Tripling again after 14 more years, the $7,500 will have grown to 3 × $7,500, or $22,500.

The correct answer choice is (E).

113. B

Translate the given information into an algebraic equation and solve for x.

The square root of $\left[\frac{6x}{4}\right] = x$

$$\frac{6x}{4} = x^2$$

$$6x = 4x^2$$

$$6 = 4x$$

$$\frac{6}{4} = \frac{3}{2} = x$$

You could plug in the answer choices to see which value satisfies the given information, but if the first answer choice you try doesn't work, you've got some ugly arithmetic ahead of you. Better to approach this one algebraically.

The correct answer choice is (B).

114. D

Questions that ask you to substitute a value for a variable are really arithmetic questions and are primarily concerned with the order of operations.

Substitute –2 for x in the expression and solve for the value of the expression. Be sure to place the –2 in parentheses when you substitute and respect those parentheses when you apply the order of operations.

$$\frac{-2+1}{(-2)^3-(-2)^2+(-2)} = \frac{-1}{-8-4-2}$$
$$= \frac{-1}{-14}$$
$$= \frac{1}{14}$$

The correct answer choice is (D).

115. E

If the square root of x is greater than 16, then $x > 16^2$, or $x > 256$.

If $x > 256$, then $\frac{x}{16} > \frac{256}{16}$, or $x > 16$.

Only choice (E), 17, satisfies this inequality.

116. C

Perimeter of a rectangle = 2 × *length* + 2 × *width*.

If we call the width of the photograph w, then the length (l) would be (w + 2).

So:

$$\begin{aligned} 2w + 2(w+2) &= 18 \\ 4w + 4 &= 18 \\ 4w &= 14 \\ 2w &= 7 \\ w &= \frac{7}{2} \end{aligned}$$

And since $l = w + 2$, we can determine that

$$l = \frac{7}{2} + 2; \quad l = \frac{7}{2} + \frac{4}{2}; \quad l = \frac{11}{2}$$

Also, although it's not particularly elegant, this question does allow you to work backward from answer choices. Applying the formula for perimeter, which is Perimeter of a rectangle = 2 × (*length* + *width*), we know the dimensions should add up to half the perimeter. Which dimensions add to 9?

The correct answer choice is (C).

117. C

There are a total of two roads that can initially be taken. At the next choice point, travelers have a choice of two roads, and at the third and final choice point, travelers can choose any one of four roads. Thus, the total number of different routes is 2 × 2 × 4 = 16.

Alternate solution: Map out each path individually while strategically eliminating answer choices.

The correct answer choice is (C).

118. B

It's often easier to use fractions than it is to use decimals (and percents), so let's do that. In fact, you should know some common decimal-to-fraction conversions for this express purpose. If you commit $\frac{1}{2}$, $\frac{1}{3}$, $\frac{1}{4}$, $\frac{1}{5}$, and $\frac{1}{10}$ to memory (if you haven't already), just about every other fraction you'll need on the GMAT is a multiple of one or more of those.

Instead of 25% or 0.25, let's use $\frac{1}{4}$, and instead of 30% (or 0.3), let's use $\frac{3}{10}$.

We're told that $\frac{1}{4}$ of Shana's current 56-pair shoe collection consists of sneakers, so 14 pairs are sneakers. But she's buying 14 more pairs, which will bring the collection to a total of 70 pairs, $\frac{3}{10}$ of which should be sneakers. Reducing out the 10s, we find that she'll have a total of 7 × 3 = 21 sneakers, 14 of which are old. Thus, she'll need to buy 7 more pairs.

The correct answer choice is (B).

119. A

The three relevant values are related by this formula for passenger miles per gallon:

$$\frac{\text{total passenger miles}}{\text{total fuel consumed}} = \frac{3.2 \times 10^9}{200 \text{ million}}$$

Because some of the information is given in scientific notation and some is given in standard notation, you have to decide which notation to use. If you're good at manipulating exponents, you might try scientific notation:

$$\frac{3.2 \times 10^9}{2.0 \times 10^8} = \frac{3.2 \times 10^1}{2.0} = \frac{32}{2} = 16$$

If you'd prefer standard notation, you can just barely get away with it here. If the power of ten were much larger, it would be pretty awkward:

$$\frac{3{,}200{,}000{,}000}{200{,}000{,}000} = \frac{32}{2} = 16$$

The correct answer choice is (A).

120. A

You could try out each answer choice by finding permissible values for x and y, such that xy yields the product in the answer choice, then eliminate all answer choices for which the product xy could produce this value.

However, it's more efficient to notice that, since y is greater than 9, it must be positive. Similarly, since x is greater than or equal to 0, it cannot be negative. The product of any two non-negative numbers is also non-negative, and noticing that there's only one negative value provided, we can make light work of this one.

The correct answer choice is (A).

121. D

Calculate the total price of the purchase with a 3% sales tax:

3% sales tax on \$366 = 1.03 × \$366 = \$376.98.

Now calculate the total price of the purchase with a 6% sales tax:

6% sales tax on \$366 = 1.06 × \$366 = \$387.96.

The range described by the correct response must contain all the possible values from \$376.98 to \$387.96. Just to be clear, even a very large range—say \$10 to \$10,000—could be correct, so long as it contained all the values from \$376.98 to \$387.96.

The correct answer choice is (D).

122. D

Note that the borrower will have to pay a max of 9% interest (and we want the max here), so that would be 100% of the \$250 base + 9% interest on the 250 + a 1% surcharge on the base plus interest. Simplified, here's how that would look: 1.01(1.09 × \$250).

It may be easier to do this in steps:

1.09(\$250) = \$272.50

1% of \$272.50 = \$2.73

\$272.50 + \$2.73 = \$275.23

The correct answer choice is (D).

123. D

First calculate the actual number of kilograms of sugar in the 40 kilograms of syrup.

35% of 40 = (0.35)(40) = 14 kilograms of sugar

If 10 kilograms of sugar are added, the total amount of sugar would be 14 + 10 = 24, and the total weight of syrup would be 40 + 10 = 50.

Percentage can be calculated by $\frac{x}{100} = \frac{\text{part}}{\text{whole}}$.

So $\frac{x}{100} = \frac{24}{50} = \frac{48}{100}$.

The percentage of sugar by weight in the new solution is 48%.

The correct answer choice is (D).

124. E

The entire pattern is four shapes long, after which it repeats. The circle is the third shape in this pattern. Therefore, the number of shapes in a pattern that ends in a circle must be 3 more than a multiple of 4.

This can be expressed as $4n + 3$.

Subtract 3 from each answer choice and choose the one the one that yields a multiple of 4. Choice (E), 47, works.

The correct answer choice is (E).

125. E

Simplify and solve: $(10^5 - 10^3)(0.00037)$

Distribute the 0.00037:

$(10^5)(0.00037) - (10^3)(0.00037)$

$= (100{,}000)(0.00037) - (1{,}000)(0.00037)$

$= 37.3737373737 - 0.373737373737$

$= 37.0$

The correct answer choice is (E).

126. D

$$A_{rectangle} = length \times width$$

To find the fraction of the unraised portion of the sandbox, we'll need to calculate the overall area, subtract the raised portions from that area, and then formulate the appropriate fraction. The area of the sandbox is $20 \times 10 = 200$ ft^2, and the area of each of the 3 raised squares is $4 \times 4 = 16$ ft^2, so the total raised area is $3 \times 16 = 48$ ft^2, which leaves 152 ft^2 of unraised area. So the fraction of the sandbox that is not raised is

$$\frac{152}{200} = \frac{76}{100} = \frac{38}{50} = \frac{19}{25}$$

The correct answer choice is (D).

127. B

Translate the given information into an algebraic equation. Since we're asked for Nancy's age in 2 years, solve in terms of N. Let Nancy's age = N and Devon's age = D.

Here's what we know:

$$N + 20 = D \text{ and } N + 6 = \left(\frac{1}{3}\right)(D + 6)$$

[Note: Remember to add 6 years to Devon's age, too.]

Substitute $(N + 20)$ in place of D, which makes the second equation: $N + 6 = \left(\frac{1}{3}\right)[(N + 20) + 6]$

Simplify:

$$N+6 = \left(\frac{1}{3}\right)\left(N+26\right)$$
$$3(N+6) = N+26$$
$$3N+18 = N+26$$

Manipulate the equation to get just Ns on one side and just values on the other:

Subtract N from both sides: $3N + 18 = N + 26$; $2N + 18 = 26$.

Then subtract 18 from both sides: $2N = 8$; $N = 4$.

Finally, remember to add 2: $N + 2 = 6$.

The correct answer choice is (B).

128. A

This question requires almost no computation once the translation is complete, so if you are good at algebra translation, you should definitely use that skill here: $\frac{d}{200}$ equals the original cost per bag. The wholesale club resells it at a markup of 40% or $(1.4)\left(\frac{d}{200}\right) = \frac{1.4d}{200}$. This fractional value is equivalent to $\frac{7d}{1{,}000}$.

Alternatively, you can pick a number for the unknown value. For instance, in this case, you could stipulate that $d = 200$ so that each bag costs \$1.00 before the markup and \$1.40 after. Then plug 200 in place of d in each of the answer choices and see which gives you \$1.40.

The correct answer choice is (A).

129. B

There are a number of different ways to arrive at the correct answer. We'll look at two.

First, label the students A, B, C, etc. You could say A has to play 18 other students. B, though, has to play only 17 others (because you've already counted her game against A). And C has to play 16 others (because you've already counted her games against both A and B).

Follow this pattern and you will count down to 1, like this:

$18 + 17 + 16 + 15 + 14 + 13 + 12 + 11 + 10 + 9 + 8 + 7 + 6 + 5 + 4 + 3 + 2 + 1 = 171$

A simpler way to do the problem, though, is to note that every student plays every other student, so every student has 18 games. This would seem to yield 19 × 18 games, or 342 games. But, of course, this counts every game twice. For instance, it counts the first game as a game between A and B, and as a game between B and A. Correct for this by dividing by 2.

The formula for this sort of situation, where you have *N* players, each of whom must play each of the others, is $\frac{N \times (N-1)}{2}$

The correct answer choice is (B).

130. C

In questions like this that present us with an unknown function—represented by an unusual symbol—our task is merely to plug the numbers in the question into the function as it is defined. It's like substitution, but for the operation instead of the values. Be sure to follow the same order of operations we always use, in this case, starting inside the parentheses. Here's how it works out:

$$6 \triangle 9 = \frac{6^2}{9} = \frac{36}{9} = 4$$

Now complete it:

$$4 \triangle 2 = \frac{4^2}{2} = \frac{16}{2} = 8$$

The correct answer choice is (C).

131. B

Let's use some common sense here. The company pays an elevated rate for the first hour of work, so it would definitely save money by paying the contractor in one lump sum rather than paying per project (it would have to pay the first hour rate twice instead of once).

How much would the company save? Well, it can't short on overall hours, but it can swap out the increased rate on the second project's first hour for a regular additional hour. So the difference in overall pay is the difference between the pay rates for the one hour in question: $\$(a - b)$.

To make this less abstract, pick real values for *a* and *b*, then figure out the difference between the two scenarios: Let's say *a* is 10 and *b* is 5.

Paying on a per-project basis, we have a 2-hour project being paid $(10 + 5) plus a 4-hour project being paid $(10 + 5 + 5 + 5) for a total of $40.

Paying a lump sum for all hours, we have 6 hours being paid $(10 + 5 + 5 + 5 + 5 + 5) = $35.

Thus, the difference is $5, or $\$(a - b)$.

The correct answer choice is (B).

132. B

We need to recall a few coordinate geometry formulas in order to work this one out:

Coordinates of a point: (x, y)

Slope-intercept formula for a line: $y = mx + b$, where

m is the slope $\left(\frac{\text{rise}}{\text{run}}\right)$,

b is the *y*-intercept,

and x and y represent the *x*- and *y*-coordinates relative to one another.

$$m = \text{slope} = \frac{\text{rise}}{\text{run}} = \frac{(y_2 - y_1)}{(x_2 - x_1)}$$

We're given $x = 2y + 8$, so let's put that in slope-intercept form so we can pull out what we need:

$$2y = x - 8; \quad y = \frac{1}{2}x - 4$$

So now we know that the slope of the described line $= \frac{1}{2}$.

Finally, let's use the formula for slope with two known points to solve for k:

Point 1: (a, b), so $x_1 = a$ and $y_1 = b$.

Point 2: $(a - 4, b + k)$, so $x_2 = (a - 4)$ and $y_2 = (b + k)$.

We know slope $= \frac{(y_2 - y_1)}{(x_2 - x_1)}$, so . . .

$y_2 - y_1 = (b + k) - b = k$

And . . .

$x_2 - x_1 = (a - 4) - a = -4$

So $\frac{(y_2 - y_1)}{(x_2 - x_1)} = \frac{k}{-4}$.

Using the known value for m from above:

$$\frac{k}{-4} = \frac{1}{2}; \quad k = \left(\frac{1}{2}\right)\left(\frac{-4}{1}\right) = \frac{-4}{2} = -2$$

The correct answer choice is (B).

133. C

Don't be put off by the odd appearance of symbol questions; they're just strange-looking functions (substitution questions). To handle this one, simply plug the given information into the algebraic expression and solve:

$$\frac{1}{(x+c)} = \frac{1}{x}$$

$$x = x + c$$

$$0 = c$$

The correct answer choice is (C).

134. C

Since the flagpole stands at a 90-degree angle to the ground, we know that the distance between the end of its shadow and the top of the flagpole is the hypotenuse of a right triangle. The Pythagorean theorem states that hypotenuse^2 = side^2 + side^2. Use this formula to find the ground length from the base of the flagpole to the end of its shadow:

$$8^2 = x^2 + 5^2$$

$$64 = x^2 + 25$$

$$39 = x^2$$

$$x = \sqrt{39}$$

Subtract this distance from the total distance between the base of the flagpole and the school to find the total distance from the flagpole's shadow to the school: $15 - \sqrt{39}$.

The correct answer choice is (C).

135. D

Often when we see odd shapes, we can break them up into two or more smaller and more familiar shapes. Draw a horizontal line across the bottom of the wedge to form two shapes, the upper one a triangle with a height of 5 and an unknown base, and the lower one a rectangle with a width of 1 and an unknown length. The area of the entire wedge will equal the sum of the area of these two shapes. To find the length of the unknown side of the triangle, use the Pythagorean theorem: In a right triangle, $a^2 + b^2 = c^2$, where c is the hypotenuse:

$$a^2 + 5^2 = (\sqrt{61})^2$$
$$a^2 + 25 = 61$$
$$a^2 = 36$$
$$a = 6$$

Now let's use that to calculate the area of the triangular portion:

$\left(\frac{1}{2}\right)$(base)(height) = $\left(\frac{1}{2}\right)(6)(5) = (3)(5) = 15$

Next, we need to calculate the area of the rectangle: length × width. We now know the length is 6, so the area is (6)(1) = 6.

Finally, let's add everything up: The area of the entire shape is equal to the area of the triangle plus the area of the rectangle: 15 + 6 = 21.

The correct answer choice is (D).

136. E

This is a basic algebraic equation. You can begin by multiplying both sides by x to get rid of the fractions: $3x + 3 = 4x - 4$.

Next, add 4 to both sides, and then subtract $3x$ from both sides to solve: $7 = x$.

And if you're not a fan of algebra, you could always plug the answer choices into the given equation and see which one works out.

The correct answer choice is (E).

137. C

If a question presents the very same rate or ratio using two different sets of terms, it's usually best to set up a proportion. In this question, the rate of sets returned to sets sold is given as 73 to 100,000, and the actual number of sets sold is 5,000,000. So the proportion will look like this: $\frac{73}{100{,}000} = \frac{x}{5{,}000{,}000}$.

The standard way to handle proportions is to cross multiply, then solve for the variable. That's fine, but there are often easier ways. Here, for instance, we know that whatever multiplier gets us from denominator to denominator will also get us from numerator to numerator. Since 100,000 × 50 = 5,000,000, 73 × 50 = x; therefore, x = 3,650.

The correct answer choice is (C).

138. A

Since we're told that 20% of the members of the class have been accepted, we know that the remainder who have not been accepted must account for 80% of the class. We also know that this 80% is 640 students: the 200 who have applied but not been accepted, plus the 440 who have not applied.

Let x = the number of students in the class.

$0.8x = 640$; $x = \frac{640}{0.8} = \frac{6{,}400}{8} = 800$

The correct answer choice is (A).

139. D

We're given the current ratio of cooks to waiters, $\frac{3}{13}$, but the actual number of cooks and waiters could be any multiple of 3 and 13, respectively. If we call the unknown multiplier x, we can say that the original number of cooks was $3x$, and the original number of waiters was $13x$ (i.e., $\frac{3}{13} = \frac{3x}{13x}$). When 12 more waiters are added, the resulting ratio is $\frac{3x}{13x + 12}$, which we're told is equal to $\frac{3}{16}$.

$$\frac{3x}{13x + 12} = \frac{3}{16}$$

Cross multiply to get $16(3x) = 3(13x + 12)$.

Distribute to get $48x = 39x + 36$.

Subtract $39x$ from both sides to get $9x = 36$.

Divide to get $x = 4$.

Remember, we're solving for the number of cooks, so solve for $3x$: $3x = 12$.

The correct answer choice is (D).

140. C

To determine the value of $x - 9$, you must of course solve the other equation for x. The fact that the question asks "which . . . *could* be the value" indicates that x could have more than one solution, thus cluing you in to what your first step should be.

$(x - 2)^2 = 900$

Begin by taking the square root of both sides: $(x - 2) = 30$ or $(x - 2) = -30$.

Add 2 to both sides to determine the two possible values of x:

$x = 32$ or $x = -28$

Now, for the final step, substitute each of these into $x - 9$ to see which one will give us an answer that appears in one of the choices:

$32 - 9 = 23$

And . . .

$-28 - 9 = -37$

Since 23 is not a choice given, −37 is the correct choice.

The correct answer choice is (C).

141. A

There are a couple of ways to approach this one.

You might rewrite the original inequality as $w^2 < 9$. Keeping in mind that the square root of w can either be a positive or a negative number, take the square root of both sides to get $w < 3$ and $w > -3$.

On the other hand, you might notice here that the left side of the inequality is a classic quadratic—a factorable expression of the form $x^2 - y^2$. Such an expression always factors to $(x + y)(x - y)$. Applying that model here yields $(3 + w)(3 - w) = 0$.

Solve the equation $(3 + w)(3 - w) = 0$. If the product of these two expressions is 0, then one of them must be 0. This means that w is either 3 or −3.

So the inequality is true for all values of w equal to or greater than −3 and less than or equal to 3.

Thus, $-3 < w < 3$.

The correct answer choice is (A).

142. E

To solve for the probability that the businessman will wear a white shirt at least once, traditional methods will be highly inefficient. The traditional approach would be to figure out all the different possible combinations of shirt selections that would include at least one white shirt, calculate the probability for each, then add them up.

The good news: There's a faster way. Look at this problem from the opposite viewpoint. Instead of calculating the desired outcomes—which here are too numerous to be manageable—let's instead calculate the undesirable outcomes and subtract those from the total probability of 1. In other words, determine what the probability is that the man will wear a blue or gray shirt on all four days (i.e., wear no white shirt at all), which is represented by $\left(\frac{2}{3}\right)^4$ or $\frac{16}{81}$. Subtracting this fraction from 1 will show the "other side" of the probability, the chance that the man *will* wear a white shirt at least once: $1 - \frac{16}{81} = \frac{81}{81} - \frac{16}{81} = \frac{65}{81}$.

The correct answer choice is (E).

143. D

This problem requires you to combine the four groups of students to determine the total number who took the exam. Since three of these groups are represented as fractions, represent them in conjunction with the variable that represents the total number of students: $\frac{1}{8}x + \frac{1}{6}x + \frac{2}{3}x + 20 = x$. Find a common denominator for the fractions of x and add them together:

$\frac{3}{24}x + \frac{4}{24}x + \frac{16}{24}x + 20 = x$; $\frac{23}{24}x + 20 = x$

Subtract $\frac{23}{24}x$ from each side: $20 = \frac{1}{24}x$.

Multiply each side by 24 to get rid of the fraction and solve: $480 = x$.

And if this is a bit tough for you, you could always work backward from the answer choices, looking for a value of x that works in the scenario presented.

The correct answer choice is (D).

144. C

You could answer this question by solving each equation with the two values, 98 and 99, or, considering that any increase by 1 would have the same result, you could solve each equation with smaller values, such as 2 and 3. Or, better yet, you could just apply common sense to each of the equations.

Begin by assessing the statement that shows up most often in the answer choices. If it does not match the requirements of the question stem, all answer choices containing that statement can be eliminated.

Statement II shows up most often in the answer choices, so assess this statement first.

Statement II: If you increase the value of a denominator in a positive fraction, the value that the fraction represents will be smaller ($\frac{1}{99}$ is a smaller value than $\frac{1}{98}$). However, with a negative fraction, the reverse is true ($\frac{-1}{98}$ is less than $\frac{-1}{99}$). This will increase. You must keep all the answer choices that contain Statement II. Eliminate (B).

Statement I: If you multiply a number by a higher number, its value will increase, and even if you then subtract a constant from it, its value will still be higher than if you had multiplied the number by a lower number. This will increase. So, the correct answer must contain Statement I. Eliminate (A) and (D).

Statement III: Since this expression will always be a positive fraction, the higher the value of the denominator, the lower the overall value of the fraction. This will *not* increase. Eliminate (E).

Thus, only Statements I and II result in a higher value.

The correct answer choice is (C).

145. B

The greatest distance d across the monolith will be from one corner to another. You'll want to use the Pythagorean theorem to calculate the diagonal. Note: the diagonal of a box is the same as the diagonal of a rectangle, but you'll have to account for the extra dimension. Then solve for d.

Rectangle: $x^2 + y^2 = d^2$

Box: $x^2 + y^2 + z^2 = d^2$

Adding in the dimensions:

$$1^2 + 4^2 + 9^2 = d^2$$
$$98 = d^2$$
$$\sqrt{98} = AD$$
$$\sqrt{49}\sqrt{2} = AD$$
$$7\sqrt{2} = AD$$

The correct answer choice is (B).

146. B

Take the percentage given for each of the 1998 figures, make the appropriate increase or decrease, and then add the resulting values.

Amt. spent on health insurance 1998: \$8,700

Amt. spent on health insurance 1999: 1.3 × \$8,700 = \$11,310

Amt. spent on bonuses 1998: \$3,000

Amt. spent on bonuses 1999: 0.55 × $3,000 = $1,650

$11,310 + $1,650 = $12,960

The correct answer choice is (B).

147. B

This problem may seem odd at first, but it's actually fairly uncomplicated. All you have to do is substitute –5 for *w* and 4 for *z* in the expression given:

$wz - 5(w + z) = -5(4) - 5(-5 + 4) = -20 - 5(-1) = -20 + 5 = -15$

The correct answer choice is (B).

148. C

One way to solve this problem is to create a Venn diagram. Place the number of coaches who teach more than one team into the appropriate overlapping sections, 3 in the track-tennis intersection, 2 in the track-baseball intersection, and 1 in the tennis-baseball intersection. Then, it's only a matter of subtracting the intersecting quantities from the number of coaches given in the chart for each sport.

For example, there are 5 coaches in the overlapping part of the track set. Subtracting 5 from the number of coaches who work with the track team (8) will indicate that only 3 work exclusively with the track team.

Enter this number into the diagram and then do the same for the other two teams. Finally, add all the numbers in the diagram: 3 + 1 + 1 + 3 + 2 + 1 = 11.

However, there's an even quicker way: Forget about drawing a Venn diagram. Instead, add the number of coaching jobs as listed on the chart provided: 8 + 5 + 4 = 17. Now add up the total number of people who hold two coaching positions per the question's setup: 3 + 2 + 1 = 6. Finally, 17 jobs – 6 people counted twice (because they hold two different coaching positions) = 11 different coaches.

The correct answer choice is (C).

149. D

The fact that $\frac{1}{5}$ of the students answered the first question correctly can be represented as $\left(\frac{1}{5}\right)x$. Next, multiply this by the fraction who also got the second question correct, $\frac{1}{2}$, to get $\left(\frac{1}{2}\right)\left(\frac{1}{5}\right)x = \frac{x}{10}$.

Finally, answer the right question. Since $\frac{x}{10}$ represents the number of students who answered both questions correctly, the number of students who didn't answer both questions correctly can be represented as $x - \frac{x}{10} = \frac{9x}{10}$.

If this was tricky for you, pick a number for *x* and plug it into the scenario and answer choices to make things more concrete (and, therefore, easier). Pick an easy number that is divisible by both 2 and 5—like 10.

The correct answer choice is (D).

150. E

The information given is the ratio of ties to shirts $\left(\frac{3}{5}\right)$ and the fact that the man bought 4 new ties and 4 new shirts.

However, since neither the original number of either shirts or ties is given, there is no way to calculate the new ratio—it could be that he actually had 3 ties and 5 shirts before the new purchase, or he could have had 6 and 10, or 30 and 50, respectively, or some other number.

If either number had been given, the new ratio could be determined, but since neither number is given, the new ratio cannot be determined.

The correct answer choice is (E).

Data Sufficiency

PREVIEWING DATA SUFFICIENCY

A Data Sufficiency question stem will never give you enough information to solve for an answer, which is very different from typical math problems. You're probably used to having a lot of information presented up front, followed by the actual question. But Data Sufficiency works differently: The other data are presented after the initial question; these are called the "statements."

Your goal in a Data Sufficiency question is to determine whether the data in the statements are enough to allow you to answer the question. Many Data Sufficiency questions can be solved without finding the specific answer to the question presented in the stem.

QUESTION FORMAT AND STRUCTURE

The instructions for the Data Sufficiency section on the GMAT look like this:

> **Directions:** In each of the problems, a question is followed by two statements containing certain data. You are to determine whether the data provided by the statements are sufficient to answer the question. Choose the correct answer based upon the statements' data, your knowledge of mathematics, and your familiarity with everyday facts (such as the number of minutes in an hour or cents in a dollar). You must indicate whether
>
> - Statement (1) ALONE is sufficient, but statement (2) is not sufficient.
> - Statement (2) ALONE is sufficient, but statement (1) is not sufficient.
> - BOTH statements TOGETHER are sufficient, but NEITHER statement ALONE is sufficient.
> - EACH statement ALONE is sufficient.
> - Statements (1) and (2) TOGETHER are NOT sufficient.
>
> **Note:** Diagrams accompanying problems agree with information given in the question but may not agree with additional information given in statements (1) and (2).
>
> All numbers used are real numbers.

On the Quantitative section, you'll see about 15 Data Sufficiency questions, which ask you to assess whether certain statements provide enough information to answer a question. Often the question requires little or no mathematical work. The key to solving the question is understanding how the question type is structured and using that knowledge to work efficiently.

The directions may seem confusing at first, but they become clear with use. Let's walk through a straightforward example:

Is x greater than 2.7?

(1) $x > 2.6$

(2) $x > 2.8$

- Statement (1) ALONE is sufficient, but statement (2) is not sufficient.
- Statement (2) ALONE is sufficient, but statement (1) is not sufficient.
- BOTH statements TOGETHER are sufficient, but NEITHER statement ALONE is sufficient.
- EACH statement ALONE is sufficient.
- Statements (1) and (2) TOGETHER are NOT sufficient.

This question asks whether the information in one or both statements is sufficient to answer a yes or no question. The interesting thing about this type of Data Sufficiency question is that a "no" is just as conclusive as a "yes." As long as the answer is always a "yes" or always a "no," the information is sufficient.

Statement (1) notes that $x > 2.6$. If $x > 2.6$, it is uncertain whether x is greater than 2.7. The value of x could be 2.65, or it could be 2.8. Statement (1) is not sufficient to answer the question.

Statement (2), on the other hand, is sufficient. If $x > 2.8$, then we know with certainty that the value of x will be greater than 2.7. Values greater than 2.8 will always be greater than 2.7.

The credited response is (B). The information provided in statement (2) leads to a definite answer (for the record here, an absolute "yes" in all possible circumstances), but statement (1) allows for both "yes" and "no" answers. There's no need to combine the answers in a case where only one or each of the statements, taken individually, is sufficient to answer the question.

Data Sufficiency Practice

1. If a and b are positive integers, a is what percent of b?

(1) $\frac{1}{4}b = a$

(2) $\frac{a}{b} = \frac{20}{80}$

- Statement (1) ALONE is sufficient, but statement (2) alone is not sufficient.
- Statement (2) ALONE is sufficient, but statement (1) alone is not sufficient.
- BOTH statements TOGETHER are sufficient, but NEITHER statement ALONE is sufficient.
- EACH statement ALONE is sufficient.
- Statements (1) and (2) TOGETHER are NOT sufficient to answer the question asked, and additional data are needed.

2. Is it true that $a < b$?

(1) $a - c < b - c$

(2) $\frac{a}{2} < \frac{20}{80}$

- Statement (1) ALONE is sufficient, but statement (2) alone is not sufficient.
- Statement (2) ALONE is sufficient, but statement (1) alone is not sufficient.
- BOTH statements TOGETHER are sufficient, but NEITHER statement ALONE is sufficient.
- EACH statement ALONE is sufficient.
- Statements (1) and (2) TOGETHER are NOT sufficient to answer the question asked, and additional data are needed.

3. On a certain soccer team, one team member is to be chosen at random to play in the goalie position. What is the probability that a girl will be chosen?
   (1) One-quarter of the team members are girls.
   (2) 16 of the team members are boys.

   - Statement (1) ALONE is sufficient, but statement (2) alone is not sufficient.
   - Statement (2) ALONE is sufficient, but statement (1) alone is not sufficient.
   - BOTH statements TOGETHER are sufficient, but NEITHER statement ALONE is sufficient.
   - EACH statement ALONE is sufficient.
   - Statements (1) and (2) TOGETHER are NOT sufficient to answer the question asked, and additional data are needed.

4. A rope has four knots labeled *A, B, C*, and *D*, in that order. What is the rope distance between knots *B* and *C*?
   (1) The rope distance between knots *A* and *C* is 5 feet.
   (2) The rope distance between knots *B* and *D* is 7 feet.

   - Statement (1) ALONE is sufficient, but statement (2) alone is not sufficient.
   - Statement (2) ALONE is sufficient, but statement (1) alone is not sufficient.
   - BOTH statements TOGETHER are sufficient, but NEITHER statement ALONE is sufficient.
   - EACH statement ALONE is sufficient.
   - Statements (1) and (2) TOGETHER are NOT sufficient to answer the question asked, and additional data are needed.

5. Is x greater than 2.7 ?

(1) $x > 2.6$

(2) $x > 2.8$

- o Statement (1) ALONE is sufficient, but statement (2) alone is not sufficient.
- o Statement (2) ALONE is sufficient, but statement (1) alone is not sufficient.
- o BOTH statements TOGETHER are sufficient, but NEITHER statement ALONE is sufficient.
- o EACH statement ALONE is sufficient.
- o Statements (1) and (2) TOGETHER are NOT sufficient to answer the question asked, and additional data are needed.

6. If n is an integer, is $n - 1$ even?

(1) $n - 2$ is odd.

(2) $n + 1$ is even.

- o Statement (1) ALONE is sufficient, but statement (2) alone is not sufficient.
- o Statement (2) ALONE is sufficient, but statement (1) alone is not sufficient.
- o BOTH statements TOGETHER are sufficient, but NEITHER statement ALONE is sufficient.
- o EACH statement ALONE is sufficient.
- o Statements (1) and (2) TOGETHER are NOT sufficient to answer the question asked, and additional data are needed.

7. Is $3 < x < 4$?

    (1) $1 < x$
    (2) $x < 5$

    - Statement (1) ALONE is sufficient, but statement (2) alone is not sufficient.
    - Statement (2) ALONE is sufficient, but statement (1) alone is not sufficient.
    - BOTH statements TOGETHER are sufficient, but NEITHER statement ALONE is sufficient.
    - EACH statement ALONE is sufficient.
    - Statements (1) and (2) TOGETHER are NOT sufficient to answer the question asked, and additional data are needed.

8. Milk flows into a vat at a constant rate through a metal pipe. At the same time, milk is pumped out of the vat at a constant rate through another metal pipe. At what rate, in liters per minute, is the amount of milk in the vat decreasing?

    (1) The amount of milk initially in the vat was 100 liters.
    (2) Milk flows into the vat at a rate of 5 gallons every 5 minutes and out of the vat at a rate of 5 gallons per minute.

    - Statement (1) ALONE is sufficient, but statement (2) alone is not sufficient.
    - Statement (2) ALONE is sufficient, but statement (1) alone is not sufficient.
    - BOTH statements TOGETHER are sufficient, but NEITHER statement ALONE is sufficient.
    - EACH statement ALONE is sufficient.
    - Statements (1) and (2) TOGETHER are NOT sufficient to answer the question asked, and additional data are needed.

9. Is x a positive number?
   (1) $8x > 7x$
   (2) $x - 2$ is negative.

   - Statement (1) ALONE is sufficient, but statement (2) alone is not sufficient.
   - Statement (2) ALONE is sufficient, but statement (1) alone is not sufficient.
   - BOTH statements TOGETHER are sufficient, but NEITHER statement ALONE is sufficient.
   - EACH statement ALONE is sufficient.
   - Statements (1) and (2) TOGETHER are NOT sufficient to answer the question asked, and additional data are needed.

10. Does $3r - 4s = 0$?
   (1) $s \neq 0$
   (2) $6r = 8s$

   - Statement (1) ALONE is sufficient, but statement (2) alone is not sufficient.
   - Statement (2) ALONE is sufficient, but statement (1) alone is not sufficient.
   - BOTH statements TOGETHER are sufficient, but NEITHER statement ALONE is sufficient.
   - EACH statement ALONE is sufficient.
   - Statements (1) and (2) TOGETHER are NOT sufficient to answer the question asked, and additional data are needed.

11. What is the value of integer $-x$?

    (1) x is a prime number.
    (2) $23 \leq x \leq 29$

    - Statement (1) ALONE is sufficient, but statement (2) alone is not sufficient.
    - Statement (2) ALONE is sufficient, but statement (1) alone is not sufficient.
    - BOTH statements TOGETHER are sufficient, but NEITHER statement ALONE is sufficient.
    - EACH statement ALONE is sufficient.
    - Statements (1) and (2) TOGETHER are NOT sufficient to answer the question asked, and additional data are needed.

12. If j and k are integers, is $j + k$ an odd integer?

    (1) $j > 12$
    (2) $j = k - 1$

    - Statement (1) ALONE is sufficient, but statement (2) alone is not sufficient.
    - Statement (2) ALONE is sufficient, but statement (1) alone is not sufficient.
    - BOTH statements TOGETHER are sufficient, but NEITHER statement ALONE is sufficient.
    - EACH statement ALONE is sufficient.
    - Statements (1) and (2) TOGETHER are NOT sufficient to answer the question asked, and additional data are needed.

13. If $x - y = z$, what is the value of y?

(1) $x = 7$

(2) $z = x + 4$

- Statement (1) ALONE is sufficient, but statement (2) alone is not sufficient.
- Statement (2) ALONE is sufficient, but statement (1) alone is not sufficient.
- BOTH statements TOGETHER are sufficient, but NEITHER statement ALONE is sufficient.
- EACH statement ALONE is sufficient.
- Statements (1) and (2) TOGETHER are NOT sufficient to answer the question asked, and additional data are needed.

14. Is n an integer?

(1) $\frac{n}{3}$ is an integer.

(2) $3n$ is an integer.

- Statement (1) ALONE is sufficient, but statement (2) alone is not sufficient.
- Statement (2) ALONE is sufficient, but statement (1) alone is not sufficient.
- BOTH statements TOGETHER are sufficient, but NEITHER statement ALONE is sufficient.
- EACH statement ALONE is sufficient.
- Statements (1) and (2) TOGETHER are NOT sufficient to answer the question asked, and additional data are needed.

15. What is the value of $\frac{1}{x} + \frac{1}{y}$?

(1) $x + y = 15$
(2) $xy = 50$

- o Statement (1) ALONE is sufficient, but statement (2) alone is not sufficient.
- o Statement (2) ALONE is sufficient, but statement (1) alone is not sufficient.
- o BOTH statements TOGETHER are sufficient, but NEITHER statement ALONE is sufficient.
- o EACH statement ALONE is sufficient.
- o Statements (1) and (2) TOGETHER are NOT sufficient to answer the question asked, and additional data are needed.

16. In triangle *ABC*, if $AB = x$, $BC = x - 1$, $AC = y$, which of the three angles of triangle *ABC* has the smallest degree measure?

(1) $y = x - 2$
(2) $y = 5$

- o Statement (1) ALONE is sufficient, but statement (2) alone is not sufficient.
- o Statement (2) ALONE is sufficient, but statement (1) alone is not sufficient.
- o BOTH statements TOGETHER are sufficient, but NEITHER statement ALONE is sufficient.
- o EACH statement ALONE is sufficient.
- o Statements (1) and (2) TOGETHER are NOT sufficient to answer the question asked, and additional data are needed.

17. What distance did Marty drive?
    (1) Wendy drove 15 miles in 20 minutes.
    (2) Marty drove at the same average speed as Wendy.

- O Statement (1) ALONE is sufficient, but statement (2) alone is not sufficient.
- O Statement (2) ALONE is sufficient, but statement (1) alone is not sufficient.
- O BOTH statements TOGETHER are sufficient, but NEITHER statement ALONE is sufficient.
- O EACH statement ALONE is sufficient.
- O Statements (1) and (2) TOGETHER are NOT sufficient to answer the question asked, and additional data are needed.

18. What number is 12 percent of x?
    (1) 8 is 5 percent of x.
    (1) $\frac{1}{4}$ of x is 40.

- O Statement (1) ALONE is sufficient, but statement (2) alone is not sufficient.
- O Statement (2) ALONE is sufficient, but statement (1) alone is not sufficient.
- O BOTH statements TOGETHER are sufficient, but NEITHER statement ALONE is sufficient.
- O EACH statement ALONE is sufficient.
- O Statements (1) and (2) TOGETHER are NOT sufficient to answer the question asked, and additional data are needed.

19. 4.7☆◎3

If ☆ and ◎ each represent single digits in the decimal above, what digit does ☆ represent?

(1) When the decimal is rounded to the nearest tenth, 4.8 is the result.
(2) When the decimal is rounded to the nearest hundredth, 4.77 is the result.

- o Statement (1) ALONE is sufficient, but statement (2) alone is not sufficient.
- o Statement (2) ALONE is sufficient, but statement (1) alone is not sufficient.
- o BOTH statements TOGETHER are sufficient, but NEITHER statement ALONE is sufficient.
- o EACH statement ALONE is sufficient.
- o Statements (1) and (2) TOGETHER are NOT sufficient to answer the question asked, and additional data are needed.

20. What is the value of $ab + bc$?

(1) $b = 5$
(2) $a + c = 8$

- o Statement (1) ALONE is sufficient, but statement (2) alone is not sufficient.
- o Statement (2) ALONE is sufficient, but statement (1) alone is not sufficient.
- o BOTH statements TOGETHER are sufficient, but NEITHER statement ALONE is sufficient.
- o EACH statement ALONE is sufficient.
- o Statements (1) and (2) TOGETHER are NOT sufficient to answer the question asked, and additional data are needed.

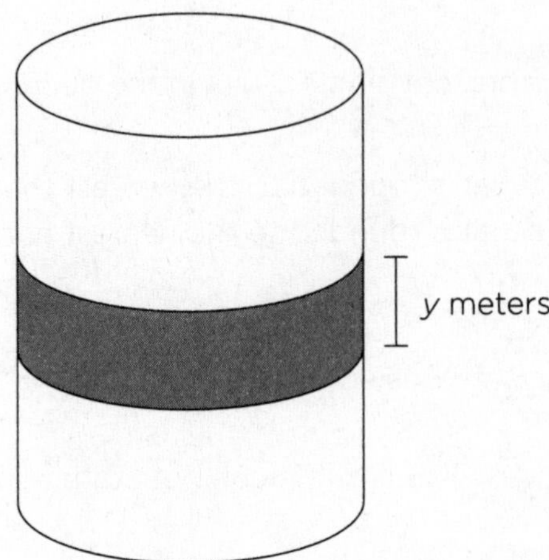

21. A cylindrical water tank has a stripe painted around its circumference, as shown in the figure provided. What is the surface area of this stripe?

    (1) $y = 0.7$
    (2) The height of the tank is 2 meters.

    - O Statement (1) ALONE is sufficient, but statement (2) alone is not sufficient.
    - O Statement (2) ALONE is sufficient, but statement (1) alone is not sufficient.
    - O BOTH statements TOGETHER are sufficient, but NEITHER statement ALONE is sufficient.
    - O EACH statement ALONE is sufficient.
    - O Statements (1) and (2) TOGETHER are NOT sufficient to answer the question asked, and additional data are needed.

22. What is the value of integer k?

    (1) $k(k - 1) = 2$
    (2) $2^{3k} = 64$

    - O Statement (1) ALONE is sufficient, but statement (2) alone is not sufficient.
    - O Statement (2) ALONE is sufficient, but statement (1) alone is not sufficient.
    - O BOTH statements TOGETHER are sufficient, but NEITHER statement ALONE is sufficient.
    - O EACH statement ALONE is sufficient.
    - O Statements (1) and (2) TOGETHER are NOT sufficient to answer the question asked, and additional data are needed.

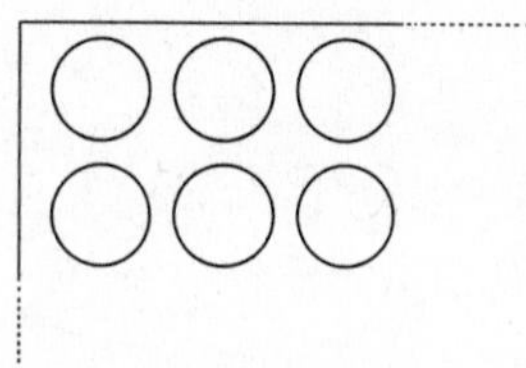

23. The interior of a rectangular box is 54 inches long, 27 inches wide, and 9 inches high. The box is filled with x cylindrical tubes of tennis balls that stand upright in rows and columns such that all the cylinders are touching and there is no additional space for extra tubes. If the tubes are 9 inches high, what is the value of x?

    (1) 18 tubes fit exactly along the interior length of the box.
    (2) Each of the tubes has a diameter of 3 inches.

    - Statement (1) ALONE is sufficient, but statement (2) alone is not sufficient.
    - Statement (2) ALONE is sufficient, but statement (1) alone is not sufficient.
    - BOTH statements TOGETHER are sufficient, but NEITHER statement ALONE is sufficient.
    - EACH statement ALONE is sufficient.
    - Statements (1) and (2) TOGETHER are NOT sufficient to answer the question asked, and additional data are needed.

$$\begin{cases} c+2 = a \\ a-9 = b \\ d+c = 12 \end{cases}$$

24. For the system of equations given, what is the value of c?

(1) $a = 8$
(2) $d = 6$

- Statement (1) ALONE is sufficient, but statement (2) alone is not sufficient.
- Statement (2) ALONE is sufficient, but statement (1) alone is not sufficient.
- BOTH statements TOGETHER are sufficient, but NEITHER statement ALONE is sufficient.
- EACH statement ALONE is sufficient.
- Statements (1) and (2) TOGETHER are NOT sufficient to answer the question asked, and additional data are needed.

25. Is n equal to 7?

(1) $n \geq 7$
(2) $n \leq 7$

- Statement (1) ALONE is sufficient, but statement (2) alone is not sufficient.
- Statement (2) ALONE is sufficient, but statement (1) alone is not sufficient.
- BOTH statements TOGETHER are sufficient, but NEITHER statement ALONE is sufficient.
- EACH statement ALONE is sufficient.
- Statements (1) and (2) TOGETHER are NOT sufficient to answer the question asked, and additional data are needed.

	A	B	C	D
A	0	m	12	n
B	m	0	18	24
C	12	18	0	24
D	n	21	24	0

26. The table provided shows the distance, in city blocks by the most direct route, between key city landmarks represented by A, B, C, and D. For example, the distance between A and C is 12 city blocks. What is the value of *m*?

    (1) By the most direct route, the distance between B and C is half the distance between A and D.

    (2) By the most direct route, the distance between D and C is half the distance between A and B.

- Statement (1) ALONE is sufficient, but statement (2) alone is not sufficient.
- Statement (2) ALONE is sufficient, but statement (1) alone is not sufficient.
- BOTH statements TOGETHER are sufficient, but NEITHER statement ALONE is sufficient.
- EACH statement ALONE is sufficient.
- Statements (1) and (2) TOGETHER are NOT sufficient to answer the question asked, and additional data are needed.

27. What is the value of the two-digit integer n?
    (1) The sum of the two digits is 6.
    (2) n is divisible by 4.

- O Statement (1) ALONE is sufficient, but statement (2) alone is not sufficient.
- O Statement (2) ALONE is sufficient, but statement (1) alone is not sufficient.
- O BOTH statements TOGETHER are sufficient, but NEITHER statement ALONE is sufficient.
- O EACH statement ALONE is sufficient.
- O Statements (1) and (2) TOGETHER are NOT sufficient to answer the question asked, and additional data are needed.

28. What is the tenths digit in the decimal representation of x?
    (1) x is greater than $\frac{3}{8}$.
    (2) x is less than $\frac{3}{7}$.

- O Statement (1) ALONE is sufficient, but statement (2) alone is not sufficient.
- O Statement (2) ALONE is sufficient, but statement (1) alone is not sufficient.
- O BOTH statements TOGETHER are sufficient, but NEITHER statement ALONE is sufficient.
- O EACH statement ALONE is sufficient.
- O Statements (1) and (2) TOGETHER are NOT sufficient to answer the question asked, and additional data are needed.

29. A 40-foot-long platform connects two adjacent buildings, and the platform is made up of a one-plank-wide strip of square-shaped planks. How many planks comprose the platform?

(1) Each plank has a diagonal of $5\sqrt{2}$ feet.
(2) Each plank has a width of 5 feet.

- Statement (1) ALONE is sufficient, but statement (2) alone is not sufficient.
- Statement (2) ALONE is sufficient, but statement (1) alone is not sufficient.
- BOTH statements TOGETHER are sufficient, but NEITHER statement ALONE is sufficient.
- EACH statement ALONE is sufficient.
- Statements (1) and (2) TOGETHER are NOT sufficient to answer the question asked, and additional data are needed.

30. How many members are in both Club X and Club Y?

(1) There were 15 members at the joint conference for members of Club X and Club Y, and no members were absent.
(2) Club X has 6 members and Club Y has 12 members.

- Statement (1) ALONE is sufficient, but statement (2) alone is not sufficient.
- Statement (2) ALONE is sufficient, but statement (1) alone is not sufficient.
- BOTH statements TOGETHER are sufficient, but NEITHER statement ALONE is sufficient.
- EACH statement ALONE is sufficient.
- Statements (1) and (2) TOGETHER are NOT sufficient to answer the question asked, and additional data are needed.

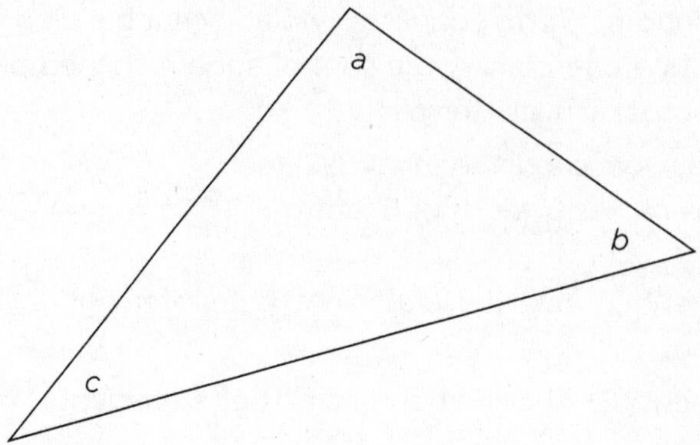

31. What is the value of c in the triangle presented?

(1) $a + b = 128$

(2) $a + c = 112$

- Statement (1) ALONE is sufficient, but statement (2) alone is not sufficient.
- Statement (2) ALONE is sufficient, but statement (1) alone is not sufficient.
- BOTH statements TOGETHER are sufficient, but NEITHER statement ALONE is sufficient.
- EACH statement ALONE is sufficient.
- Statements (1) and (2) TOGETHER are NOT sufficient to answer the question asked, and additional data are needed.

32. If a, b, and c are nonzero numbers, is $bc = 16$?

(1) $\frac{b}{8} = \frac{2}{c}$

(2) $ab^2c = 16ab$

- Statement (1) ALONE is sufficient, but statement (2) alone is not sufficient.
- Statement (2) ALONE is sufficient, but statement (1) alone is not sufficient.
- BOTH statements TOGETHER are sufficient, but NEITHER statement ALONE is sufficient.
- EACH statement ALONE is sufficient.
- Statements (1) and (2) TOGETHER are NOT sufficient to answer the question asked, and additional data are needed.

33. What is the value of x in the equation $-18 + 24 - x = y$?

(1) $\frac{y}{x} = 5$

(2) $y = 5$

- Statement (1) ALONE is sufficient, but statement (2) alone is not sufficient.
- Statement (2) ALONE is sufficient, but statement (1) alone is not sufficient.
- BOTH statements TOGETHER are sufficient, but NEITHER statement ALONE is sufficient.
- EACH statement ALONE is sufficient.
- Statements (1) and (2) TOGETHER are NOT sufficient to answer the question asked, and additional data are needed.

34. What is the value of xy^2?

(1) $y = x - 2$

(2) $y = x^2 - 2$

- Statement (1) ALONE is sufficient, but statement (2) alone is not sufficient.
- Statement (2) ALONE is sufficient, but statement (1) alone is not sufficient.
- BOTH statements TOGETHER are sufficient, but NEITHER statement ALONE is sufficient.
- EACH statement ALONE is sufficient.
- Statements (1) and (2) TOGETHER are NOT sufficient to answer the question asked, and additional data are needed.

35. If k denotes a decimal, is $k < 0.5$?

(1) When k is rounded to the nearest tenth, the result is 0.5.
(2) When k is rounded to the nearest integer, the result is 0.

- Statement (1) ALONE is sufficient, but statement (2) alone is not sufficient.
- Statement (2) ALONE is sufficient, but statement (1) alone is not sufficient.
- BOTH statements TOGETHER are sufficient, but NEITHER statement ALONE is sufficient.
- EACH statement ALONE is sufficient.
- Statements (1) and (2) TOGETHER are NOT sufficient to answer the question asked, and additional data are needed.

36. If a broker receives a 4 percent commission on a trading deal, what was the dollar amount of the trading deal?

(1) The trading deal minus the broker's commission was $61,440.
(2) The trading deal was 80 percent of the consensus market value of $80,000.

- Statement (1) ALONE is sufficient, but statement (2) alone is not sufficient.
- Statement (2) ALONE is sufficient, but statement (1) alone is not sufficient.
- BOTH statements TOGETHER are sufficient, but NEITHER statement ALONE is sufficient.
- EACH statement ALONE is sufficient.
- Statements (1) and (2) TOGETHER are NOT sufficient to answer the question asked, and additional data are needed.

37. If $\frac{\sqrt{x}}{y} = k$, what is the value of x?

(1) $yk = 12$

(2) $y = 3$ and $k = 4$

- O Statement (1) ALONE is sufficient, but statement (2) alone is not sufficient.
- O Statement (2) ALONE is sufficient, but statement (1) alone is not sufficient.
- O BOTH statements TOGETHER are sufficient, but NEITHER statement ALONE is sufficient.
- O EACH statement ALONE is sufficient.
- O Statements (1) and (2) TOGETHER are NOT sufficient to answer the question asked, and additional data are needed.

38. How many integers are there between, but not including, integers a and b?

(1) $b - a = 8$

(2) There are 7 integers between, but not including, $a - 1$ and $b - 1$.

- O Statement (1) ALONE is sufficient, but statement (2) alone is not sufficient.
- O Statement (2) ALONE is sufficient, but statement (1) alone is not sufficient.
- O BOTH statements TOGETHER are sufficient, but NEITHER statement ALONE is sufficient.
- O EACH statement ALONE is sufficient.
- O Statements (1) and (2) TOGETHER are NOT sufficient to answer the question asked, and additional data are needed.

39. What is the number of members of the Booster Club who are under 21 years old?

(1) Exactly $\frac{2}{3}$ of the members of the Booster Club are at least 21 years old.

(2) The 15 males in the Booster Club account for 50 percent of the club's membership.

- O Statement (1) ALONE is sufficient, but statement (2) alone is not sufficient.
- O Statement (2) ALONE is sufficient, but statement (1) alone is not sufficient.
- O BOTH statements TOGETHER are sufficient, but NEITHER statement ALONE is sufficient.
- O EACH statement ALONE is sufficient.
- O Statements (1) and (2) TOGETHER are NOT sufficient to answer the question asked, and additional data are needed.

40. Is $x > y$?

(1) $x = y - 1$

(2) $\frac{x}{3} = y - 5$

- O Statement (1) ALONE is sufficient, but statement (2) alone is not sufficient.
- O Statement (2) ALONE is sufficient, but statement (1) alone is not sufficient.
- O BOTH statements TOGETHER are sufficient, but NEITHER statement ALONE is sufficient.
- O EACH statement ALONE is sufficient.
- O Statements (1) and (2) TOGETHER are NOT sufficient to answer the question asked, and additional data are needed.

41. If n is an integer, is n even?

(1) $\frac{n}{2}$ is NOT an odd integer.

(2) $n + 4$ is an even integer.

- o Statement (1) ALONE is sufficient, but statement (2) alone is not sufficient.
- o Statement (2) ALONE is sufficient, but statement (1) alone is not sufficient.
- o BOTH statements TOGETHER are sufficient, but NEITHER statement ALONE is sufficient.
- o EACH statement ALONE is sufficient.
- o Statements (1) and (2) TOGETHER are NOT sufficient to answer the question asked, and additional data are needed.

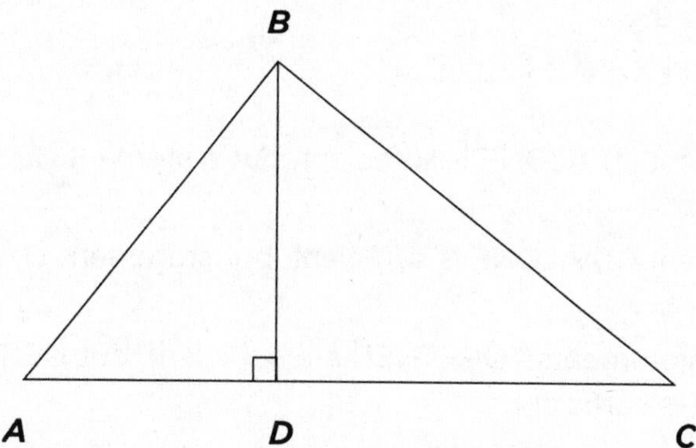

42. What is the area of the triangular region ABC provided?

(1) The length of AC is 18, and the length of BD is 8.

(2) $x = 30$

- o Statement (1) ALONE is sufficient, but statement (2) alone is not sufficient.
- o Statement (2) ALONE is sufficient, but statement (1) alone is not sufficient.
- o BOTH statements TOGETHER are sufficient, but NEITHER statement ALONE is sufficient.
- o EACH statement ALONE is sufficient.
- o Statements (1) and (2) TOGETHER are NOT sufficient to answer the question asked, and additional data are needed.

43. What is the average (arithmetic mean) of a and b?

(1) The average of $a + 3$ and $b + 5$ is 16.

(2) The average (arithmetic mean) of a, b, and 21 is 15.

- o Statement (1) ALONE is sufficient, but statement (2) alone is not sufficient.
- o Statement (2) ALONE is sufficient, but statement (1) alone is not sufficient.
- o BOTH statements TOGETHER are sufficient, but NEITHER statement ALONE is sufficient.
- o EACH statement ALONE is sufficient.
- o Statements (1) and (2) TOGETHER are NOT sufficient to answer the question asked, and additional data are needed.

44. Does $jx = 5 + kx$?

(1) $x(j - k) = 5$

(2) $j = 6$ and $k = x = 1$.

- o Statement (1) ALONE is sufficient, but statement (2) alone is not sufficient.
- o Statement (2) ALONE is sufficient, but statement (1) alone is not sufficient.
- o BOTH statements TOGETHER are sufficient, but NEITHER statement ALONE is sufficient.
- o EACH statement ALONE is sufficient.
- o Statements (1) and (2) TOGETHER are NOT sufficient to answer the question asked, and additional data are needed.

45. A certain number of people randomly and independently wrote down a single letter of the 26-letter alphabet. Was any one letter written down by more than one person?

(1) The number of people who wrote down a letter was greater than 30.
(2) The number of people who wrote down a letter was less than 80.

- Statement (1) ALONE is sufficient, but statement (2) alone is not sufficient.
- Statement (2) ALONE is sufficient, but statement (1) alone is not sufficient.
- BOTH statements TOGETHER are sufficient, but NEITHER statement ALONE is sufficient.
- EACH statement ALONE is sufficient.
- Statements (1) and (2) TOGETHER are NOT sufficient to answer the question asked, and additional data are needed.

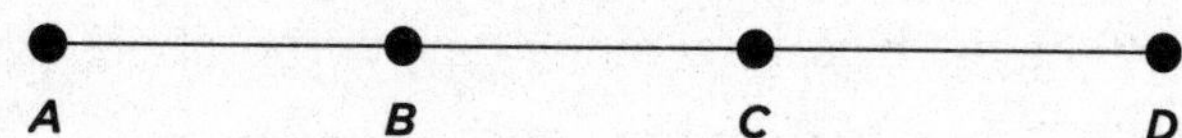

46. In the figure provided, is $AB > CD$?

(1) $AD = 30$
(2) $BC = CD$

- Statement (1) ALONE is sufficient, but statement (2) alone is not sufficient.
- Statement (2) ALONE is sufficient, but statement (1) alone is not sufficient.
- BOTH statements TOGETHER are sufficient, but NEITHER statement ALONE is sufficient.
- EACH statement ALONE is sufficient.
- Statements (1) and (2) TOGETHER are NOT sufficient to answer the question asked, and additional data are needed.

47. How much was Michael's legal fee?

(1) Michael's lawyer billed him for 2 hours of legal counsel.

(2) The fee for the second hour of legal counsel is half that for the first hour.

- Statement (1) ALONE is sufficient, but statement (2) alone is not sufficient.
- Statement (2) ALONE is sufficient, but statement (1) alone is not sufficient.
- BOTH statements TOGETHER are sufficient, but NEITHER statement ALONE is sufficient.
- EACH statement ALONE is sufficient.
- Statements (1) and (2) TOGETHER are NOT sufficient to answer the question asked, and additional data are needed.

48. At a certain university, 75 percent of the faculty have PhDs, and 50 percent of the faculty are over 45 years old. If 90 percent of those members of the faculty over 45 have PhDs, how many faculty members over 45 have PhDs?

(1) There are 180 faculty members at the university.

(2) Of the faculty aged 45 years old or less, 60 percent have PhDs.

- Statement (1) ALONE is sufficient, but statement (2) alone is not sufficient.
- Statement (2) ALONE is sufficient, but statement (1) alone is not sufficient.
- BOTH statements TOGETHER are sufficient, but NEITHER statement ALONE is sufficient.
- EACH statement ALONE is sufficient.
- Statements (1) and (2) TOGETHER are NOT sufficient to answer the question asked, and additional data are needed.

49. If A, B, and C are three distinct points, do line segments AB and AC have the same lengths?

(1) A, B, and C are vertices of the equilateral triangle ABC.

(2) $AB - BC = 0$ and $AC - BC = 0$.

- Statement (1) ALONE is sufficient, but statement (2) alone is not sufficient.
- Statement (2) ALONE is sufficient, but statement (1) alone is not sufficient.
- BOTH statements TOGETHER are sufficient, but NEITHER statement ALONE is sufficient.
- EACH statement ALONE is sufficient.
- Statements (1) and (2) TOGETHER are NOT sufficient to answer the question asked, and additional data are needed.

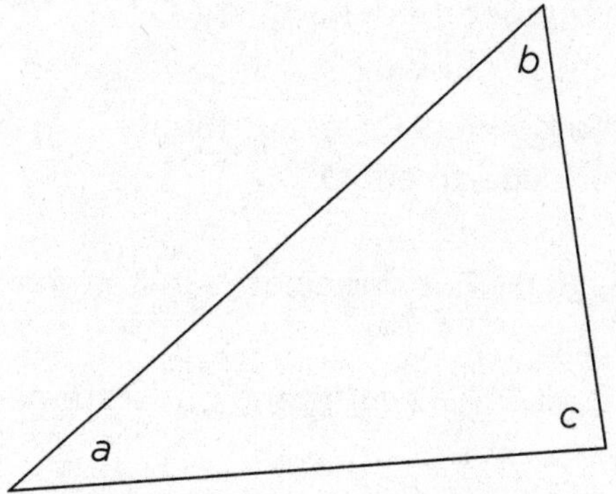

50. Is the triangle provided an isosceles right triangle?

(1) $c = 2b$

(2) $a = 45$

- Statement (1) ALONE is sufficient, but statement (2) alone is not sufficient.
- Statement (2) ALONE is sufficient, but statement (1) alone is not sufficient.
- BOTH statements TOGETHER are sufficient, but NEITHER statement ALONE is sufficient.
- EACH statement ALONE is sufficient.
- Statements (1) and (2) TOGETHER are NOT sufficient to answer the question asked, and additional data are needed.

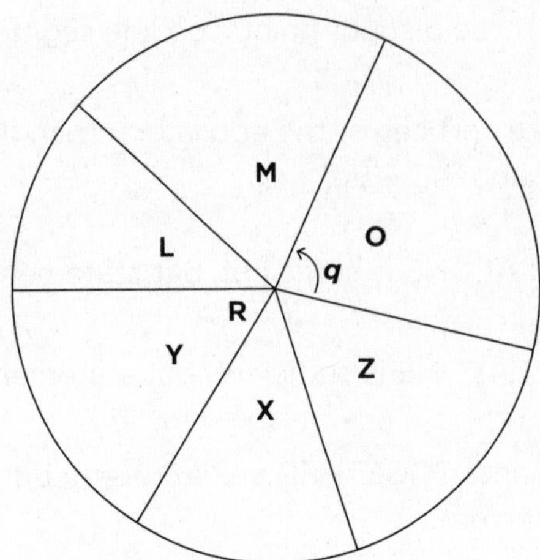

51. The circle graph shown represents the total budget for State School T, broken down by the budget allotted to each of its 6 departments. If State School T's total budget is $6,750,000 and R represents the center of the circle, what is the budget for department O?

(1) $q = 92$

(2) The sum of the budgets for departments X, Y, and L is twice as much as the budget for department O.

- Statement (1) ALONE is sufficient, but statement (2) alone is not sufficient.
- Statement (2) ALONE is sufficient, but statement (1) alone is not sufficient.
- BOTH statements TOGETHER are sufficient, but NEITHER statement ALONE is sufficient.
- EACH statement ALONE is sufficient.
- Statements (1) and (2) TOGETHER are NOT sufficient to answer the question asked, and additional data are needed.

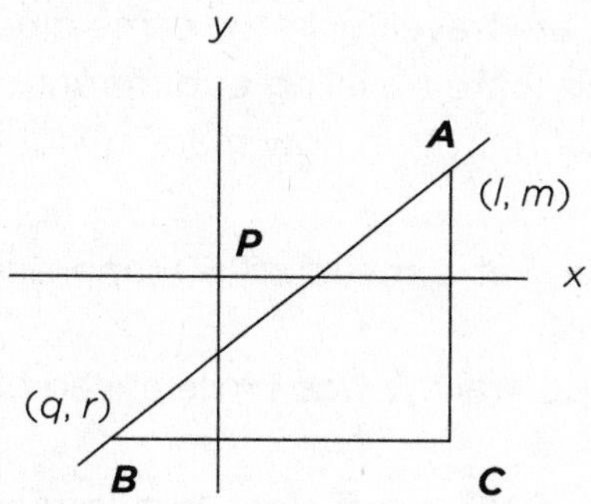

52. In the graph shown, segments BC and AC are parallel to the the x- and y-axes, respectively. Is the ratio of the length of AC to the length of BC equal to 1?

(1) $q = -2$ and $r = -4$

(2) $l = 3$, $m = 1$

- O Statement (1) ALONE is sufficient, but statement (2) alone is not sufficient.
- O Statement (2) ALONE is sufficient, but statement (1) alone is not sufficient.
- O BOTH statements TOGETHER are sufficient, but NEITHER statement ALONE is sufficient.
- O EACH statement ALONE is sufficient.
- O Statements (1) and (2) TOGETHER are NOT sufficient to answer the question asked, and additional data are needed.

53. Two trains, Q and P, are traveling in the same direction on straight and parallel tracks. Q and P are traveling at different constant rates. If train Q is now 3 miles ahead of train P, in how many minutes will train Q be 6 miles ahead of train P?

(1) Train Q is traveling at a speed of 150 mph, and train P is traveling at a speed of 120 mph.

(2) Four minutes ago, train Q was 1 mile ahead of train P.

- Statement (1) ALONE is sufficient, but statement (2) alone is not sufficient.
- Statement (2) ALONE is sufficient, but statement (1) alone is not sufficient.
- BOTH statements TOGETHER are sufficient, but NEITHER statement ALONE is sufficient.
- EACH statement ALONE is sufficient.
- Statements (1) and (2) TOGETHER are NOT sufficient to answer the question asked, and additional data are needed.

54. If x, y, and z are integers, is $x + y - z$ less than $x - y + z$?

(1) $y < 0$

(2) $z > 0$

- Statement (1) ALONE is sufficient, but statement (2) alone is not sufficient.
- Statement (2) ALONE is sufficient, but statement (1) alone is not sufficient.
- BOTH statements TOGETHER are sufficient, but NEITHER statement ALONE is sufficient.
- EACH statement ALONE is sufficient.
- Statements (1) and (2) TOGETHER are NOT sufficient to answer the question asked, and additional data are needed.

55. If a certain file has a size of 960 kilobytes, how many seconds will it take to download the file over a certain Internet connection? (Note that 1 kilobyte = 8 kilobits.)

(1) Over this Internet connection, the file downloads uninterrupted at a constant speed of 512 kilobits per second.

(2) Over this Internet connection, it takes 4 times as long to upload the file as it does to download the file, and it takes 75 seconds to do both.

- Statement (1) ALONE is sufficient, but statement (2) alone is not sufficient.
- Statement (2) ALONE is sufficient, but statement (1) alone is not sufficient.
- BOTH statements TOGETHER are sufficient, but NEITHER statement ALONE is sufficient.
- EACH statement ALONE is sufficient.
- Statements (1) and (2) TOGETHER are NOT sufficient to answer the question asked, and additional data are needed.

56. An ice cream truck is passing out free ice cream to each child at a playground. The driver randomly hands out only chocolate, vanilla, and strawberry ice cream. What is the probability that a certain child will receive either chocolate or strawberry ice cream?

(1) The probability that a certain child will receive chocolate ice cream is $\frac{1}{10}$.

(2) The probability that a certain child will receive vanilla is $\frac{1}{4}$.

- Statement (1) ALONE is sufficient, but statement (2) alone is not sufficient.
- Statement (2) ALONE is sufficient, but statement (1) alone is not sufficient.
- BOTH statements TOGETHER are sufficient, but NEITHER statement ALONE is sufficient.
- EACH statement ALONE is sufficient.
- Statements (1) and (2) TOGETHER are NOT sufficient to answer the question asked, and additional data are needed.

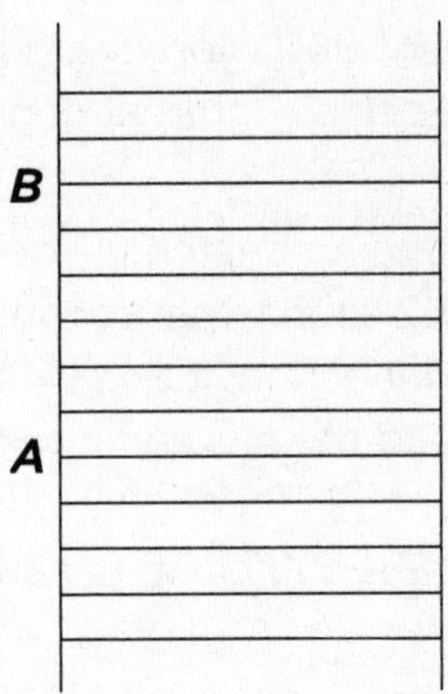

57. The figure provided represents a toy ladder, attached vertically to the side of a dollhouse, with the bottom resting on the ground. The rungs are spaced equally apart, and the distance from the ground to the top of the first rung is the same as from the top of the first rung to the top of the second. *A* and *B* represent rungs on the ladder. How far from the ground is the top of *B*?

(1) The top of *A* is $\frac{1}{2}$ foot above the ground.

(2) The top of *B* is $\frac{3}{5}$ foot above the top of *A*.

- Statement (1) ALONE is sufficient, but statement (2) alone is not sufficient.
- Statement (2) ALONE is sufficient, but statement (1) alone is not sufficient.
- BOTH statements TOGETHER are sufficient, but NEITHER statement ALONE is sufficient.
- EACH statement ALONE is sufficient.
- Statements (1) and (2) TOGETHER are NOT sufficient to answer the question asked, and additional data are needed.

58. At a junior/senior prom, $\frac{9}{10}$ of the attendees were junior or senior students and the remaining attendees were faculty. If $\frac{2}{3}$ of the student attendees were seniors, what number of attendees were juniors?

(1) There was a total of 270 attendees at the prom.
(2) The total number of faculty at the prom was 27.

- Statement (1) ALONE is sufficient, but statement (2) alone is not sufficient.
- Statement (2) ALONE is sufficient, but statement (1) alone is not sufficient.
- BOTH statements TOGETHER are sufficient, but NEITHER statement ALONE is sufficient.
- EACH statement ALONE is sufficient.
- Statements (1) and (2) TOGETHER are NOT sufficient to answer the question asked, and additional data are needed.

59. A circular Jacuzzi *X* has $\frac{1}{4}$ the circumference of the circular pool *Y*. Each structure is surrounded by a tile border with negligible width. What is the surface area of Jacuzzi *X*?

(1) The surface area of *Y* is 900π square feet.
(2) The length of the border immediately surrounding *Y* is 60π ft.

- Statement (1) ALONE is sufficient, but statement (2) alone is not sufficient.
- Statement (2) ALONE is sufficient, but statement (1) alone is not sufficient.
- BOTH statements TOGETHER are sufficient, but NEITHER statement ALONE is sufficient.
- EACH statement ALONE is sufficient.
- Statements (1) and (2) TOGETHER are NOT sufficient to answer the question asked, and additional data are needed.

60. A daycare center charges 125% of the regular daily tuition fee for children under five years of age, with the exception of children under two, who incur a rate of twice the regular daily tuition fee. What amount did the daycare charge last week in total tuition fees?

(1) The regular daily tuition fee is $20.

(2) There was a total of 15 children attending the daycare each day last week, and there were no children who were under two years of age.

- Statement (1) ALONE is sufficient, but statement (2) alone is not sufficient.
- Statement (2) ALONE is sufficient, but statement (1) alone is not sufficient.
- BOTH statements TOGETHER are sufficient, but NEITHER statement ALONE is sufficient.
- EACH statement ALONE is sufficient.
- Statements (1) and (2) TOGETHER are NOT sufficient to answer the question asked, and additional data are needed.

61. At a clothing sale, the entire inventory of 56 identical leather jackets was sold. Most of the jackets sold at the sale price, and the rest were sold to employees at a lower price. What was the revenue from the jackets?

(1) The total number of jackets sold at the sale price was $\frac{3}{4}$ of the total number of jackets sold.

(2) At the sale price, the jackets sold for $120 each.

- Statement (1) ALONE is sufficient, but statement (2) alone is not sufficient.
- Statement (2) ALONE is sufficient, but statement (1) alone is not sufficient.
- BOTH statements TOGETHER are sufficient, but NEITHER statement ALONE is sufficient.
- EACH statement ALONE is sufficient.
- Statements (1) and (2) TOGETHER are NOT sufficient to answer the question asked, and additional data are needed.

62. Given that the symbol ◇ represents one of the operations multiplication, addition, or subtraction, is the following true for all nonzero numbers a, b, and c: $a \diamond (b + c) = (a \diamond b) + (a \diamond c)$?

(1) There exist some values a for which $a \diamond 1$ is not equal to $1 \diamond a$.
(2) The symbol ◇ represents subtraction.

- Statement (1) ALONE is sufficient, but statement (2) alone is not sufficient.
- Statement (2) ALONE is sufficient, but statement (1) alone is not sufficient.
- BOTH statements TOGETHER are sufficient, but NEITHER statement ALONE is sufficient.
- EACH statement ALONE is sufficient.
- Statements (1) and (2) TOGETHER are NOT sufficient to answer the question asked, and additional data are needed.

63. From 2005 to 2006, by what percent did the sales of Company A increase?

(1) In 2005, the sales for Company A were $\frac{1}{4}$ of the sales of Company B.

(2) In 2006, the sales for Company A were $\frac{3}{4}$ of the sales of Company B.

- Statement (1) ALONE is sufficient, but statement (2) alone is not sufficient.
- Statement (2) ALONE is sufficient, but statement (1) alone is not sufficient.
- BOTH statements TOGETHER are sufficient, but NEITHER statement ALONE is sufficient.
- EACH statement ALONE is sufficient.
- Statements (1) and (2) TOGETHER are NOT sufficient to answer the question asked, and additional data are needed.

64. Before a charity run, a certain volunteer runner had donation contracts that totaled x dollars for each mile she ran. What was the amount the runner was expected to collect in donations?

 (1) The runner was expected to run a total of 21 miles.
 (2) Because the runner ran 5 more miles than expected, she collected a total of $3,900.

 o Statement (1) ALONE is sufficient, but statement (2) alone is not sufficient.
 o Statement (2) ALONE is sufficient, but statement (1) alone is not sufficient.
 o BOTH statements TOGETHER are sufficient, but NEITHER statement ALONE is sufficient.
 o EACH statement ALONE is sufficient.
 o Statements (1) and (2) TOGETHER are NOT sufficient to answer the question asked; and additional data are needed.

65. During a U.S. domestic flight, did a certain Boeing 757 aircraft ever exceed the economical cruising speed of 850 kilometers per hour?

 (1) The total flight time was 3 hours.
 (2) The aircraft flew a distance of 2,463 kilometers during the flight.

 o Statement (1) ALONE is sufficient, but statement (2) alone is not sufficient.
 o Statement (2) ALONE is sufficient, but statement (1) alone is not sufficient.
 o BOTH statements TOGETHER are sufficient, but NEITHER statement ALONE is sufficient.
 o EACH statement ALONE is sufficient.
 o Statements (1) and (2) TOGETHER are NOT sufficient to answer the question asked, and additional data are needed.

66. In a certain rural town, 250 households contain a dog or a cat or both. How many of these households contain both a dog and a cat if 75 of the 250 households do not contain a dog?

(1) 150 of the 250 households do not contain a cat.
(2) The total number of households that contain a cat is 100.

- Statement (1) ALONE is sufficient, but statement (2) alone is not sufficient.
- Statement (2) ALONE is sufficient, but statement (1) alone is not sufficient.
- BOTH statements TOGETHER are sufficient, but NEITHER statement ALONE is sufficient.
- EACH statement ALONE is sufficient.
- Statements (1) and (2) TOGETHER are NOT sufficient to answer the question asked, and additional data are needed.

67. Mary's employer reimburses her driving expenses according to a certain formula. Mary receives a fixed dollar amount for each day she drives for work, plus a certain dollar amount for each client she visits that day. If Mary visits 16 clients on one day, how much will she be reimbursed?

(1) Mary visited 12 clients last Monday.
(2) Mary's was reimbursed $76 for the driving she did last Monday.

- Statement (1) ALONE is sufficient, but statement (2) alone is not sufficient.
- Statement (2) ALONE is sufficient, but statement (1) alone is not sufficient.
- BOTH statements TOGETHER are sufficient, but NEITHER statement ALONE is sufficient.
- EACH statement ALONE is sufficient.
- Statements (1) and (2) TOGETHER are NOT sufficient to answer the question asked, and additional data are needed.

68. Jessica had a meeting on a certain day of the week. Was it on a Friday?
   (1) The meeting took place at a certain hour between 9:00 a.m. and 5:00 p.m.
   (2) If the meeting had taken place exactly 66 hours before its actual commencement time, it would have been on a Tuesday.

- o Statement (1) ALONE is sufficient, but statement (2) alone is not sufficient.
- o Statement (2) ALONE is sufficient, but statement (1) alone is not sufficient.
- o BOTH statements TOGETHER are sufficient, but NEITHER statement ALONE is sufficient.
- o EACH statement ALONE is sufficient.
- o Statements (1) and (2) TOGETHER are NOT sufficient to answer the question asked, and additional data are needed.

69. Is $x \neq y$?
   (1) $x + y > 0$
   (2) $xy < 0$

- o Statement (1) ALONE is sufficient, but statement (2) alone is not sufficient.
- o Statement (2) ALONE is sufficient, but statement (1) alone is not sufficient.
- o BOTH statements TOGETHER are sufficient, but NEITHER statement ALONE is sufficient.
- o EACH statement ALONE is sufficient.
- o Statements (1) and (2) TOGETHER are NOT sufficient to answer the question asked, and additional data are needed.

70. If the infinite sequence M is defined as $M_1 = 6$, $M_2 = 96$, $M_3 = 996$, . . . , $M_k = 10^k - 4$, is every term in this sequence divisible by q, if q is an even number?

(1) q is less than 45.

(2) At least 2 terms in the sequence are divisible by q.

- O Statement (1) ALONE is sufficient, but statement (2) alone is not sufficient.
- O Statement (2) ALONE is sufficient, but statement (1) alone is not sufficient.
- O BOTH statements TOGETHER are sufficient, but NEITHER statement ALONE is sufficient.
- O EACH statement ALONE is sufficient.
- O Statements (1) and (2) TOGETHER are NOT sufficient to answer the question asked, and additional data are needed.

71. If the numbers l and m are both greater than 0, is $\frac{l}{m}$ an integer?

(1) l and m are both integers.

(2) l^2 and m^2 are both integers.

- O Statement (1) ALONE is sufficient, but statement (2) alone is not sufficient.
- O Statement (2) ALONE is sufficient, but statement (1) alone is not sufficient.
- O BOTH statements TOGETHER are sufficient, but NEITHER statement ALONE is sufficient.
- O EACH statement ALONE is sufficient.
- O Statements (1) and (2) TOGETHER are NOT sufficient to answer the question asked, and additional data are needed.

72. Mrs. K's class has 10 students. If the average age of the students is 12, then how many of the students are 12 years of age?
(1) None of the students are younger than 12.
(2) None of the students are older than 12.

- Statement (1) ALONE is sufficient, but statement (2) alone is not sufficient.
- Statement (2) ALONE is sufficient, but statement (1) alone is not sufficient.
- BOTH statements TOGETHER are sufficient, but NEITHER statement ALONE is sufficient.
- EACH statement ALONE is sufficient.
- Statements (1) and (2) TOGETHER are NOT sufficient to answer the question asked, and additional data are needed.

73. Is $|a| = b - c$?
(1) $c = a + b$
(2) $a < 0$

- Statement (1) ALONE is sufficient, but statement (2) alone is not sufficient.
- Statement (2) ALONE is sufficient, but statement (1) alone is not sufficient.
- BOTH statements TOGETHER are sufficient, but NEITHER statement ALONE is sufficient.
- EACH statement ALONE is sufficient.
- Statements (1) and (2) TOGETHER are NOT sufficient to answer the question asked, and additional data are needed.

74. A certain student sold key lime pies to raise money for her school. If she sold a total of 75 pies, and some sold at full price while the rest sold at x percent of the full price, what was the total revenue the student generated for the school?

(1) $x = 80$

(2) The full price of each pie was $30.

- Statement (1) ALONE is sufficient, but statement (2) alone is not sufficient.
- Statement (2) ALONE is sufficient, but statement (1) alone is not sufficient.
- BOTH statements TOGETHER are sufficient, but NEITHER statement ALONE is sufficient.
- EACH statement ALONE is sufficient.
- Statements (1) and (2) TOGETHER are NOT sufficient to answer the question asked, and additional data are needed.

75. A terminating decimal is defined as a decimal that has a finite number of nonzero digits. Examples of terminating decimals are 0.24, 52, and 6.0314. x and y are positive integers. If $\frac{x}{y}$ is expressed as a decimal, is it a terminating decimal?

(1) $40 < x < 45$

(2) $y = 8$

- Statement (1) ALONE is sufficient, but statement (2) alone is not sufficient.
- Statement (2) ALONE is sufficient, but statement (1) alone is not sufficient.
- BOTH statements TOGETHER are sufficient, but NEITHER statement ALONE is sufficient.
- EACH statement ALONE is sufficient.
- Statements (1) and (2) TOGETHER are NOT sufficient to answer the question asked, and additional data are needed.

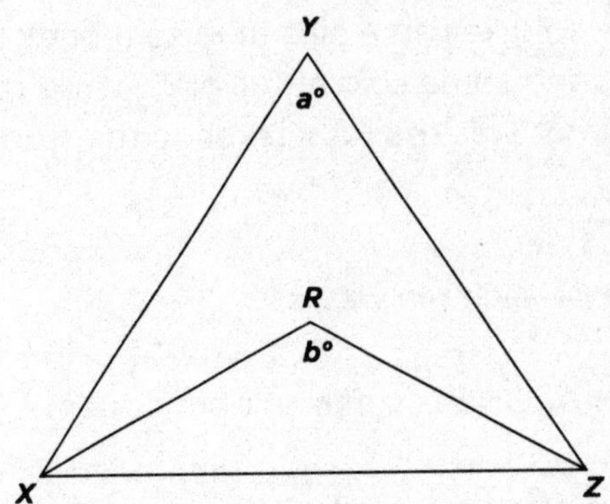

76. In the figure provided, what is the value of $b - a$?
    (1) Triangle *XYZ* and triangle *XRZ* are isosceles triangles.
    (2) The value of *a* is 50.

- Statement (1) ALONE is sufficient, but statement (2) alone is not sufficient.
- Statement (2) ALONE is sufficient, but statement (1) alone is not sufficient.
- BOTH statements TOGETHER are sufficient, but NEITHER statement ALONE is sufficient.
- EACH statement ALONE is sufficient.
- Statements (1) and (2) TOGETHER are NOT sufficient to answer the question asked, and additional data are needed.

77. If two numbers, *l* and *m*, are both positive integers, are both *l* and *m* greater than *r*?
    (1) *m* is greater than *l*.
    (2) $l - m > r$

- Statement (1) ALONE is sufficient, but statement (2) alone is not sufficient.
- Statement (2) ALONE is sufficient, but statement (1) alone is not sufficient.
- BOTH statements TOGETHER are sufficient, but NEITHER statement ALONE is sufficient.
- EACH statement ALONE is sufficient.
- Statements (1) and (2) TOGETHER are NOT sufficient to answer the question asked, and additional data are needed.

78. When Mrs. T's students answer the bonus question correctly, she awards a bonus. If the base score is between 10 and 99, the bonus is equal to 2 times the tens digit in the base score. The last test Mrs. T scored was between 10 and 99, and the student answered the bonus question correctly. Was the bonus given greater than 17% of the base score?

(1) The base score of the test was between 50 and 90.
(2) Mrs. T added 16 bonus points to the last test she graded.

- Statement (1) ALONE is sufficient, but statement (2) alone is not sufficient.
- Statement (2) ALONE is sufficient, but statement (1) alone is not sufficient.
- BOTH statements TOGETHER are sufficient, but NEITHER statement ALONE is sufficient.
- EACH statement ALONE is sufficient.
- Statements (1) and (2) TOGETHER are NOT sufficient to answer the question asked, and additional data are needed.

79. At a certain convenience store, the revenue from Brand A hot dogs decreased by 5% from April to May, while the revenue from Brand B hot dogs increased by 5% from April to May. The revenue from Brand A in May was what percentage of the revenue from Brand B in April?

(1) The increase in revenue of Brand B was $\frac{19}{20}$ the decrease in revenue of Brand A.
(2) The revenue in April from Brand A was equal to $\frac{20}{19}$ the revenue in April from Brand B.

- Statement (1) ALONE is sufficient, but statement (2) alone is not sufficient.
- Statement (2) ALONE is sufficient, but statement (1) alone is not sufficient.
- BOTH statements TOGETHER are sufficient, but NEITHER statement ALONE is sufficient.
- EACH statement ALONE is sufficient.
- Statements (1) and (2) TOGETHER are NOT sufficient to answer the question asked, and additional data are needed.

80. Is $q > r$?

(1) $qr = 32$

(2) $q^2 > r^2$

- Statement (1) ALONE is sufficient, but statement (2) alone is not sufficient.
- Statement (2) ALONE is sufficient, but statement (1) alone is not sufficient.
- BOTH statements TOGETHER are sufficient, but NEITHER statement ALONE is sufficient.
- EACH statement ALONE is sufficient.
- Statements (1) and (2) TOGETHER are NOT sufficient to answer the question asked, and additional data are needed.

81. If a number n is pulled out of a hat at random, what is the probability that $\left(\frac{1}{2}\right)n - 2 \geq 0$?

(1) There are 6 numbers in the hat, and each number is an integer.

(2) For every value of n in the hat, $1 \leq n \leq 30$.

- Statement (1) ALONE is sufficient, but statement (2) alone is not sufficient.
- Statement (2) ALONE is sufficient, but statement (1) alone is not sufficient.
- BOTH statements TOGETHER are sufficient, but NEITHER statement ALONE is sufficient.
- EACH statement ALONE is sufficient.
- Statements (1) and (2) TOGETHER are NOT sufficient to answer the question asked, and additional data are needed.

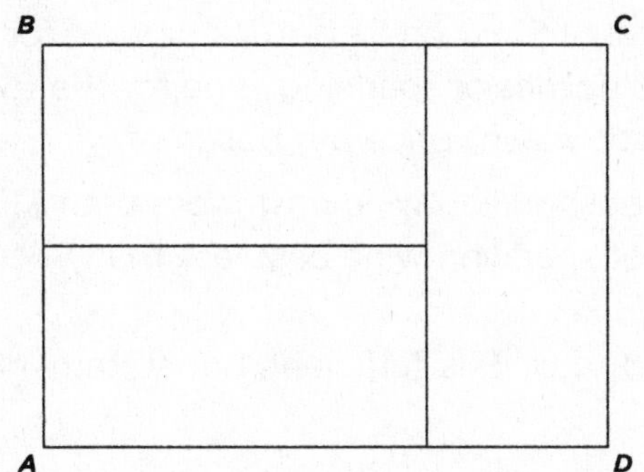

82. In the figure provided, what is the ratio $\frac{CD}{AD}$?

(1) The area of the rectangular region *ABCD* is 36.

(2) Each of the three small rectangles within the rectangular region *ABCD* has the same dimensions.

- Statement (1) ALONE is sufficient, but statement (2) alone is not sufficient.
- Statement (2) ALONE is sufficient, but statement (1) alone is not sufficient.
- BOTH statements TOGETHER are sufficient, but NEITHER statement ALONE is sufficient.
- EACH statement ALONE is sufficient.
- Statements (1) and (2) TOGETHER are NOT sufficient to answer the question asked, and additional data are needed.

83. Given that x is an integer and x is positive, is $\frac{210}{x}$ also an integer?

(1) x is a prime number.

(2) $x < 8$

- Statement (1) ALONE is sufficient, but statement (2) alone is not sufficient.
- Statement (2) ALONE is sufficient, but statement (1) alone is not sufficient.
- BOTH statements TOGETHER are sufficient, but NEITHER statement ALONE is sufficient.
- EACH statement ALONE is sufficient.
- Statements (1) and (2) TOGETHER are NOT sufficient to answer the question asked, and additional data are needed.

84. Anita spent a total of $780 on 52 bottles of wine for her wedding. She then decided to buy 8 bottles of sparkling wine for the toasts as well. Was the average (arithmetic mean) price per bottle of wine less than $20?

(1) Each bottle of sparkling wine cost more than $15.
(2) Each bottle of sparkling wine cost less than $40.

- Statement (1) ALONE is sufficient, but statement (2) alone is not sufficient.
- Statement (2) ALONE is sufficient, but statement (1) alone is not sufficient.
- BOTH statements TOGETHER are sufficient, but NEITHER statement ALONE is sufficient.
- EACH statement ALONE is sufficient.
- Statements (1) and (2) TOGETHER are NOT sufficient to answer the question asked, and additional data are needed.

85. If $\frac{5}{b} = \frac{a}{4}$, is $b > a$?

(1) $b \geq 5$
(2) $b \leq 7$

- Statement (1) ALONE is sufficient, but statement (2) alone is not sufficient.
- Statement (2) ALONE is sufficient, but statement (1) alone is not sufficient.
- BOTH statements TOGETHER are sufficient, but NEITHER statement ALONE is sufficient.
- EACH statement ALONE is sufficient.
- Statements (1) and (2) TOGETHER are NOT sufficient to answer the question asked, and additional data are needed.

86. If q and r are two integers and $q \neq r$, does $q = 0$?

(1) $q^2 = qr$

(2) $r = 5$

- Statement (1) ALONE is sufficient, but statement (2) alone is not sufficient.
- Statement (2) ALONE is sufficient, but statement (1) alone is not sufficient.
- BOTH statements TOGETHER are sufficient, but NEITHER statement ALONE is sufficient.
- EACH statement ALONE is sufficient.
- Statements (1) and (2) TOGETHER are NOT sufficient to answer the question asked, and additional data are needed.

87. What is the value of $25{,}850(2.75)^k$?

(1) $k^2 - 6k + 8 = 0$

(2) $k - 4 \neq 0$

- Statement (1) ALONE is sufficient, but statement (2) alone is not sufficient.
- Statement (2) ALONE is sufficient, but statement (1) alone is not sufficient.
- BOTH statements TOGETHER are sufficient, but NEITHER statement ALONE is sufficient.
- EACH statement ALONE is sufficient.
- Statements (1) and (2) TOGETHER are NOT sufficient to answer the question asked, and additional data are needed.

88. If the integers v and w are both positive, is $\frac{v}{w}$ an integer?

(1) For every factor n of w, n is also a factor of v.
(2) For every prime factor p of w, p is also a prime factor of v.

- Statement (1) ALONE is sufficient, but statement (2) alone is not sufficient.
- Statement (2) ALONE is sufficient, but statement (1) alone is not sufficient.
- BOTH statements TOGETHER are sufficient, but NEITHER statement ALONE is sufficient.
- EACH statement ALONE is sufficient.
- Statements (1) and (2) TOGETHER are NOT sufficient to answer the question asked, and additional data are needed.

89. What is the value of a if $a^x = 1$?

(1) $a > 0$
(2) x is an integer not equal to 0.

- Statement (1) ALONE is sufficient, but statement (2) alone is not sufficient.
- Statement (2) ALONE is sufficient, but statement (1) alone is not sufficient.
- BOTH statements TOGETHER are sufficient, but NEITHER statement ALONE is sufficient.
- EACH statement ALONE is sufficient.
- Statements (1) and (2) TOGETHER are NOT sufficient to answer the question asked, and additional data are needed.

$$R = \frac{\frac{3}{a}}{\frac{2}{b} + \frac{4}{5b}}$$

90. Referring to the equation shown, if $ab \neq 0$, what is the value of R?

(1) $b = 4a$

(2) $a = \frac{2}{3}$

- O Statement (1) ALONE is sufficient, but statement (2) alone is not sufficient.
- O Statement (2) ALONE is sufficient, but statement (1) alone is not sufficient.
- O BOTH statements TOGETHER are sufficient, but NEITHER statement ALONE is sufficient.
- O EACH statement ALONE is sufficient.
- O Statements (1) and (2) TOGETHER are NOT sufficient to answer the question asked, and additional data are needed.

91. Given that n is an integer, is $|n| \times n < 2^n$?

(1) $n < 0$

(2) $n = -6$

- O Statement (1) ALONE is sufficient, but statement (2) alone is not sufficient.
- O Statement (2) ALONE is sufficient, but statement (1) alone is not sufficient.
- O BOTH statements TOGETHER are sufficient, but NEITHER statement ALONE is sufficient.
- O EACH statement ALONE is sufficient.
- O Statements (1) and (2) TOGETHER are NOT sufficient to answer the question asked, and additional data are needed.

92. If a and b are both positive integers, is the square root of $(b - a)$ also an integer?

(1) $b > a + 21$

(2) $b = a(a + 1)$

- o Statement (1) ALONE is sufficient, but statement (2) alone is not sufficient.
- o Statement (2) ALONE is sufficient, but statement (1) alone is not sufficient.
- o BOTH statements TOGETHER are sufficient, but NEITHER statement ALONE is sufficient.
- o EACH statement ALONE is sufficient.
- o Statements (1) and (2) TOGETHER are NOT sufficient to answer the question asked, and additional data are needed.

93. If $s < 0$, is $t > 0$?

(1) $t + s < 0$

(2) $\frac{s}{t} < 0$

- o Statement (1) ALONE is sufficient, but statement (2) alone is not sufficient.
- o Statement (2) ALONE is sufficient, but statement (1) alone is not sufficient.
- o BOTH statements TOGETHER are sufficient, but NEITHER statement ALONE is sufficient.
- o EACH statement ALONE is sufficient.
- o Statements (1) and (2) TOGETHER are NOT sufficient to answer the question asked, and additional data are needed.

94. For each month, the number of accounts, a, that a certain salesperson has contracted that month is directly proportional to his efficiency score, e, which is directly proportional to his commission rate, c. What is a if $c = 3.0$?

(1) Whenever $c = 4.0$, $e = 0.3$.
(2) Whenever $c = 6.0$, $a = 80$.

- Statement (1) ALONE is sufficient, but statement (2) alone is not sufficient.
- Statement (2) ALONE is sufficient, but statement (1) alone is not sufficient.
- BOTH statements TOGETHER are sufficient, but NEITHER statement ALONE is sufficient.
- EACH statement ALONE is sufficient.
- Statements (1) and (2) TOGETHER are NOT sufficient to answer the question asked, and additional data are needed.

95. If $m \neq -n$, is $\frac{(m-n)}{(m+n)} > 1$?

(1) $n < 0$
(2) $m > 0$

- Statement (1) ALONE is sufficient, but statement (2) alone is not sufficient.
- Statement (2) ALONE is sufficient, but statement (1) alone is not sufficient.
- BOTH statements TOGETHER are sufficient, but NEITHER statement ALONE is sufficient.
- EACH statement ALONE is sufficient.
- Statements (1) and (2) TOGETHER are NOT sufficient to answer the question asked, and additional data are needed.

96. For a certain company X, the average daily payroll for each 30-day payroll cycle is the average (arithmetic mean) of the daily payroll totals for each of the 30 days. During the first part of a recent 30-day payroll cycle, the daily payroll was a constant \$5,750. When a new employee was hired during this 30-day cycle, the total payroll for each day rose by \$280. If the new daily payroll total remained constant for the remainder of the cycle, what was the average daily payroll for the 30-day cycle?

(1) The new employee was hired on the 11th day of the payroll cycle.

(2) The average daily payroll was \$5,890 through the first 20 days of the cycle.

- o Statement (1) ALONE is sufficient, but statement (2) alone is not sufficient.
- o Statement (2) ALONE is sufficient, but statement (1) alone is not sufficient.
- o BOTH statements TOGETHER are sufficient, but NEITHER statement ALONE is sufficient.
- o EACH statement ALONE is sufficient.
- o Statements (1) and (2) TOGETHER are NOT sufficient to answer the question asked, and additional data are needed.

97. Is $\frac{1}{x} > \frac{y}{y^2+3}$?

(1) $y > 0$

(2) $x = y$

- o Statement (1) ALONE is sufficient, but statement (2) alone is not sufficient.
- o Statement (2) ALONE is sufficient, but statement (1) alone is not sufficient.
- o BOTH statements TOGETHER are sufficient, but NEITHER statement ALONE is sufficient.
- o EACH statement ALONE is sufficient.
- o Statements (1) and (2) TOGETHER are NOT sufficient to answer the question asked, and additional data are needed.

98. Is a certain number p an integer?

(1) $\sqrt{p}$ is an integer.
(2) p^2 is an integer.

- Statement (1) ALONE is sufficient, but statement (2) alone is not sufficient.
- Statement (2) ALONE is sufficient, but statement (1) alone is not sufficient.
- BOTH statements TOGETHER are sufficient, but NEITHER statement ALONE is sufficient.
- EACH statement ALONE is sufficient.
- Statements (1) and (2) TOGETHER are NOT sufficient to answer the question asked, and additional data are needed.

99. If y is an integer greater than 0, is $(y^3 - y)$ divisible by 4?

(1) $y^2 + y$ is divisible by 10.
(2) For a certain integer k, $y = 2k + 1$.

- Statement (1) ALONE is sufficient, but statement (2) alone is not sufficient.
- Statement (2) ALONE is sufficient, but statement (1) alone is not sufficient.
- BOTH statements TOGETHER are sufficient, but NEITHER statement ALONE is sufficient.
- EACH statement ALONE is sufficient.
- Statements (1) and (2) TOGETHER are NOT sufficient to answer the question asked, and additional data are needed.

100. What is the tens digit of a certain positive integer n?

(1) When n is divided by 230, the remainder is 30.
(2) When n is divided by 200, the remainder is 30.

- Statement (1) ALONE is sufficient, but statement (2) alone is not sufficient.
- Statement (2) ALONE is sufficient, but statement (1) alone is not sufficient.
- BOTH statements TOGETHER are sufficient, but NEITHER statement ALONE is sufficient.
- EACH statement ALONE is sufficient.
- Statements (1) and (2) TOGETHER are NOT sufficient to answer the question asked, and additional data are needed.

101. Mrs. K is paid at a reduced rate for contracts completed late, and the contract prices may vary. Her compensation for the first two late contracts in any month is reduced by 10%, and her compensation for any subsequent late contracts in the same month is reduced by 15%. If Mrs. K completed three contracts late, in the same month, was her total compensation for those three contracts reduced by more than 11%?

(1) Without any reduction, she would have received $550 for the last of the three late contracts and at least $1,200 for each of the others.
(2) Without any reduction, she would have received $1,500 for the first of the three late contracts.

- Statement (1) ALONE is sufficient, but statement (2) alone is not sufficient.
- Statement (2) ALONE is sufficient, but statement (1) alone is not sufficient.
- BOTH statements TOGETHER are sufficient, but NEITHER statement ALONE is sufficient.
- EACH statement ALONE is sufficient.
- Statements (1) and (2) TOGETHER are NOT sufficient to answer the question asked, and additional data are needed.

102. Given that a and b are positive, is the ratio $a:b$ greater than 5?

(1) a is 3 more than 5 times b.

(2) The ratio of $4a$ to $5b$ is greater than 4.

- Statement (1) ALONE is sufficient, but statement (2) alone is not sufficient.
- Statement (2) ALONE is sufficient, but statement (1) alone is not sufficient.
- BOTH statements TOGETHER are sufficient, but NEITHER statement ALONE is sufficient.
- EACH statement ALONE is sufficient.
- Statements (1) and (2) TOGETHER are NOT sufficient to answer the question asked, and additional data are needed.

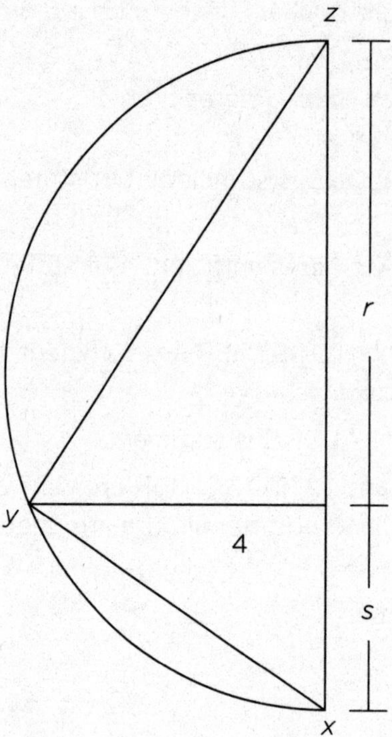

103. In the figure provided, if arc *XYZ* forms a semicircle, what is the length of its diameter *XZ*?

(1) $r = 8$

(2) $s = 2$

- Statement (1) ALONE is sufficient, but statement (2) alone is not sufficient.
- Statement (2) ALONE is sufficient, but statement (1) alone is not sufficient.
- BOTH statements TOGETHER are sufficient, but NEITHER statement ALONE is sufficient.
- EACH statement ALONE is sufficient.
- Statements (1) and (2) TOGETHER are NOT sufficient to answer the question asked, and additional data are needed.

104. If x is an integer, does x have a factor n such that $1 < n < x$?

(1) $x > 3!$

(2) $15! + 2 \leq x \leq 15! + 15$

- Statement (1) ALONE is sufficient, but statement (2) alone is not sufficient.
- Statement (2) ALONE is sufficient, but statement (1) alone is not sufficient.
- BOTH statements TOGETHER are sufficient, but NEITHER statement ALONE is sufficient.
- EACH statement ALONE is sufficient.
- Statements (1) and (2) TOGETHER are NOT sufficient to answer the question asked, and additional data are needed.

105. Is p a negative number?

(1) $p^3(1 - p^2) < 0$

(2) $p^2 - 1 < 0$

- Statement (1) ALONE is sufficient, but statement (2) alone is not sufficient.
- Statement (2) ALONE is sufficient, but statement (1) alone is not sufficient.
- BOTH statements TOGETHER are sufficient, but NEITHER statement ALONE is sufficient.
- EACH statement ALONE is sufficient.
- Statements (1) and (2) TOGETHER are NOT sufficient to answer the question asked, and additional data are needed.

106. What is the maximum number of gallons of water that the Smiths' backyard pool can hold?

(1) The pool currently contains 3,700 gallons of water.

(2) When the pool is $\frac{3}{4}$ full of water and 500 gallons of water are added, the amount of water in the pool increases by $\frac{1}{9}$.

- O Statement (1) ALONE is sufficient, but statement (2) alone is not sufficient.
- O Statement (2) ALONE is sufficient, but statement (1) alone is not sufficient.
- O BOTH statements TOGETHER are sufficient, but NEITHER statement ALONE is sufficient.
- O EACH statement ALONE is sufficient.
- O Statements (1) and (2) TOGETHER are NOT sufficient to answer the question asked, and additional data are needed.

107. The prices of a van and a truck were both decreased. Which vehicle had the greater dollar decrease in price?

(1) The price of the truck decreased by 8 percent.

(2) The price of the van decreased by 12 percent.

- O Statement (1) ALONE is sufficient, but statement (2) alone is not sufficient.
- O Statement (2) ALONE is sufficient, but statement (1) alone is not sufficient.
- O BOTH statements TOGETHER are sufficient, but NEITHER statement ALONE is sufficient.
- O EACH statement ALONE is sufficient.
- O Statements (1) and (2) TOGETHER are NOT sufficient to answer the question asked, and additional data are needed.

108. What is the value of $\frac{a}{3} - \frac{b}{3}$?

(1) $a - b = 12$

(2) $\frac{a-b}{3} = 4$

- o Statement (1) ALONE is sufficient, but statement (2) alone is not sufficient.
- o Statement (2) ALONE is sufficient, but statement (1) alone is not sufficient.
- o BOTH statements TOGETHER are sufficient, but NEITHER statement ALONE is sufficient.
- o EACH statement ALONE is sufficient.
- o Statements (1) and (2) TOGETHER are NOT sufficient to answer the question asked, and additional data are needed.

109. How many positive integer factors does *k* have?

(1) *k* has the same number of positive integer factors as 3^3.

(2) $k = rs$, where *r* and *s* are different prime numbers.

- o Statement (1) ALONE is sufficient, but statement (2) alone is not sufficient.
- o Statement (2) ALONE is sufficient, but statement (1) alone is not sufficient.
- o BOTH statements TOGETHER are sufficient, but NEITHER statement ALONE is sufficient.
- o EACH statement ALONE is sufficient.
- o Statements (1) and (2) TOGETHER are NOT sufficient to answer the question asked, and additional data are needed.

110. What is the perimeter of a rectangle with length l and width w?

(1) $l - w = 15$
(2) $l + w = 35$

- Statement (1) ALONE is sufficient, but statement (2) alone is not sufficient.
- Statement (2) ALONE is sufficient, but statement (1) alone is not sufficient.
- BOTH statements TOGETHER are sufficient, but NEITHER statement ALONE is sufficient.
- EACH statement ALONE is sufficient.
- Statements (1) and (2) TOGETHER are NOT sufficient to answer the question asked, and additional data are needed.

111. On a recent test, Kevin scored m percent higher than the class average, while Katherine scored n percent higher than the class average. What was the class average?

(1) $n - m = 7$
(2) $m = 12$

- Statement (1) ALONE is sufficient, but statement (2) alone is not sufficient.
- Statement (2) ALONE is sufficient, but statement (1) alone is not sufficient.
- BOTH statements TOGETHER are sufficient, but NEITHER statement ALONE is sufficient.
- EACH statement ALONE is sufficient.
- Statements (1) and (2) TOGETHER are NOT sufficient to answer the question asked, and additional data are needed.

112. What is the value of g?

(1) $h = 11.83$

(2) $g = \frac{h}{5.49}$

- O Statement (1) ALONE is sufficient, but statement (2) alone is not sufficient.
- O Statement (2) ALONE is sufficient, but statement (1) alone is not sufficient.
- O BOTH statements TOGETHER are sufficient, but NEITHER statement ALONE is sufficient.
- O EACH statement ALONE is sufficient.
- O Statements (1) and (2) TOGETHER are NOT sufficient to answer the question asked, and additional data are needed.

113. A number is selected from the set {21, 24, 27, 28, 30, 36, 45}. Which number was selected?

(1) The number selected is a multiple of 9.

(2) The number selected is odd.

- O Statement (1) ALONE is sufficient, but statement (2) alone is not sufficient.
- O Statement (2) ALONE is sufficient, but statement (1) alone is not sufficient.
- O BOTH statements TOGETHER are sufficient, but NEITHER statement ALONE is sufficient.
- O EACH statement ALONE is sufficient.
- O Statements (1) and (2) TOGETHER are NOT sufficient to answer the question asked, and additional data are needed.

114. Alan, Becky, Chris, and Darla need to schedule a two-hour meeting on Saturday to finish a group project. Is there a two-hour time block on Saturday during which everyone is free to meet?

(1) On Saturday, Alan can meet any time between 10:00 a.m. and 3:00 p.m., while Darla can meet any time after 1:00 p.m.
(2) On Saturday, Becky and Chris can meet any time between noon and 4:00 p.m.

- Statement (1) ALONE is sufficient, but statement (2) alone is not sufficient.
- Statement (2) ALONE is sufficient, but statement (1) alone is not sufficient.
- BOTH statements TOGETHER are sufficient, but NEITHER statement ALONE is sufficient.
- EACH statement ALONE is sufficient.
- Statements (1) and (2) TOGETHER are NOT sufficient to answer the question asked, and additional data are needed.

115. What is the value of a if $2b(a + 1) = 3$?

(1) $b = 5$
(2) $b^2 = 25$

- Statement (1) ALONE is sufficient, but statement (2) alone is not sufficient.
- Statement (2) ALONE is sufficient, but statement (1) alone is not sufficient.
- BOTH statements TOGETHER are sufficient, but NEITHER statement ALONE is sufficient.
- EACH statement ALONE is sufficient.
- Statements (1) and (2) TOGETHER are NOT sufficient to answer the question asked, and additional data are needed.

116. Last year, 625 new students enrolled in a certain school. How many of the new students were female?

(1) In total, 1,770 females attended the school last year.
(2) Exactly 60% of all students at the school are female.

- o Statement (1) ALONE is sufficient, but statement (2) alone is not sufficient.
- o Statement (2) ALONE is sufficient, but statement (1) alone is not sufficient.
- o BOTH statements TOGETHER are sufficient, but NEITHER statement ALONE is sufficient.
- o EACH statement ALONE is sufficient.
- o Statements (1) and (2) TOGETHER are NOT sufficient to answer the question asked, and additional data are needed.

117. What is the ratio of *b* to *c*?

(1) b is 2 more than half of c.
(2) $\frac{2b}{5c} = \frac{1}{2}$

- o Statement (1) ALONE is sufficient, but statement (2) alone is not sufficient.
- o Statement (2) ALONE is sufficient, but statement (1) alone is not sufficient.
- o BOTH statements TOGETHER are sufficient, but NEITHER statement ALONE is sufficient.
- o EACH statement ALONE is sufficient.
- o Statements (1) and (2) TOGETHER are NOT sufficient to answer the question asked, and additional data are needed.

118. What was the net profit of a certain company during its fourth year of operation?

(1) Net profit during the third year was half as much as during the fifth year.
(2) Net profit during the fourth year was $12 million more than during the third year.

- Statement (1) ALONE is sufficient, but statement (2) alone is not sufficient.
- Statement (2) ALONE is sufficient, but statement (1) alone is not sufficient.
- BOTH statements TOGETHER are sufficient, but NEITHER statement ALONE is sufficient.
- EACH statement ALONE is sufficient.
- Statements (1) and (2) TOGETHER are NOT sufficient to answer the question asked, and additional data are needed.

119. Positive integers j and k are added together. What is the remainder when $j + k$ is divided by 5?

(1) When j is divided by 5, the remainder is 0.
(2) When k is divided by 5, the remainder is 0.

- Statement (1) ALONE is sufficient, but statement (2) alone is not sufficient.
- Statement (2) ALONE is sufficient, but statement (1) alone is not sufficient.
- BOTH statements TOGETHER are sufficient, but NEITHER statement ALONE is sufficient.
- EACH statement ALONE is sufficient.
- Statements (1) and (2) TOGETHER are NOT sufficient to answer the question asked, and additional data are needed.

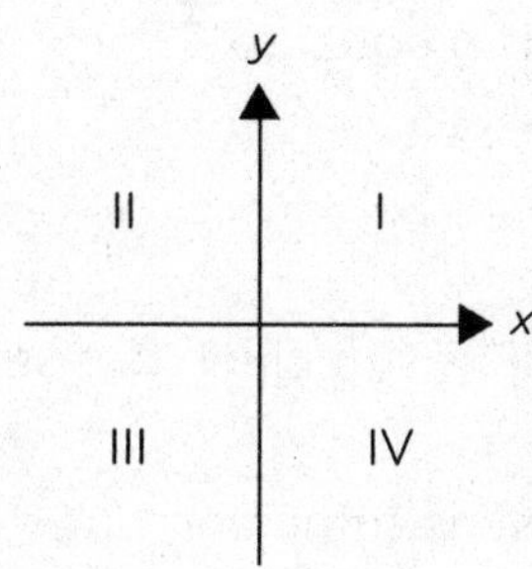

120. If the coordinates of point A are (m, n), in which quadrant of the rectangular coordinate plane provided does point A lie?

(1) $m = -n$

(2) $m = -4$ and $n = 4$

- O Statement (1) ALONE is sufficient, but statement (2) alone is not sufficient.
- O Statement (2) ALONE is sufficient, but statement (1) alone is not sufficient.
- O BOTH statements TOGETHER are sufficient, but NEITHER statement ALONE is sufficient.
- O EACH statement ALONE is sufficient.
- O Statements (1) and (2) TOGETHER are NOT sufficient to answer the question asked, and additional data are needed.

121. What is the value of p?

(1) $\frac{24}{p} = -3$

(2) $5p + 6 - p = 3p - 2$

- O Statement (1) ALONE is sufficient, but statement (2) alone is not sufficient.
- O Statement (2) ALONE is sufficient, but statement (1) alone is not sufficient.
- O BOTH statements TOGETHER are sufficient, but NEITHER statement ALONE is sufficient.
- O EACH statement ALONE is sufficient.
- O Statements (1) and (2) TOGETHER are NOT sufficient to answer the question asked, and additional data are needed.

122. If n is a positive integer, is n equal to 6?

(1) $n^2 + 1$ is a prime number.

(2) $n > 2$

- Statement (1) ALONE is sufficient, but statement (2) alone is not sufficient.
- Statement (2) ALONE is sufficient, but statement (1) alone is not sufficient.
- BOTH statements TOGETHER are sufficient, but NEITHER statement ALONE is sufficient.
- EACH statement ALONE is sufficient.
- Statements (1) and (2) TOGETHER are NOT sufficient to answer the question asked, and additional data are needed.

123. How many total units were produced at a certain factory?

(1) The factory produced 16,000 nondefective units.

(2) 20% of all units produced were defective.

- Statement (1) ALONE is sufficient, but statement (2) alone is not sufficient.
- Statement (2) ALONE is sufficient, but statement (1) alone is not sufficient.
- BOTH statements TOGETHER are sufficient, but NEITHER statement ALONE is sufficient.
- EACH statement ALONE is sufficient.
- Statements (1) and (2) TOGETHER are NOT sufficient to answer the question asked, and additional data are needed.

124. If k is a positive integer, what is the value of k?

(1) $k^3 < 60$

(2) When k^3 is divided by 2, the remainder is 0.

- Statement (1) ALONE is sufficient, but statement (2) alone is not sufficient.
- Statement (2) ALONE is sufficient, but statement (1) alone is not sufficient.
- BOTH statements TOGETHER are sufficient, but NEITHER statement ALONE is sufficient.
- EACH statement ALONE is sufficient.
- Statements (1) and (2) TOGETHER are NOT sufficient to answer the question asked, and additional data are needed.

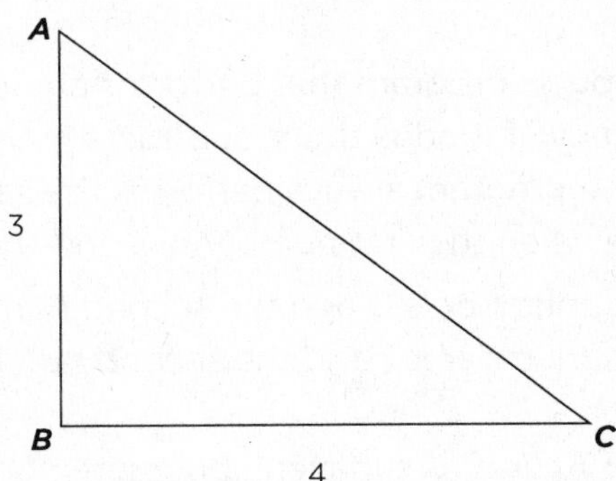

125. In the triangle provided, is $AC = 5$?

(1) The sum of the measures of angles BAC and ACB is 90.

(2) $AC > AB$ and $AC > BC$

- Statement (1) ALONE is sufficient, but statement (2) alone is not sufficient.
- Statement (2) ALONE is sufficient, but statement (1) alone is not sufficient.
- BOTH statements TOGETHER are sufficient, but NEITHER statement ALONE is sufficient.
- EACH statement ALONE is sufficient.
- Statements (1) and (2) TOGETHER are NOT sufficient to answer the question asked, and additional data are needed.

126. Are integers *d*, *e*, and *f* consecutive integers?

(1) The difference between *d* and *e* is equal to the difference between *e* and *f*.

(2) The difference between *d* and *f* is equal to 2.

- Statement (1) ALONE is sufficient, but statement (2) alone is not sufficient.
- Statement (2) ALONE is sufficient, but statement (1) alone is not sufficient.
- BOTH statements TOGETHER are sufficient, but NEITHER statement ALONE is sufficient.
- EACH statement ALONE is sufficient.
- Statements (1) and (2) TOGETHER are NOT sufficient to answer the question asked, and additional data are needed.

127. Ming finds a computer program that performs an operation on two numbers, but she doesn't know if it adds them, subtracts them, multiplies them, or divides them. If the program always performs the same operation, what answer will it give when the first number is 5 and the second number is 3?

(1) When the first number is 0 and the second number is 1, the answer is −1.

(2) When the first number is 1 and the second number is 0, the answer is 1.

- Statement (1) ALONE is sufficient, but statement (2) alone is not sufficient.
- Statement (2) ALONE is sufficient, but statement (1) alone is not sufficient.
- BOTH statements TOGETHER are sufficient, but NEITHER statement ALONE is sufficient.
- EACH statement ALONE is sufficient.
- Statements (1) and (2) TOGETHER are NOT sufficient to answer the question asked, and additional data are needed.

128. What is the value of a?

(1) $2b - 2 = b - \left(\frac{a}{3}\right) + b$

(2) $a - b = -4$

- O Statement (1) ALONE is sufficient, but statement (2) alone is not sufficient.
- O Statement (2) ALONE is sufficient, but statement (1) alone is not sufficient.
- O BOTH statements TOGETHER are sufficient, but NEITHER statement ALONE is sufficient.
- O EACH statement ALONE is sufficient.
- O Statements (1) and (2) TOGETHER are NOT sufficient to answer the question asked, and additional data are needed.

129. Farmer John fills an empty bag with 5 pounds of barley and oats. The bag then contains m pounds of barley and n pounds of oats. How many pounds of oats are in the bag?

(1) $\frac{3}{m} = \frac{6}{7}$

(2) $\frac{n}{5} = \frac{3}{10}$

- O Statement (1) ALONE is sufficient, but statement (2) alone is not sufficient.
- O Statement (2) ALONE is sufficient, but statement (1) alone is not sufficient.
- O BOTH statements TOGETHER are sufficient, but NEITHER statement ALONE is sufficient.
- O EACH statement ALONE is sufficient.
- O Statements (1) and (2) TOGETHER are NOT sufficient to answer the question asked, and additional data are needed.

130. If m and n are positive integers, what is the value of $m - n$?

(1) $mn = 16$
(2) $m = n^3$

- o Statement (1) ALONE is sufficient, but statement (2) alone is not sufficient.
- o Statement (2) ALONE is sufficient, but statement (1) alone is not sufficient.
- o BOTH statements TOGETHER are sufficient, but NEITHER statement ALONE is sufficient.
- o EACH statement ALONE is sufficient.
- o Statements (1) and (2) TOGETHER are NOT sufficient to answer the question asked, and additional data are needed.

131. How many years ago was Lisa born?

(1) Six years ago, Lisa was half as old as she is now.
(2) Eight years from now, Lisa will be exactly twice as old as her brother Carl is now.

- o Statement (1) ALONE is sufficient, but statement (2) alone is not sufficient.
- o Statement (2) ALONE is sufficient, but statement (1) alone is not sufficient.
- o BOTH statements TOGETHER are sufficient, but NEITHER statement ALONE is sufficient.
- o EACH statement ALONE is sufficient.
- o Statements (1) and (2) TOGETHER are NOT sufficient to answer the question asked, and additional data are needed.

132. If both a and b are nonzero integers, what is the value of ab?

(1) $a^2 = b^2$

(2) $\sqrt{b} = 2$

- Statement (1) ALONE is sufficient, but statement (2) alone is not sufficient.
- Statement (2) ALONE is sufficient, but statement (1) alone is not sufficient.
- BOTH statements TOGETHER are sufficient, but NEITHER statement ALONE is sufficient.
- EACH statement ALONE is sufficient.
- Statements (1) and (2) TOGETHER are NOT sufficient to answer the question asked, and additional data are needed.

133. Jack's school has a hallway with 100 lockers numbered 1–100. How many of the lockers are currently open?

(1) Currently, the number of open odd-numbered lockers is 5 less than the number of open even-numbered lockers.

(2) Currently, exactly $\frac{1}{5}$ of the even-numbered lockers and $\frac{1}{10}$ of the odd-numbered lockers are open.

- Statement (1) ALONE is sufficient, but statement (2) alone is not sufficient.
- Statement (2) ALONE is sufficient, but statement (1) alone is not sufficient.
- BOTH statements TOGETHER are sufficient, but NEITHER statement ALONE is sufficient.
- EACH statement ALONE is sufficient.
- Statements (1) and (2) TOGETHER are NOT sufficient to answer the question asked, and additional data are needed.

134. The number k is a three-digit integer that has A as its hundreds digit, B as its tens digit, and C as its units digit. If none of the three digits is 0, what is the value of $2k$?

(1) $A = 3B = 9C$

(2) $\frac{A}{B} = \frac{B}{C}$

- Statement (1) ALONE is sufficient, but statement (2) alone is not sufficient.
- Statement (2) ALONE is sufficient, but statement (1) alone is not sufficient.
- BOTH statements TOGETHER are sufficient, but NEITHER statement ALONE is sufficient.
- EACH statement ALONE is sufficient.
- Statements (1) and (2) TOGETHER are NOT sufficient to answer the question asked, and additional data are needed.

135. A city's water tower is in the shape of a regular cylinder. If the tower is currently full of water, how long will it take to empty it completely?

(1) The tower's circular base has a radius of 15 feet.

(2) Water is drained from the tower at a constant rate of 100 gallons per hour (1 gallon = 7.5 cubic feet).

- Statement (1) ALONE is sufficient, but statement (2) alone is not sufficient.
- Statement (2) ALONE is sufficient, but statement (1) alone is not sufficient.
- BOTH statements TOGETHER are sufficient, but NEITHER statement ALONE is sufficient.
- EACH statement ALONE is sufficient.
- Statements (1) and (2) TOGETHER are NOT sufficient to answer the question asked, and additional data are needed.

136. Is the value of x positive?

(1) $x - (-10) < 10 - x$

(2) $x < 3$

- O Statement (1) ALONE is sufficient, but statement (2) alone is not sufficient.
- O Statement (2) ALONE is sufficient, but statement (1) alone is not sufficient.
- O BOTH statements TOGETHER are sufficient, but NEITHER statement ALONE is sufficient.
- O EACH statement ALONE is sufficient.
- O Statements (1) and (2) TOGETHER are NOT sufficient to answer the question asked, and additional data are needed.

137. Given that k is an integer, is $\frac{k + 30}{k}$ an integer?

(1) $k^2 = 9$

(2) $k < 5$

- O Statement (1) ALONE is sufficient, but statement (2) alone is not sufficient.
- O Statement (2) ALONE is sufficient, but statement (1) alone is not sufficient.
- O BOTH statements TOGETHER are sufficient, but NEITHER statement ALONE is sufficient.
- O EACH statement ALONE is sufficient.
- O Statements (1) and (2) TOGETHER are NOT sufficient to answer the question asked, and additional data are needed.

138. Which of the five values in the set $\{a, b, c, d, e\}$ is the minimum, given that all five values are positive?

(1) $a - c = e$

(2) $b > d$

- Statement (1) ALONE is sufficient, but statement (2) alone is not sufficient.
- Statement (2) ALONE is sufficient, but statement (1) alone is not sufficient.
- BOTH statements TOGETHER are sufficient, but NEITHER statement ALONE is sufficient.
- EACH statement ALONE is sufficient.
- Statements (1) and (2) TOGETHER are NOT sufficient to answer the question asked, and additional data are needed.

139. Given that $kp = 48$, what is the value of $k + p$?

(1) k and p are consecutive even integers.

(2) k and p are both positive integers.

- Statement (1) ALONE is sufficient, but statement (2) alone is not sufficient.
- Statement (2) ALONE is sufficient, but statement (1) alone is not sufficient.
- BOTH statements TOGETHER are sufficient, but NEITHER statement ALONE is sufficient.
- EACH statement ALONE is sufficient.
- Statements (1) and (2) TOGETHER are NOT sufficient to answer the question asked, and additional data are needed.

140. When an certain auction company sells an item, it charges the seller a flat fee plus a percentage of the selling price. If Julie sold an item through this auction house, how much did the company charge Julie to sell the item?

(1) The auction company charges sellers 25% of the item's selling price.
(2) The flat fee for each sale is $25.

- Statement (1) ALONE is sufficient, but statement (2) alone is not sufficient.
- Statement (2) ALONE is sufficient, but statement (1) alone is not sufficient.
- BOTH statements TOGETHER are sufficient, but NEITHER statement ALONE is sufficient.
- EACH statement ALONE is sufficient.
- Statements (1) and (2) TOGETHER are NOT sufficient to answer the question asked, and additional data are needed.

141. What is the value of $x + y$?

(1) $x + 2 = 5 - y$
(2) $(x + y)^2 = 9$

- Statement (1) ALONE is sufficient, but statement (2) alone is not sufficient.
- Statement (2) ALONE is sufficient, but statement (1) alone is not sufficient.
- BOTH statements TOGETHER are sufficient, but NEITHER statement ALONE is sufficient.
- EACH statement ALONE is sufficient.
- Statements (1) and (2) TOGETHER are NOT sufficient to answer the question asked, and additional data are needed.

142. Working at a constant rate, Keith can paint 7,200 linear feet of shelving in 90 minutes. How long would it take Keith and Samantha, working together, to paint 7,200 linear feet of shelving?

(1) Working alone, it takes Keith twice as long to paint the shelving as it takes Keith and Samantha working together.

(2) Both Keith and Samantha paint the shelving at the same rate.

- Statement (1) ALONE is sufficient, but statement (2) alone is not sufficient.
- Statement (2) ALONE is sufficient, but statement (1) alone is not sufficient.
- BOTH statements TOGETHER are sufficient, but NEITHER statement ALONE is sufficient.
- EACH statement ALONE is sufficient.
- Statements (1) and (2) TOGETHER are NOT sufficient to answer the question asked, and additional data are needed.

143. If z is a positive integer, does z have more than two positive integer factors?

(1) $23 < z < 29$

(2) z is odd.

- Statement (1) ALONE is sufficient, but statement (2) alone is not sufficient.
- Statement (2) ALONE is sufficient, but statement (1) alone is not sufficient.
- BOTH statements TOGETHER are sufficient, but NEITHER statement ALONE is sufficient.
- EACH statement ALONE is sufficient.
- Statements (1) and (2) TOGETHER are NOT sufficient to answer the question asked, and additional data are needed.

144. Is $g = h$?

(1) $a + g > 10$

(2) $a + h > 10$

- Statement (1) ALONE is sufficient, but statement (2) alone is not sufficient.
- Statement (2) ALONE is sufficient, but statement (1) alone is not sufficient.
- BOTH statements TOGETHER are sufficient, but NEITHER statement ALONE is sufficient.
- EACH statement ALONE is sufficient.
- Statements (1) and (2) TOGETHER are NOT sufficient to answer the question asked, and additional data are needed.

145. Is the range of the set of numbers $\{j, k, m, n, p\}$ greater than 5?

(1) $k - n > 5$

(2) k is the greatest number in the set.

- Statement (1) ALONE is sufficient, but statement (2) alone is not sufficient.
- Statement (2) ALONE is sufficient, but statement (1) alone is not sufficient.
- BOTH statements TOGETHER are sufficient, but NEITHER statement ALONE is sufficient.
- EACH statement ALONE is sufficient.
- Statements (1) and (2) TOGETHER are NOT sufficient to answer the question asked, and additional data are needed.

146. If a is less than 80% of b, is a less than 50?

(1) $b - a = 20$

(2) $b < 50$

- Statement (1) ALONE is sufficient, but statement (2) alone is not sufficient.
- Statement (2) ALONE is sufficient, but statement (1) alone is not sufficient.
- BOTH statements TOGETHER are sufficient, but NEITHER statement ALONE is sufficient.
- EACH statement ALONE is sufficient.
- Statements (1) and (2) TOGETHER are NOT sufficient to answer the question asked, and additional data are needed.

147. Is k positive?

(1) $k^5 > 0$

(2) $-3k < 0$

- Statement (1) ALONE is sufficient, but statement (2) alone is not sufficient.
- Statement (2) ALONE is sufficient, but statement (1) alone is not sufficient.
- BOTH statements TOGETHER are sufficient, but NEITHER statement ALONE is sufficient.
- EACH statement ALONE is sufficient.
- Statements (1) and (2) TOGETHER are NOT sufficient to answer the question asked, and additional data are needed.

148. If t is a two-digit positive integer, what is the value of t?

(1) One digit of t is the square of the other digit, and the two digits add to 6.

(2) $t > 30$

- O Statement (1) ALONE is sufficient, but statement (2) alone is not sufficient.
- O Statement (2) ALONE is sufficient, but statement (1) alone is not sufficient.
- O BOTH statements TOGETHER are sufficient, but NEITHER statement ALONE is sufficient.
- O EACH statement ALONE is sufficient.
- O Statements (1) and (2) TOGETHER are NOT sufficient to answer the question asked, and additional data are needed.

149. Is $mn < 11$?

(1) $m + n = 7$

(2) $5 \geq m \geq 3$ and $4 \geq n \geq 2$

- O Statement (1) ALONE is sufficient, but statement (2) alone is not sufficient.
- O Statement (2) ALONE is sufficient, but statement (1) alone is not sufficient.
- O BOTH statements TOGETHER are sufficient, but NEITHER statement ALONE is sufficient.
- O EACH statement ALONE is sufficient.
- O Statements (1) and (2) TOGETHER are NOT sufficient to answer the question asked, and additional data are needed.

150. A certain company's net profit in September was equal to 9.8% of that month's total sales, while its net profit in October was equal to 10.3% of that month's total sales. If total sales for both months were equal, how much net profit did the company earn in October?

(1) The company's October net profit was $19,600 higher than its September net profit.

(2) The company's net profit in September was $384,160.

- Statement (1) ALONE is sufficient, but statement (2) alone is not sufficient.
- Statement (2) ALONE is sufficient, but statement (1) alone is not sufficient.
- BOTH statements TOGETHER are sufficient, but NEITHER statement ALONE is sufficient.
- EACH statement ALONE is sufficient.
- Statements (1) and (2) TOGETHER are NOT sufficient to answer the question asked, and additional data are needed.

Answers and explanations begin on the next page.

Answer Key

DATA SUFFICIENCY PRACTICE

1. D
2. D
3. A
4. E
5. B
6. D
7. E
8. B
9. A
10. B
11. E
12. B
13. B
14. A
15. C
16. A
17. E
18. D
19. E
20. C
21. E
22. B
23. D
24. D
25. C
26. B
27. E
28. E
29. D
30. C
31. A
32. D
33. D
34. E
35. B
36. D
37. D
38. D
39. C
40. A
41. B
42. A
43. D
44. D
45. A
46. E
47. E
48. A
49. D
50. C
51. A
52. C
53. D
54. C
55. D
56. B
57. D
58. D
59. D
60. E
61. E
62. D
63. E
64. C
65. E
66. D
67. E
68. C
69. B
70. E
71. E
72. D
73. C
74. E
75. B
76. E
77. C
78. B
79. D
80. E
81. E
82. B
83. C
84. B
85. A
86. A
87. C
88. A
89. C
90. A
91. D
92. B
93. B
94. B
95. E
96. D
97. C
98. A
99. B
100. B
101. A
102. D
103. D
104. B
105. C
106. B
107. E
108. D
109. D
110. B
111. E
112. C
113. E
114. C
115. A
116. E
117. B

118. E
119. C
120. B
121. D
122. E
123. C
124. C
125. A
126. C
127. A
128. A
129. D
130. C
131. A
132. E
133. B
134. A
135. E
136. A
137. A
138. E
139. C
140. E
141. A
142. D
143. A
144. E
145. A
146. B
147. D
148. C
149. E
150. D

Answers and Explanations

DATA SUFFICIENCY PRACTICE

1. D

This question asks whether the information in one or both statements is sufficient to find a specific value.

To find a as a percentage of b is the same as finding the ratio of a to b. Simply stated, we need to know one value in terms of the other, which is given to us in each statement. Don't do the math! Just note the fact that you *could* do it using the information in either statement, select choice (D) (each is sufficient independently), and move on.

If you're having trouble, just make up a value for either a or b and test it out for yourself.

The credited response is (D): Each statement, taken independently, is sufficient to find the value in question.

2. D

This question asks whether the information in one or both statements is sufficient to answer a yes or no question.

With statement (1), if we add c to each side, we are left with $a < b$ verifying the question (SUFFICIENT).

With statement (2), we can take the same approach by multiplying both sides of the equation by 2: $a < b$ (SUFFICIENT).

The credited response is (D): Each statement, when considered independently, leads to an absolute answer in all circumstances (for the record here, both "yes").

3. A

This question asks whether the information in one or both statements is sufficient to find a specific value.

Since $\frac{1}{4}$ of the team members are girls, the probability of a girl being chosen would be $\frac{1}{4}$. Thus, statement (1) is SUFFICIENT.

Statement (2) is no good because we wouldn't know the total number of teammates. Without that information, we can't use the number of boys on the team alone to determine the probability. Statement (2) is NOT sufficient.

The credited response is (A): Statement (1), taken independently, is sufficient to find the value in question, but statement (2) is not.

4. E

This question asks whether the information in one or both statements is sufficient to find a specific value.

Neither of the statements alone is sufficient. It may be tempting to think that together the statements can answer the question—by subtracting the two distances. Even combined, however, the information is insufficient. We have no information about the distances between A and B or between C and D. If you're having a tough time understanding this one, try drawing a couple examples where the distance of $\underline{BC}$ varies even when $\underline{AC}$ is 5 and $\underline{BD}$ is 7 to prove it.

Draw a picture, and create two conflicting scenarios:

A – B	B – C	C – D
3	2	5
4	1	6

The credited response is (E): The statements don't provide sufficient information to find the value in question, not even when considered together.

5. B

This question asks whether the information in one or both statements is sufficient to answer a yes or no question.

If $x > 2.6$, we still can't be sure it is greater than 2.7. It could be 2.65, or 2.8 . . . so statement (1) is not sufficient.

Statement (2), on the other hand, is sufficient. If $x > 2.8$, then we know with certainty that it is greater than 2.7.

The credited response is (B): The information provided in statement (2) leads to a definite answer (for the record here, an absolute "yes" in all possible circumstances), but statement (1) allows for both "yes" and "no" answers.

6. D

This question asks whether the information in one or both statements is sufficient to answer a yes or no question.

If $n - 2$ is odd, then we know that n itself must be odd. Not sure about that? Make up some numbers and test it out. So if n is odd, then $n - 1$ must be even. Statement (1) is sufficient.

Statement (2) tells us that $n + 1$ is even. That means that n is odd, which means that $n - 1$ is also even. Statement (2) is also sufficient!

The credited response is (D): Each statement, when considered independently, leads to an absolute answer in all circumstances (for the record here, both "yes").

7. E

This question asks whether the information in one or both statements is sufficient to answer a yes or no question.

Statement (1): Some values greater than 1 are between 3 and 4, but not all are. x could be, say, 3.5 or 7. Not sufficient. Eliminate answers (A) and (D).

Statement (2): Some values less than 5 are between 3 and 4, but not all are. Not sufficient. Eliminate answer (B).

Even taken together, the two statements don't yield a definite answer, either "yes" or "no." Combined, they give a range for x of $1 < x < 5$. x could be 2 (no) or 4 (yes).

The credited response is (E): Statements (1) and (2) TOGETHER are NOT sufficient to answer the question asked, and additional data are needed.

8. B

This question asks whether the information in one or both statements is sufficient to find a specific value.

The amount of milk initially in the vat is irrelevant, since we're only interested in the rate of milk decrease, so statement (1) is not sufficient. Statement (2) tells us separate rates for the milk flowing into and out of the vat. Using these rates, we can find an overall rate for the decrease of milk volume. Don't bother finding the actual rate! To answer this question, you just need to confirm that it is possible to calculate—don't waste time actually doing the math. Statement (2) alone is sufficient.

The credited response is (B): Statement (2), taken independently, is sufficient to find the value in question, but statement (1) is not.

9. A

This question asks whether the information in one or both statements is sufficient to answer a yes or no question.

Statement (1) is sufficient, since that inequality would only hold true for a positive value of x. Make up some numbers to test it out. We know statement (2) is not sufficient because there are both positive and negative values of x that satisfy the statement "$x - 2$ is negative."

The credited response is (A): The information provided in statement (1) leads to a definite answer (for the record here, an absolute "yes" in all possible circumstances), but statement (2) allows for both "yes" and "no" answers.

10. B

This question asks whether the information in one or both statements is sufficient to answer a yes or no question.

Statement (1) is totally irrelevant, since it doesn't narrow down the infinite possible values of r and s that could satisfy (or not satisfy) the given equation. Not sufficient.

Statement (2) lets us substitute for r in the given equation, as follows: $3r - 4s = 0$. We know that $6r = 8s$, which means:

$$3r = 4s$$
$$4s - 4s = 0$$
$$0 = 0 \rightarrow \text{Sufficiency!}$$

The credited response is (B): The information provided in statement (2) leads to a definite answer (for the record here, an absolute "yes" in all possible circumstances), but statement (1) allows for both "yes" and "no" answers.

11. E

This question asks whether the information in one or both statements is sufficient to find a specific value.

Statement (1) alone clearly isn't going to be enough, since there are many prime numbers.

Statement (2) alone gives us a range of 7 possible integers. If we combine the two statements, can we narrow down to one possible value? Well, no. There are two prime numbers in the given range, 23 and 29, so the information provided is not sufficient to find the value of $-x$.

The credited response is (E): The information provided in the statements, taken independently or together, is insufficient; both "yes" and "no" answers are still possible (in other words, the answer is always "maybe").

12. B

This question asks whether the information in one or both statements is sufficient to answer a yes or no question.

This is a pretty straightforward number properties question drilling us on our odds and evens rules. Remember that when adding, the only way to end up with an odd sum is to have an odd number of odd values in the list of numbers to be added together. If this is unclear, pick a few different values—odds and evens—and test it out.

Statement (1) doesn't give us much to work with. It's certainly not sufficient.

Statement (2) is enough to know for certain that the sum of j and k would be odd. An even plus an odd will always be odd. Make up a few numbers to check it out. You'll find that the sum of consecutive integers is always odd. Sufficient.

The credited response is (B): The information provided in statement (2) leads to a definite answer (for the record here, an absolute "yes" in all possible circumstances), but statement (1) allows for both "yes" and "no" answers.

13. B

This question asks whether the information in one or both statements is sufficient to find a specific value.

Statement (1) is insufficient because if we plug in $x = 7$, we are left with $7 - y = z\ldots$ and we still are unable to solve for y's value.

Let's try plugging in statement (2): $x - y = z$; $x - y = (x + 4)$; $-y = 4$; $y = -4$: Statement (2) alone is sufficient.

The credited response is (B): Statement (2), taken independently, is sufficient to find the value in question, but statement (1) is not.

14. A

This question asks whether the information in one or both statements is sufficient to answer a yes or no question.

If $\frac{n}{3}$ is an integer, we know that n is a multiple of 3, and we can be certain that n is an integer. The best way to test this is through some trial and error. Statement (1) is sufficient.

Statement (2), however, is not sufficient. All we know from this one is that a multiple of n is an integer, which doesn't clarify whether or not n itself is one. Take for example, $n = \frac{1}{3}$. In this case, n is not an integer, but $3n$ still is an integer. We cannot be certain whether n is an integer or not.

The credited response is (A): The information provided in statement (1) leads to a definite answer (for the record here, an absolute "yes" in all possible circumstances), but statement (2) allows for both "yes" and "no" answers.

15. C

This question asks whether the information in one or both statements is sufficient to find a specific value.

We can rewrite the expression $\frac{1}{x} + \frac{1}{y}$ to read:

$$\frac{1}{x} + \frac{1}{y} = \frac{y}{xy} + \frac{x}{xy} = \frac{(x + y)}{xy}$$

Statement (1) gives us a value for $(x + y)$. We can plug it into the fraction we've formed above: $\frac{15}{xy}$

But we're unable to get any closer to the value. Not sufficient.

Statement (2) gives us our denominator if we plug this in by itself: $\frac{x + y}{50}$

This too is insufficient to solve the fraction in itself. But combined, we *are* able to find the value: $\frac{x + y}{xy} = \frac{15}{50} = \frac{3}{10}$.

The credited response is (C): Taken together, statements (1) and (2) are sufficient to find the value in question, but neither statement is sufficient when considered independently.

16. A

This question asks whether the information in one or both statements is sufficient to find a specific value.

In a triangle, the smallest side will be opposite the angle with the smallest degree measure. If we can identify which side is shortest, we can identify the smallest angle.

Statement (1) tells us that $\underline{AC} = y = x - 2$. Since the other sides have measures of x and $x - 1$, we know that $\underline{AC}$ will be the smallest side. You can test this out by making up a value for x. Since we know $\underline{AC}$ is the smallest side, we can find the angle with the smallest degree measure. Sufficient.

Statement (2) tells us the length of y. This does not help us determine which side is smallest, so it is not sufficient.

The credited response is (A): Statement (1), taken independently, is sufficient to find the value in question, but statement (2) is not.

17. E

This question asks whether the information in one or both statements is sufficient to find a specific value.

We know that statement (1) is not sufficient because it doesn't tell us anything about Marty.

Statement (2) by itself also fails to provide enough information, since statement (2) doesn't tell us anything about Wendy's distance.

Would it, combined with statement (1), give us enough information to answer the question? We know how far Marty would get in any 20-minute interval, but the problem is that we don't know how long Marty drove.

The credited response is (E): The statements don't provide sufficient information to find the value in question, not even when considered together.

18. D

This question asks whether the information in one or both statements is sufficient to find a specific value.

We can answer the question if we can find x. Each statement alone gives us enough information to find x.

Statement (1): $0.05x = 8$. No need to do the math. We know we *could* successfully solve this. Sufficient.

Statement (2): $\left(\frac{1}{4}\right)x = 40$. Again, we know we can solve for x here. Sufficient.

The real feat here is avoiding calculations. Doing the math here would burn up valuable time that we don't want to spare.

The credited response is (D): Each statement, taken independently, is sufficient to find the value in question.

19. E

This question asks whether the information in one or both statements is sufficient to find a specific value.

From statement (1), we know that the hundredths digit (represented by ☆) must be equal to 5, 6, 7, 8, or 9. We cannot narrow it down further than that, so statement (1) is not sufficient.

Statement (2) shows us the hundredths digit, but it has been rounded. Since we do not know the thousandths digit, we cannot be sure whether the hundredths digit is indeed 7, or if it was rounded up from 6. Because we cannot be sure of ☆'s value, this is not sufficient.

Even combined, we do not have enough information to answer the question.

The credited response is (E): The statements don't provide sufficient information to find the value in question, not even when considered together.

20. C

This question asks whether the information in one or both statements is sufficient to find a specific value.

Statement (1) is not sufficient to answer the question. If we substitute in the given value, we can see that we still know nothing about a and c.

Statement (2) gives us the info we need about a and c. Lack of info about b makes this answer alone also not sufficient.

But before we think about the statements combined, let's simplify the given information: $ab + bc = b(a + c)$. Now looking at the statements in conjunction, we can get to the value by substituting in the given values in the statements.

The credited response is (C): Taken together, statements (1) and (2) are sufficient to find the value in question, but neither statement is sufficient when considered independently.

21. E

This question asks whether the information in one or both statements is sufficient to find a specific value.

The surface area of a cylinder = circumference × height, but we're not interested in the surface area of the whole cylinder, only the surface area of the stripe. So what we'll need to know in order to find this is the circumference of the cylinder (or radius or diameter of the circle at its base or top, which would allow us to find circumference) *and* the width of the stripe (here, y). Neither statement has any information about the circumference of the tank. The information provided only pertains to the tank/stripe's height. Thus, we do not have enough information to answer this question.

The credited response is (E): The statements don't provide sufficient information to find the value in question, not even when considered together.

22. B

This question asks whether the information in one or both statements is sufficient to find a specific value.

Let's rearrange statement (1) to solve for k: $k(k - 1) = 2$; $k^2 - k - 2 = 0$. We now need to factor to solve this quadratic equation: $(k - 2)(k + 1) = 0$. So k could equal –1 or 2 to satisfy the equation. Since we cannot be sure which value is correct, statement (1) is not sufficient.

In statement (2), $2^{(3k)} = 64$. This must equal 2^6, since that equals 64. So we can say: $6 = 3k$; $k = 2$. This is sufficient.

The credited response is (B): Statement (2), taken independently, is sufficient to find the value in question, but statement (1) is not.

23. D

This question asks whether the information in one or both statements is sufficient to find a specific value.

With statement (1), we can determine x by finding the diameter of each tube. We know the length is 54 inches. If 18 tubes fit along that edge, we know the diameter is: $\frac{54}{18} = 3$. We can then figure out that $\frac{27}{3} = 9$ tubes would fit along the width. And from there, we can determine x (but to save time, we won't work out the math). Sufficient.

And statement (2) gives us the diameter outright, and we already know we can find x using the diameter with the given dimensions. Sufficient.

The credited response is (D): Each statement, taken independently, is sufficient to find the value in question.

24. D

This question asks whether the information in one or both statements is sufficient to find a specific value.

Statement (1) is sufficient because if we plug in $a = 8$ to the top equation, $c + 2 = a$; $c + 2 = 8$; $c = 6$.

And statement (2) is also sufficient: We can plug in the d value to the third equation to find c: $d + c = 12$; $6 + c = 12$; $c = 6$. They're using the concept of "system of equations" to make the question seem harder than it is.

The credited response is (D): Each statement, taken independently, is sufficient to find the value in question.

25. C

This question asks whether the information in one or both statements is sufficient to answer a yes or no question.

Since each statement, considered independently, merely provides a range that extends infinitely in one direction—greater in statement (1), less than in statement (2)—either of these statements taken alone is not sufficient. Combined, however, we can declare the following range for n: $7 \leq n \leq 7$, which is equivalent to $n = 7$.

The credited response is (C): When taken together, the information provided in the statements leads to a definite answer (for the record here, an absolute "yes" in all possible circumstances), but when considered independently, each statement still allows both "yes" and "no" answers.

26. B

This question asks whether the information in one or both statements is sufficient to find a specific value.

Statement (1) pertains to n, not m, so it is *not* sufficient to find the value of m.

Statement (2) tells us that the distance between D and C (which, according to the table, is 12) is half the distance between A and B. Using this information, we can successfully solve for m. Sufficient.

The credited response is (B): Statement (2), taken independently, is sufficient to find the value in question, but statement (1) is not.

27. E

This question asks whether the information in one or both statements is sufficient to find a specific value.

It should quickly become clear that this question will only be answerable, if at all possible, by combining the two statements. Based on statement (1), n could equal 60, 51, 42, 33, 24, or 15 (not 06—it's not a two-digit number). And based upon statement (2), any multiple of 4 will do. So neither statement alone will work.

All we need to do in order to go with choice (E) and move on is show that there is more than one possible value that satisfies both statements. Use the list you created in statement (1) and eliminate anything that isn't a multiple of 4—doing so leaves us with 60 and 24, so even combining the two statements isn't enough.

The credited response is (E): The statements don't provide sufficient information to find the value in question, not even when considered together.

28. E

This question asks whether the information in one or both statements is sufficient to find a specific value.

Without even calculating, it should be apparent that each statement, considered independently, merely provides a range of possible values, so neither one could possibly be sufficient on its own. But in combination, we need to get a little bit closer. First, let's change the statements' fractions to decimals:

$$\text{Statement (1)} = x > \frac{3}{8}, \text{ so } x > 0.375$$

$$\text{Statement (2)} = x < \frac{3}{7}, \text{ so } x < 0.429$$

Combined: $0.375 < x < 0.429$. Since the range includes 3 and 4 as possible tenths digits, there is not sufficient information to answer this question.

The credited response is (E): The statements don't provide sufficient information to find the value in question, not even when considered together.

29. D

This question asks whether the information in one or both statements is sufficient to find a specific value.

Statement (1) is sufficient because we can determine that the square-shaped planks have sides of length 5. Therefore, 8 square planks of length 5 would make a 40-foot long sidewalk. Remember that the diagonal of a square is side length × $\sqrt{2}$.

Statement (2) provides the same information as Statement 1, and knowing the width (or length) of each plank will tell you the total number of planks needed to make up the total platform.

The credited response is (D): EACH statement ALONE is sufficient.

30. C

This question asks whether the information in one or both statements is sufficient to find a specific value.

Neither statement (1) or statement (2) alone is sufficient. Combined, however, we can determine the overlap between clubs. If the joint conference consisted of 15 Club X and Club Y members, we can use the information for the individual clubs: 6 Club X members + 12 Club Y members = 18 memberships. If there were only 15 members at the joint conference, there must be 3 members who belong to both clubs.

The credited response is (C): Taken together, statements (1) and (2) are sufficient to find the value in question, but neither statement is sufficient when considered independently.

31. A

This question asks whether the information in one or both statements is sufficient to find a specific value.

The sum of the interior angles of a triangle is always 180. In statement (1), we learn that the two other angles total 128. We can create an equation to find the value of c: $a + b + c = 180$; $128 + c = 180$; $c = 52$. Sufficient. But if we apply the same formula to the information given in statement (2), we'll find that we can find the value of b but not the value of c. Not sufficient.

The credited response is (A): Statement (1), taken independently, is sufficient to find the value in question, but statement (2) is not.

32. D

This question asks whether the information in one or both statements is sufficient to answer a yes or no question.

Statement (1): If we cross multiply the equation, we get $bc = 16$. Sufficient.

Statement (2): If we divide each side of the equation by ab, we are left with $bc = 16$. Also sufficient.

The credited response is (D): Each statement, when considered independently, leads to an absolute answer in all circumstances (for the record here, both "yes").

33. D

This question asks whether the information in one or both statements is sufficient to find a specific value.

From statement (1), we can solve for y: $\frac{y}{x} = 5$; $y = 5x$. Then we can substitute that value in for y in the given equation: $-18 + 24 - x = y$; $6 - x = 5x$; $6 = 6x$; $x = 1$. Sufficient.

Statement (2) allows us to simply plug in the value for y directly and solve. In the original equation $-18 + 24 - x = y$. And in this statement, $y = 5$. So $-18 + 24 - x = 5$; $6 - x = 5$; $1 - x = 0$; $x = 1$. Sufficient.

The credited response is (D): Each statement, taken independently, is sufficient to find the value in question.

34. E

This question asks whether the information in one or both statements is sufficient to find a specific value.

Neither statement (1) or statement (2) alone can help us determine the value of xy^2. If we combine the two statements, we can substitute for y as follows: $x - 2 = x^2 - 2$; $x = x^2$. Thus, x equals either 1 or 0. Since $y = x - 2$, y equals either −1 or −2. That means xy^2 equals either −1 or 0. Since we cannot definitely find a single value, we do not have enough information to answer the question.

The credited response is (E): The statements don't provide sufficient information to find the value in question, not even when considered together.

35. B

This question asks whether the information in one or both statements is sufficient to answer a yes or no question.

This one's drilling us on an old-school concept: rounding. Statement (1) is not sufficient because k could equal 0.52 or 0.48, satisfying the statement, and we would still be unable to answer the question with certainty. Statement (2), however, is sufficient because k must be less than 0.5 in order to round down (or up) to 0.

The credited response is (B): The information provided in statement (2) leads to a definite answer (for the record here, an absolute "yes" in all possible circumstances), but statement (1) allows for both "yes" and "no" answers.

36. D

This question asks whether the information in one or both statements is sufficient to find a specific value.

To figure this one out, we'll need to know the dollar amount of the broker's commission, or we'll need to be able to figure it out somehow. Statement (1) is sufficient. We can set up an equation using the information in this statement. The dollar amount of the deal minus the broker's commission represents 96% of the deal amount (100% less the 4% commission): $\frac{61,440}{\text{deal amount}} = \frac{96}{100}$. From here, we can solve for the deal amount. And statement (2) is also sufficient. If the market value is $80,000 and the deal was 80% of that value, then 80,000 × 0.8 = deal amount.

The credited response is (D): Each statement, taken independently, is sufficient to find the value in question.

37. D

This question asks whether the information in one or both statements is sufficient to find a specific value.

To find x, we need to know $\sqrt{x}$ or have a way of figuring it out. Here are two scenarios that would give us enough information: (1) knowing the values of y and k or (2) knowing the value of yk (cross multiply to determine that $\frac{\sqrt{x}}{y} = k$ simplifies to $\sqrt{x} = yk$).

In statement (1), we have the information needed in the second scenario. No need to do the math to know it is sufficient, but for the record:

$$\frac{\sqrt{x}}{y} = k; \quad \sqrt{x} = yk; \quad \sqrt{x} = 12; \quad x = 144$$

And in statement (2), we have the information needed in the first scenario. Again, no need for actual math work to prove it's sufficient, but if you want to see it :

$\frac{\sqrt{x}}{y} = k;\quad \frac{\sqrt{x}}{3} = 4;\quad \sqrt{x} = 12;\quad x = 144$

The credited response is (D): Each statement, taken independently, is sufficient to find the value in question.

38. D

This question asks whether the information in one or both statements is sufficient to find a specific value.

This is a very direct number properties question. If you don't remember the rules, the easiest way to work out a number properties question is to pick some numbers and try out the math.

From statement (1), we know $b - a$ must equal 8. If you remember that subtraction is inclusive of one of the two numbers, then no more work is needed to prove this is sufficient information. But in case you forgot that, let's say $a = 1$ and $b = 9$. And we can count that there are 7 integers in between. We know that this won't change based on the numbers we choose (with a difference of 8). If you're not sure, try some other numbers out to test it for yourself.

In statement (2), we're given the exact relationship, but one value less for each variable . . . so it must be the same. But if you're not convinced, let's take the same approach and say $a = 1$ and $b = 9$. That means $a - 1$ would be 0 and b - 1 would be 8. Once again, we can count seven integers between 0 and 8, and we can always do the same for any integer values of *a* and *b*.

The credited response is (D): Each statement, taken independently, is sufficient to find the value in question.

39. C

This question asks whether the information in one or both statements is sufficient to find a specific value.

To solve this one, we'll need to know the number of members in the Booster Club *and* what percentage of the club is 21+ (or what percentage is under 21)—that is, if we're not told outright how many are under 21 (we're not usually so lucky).

Using statement (1), we can determine the *ratio* of club members who are under 21 years old, but we cannot determine an actual *number* of members in that age group. Not sufficient. Statement (2) provides just the opposite: Using the information here, we can determine the total number of club members, but no information about age is provided.

Taken together, however, we can determine both the percentage that is under 21 (first statement) and the total number of members (second statement), which is enough to make the requested calculation in the stimulus. Don't actually do the math . . . but if you want to see it, here it is:

Statement (2): $15 = 0.5m;\ m = 30$.

Statement (1): $\frac{2}{3}m = 21^{+};\ \frac{1}{3}m =$ under 21

Combined: $\frac{1}{3}m = \frac{1}{3}(30) = 10$

There are 10 Booster Club members under 21.

The credited response is (C): Taken together, statements (1) and (2) are sufficient to find the value in question, but neither statement is sufficient when considered independently.

40. A

This question asks whether the information in one or both statements is sufficient to answer a yes or no question.

In order to answer this with a definite yes or no, we need to know either the values for x and y or the relationship between them. Statement (1) is sufficient, because it basically tells us the relationship between them: x is exactly one integer less than y. Granted, the answer is "no," but it's a definite "no," and that's sufficient.

In statement (2), however, we first need to simplify:

$$\frac{x}{3} = y - 5$$

$$x = 3(y - 5)$$

$$x = 3y - 15$$

The easiest way to test this one is to plug in two very different values for y (preferably ones that are easy to calculate): Try 10 and -10. When $y = 10$, x is greater than y ($x = 15$); when $y = -10$, x is less than y ($x = -45$). Insufficient.

The credited response is (A): The information provided in statement (1) leads to a definite answer (for the record here, an absolute "no" in all possible circumstances), but statement (2) allows for both "yes" and "no" answers.

41. B

This question asks whether the information in one or both statements is sufficient to answer a yes or no question.

Statement (1): It's probably fastest to pick two values, one odd and one even, and then test. Let's try out 3 and 4, both of which satisfy this condition. If $n = 3$, then it's true that $\frac{n}{2}$ is *not* an odd integer because it's a fraction . . . so n could be odd. Next, if $n = 4$, then it's true that $\frac{n}{2}$ is *not* an odd integer because it is an even integer (2). So n could be odd or even. Statement (1) does not answer the question. Insufficient.

Statement (2): An even number plus an even number is always even; an odd plus an even number is always odd. So Statement (2) implies that n is even. Sufficient.

The credited response is (B): The information provided in statement (2) leads to a definite answer (for the record here, an absolute "yes" in all possible circumstances), but statement (1) allows for both "yes" and "no" answers.

42. A

This question asks whether the information in one or both statements is sufficient to find a specific value.

Statement (1) provides enough info to calculate the triangle area using the formula: $\frac{1}{2} \times$ base $\times$ height. Though you needn't bother to calculate it, the area is $\frac{(8 \times 18)}{2}$, or 72. Sufficient.

Statement (2) lets us know that triangle BDC is a 30°-60°-90° triangle, and from that we can determine the ratios among the side lengths of that triangle. Without knowing any actual side lengths, however, we do not have the information necessary to calculate the area. Insufficient.

The credited response is (A): Statement (1), taken independently, is sufficient to find the value in question, but statement (2) is not.

43. D

This question asks whether the information in one or both statements is sufficient to find a specific value.

For many questions about averages, the best approach is the math-class approach; just plug the given values into the formula for the arithmetic mean, then solve for the unknown (or, for Data Sufficiency, determine whether you could solve for the unknown. The formula for the mean is $\text{average} = \frac{\text{sum of } n \text{ numbers}}{n}$.

Because the question tells us that $n = 2$ in this case, we can rewrite the question as "$a + b =$?"

Statement (1): Let's express the average mathematically: $\frac{(a+3)+(b+5)}{2} = 16$. Now let's simplify this to isolate a and b:

$$a + b + 8 = 32;\ a + b = 24$$

Stop here: Sufficient. Eliminate (B), (C), and (E).

Statement (2):

$$\frac{a + b + 21}{3} = 15$$

$a + b + 21 = 45$; $a + b = 24$. Stop here: Sufficient.

The credited response is (D): Each statement, taken independently, is sufficient to find the value in question.

44. D

This question asks whether the information in one or both statements is sufficient to answer a yes or no question.

Start with Statement 2, since it is obviously sufficient.

Statement (2): Gives you values for all of the variables. Once you replace those variables, you have an equation relating constants. Even without any arithmetic manipulation to determine whether the equation is true, you can see that it is either necessarily true or necessarily false. The answer cannot be "maybe." If you want to go ahead and do the arithmetic:

$(6)(1) = 5 + (1)(1)$; $6 = 5 + 1$; $6 = 6$. This answers the question with a "yes" and is sufficient. Eliminate (A), (C), and (E).

Statement (1): We can manipulate the equation to isolate jx, just as jx is isolated in the question:

$x(j - k) = 5$; $jx - kx = 5$; $jx = 5 + kx$. This also answers the question with a "yes" and is sufficient.

The credited response is (D): Each statement, when considered independently, leads to an absolute answer in all circumstances (for the record here, both "yes").

45. A

This question asks whether the information in one or both statements is sufficient to answer a yes or no question.

Since there are 26 letters in the alphabet, it is possible that 26 people could write down letters without anyone writing the same letter as someone else. Beyond 26 people, repeated letters are unavoidable. Since statement (1) says that more than 30 people wrote down letters, we know that 4 or more people (beyond 26) must have written the same letter as someone from the first 26. This is sufficient. Eliminate (B), (C), and (E).

Statement (2) is *not* sufficient because, if the number of people is less than 80, we can't be sure whether the number is less than or greater than 26, and even if we know it's less, we don't know that some of those people haven't picked the same letter selection as others.

The credited response is (A): The information provided in statement (1) leads to a definite answer (for the record here, an absolute "yes" in all possible circumstances), but statement (2) allows for both "yes" and "no" answers.

46. E

This question asks whether the information in one or both statements is sufficient to answer a yes or no question.

Although you could solve this question algebraically, the best approach here is to assign different lengths to *AB*, *BC*, and *CD*, consistent with the information in the statements, and check whether that information determines the relationship between *AB* and *CD*. You might wish to redraw the line *AD* as you consider different possibilities.

Statement (1): If *AD* is 30, *AB* might be greater than *CD*. If *AB* = 20, *BC* = *CD* = 5. But *AB* might be equal to CD, if *AB* = *BC* = *CD* = 10. If all values give you an answer of "yes," the statement is sufficient; if all possible values give you an answer of "no," the statement is sufficient. Here, different values give you different results, so statement (1) is insufficient. Eliminate (A) and (D).

Statement (2): If *BC* = *CD*, perhaps *AB* = 20 and *BC* = *CD* = 10, or perhaps *AB* = 10 and *BC* = *CD* = 20. Insufficient. Eliminate (B).

What if both statement (1) and statement (2) are true? Perhaps *AB* = *BC* = *CD* = 10 (which gives us an answer of "no"). Perhaps *AB* = 20 and *BC* = *CD* = 5 (which gives us an answer of "yes"). Insufficient.

The credited response is (E): The information provided in the statements, taken independently or together, is insufficient; both "yes" and "no" answers are still possible (in other words, the answer is always "maybe").

47. E

This question asks whether the information in one or both statements is sufficient to find a specific value.

To know how much Michael's legal fee was, we'll need two pieces of information: the pay rate for any services (or hours) provided and the number of services (or hours) provided at that (or those) rate(s).

Statement (1): Gives us information about numbers of hours billed, but no pay rate. Insufficient. Eliminate (A) and (D).

Statement (2): Gives us neither a formula nor the number of hours. Insufficient. Eliminate (B).

The two statements together provide important information, but no dollar amounts with which we could calculate actual costs. Insufficient.

The credited response is (E): The statements don't provide sufficient information to find the value in question, not even when considered together.

48. A

This question asks whether the information in one or both statements is sufficient to find a specific value.

This question rewards manipulating the information given in the question before turning to the statements. If 50% of the faculty is over 45, and 90% of that 50% have PhDs, then 45% of the faculty are over 45 *and* have PhDs. The question, though, asks about the actual number, not the percentage. You can rewrite this question as "What number is 45% of the number of faculty?" So any answer that gives you the number of faculty, however indirectly, will answer this.

Statement (1): Gives the total number of faculty, which is exactly what we want. We know this is sufficient. Even if you didn't manipulate the question as described above, you could test whether the information given was sufficient:

Start with 180 faculty members; 50% are over 45 = 90 members.

Then 90% have PhDs, so 81 members of the faculty over 45 years old have PhDs. Sufficient. Eliminate (B), (C), and (E).

Statement (2) just gives us another percentage, one that itself we could have derived from the given information, but we have no basis for converting this to an actual number of people. Insufficient.

The credited response is (A): Statement (1), taken independently, is sufficient to find the value in question, but statement (2) is not.

49. D

This question asks whether the information in one or both statements is sufficient to answer a yes or no question.

Statement (1): By definition, the sides of an equilateral triangle are equal. Thus, this statement is sufficient to show that *AB* and *AC* have the same lengths. Eliminate answers (B), (C), and (E).

In statement (2), each equation can be rewritten as follows:

$$AB - BC = 0;\ AB = BC$$

$$AC - BC = 0;\ AC = BC$$

Thus, $BC = AC = AB$, and this statement is sufficient.

The credited response is (D): Each statement, when considered independently, leads to an absolute answer in all circumstances (for the record here, both "yes").

50. C

This question asks whether the information in one or both statements is sufficient to answer a yes or no question.

An isosceles right triangle has one right angle and two angles of 45°. So the question asks whether or not we can determine the triangle is a 45°-45°-90° triangle.

Statement (1) offers that one of the angles is twice another. This is consistent with a 45°-45°-90° triangle, but it's also consistent with a 30°-60°-90° triangle—in fact with any number of triangles. Insufficient. Eliminate (A) and (D).

Statement (2) states that one of the angles is 45°. This is consistent with a 45°-45°-90° triangle, but it's also consistent with a 30°-45°-105° triangle—in fact with any number of triangles. Eliminate (B).

The two statements together are sufficient. Because the sum of the interior angles of a triangle is 180°, $a + b + c = 180$.

Statement (2) says that $a = 45$, so by substitution, $45 + b + c = 180$.

Transpose: $b + c = 135$.

Statement (1) says that $c = 2b$, so by substitution, $3b = 135$.

Divide: $b = \frac{135}{3} = 45$.

If *a* and *b* are each 45°, then *c* must be 90°. Sufficient.

The credited response is (C): When taken together, the information provided in the statements leads to a definite answer (for the record here, an absolute "yes" in all possible circumstances), but when considered independently, each statement still allows both "yes" and "no" answers.

51. A

This question asks whether the information in one or both statements is sufficient to find a specific value.

In the circle graph, department O's budget is equivalent to the value of $\frac{q}{360}$ multiplied by \$6,750,000, or \$18,750*q*. In order to determine the answer to this problem, the value of *q* must be known (or at least determinable).

Statement (1): It is given that $q = 92$, which means we can calculate the budget for O, so this is sufficient. Don't do the calculations! But for the record: The budget for department O is equal to $18,750(92) or $1,725,000—sufficient.

Statement (2): The relation given here allows for a comparison among some of the budgets; however, without providing any specific values for the given sections, it does not address the question of the value of q—insufficient.

The credited response is (A): Statement (1), taken independently, is sufficient to find the value in question, but statement (2) is not.

52. C

This question asks whether the information in one or both statements is sufficient to answer a yes or no question.

If you recognize this as a question about the slope of this line containing the segment *AB*, and you recall that you need two points on a line to determines its slope, you can see without any calculation that Statement (1) and Statement (2) are each not sufficient, but that they are sufficient together.

Since the slope of the line containing the segment *AB* is equal to the ratio of *AC* to *BC* (the slope is the ratio of change in the y-values to change in the x-values), the ratio of *AC* to *BC* can be found by determining the slope of the line containing *AB*. It is necessary to know the coordinate values of *two* points on a line in order to determine the slope of that line.

Statement (1): Only the coordinate values of one point (q, r) are given; insufficient. Eliminate (A) and (D).

Statement (2): Only the coordinate values of one point (l, m) are given; insufficient. Eliminate (B).

Statements (1) and (2) together provide the coordinate values of two points on the line, which is enough information to determine the slope of the line and thus the ratio of the length of *AC* to *BC*. Sufficient.

The credited response is (C): When taken together, the information provided in the statements leads to a definite answer (for the record here, an absolute "no" in all possible circumstances), but when considered independently, each statement still allows for both "yes" and "no" answers.

53. D

This question asks whether the information in one or both statements is sufficient to find a specific value.

The question being asked is actually, "How long will it take for train Q to be another 3 miles ahead of train P?" or, more simply, "How much faster is train Q than train P?" To answer this, we'll need to know the speed of each train, or we'll need information that would allow us to figure out their speeds (like distance from one another at a time in the past).

Statement (1): If we have the rates for each train, we can determine how long it takes Q to gain an additional three miles on P. You needn't—and shouldn't—actually perform these calculations, but . . .

Every hour, train Q will be 30 miles further ahead of train P, so train Q is increasing its distance from train P by 1 mile every 2 minutes. In 6 minutes, train Q will have gained three more miles on train P. Sufficient. Eliminate (B), (C), and (E).

Statement (2): Since train Q is now 3 miles ahead of train P, this states that train Q is increasing its distance from train P by 2 miles every 4 minutes, or 1 mile every 2 minutes. In 6 minutes, train Q will have gained 3 more miles on train P. Sufficient.

The credited response is (D): Each statement, taken independently, is sufficient to find the value in question.

54. C

This question asks whether the information in one or both statements is sufficient to answer a yes or no question.

A solution can be found by first simplifying the inequality $x + y - z < x - y + z$.

Reduce the unnecessary x on each side: $y - z < z - y$. Then simplify: $2y < 2z$; $y < z$.

If $y < z$ is true, then logically the original inequality $x + y - z < x - y + z$ is also true. Therefore, it is only necessary to determine whether $y < z$ is true.

Statement (1): This states that $y < 0$. However, since z is unknown, it cannot be determined whether $y < z$. Insufficient. Eliminate (A) and (D).

Statement (2): This states that $0 < z$. However, since z is unknown, it cannot be determined whether $y < z$. Insufficient. Eliminate (B).

Statements (1) and (2) together imply that $y < 0 < z$ and so that $y < z$. Sufficient.

The credited response is (C): When taken together, the information provided in the statements leads to a definite answer (for the record here, an absolute "yes" in all circumstances), but when considered independently, each statement still allows for both "yes" and "no" answers.

55. D

This question asks whether the information in one or both statements is sufficient to find a specific value.

Here, you could convert 960 kilobytes to kilobits, but strictly speaking, it is enough to merely recognize that you could do so and so to recognize that a statement or combination of statements is sufficient if and only if it gives the download speed in terms of either unit.

Statement (1): This gives the download speed. Don't ever do the math unless you're concerned that the value might be ambiguous (such as a range of values—not the case here). It's sufficient, but for the record, the kilobits-per-second speed is given at 512, so a file of size 7,680 kilobits would download in $\frac{7,680}{512}$, or 15, seconds. Sufficient. Eliminate (B), (C), and (E).

Statement (2): The ratio of the time to upload to the time to download = 4:1, or $\frac{4}{1}$. The ratio of upload time to download time to total time is 4:1:5. The ratio of download time to total time is 1:5. Once you have determined that you can convert the given ratio (upload time to download time) to the desired ratio (download time to total time), and that you can represent one of the terms in the desired ratio as a constant (total time = 75 seconds), you don't actually have to do the computation. Still, the file is downloading $\frac{1}{5}$ of that 75 seconds. The time it takes to download the file is $\frac{1}{5}$(75 seconds) = 15 seconds.

This statement is sufficient.

The credited response is (D): Each statement, taken independently, is sufficient to find the value in question.

56. B

This question asks whether the information in one or both statements is sufficient to find a specific value.

The three probabilities—that a child will receive chocolate ice cream, that she will receive vanilla ice cream, and that she will receive strawberry ice cream—must all add up to 1, the probability that she will receive one of these flavors.

Statement (1): This gives the probability of receiving chocolate ice cream. But we still know nothing about strawberry's chances. Insufficient. Eliminate (A) and (D).

Statement (2): The probability that a certain child will receive either chocolate or strawberry ice cream is equivalent to the probability that a child will *not* receive vanilla ice cream. Since it is given that the probability of receiving vanilla is $\frac{1}{4}$, it can be determined that the probability of receiving chocolate or strawberry ice cream is $1 - \frac{1}{4} = \frac{3}{4}$. Sufficient.

The credited response is (B): Statement (2), taken independently, is sufficient to find the value in question, but statement (1) is not.

57. D

This question asks whether the information in one or both statements is sufficient to find a specific value.

Since we can see that B is the 11th rung, and the question stipulates that all the rungs are evenly spaced, any information that tells us how far apart the rungs are spaced from one another or from the ground will allow us to calculate B's distance from the ground. So we can rephrase the question: "How far apart are the rungs?"

Statement (1): Since A—the 5th rung—is $\frac{1}{2}$ foot above the ground, each rung is $\frac{1}{10}$ of a foot above the rung immediately below (because $\frac{1}{2}$ divided by 5 is $\frac{1}{10}$). This means that the tenth rung is 1 foot above the ground. B is the 11th rung; therefore, it is $\frac{11}{10}$ feet above the ground. This statement is sufficient.

Statement (2): This states that the total distance between A and B is $\frac{3}{5}$ foot. Since B is 6 rungs above A, the distance of each rung from the rung below is $\frac{1}{6}\left(\frac{3}{5}\right) = \frac{3}{30} = \frac{1}{10}$. Sufficient.

The credited response is (D): Each statement, taken independently, is sufficient to find the value in question.

58. D

This question asks whether the information in one or both statements is sufficient to find a specific value.

If $\frac{2}{3}$ of the students are seniors, then $\frac{1}{3}$ of the students are juniors. Since $\frac{9}{10}$ of those attending are students, $\frac{3}{10}$ of those attending are juniors (since $\frac{1}{3}$ of $\frac{9}{10}$ is $\frac{9}{30}$ or $\frac{3}{10}$). Any statement or combination of statements that determines the total number of those attending or the number in any group will allow us to determine the number of juniors attending.

Statement (1): Since this gives the total number attending, we can see that this is sufficient. For the record: Since it is given that $\frac{9}{10}$ of the attendees were students, $\frac{9}{10} \times 270 = 243$ student attendees. If $\frac{2}{3}$ of the students were seniors, then $\frac{1}{3}$ of the students were juniors: $\frac{1}{3} \times 243 = 81$ juniors attending the prom. Sufficient. Eliminate (B), (C), and (E).

Statement (2): If 27 represents $\frac{1}{10}$ of the total number attending, there were 270 attending. You could calculate just as above, but why? We know this statement is sufficient.

The credited response is (D): Each statement, taken independently, is sufficient to find the value in question.

59. D

This question asks whether the information in one or both statements is sufficient to find a specific value.

You'll need a couple of formulas relating to circles here. The relevant formulas are these:

$A = \pi r^2$, where A is the area and r is the length of the radius.

$C = 2\pi r$, where C is the circumference and r is the length of the radius.

Together these formulas allow you to determine any one of A, C, and r from any other. Further, since the question itself gives the circumference of X in terms of the circumference of Y, any information about the size of Y will be as useful as information about the size of X. So there are several ways we can get sufficiency here.

Statement (1): Since we're given the surface area of the pool, we know we could calculate the radius or the circumference of Y using the formulas provided above, then find X's circumference. We can see that this sufficient. Eliminate (B), (C), and (E).

By the way, a neater way to see that Statement (1) is sufficient is to note that all circles are similar (that is, they are exactly the same shape, although perhaps different sizes). For similar figures, the $area_1:area_2$ ratio is always the square of the $line_1:line_2$ ratio. In this case, the $line_1:line_2$ ratio is 1:4, so the $area_1:area_2$ ratio must be 1:16. It is not important that $\frac{1}{16}$ of 900π is 56.25π; it is only important that it is some definite value.

If you need to see the numbers: Let A_Y mean the area of Y. Then statement (1) states that $A_Y = 900\pi$. Since $A = \pi r^2$, $r^2 = 900$. The positive square root of 900 is 30, so radius = 30. Since $2r = 60$, and $C = 2\pi r$, $C = 60\pi$. The circumference of X is $\frac{1}{4}$ the circumference of Y. The circumference of X is, therefore, 15π, which means that the radius of X is 7.5. The area of X is therefore 56.25π ft^2, since $A = \pi r^2$, or $A = \pi(7.5)^2 = 56.25\pi$ ft^2.

Statement (2): Since the length of the border around Y is equal to its circumference, and it is given that the length of the border is 60π feet, then the circumference of $Y = 60\pi$. Once the circumference is known, the area can be found following the same reasoning as we used with Statement (1). Sufficient.

The credited response is (D): Each statement, taken independently, is sufficient to find the value in question.

60. E

This question asks whether the information in one or both statements is sufficient to find a specific value.

The total amount of tuition fees charged by the daycare last week is equal to the number of children 5 years or older times the regular daily fee F, plus the number of children from ages 2 to 4 times $1.25F$, plus the number of children under 2 years times $2F$ (daily fee).

Statement (1): From this, it would be possible to calculate the amount of charges if there were information given about number of children attending each day and their respective ages. Since none is given, however, the amount of tuition fees cannot be calculated. Insufficient.

Statement (2): The number of children under 2 is given as 0, but it is still unknown how many of the attendees, if any, were 2–4 years old. Therefore, the total amount of tuition fees cannot be calculated. Insufficient.

Using the information in Statements (1) and (2) together still does not provide enough information to determine the amount of tuition fees charged last week.

The credited response is (E): The statements don't provide sufficient information to find the value in question, not even when considered together.

61. E

This question asks whether the information in one or both statements is sufficient to find a specific value.

To work this one out, we'll need three pieces of information (or ways to get them all): (1) the sale price, (2) the employee price, and (3) either the number sold at the employee price *or* the number sold at the sale price (since we know 56 jackets were sold, either number would allow us to figure the other one out).

Statement (1): Using the information given, the number of jackets sold at the sale price is $\frac{3}{4} \times 56 = 42$. The number of jackets sold at the employee price, then, is $56 - 42 = 14$. Nothing is said, however, about the actual dollar amount of the sale or employee prices, so the total revenue cannot be calculated. Insufficient. Eliminate (A) and (D).

Statement (2): There is no information given about the employee price or the number of jackets sold at each price; therefore, the total revenue cannot be calculated. Insufficient. Eliminate (B).

Using both Statements (1) and (2), it is possible to calculate the revenue generated by the jackets sold at the sale price: 42 × \$120 = \$5,040. However, in order to calculate the revenue brought in by the jackets sold at the employee price, it is necessary to know what the employee price was. Since this is still unknown, the total revenue that the sale of all the jackets generated cannot be determined. Insufficient.

The credited response is (E): The statements don't provide sufficient information to find the value in question, not even when considered together.

62. D

This question asks whether the information in one or both statements is sufficient to answer a yes or no question.

To make the given expression true, the diamond symbol would have to represent multiplication. You can prove this by trying the operations with all three options (addition, subtraction, and multiplication); multiplication is the only way to make the statements equivalent for all values.

Statement (1): If ◇ represents either operation × or +, then $a \diamond 1 = 1 \diamond a$ is always true for any value of *a*. This is because $a \times 1 = 1 \times a$, and $a + 1 = 1 + a$. It follows that ◇ must represent subtraction, which is not the operation we wanted, but it *does* give us an answer, so it's sufficient. Eliminate (B), (C), and (E).

Statement (2): This states directly that the ◇ represents subtraction. Just as in (1), it can be determined whether $a - (b + c) = (a - b) + (a - c)$. Sufficient.

The credited response is (D): Each statement, when considered independently, leads to an absolute answer in all circumstances (for the record here, both "no").

63. E

This question asks whether the information in one or both statements is sufficient to find a specific value.

In order to be sufficient, a statement or set of statements must determine the volume of sales in 2005 and in 2006.

(If you're very mathematically sophisticated, you might recognize that this is a bit of an oversimplification, but it will do for our purposes here. See the last paragraph below for a discussion.)

Statement (1): Because statement (1) gives you information about only 2005, there is no way to calculate the change in sales volume. Insufficient. Eliminate (A) and (D).

Statement (2): Because this statement gives you information about only 2006, there is no way to calculate the change in sales volume. Insufficient. Eliminate (B).

Statements (1) and (2) together provide a comparison of the sales of the two companies from 2005 to 2006; however, there are no actual sales amounts given, and Company B's sales are never provided (you can't assume they remain constant from 2005 to 2006). Therefore, it is impossible to calculate the increase in sales for Company *A* from 2005 to 2006. Insufficient, and the correct answer is (E).

By the way, to address the oversimplification mentioned in parentheses above: If we had all the information from statements (1) and (2), and we also had a comparison of the sales of Company B in 2005 to the sales of Company B in 2006, even without any constants, we could calculate the change in the sales for Company A. So strictly speaking, we don't need to determine the volume of sales for Company A in 2005 and in 2006 in order to calculate the percentage change, as long as we have information about the percentage change in sales of Company B.

The credited response is (E): The statements don't provide sufficient information to find the value in question, not even when considered together.

64. C

This question asks whether the information in one or both statements is sufficient to find a specific value.

Statement (1): Because the runner was expected to run 21 miles, the expected total amount of donations is $21x$. Without the value of x, however, $21x$ remains unknown. Insufficient. Eliminate (A) and (D).

Statement (2): Using this information, the total amount of expected donations equals the actual donations ($3,900) less the donations given on the extra miles run ($5x$). Again, without the value of x, $5x$ remains unknown and, therefore, so does the amount of expected donations. Insufficient. Eliminate (B).

Using statements (1) and (2) together, $21x + 5x = \$3{,}900$. The value of x can be calculated from this and so can $21x$, the amount of total expected donations.

The credited response is (C): Taken together, statements (1) and (2) are sufficient to find the value in question, but neither statement is sufficient when considered independently.

65. E

This question asks whether the information in one or both statements is sufficient to answer a yes or no question.

The formula for calculating distance is distance = rate × time. The question asked concerns the rate, so the rate needs to be calculated. Since rate = $\frac{\text{distance}}{\text{time}}$, it is necessary to know the distance traveled by the aircraft and the time duration of the flight. Since speed is likely to vary while in flight, it'll be next to impossible to prove a "no" on this one, even if the average speed is less than 850 km per hour. Instead, let's see if we can prove a "yes."

Statement (1): Here, the time duration of the flight is given, but no information about the distance traveled is provided. Insufficient.

Statement (2): Here, the distance traveled is given, but no information about the time duration of the flight is provided. Insufficient.

Using statements (1) and (2) together, the average rate of speed can be calculated. Since rate = $\frac{\text{distance}}{\text{time}}$, the average rate = $\frac{2{,}463}{3}$ = 821 km per hour. However, this calculates the *average* rate only. It is impossible, with the information given, to conclude whether the aircraft reached a speed that exceeded the economical cruising speed of 850 km per hour at some point during the flight and then lowered its speed to under its average speed of 821 km per hour.

The credited response is (E): The information provided in the statements, taken independently or together, is insufficient; both "yes" and "no" answers are still possible (in other words, the answer is always "maybe").

66. D

This question asks whether the information in one or both statements is sufficient to find a specific value.

This question asks you to divide a single large group, households with cats or dogs in this rural town, into a few smaller groups. You could use a Venn diagram or a tool called a double-set matrix for such a division into overlapping sets, but you can also just handle the sets more simplistically, with addition:

$D + C + CD = 250$, where D = dog only, C = cat only, and CD = cat and dog households.

From the given information, we can determine that the 75 households without a dog must be the C households, so $D + 75 + CD = 250$; $D + CD = 175$.

And since we're asked to solve for CD, perhaps it's best to rearrange: $CD = 175 - D$. So all we need for sufficiency is the number of dog-only households (or any other value that would allow us to figure that out).

Statement (1): The value of D, dog-only households, is given here; therefore, the answer can be found by substitution: $CD = 175 - D$, and $D = 150$, so $CD = 25$. Sufficient.

Statement (2): If 100 is the number of households that contain a cat, then $C + CD = 100$, and since we already know that $C = 75$, we can determine that $CD = 25$. Sufficient.

The credited response is (D): Each statement, taken independently, is sufficient to find the value in question.

67. E

This question asks whether the information in one or both statements is sufficient to find a specific value.

Mary's reimbursement (r) is equal to the fixed driving base (b) plus some number of dollars d for each client she visits, where c is the number of clients. So $r = b + dc$. The question asks for the value of r when $c = 16$. In order to calculate Mary's reimbursement, then, it is necessary to know the fixed base reimbursement, b, and the number of dollars reimbursed per client visited, d.

Statement (1): This tells us that for some value of r, $r = b + 12d$. You can't determine either b or d from this. This provides no information about the fixed base reimbursement or the number of dollars reimbursed per client visited. Insufficient.

Statement (2): This tells us that for for some value of c, $b + dc = 76$. You can't determine either b or d from this. On its own, this is totally useless.

Even together, we're not terribly far along. Last Monday, r was equal to 76. However, because there is no information given about b or d, it is impossible to determine the relationship between them and, therefore, it is impossible to calculate the rate for each element (driving and each client) to determine her pay for the 16-client day in question. Even if you pick out a couple multiples of 12 not too far beneath 76, you'll find there are still many options: If she gets paid $6/client, then she made $72 on client visits and $4 for driving, but if she gets paid $5/client, then she made $60 on client visits and $16 on driving . . . and there's no way to tell the difference. Insufficient, even when considered together.

The credited response is (E): The statements don't provide sufficient information to find the value in question, not even when considered together.

68. C

This question asks whether the information in one or both statements is sufficient to answer a yes or no question.

Considering the dearth of information provided, we'll basically need to be told whether or not the meeting is on Friday to get sufficiency here.

Statement (1): This provides information about the time of the meeting, but not about the day it took place. Insufficient.

Statement (2): To test whether this is sufficient, add 66 hours to the very beginning of Tuesday and to the very end. 66 hours is 6 less than 72 hours, or 6 less than three full days, so you could literally just pick a time early on Tuesday, then calculate the actual meeting time 3 days minus 6 hours later: If the early start hour was at 12:00 a.m. on Tuesday, then the actual meeting would be at 6:00 p.m. on Thursday—no dice. Now repeat that step again, this time choosing a much later time on Tuesday: With a start hour of Tuesday at 6:00 p.m., the actual meeting would be at noon on Friday—an affirmative. Since we have both a "no" and a "yes," this statement is insufficient.

Using the information provided in both (1) and (2) together is just a little trickier than using (2) alone; it's easier to subtract rather than to add. Subtract 66 hours (or subtract 3 days and add 6 hours) from the beginning and the end of the interval:

66 hours before any time within the interval 9:00 a.m. and 5:00 p.m. on Friday would fall between 3:00 p.m. and 11:00 p.m. on Tuesday. Sufficient.

The credited response is (C): When taken together, the information provided in the statements leads to a definite answer (for the record here, an absolute "yes" in all possible circumstances), but when considered independently, each statement still allows both "yes" and "no" answers.

69. B

This question asks whether the information in one or both statements is sufficient to answer a yes or no question.

Statement (1): In this equation, x could be equal to y, as in the example $x = 5 = y$. However, it is also possible that x is not equal to y, as in the example $x = -3$ and $y = 5$. Insufficient.

Statement (2): This states that the product of x and y is less than 0. For a product of two numbers to be negative, one and only one of the numbers must be negative, since the product of two negative values is positive. Therefore, x cannot be equal to y. Sufficient.

The credited response is (B): The information provided in statement (2) leads to a definite answer (for the record here, an absolute "yes" in all possible circumstances), but statement (1) allows for both "yes" and "no" answers.

70. E

This question asks whether the information in one or both statements is sufficient to answer a yes or no question.

If you could determine the value of q, you could say whether every term in the sequence M is divisible by q (though you might be able to say so even without determining the value of q; see below). So, when you consider the statements, try to understand what specific values of q they allow.

Statement (1): If q is less than 45, then q could be 2, 4, 6, 8, 10, and so on, through 44. While all the terms in the sequence M are divisible by 2 and by 6, the very first term, 6, is not divisible by 4, or 8, or any of the other possible values of q. Since some of the values (2 and 6) give the answer "yes" and others (4, 8, 10, etc.) give the answer "no," this statement is not sufficient.

Statement (2): This is much trickier. Clearly, at least one value of q—2—is a factor of every member of M. Is this true of every number that is a factor of at least two members? If every number that is a factor of at least two members of M is a factor of all members of M, then this is sufficient; otherwise not. Take the three smallest members of M and list some factors. If you can find some factor that two of those members share, but that the third does not, then you see that statement (2) is not sufficient, and you can eliminate (B). Testing that out, we see that 6 has the even factors 2 and 6; 96 has the even factors 2, 4, 6, 8, 12, 16, 24, 32, and 48 (you could list just the first few); 996 has the even factors 2, 4, . . . stop right there: 4 is a factor of at least two members of M, but not of all the members (not of 2, in particular). Insufficient.

Having done the hard work of sorting out statement (2), we find that we can eliminate (C) as well as (B). Why? Because the numbers we used to test statement (2)—2 and 4—are less than 45 and so satisfy statement (1) as well. We have already shown that statements (1) and (2) together describe one number that yields an answer of "yes" and another that yields an answer of "no."

The credited response is (E): The information provided in the statements, taken independently or together, is insufficient; both "yes" and "no" answers are still possible (in other words, the answer is always "maybe").

71. E

This question asks whether the information in one or both statements is sufficient to answer a yes or no question.

Although a little number properties knowledge can be helpful here, we don't have to make this too theoretical; just try out values.

Statement (1): Given that l and m are both integers, if $l = 6$ and $m = 2$, then $\frac{l}{m} = 3$, which is an integer. However, if $l = 2$ and $m = 6$, then $\frac{l}{m} = \frac{2}{6} = \frac{1}{3}$, which is not an integer. Therefore, $\frac{l}{m}$ is not an integer if m is not a factor of l. More information about l and m must be known. Insufficient.

Statement (2): Try values for l^2 and m^2 based on the values for l and m above. If $l^2 = 36$ and $m^2 = 4$, then $\frac{l}{m} = 3$, which is an integer. However, if $l^2 = 4$ and $m^2 = 36$, then $\frac{l}{m} = \frac{2}{6}$, which is not an integer. More information about l and m must be known. Insufficient.

We don't have to consider the two statements together for very long. We used the same values to test both already.

The credited response is (E): The information provided in the statements, taken independently or together, is insufficient; both "yes" and "no" answers are still possible (in other words, the answer is always "maybe").

72. D

This question asks whether the information in one or both statements is sufficient to find a specific value.

The arithmetic mean, or average, of a set of numbers can be found by taking the sum of those numbers and dividing by the total number of numbers in the set. If s represents the sum of the students' ages, then $\frac{s}{10} = 12$. Therefore, $s = 120$.

Statement (1): If none of the students are younger than 12, then each student is 12 or older. However, if the sum of the students' ages is 120 and there are 10 students, if even one student was one year older, then the sum would be 121. Therefore, every student must be 12 years of age. Sufficient. Eliminate (B), (C), and (E).

Statement (2): If none of the students are older than 12, then each student is 12 or younger. However, if the sum of the students' ages is 120 and there are 10 students, if even one student was one year younger, then the sum would be 119. Therefore, every student must be 12 years of age. Sufficient.

The credited response is (D): Each statement, taken independently, is sufficient to find the value in question.

73. C

This question asks whether the information in one or both statements is sufficient to answer a yes or no question.

Statement (1): Take this equation and put it in terms of a: $a = c - b$. In order to determine the absolute value of a, it is necessary to look at the two possible cases: a is positive or a is negative. If a is positive, then $|a| = a$. Therefore, $|a| = c - b$. If a is negative, then $|a| = -(c - b)$, which is equivalent to $|a| = b - c$.

However, it is impossible with this information to know whether a is positive or negative, so the answer cannot be reached. Insufficient.

Statement (2): While this statement provides the information that a is negative, it does not say anything about b or c, so the question of whether $|a| = b - c$ cannot possibly be answered. Insufficient.

Considered together: Since the information in statement (1) was lacking only the information about whether a was positive or negative in order to be sufficient to answer the question, it can now be solved. Statement (2) states that a is negative; therefore, the answer is yes, $|a| = b - c$. The statements together are sufficient.

The credited response is (C): When taken together, the information provided in the statements leads to a definite answer (for the record here, an absolute "yes" in all possible circumstances), but when considered independently, each statement still allows both "yes" and "no" answers.

74. E

This question asks whether the information in one or both statements is sufficient to find a specific value.

In order to determine the total revenue in the simplest, most direct way, you need to know the number of pies sold at each price, and you need to know what the prices are. Unless this question is extraordinarily tricky or subtle—and it's not—a statement or set of statements will be sufficient if and only if it gives you those values.

You could think of this in algebraic terms, but it might not be especially helpful:

Let p = the number of pies sold at full price.

Let $(75 - p)$ = the number of pies sold at discount.

Let f = price per pie without discount.

Let $x\% f\left[\text{or} \left(\frac{x}{100}\right)\times f\right]$ = price per pie without discount.

The total revenue is $pf + (75 - p)\left[\left(\frac{x}{100}\right) \times f\right]$.

If you can get that rid of those variables, you can evaluate the expression.

Statement (1): Although this gives a relationship between the discounted pies and the full-price pies (the discounted pies sold at 80% of the full price), no information is given regarding the actual price of either or the number of pies sold at each price. Insufficient. In algebraic terms, it gives you the value of only one of the three variables. Eliminate (A) and (D).

Statement (2): Although this gives the price of the pies at full price, no information is given regarding the value of x or the number of pies sold at each price. Insufficient. In algebraic terms, it gives you the value of only one of the three variables. Eliminate (B).

Using statements (1) and (2) together allows for the price of the discounted pies to be found: 25% of $30, so $22.50. However, no information is given regarding the number of pies sold at each price, so the answer cannot be determined. In algebraic terms, these statements give you the value of only two of the three variables.

The credited response is (E): The statements don't provide sufficient information to find the value in question, not even when considered together.

75. B

This question asks whether the information in one or both statements is sufficient to answer a yes or no question.

To get a yes or no answer, we'll need a value for x and a value for y.

Statement (1): The value of y is not given and cannot be determined with this information. If $x = 44$, then some values for y result in a terminating decimal while some do not. For example, $\frac{44}{4} = 11$, which is a terminating decimal, but $\frac{44}{3} = 14.666\ldots$, which is not a terminating decimal. Insufficient. Eliminate (A) and (D).

Statement (2): Any number divided by 8 results in a terminating decimal. This is because when an integer is divided by 8, the only possible remainders are 0 or 1, 2, 3, 4, 5, 6, and 7 (actually $\frac{1}{8}$, $\frac{2}{8}$, etc.). These remainders are expressed as 0.125, 0.25, 0.375, 0.5, 0.625, 0.75, and 0.875, respectively. Therefore $\frac{x}{y}$ is a terminating decimal. Sufficient.

The credited response is (B): The information provided in statement (2) leads to a definite answer (for the record here, an absolute "yes" in all possible circumstances), but statement (1) allows for both "yes" and "no" answers.

76. E

This question asks whether the information in one or both statements is sufficient to find a specific value.

Statement (1): This means that triangle XYZ and triangle XRZ each contain two congruent angles. And although we know that $b > a$, no information is given as to the measures of a and b. Therefore the value of $b - a$ cannot be found. Insufficient.

Statement (2): The value of a is given, but no information is provided as to the value of b, so the value of $b - a$ cannot be determined. Insufficient.

Taking the information in statements (1) and (2) together, the measures of angle *YXZ* and angle *YZX* each appear to equal 65, since the sum of the angles in a triangle is always 180 and the measure of *a* is given as 50. In fact, though, any two angles in this triangle might be the congruent angles; the angles might be 50 , 50, and 80 rather than 50, 65, and 65. In either event, no information is given for any of the angles in triangle *XRZ*, so the value of *b* - *a* cannot be determined.

The credited response is (E): The statements don't provide sufficient information to find the value in question, not even when considered together.

77. C

This question asks whether the information in one or both statements is sufficient to answer a yes or no question.

Statement (1): This states that $m > l$, but it does not give any information about *r*; therefore, it cannot be determined whether *l* and *m* are greater than *r*. Insufficient.

Statement (2): From this, if *m* is added to both sides of the inequality, the result is $l > m + r$. Since it is given that *m* is positive, *l* must be greater than *r*. However, whether *m* is greater than *r* cannot be determined. Insufficient.

Using the conclusions from (1) and (2) together, it is possible to determine the answer. (1) states directly that $m > l$, and (2) implies that $l > r$. Combining the two inequalities results in $m > l > r$, so both *l* and *m* are greater than *r*. Sufficient.

The credited response is (C): When taken together, the information provided in the statements leads to a definite answer (for the record here, an absolute "yes" in all possible circumstances), but when considered independently, each statement still allows for both "yes" and "no" answers.

78. B

This question asks whether the information in one or both statements is sufficient to answer a yes or no question.

For a given tens digit, the greater the units digit, the smaller a percentage the bonus will represent. For instance, if the student scored 10 points, his 2-point bonus would be 20% of his base score. On the other hand, if the student scored 19 points, his 2-point bonus would be about 11% of his base score.

Statement (1): The smallest percentage increases will come from the least tens digit with the greatest units digit; the greatest percentage increase will come from a units digit of zero. Just check 59 for the least, and any multiple of 10 for the greatest. Or, if some of this didn't occur to you, just check the extreme tens (5 and 9) with the extreme units (0 and 9)

If the base score was 90, then the bonus would have been 18 points. Since $\frac{18}{90} = 0.2$, the bonus was 20% of the base score. If the base score was 59, however, the bonus would have been 10 points. Since $\frac{10}{59}$ equals approximately 16.9%, the bonus would not have been higher than 17%. Insufficient.

Statement (2): Since the bonus was 16 points, the base score must have been between 80 and 89. Then, the base score was at most 89, which means that the bonus must have been at least $\frac{16}{89}$, which is approximately 17.97%. Sufficient.

The credited response is (B): The information provided in statement (2) leads to a definite answer (for the record here, an absolute "yes" in all possible circumstances), but statement (1) allows for both "yes" and "no" answers.

79. D

This question asks whether the information in one or both statements is sufficient to find a specific value.

First, let 0.05*a* represent the amount of decrease in revenue for Brand A, and let 0.05*b* represent the amount of increase in revenue for Brand B, where *a* and *b* represent the revenue in April for Brands A and B, respectively. It is then necessary to determine the relationship between *a* and *b* in order to solve the problem.

Statement (1): From this, we know that$0.05b = \frac{19}{20} \times 0.05a$. Since this establishes a relationship between *a* and *b*, the problem can be solved. (In fact, though you certainly should avoid the computation, since the May revenue from Brand A is $\frac{19}{20} \times a$, you need only divide each side by 0.05 to see that revenue from Brand A in May was exactly equal to the revenue from Brand B in April.) An important point here is that you can *always* express *x* as a percentage of *y*, or the ratio $\frac{x}{y}$, when given an equation of the form $cx = dx$, where *c* and *d* are constants. Sufficient.

Statement (2): This tells us that $a = 1.05b$. A relationship between *a* and *b* is again established, and the problem can be solved. Sufficient.

The credited response is (D): Each statement, taken independently, is sufficient to find the value in question.

80. E

This question asks whether the information in one or both statements is sufficient to answer a yes or no question.

Statement (1): From this information, *q* and *r* can have many values. If $q = 16$ and $r = 2$, $q > r$. However, if $q = 2$ and $r = 16$. then $q < r$. Insufficient.

Statement (2): The inequality given would provide enough information to solve the problem only if it were also given that *q* and *r* were both positive numbers. For example, if $q = -8$ and $r = -4$, $64 > 16$, but $r > q$. Insufficient.

The information provided in statements (1) and (2) together is still not sufficient to solve the problem. For example, if $q = 16$ and $r = 2$, $qr = 32$ and $q^2 > r^2$, and $q > r$; but if $q = -16$ and $r = -2$, $qr = 32$ and $q^2 > r^2$, and $q < r$.

The credited response is (E): The information provided in the statements, taken independently or together, is insufficient; both "yes" and "no" answers are still possible (in other words, the answer is always "maybe").

81. E

This question asks whether the information in one or both statements is sufficient to find a specific value.

First, the inequality $\frac{1}{2n} - 2 \geq 0 - 2 \geq 0$ is simplified to $n \geq 4$. So the problem asks us to find the probability that *n* is greater than or equal to 4. In order to evaluate this probability, you would need to know how many numbers are in the hat and how many of those are at least 4.

Statement (1): This gives the quantity of numbers in the hat (and tells us that they're integers) but does not provide any way to determine how many are at least 4. Therefore, it is not possible to determine the probability that one picked at random will be greater than or equal to 4. Insufficient.

Statement (2): Be careful here. This does not mean that all the values 1–30 are equally likely to be in the hat, just that all the values in the hat are within that range. This tells us neither the quantity of numbers in the hat nor how many are at least 4. Insufficient.

Using the information in Statements (1) and (2) together, the quantity of integers in the hat that are greater than or equal to 4 is still unknown, so the problem cannot be solved.

The credited response is (E): The statements don't provide sufficient information to find the value in question, not even when considered together.

82. B

This question asks whether the information in one or both statements is sufficient to find a specific value.

Statement (1): Since *ABCD* is a rectangle, the area is equal to the length of *AB* times the length of *AD*. So, $CD \times AD = 36$. However, no information is given about the specific lengths of any of the sides, so the length of *CD* relative to *AD* cannot be determined. Insufficient.

Statement (2): Since each rectangle has the same dimensions, and we know that $AB = CD$, then *CD* is equal to 2 times the shorter side of each rectangle. So, the shorter side of each rectangle is equal to $\frac{1}{2}CD$, and the longer dimensions are equal to *CD*. Therefore, $AD = CD + \frac{1}{2}CD$, or $AD = \frac{3}{2}CD$. Then $\frac{AD}{CD} = \frac{3}{2}$ and $\frac{CD}{AD} = \frac{2}{3}$. You could also try various values that satisfy statement 2 and see whether they all result in the same ratio. If they do, then the answer is almost certainly (B). Sufficient.

The credited response is (B): Statement (2), taken independently, is sufficient to find the value in question, but statement (1) is not.

83. C

This question asks whether the information in one or both statements is sufficient to answer a yes or no question.

Before we hit the statements, take a moment to simplify the given information and/or rephrase the question at hand. Here, we know *x* is a positive integer. We're asked, essentially, "Is *x* a factor of 210?"

Statement (1): There are some prime numbers that will divide into 210 and yield an integer. For example, if $x = 5$ or 7, $\frac{210}{x} = 42$ or 30, respectively. However, if $x = 13$ or 17, $\frac{210}{x}$ is not an integer. Insufficient.

Statement (2): From this, the only possible values for *x* are 1, 2, 3, 4, 5, 6, and 7. With the exception of 4, for each of these possible values, $\frac{210}{x}$ is an integer. Since $\frac{210}{x}$ is not an integer when $x = 4$ and no further information is given about *x*, the problem cannot be solved. Insufficient.

From statements (1) and (2) together, it is known that the only possible values for *x* are 2, 3, 5, and 7 (since 1, 4, and 6 are not prime numbers). For each of these prime number values for *x*, $\frac{210}{x}$ is, indeed, an integer.

The credited response is (C): When taken together, the information provided in the statements leads to a definite answer (for the record here, an absolute "yes" in all possible circumstances), but when considered independently, each statement still allows both "yes" and "no" answers.

84. B

This question asks whether the information in one or both statements is sufficient to answer a yes or no question.

Average = sum of values/number of values. Anita bought a total of 60 bottles. If the total price was less than $1,200, then the average price was less than $20. So, if the 8 bottles of sparkling wine cost less than $420 in total (i.e., $1,200 - $780), then the average price per bottle for all the wine was less than $20.

Statement (1): You could see in a couple of different ways that this is not sufficient. First, you might restate this as "The total cost for the sparkling wine was greater than $120." That clearly doesn't determine whether the cost was greater than $420. Greater than $15 per bottle could be $16 per bottle or $1,000 per bottle—or more for all we know. Insufficient.

Statement (2): Even if the sparkling wine was $40/bottle, rather than "less than $40," the average price per bottle would be less than $20, because the total cost for the wine would be $1,100, less than $1,200. Sufficient.

The credited response is (B): The information provided in statement (2) leads to a definite answer (for the record here, an absolute "yes" in all possible circumstances), but statement (1) allows for both "yes" and "no" answers.

85. A

This question asks whether the information in one or both statements is sufficient to answer a yes or no question.

Cross multiply to simplify: $\frac{5}{b} = \frac{a}{4}$ is equivalent to $ab = 20$. You might further note that $a = \frac{20}{b}$, though this is not necessary.

Statement (1): Since $b \geq 5$, then $a \leq 4$, because $ab = 20$. Therefore $b > a$. Also, if you had first solved for a in terms of b, you might notice here that if $b = 5$, then $a = 4$, and as b increases, a decreases. Sufficient.

Statement (2): The variables might represent fractions or negative numbers, but let's check the positive integers first. Suppose that b is 2, then a is 10, and $b < a$. But suppose that b is 5, then a is 4, and $b > a$. Insufficient.

The credited response is (A): The information provided in statement (1) leads to a definite answer (for the record here, an absolute "yes" in all possible circumstances), but statement (2) allows for both "yes" and "no" answers.

86. A

This question asks whether the information in one or both statements is sufficient to answer a yes or no question.

Statement (1): First, we should simplify this statement:

Since $q^2 = qr$, we can say that $q^2 - qr = 0$, which factors to $q \times (q - r) = 0$. Either $q = 0$, or else $q - r = 0$. So the only two cases for which this statement would be true are $q = 0$ or $q = r$. Since it is given that $q \neq r$, then q must equal 0. Sufficient.

Statement (2): This does not give us any information about q except that q does not equal 5 (since $r = 5$ and $q \neq r$). Insufficient.

The credited response is (A): The information provided in statement (1) leads to a definite answer (for the record here, an absolute "yes" in all possible circumstances), but statement (2) allows for both "yes" and "no" answers.

87. C

This question asks whether the information in one or both statements is sufficient to find a specific value.

In order to evaluate the expression, $25{,}850(2.75)^k$, it is only necessary to find the value of k. Do *not* try to work this one out. Just don't. It's totally unnecessary.

Statement (1): Factoring the equation $k^2 - 6k + 8 = 0$ will yield two possible values for k. The factored equation is $(k - 4)(k - 2) = 0$. Therefore, $k = 4$ or $k = 2$, but it is impossible from this information to know which one is the definite value of k. Insufficient.

Statement (2): This does not give us any information about k except that k does not equal 4. It could be any other number. Insufficient.

Statements (1) and (2) together: From (1), $k = 4$ or $k = 2$. In statement (2), though, it is known that $k \neq 4$; therefore, k must equal 2. Taken together, statements (1) and (2) are sufficient.

The credited response is (C): Taken together, statements (1) and (2) are sufficient to find the value in question, but neither statement is sufficient when considered independently.

88. A

This question asks whether the information in one or both statements is sufficient to answer a yes or no question.

Before we start here, we should get to the heart of the question. Since we know that both v and w are positive, we know that $\frac{v}{w}$ will also be positive. Next, the question "Is $\frac{v}{w}$ an integer?" could be rephrased as "Is v a multiple of w?" For each statement, you might want to pick some numbers that help you recall the number properties rules that are implicitly being tested. .

Statement (1): By the definition of an integer, every integer is a factor of itself. So, w is a factor of itself. Since it is given here that every factor of w is also a factor of v, then w is a factor of v and $\frac{v}{w}$ is an integer. Sufficient.

Statement (2): In the case that $w = 15$ and $v = 60$, w has the prime factors 3 and 5, both of which are prime factors of v, and $\frac{v}{w} = 4$, which is an integer. However, if $w = 18$ and $v = 60$, w has the prime factors 2 and 3, which are also both prime factors of v, but $\frac{v}{w}\left(\frac{60}{18}\right)$ is not an integer. Insufficient.

The credited response is (A): The information provided in statement (1) leads to a definite answer (for the record here, an absolute "yes" in all possible circumstances), but statement (2) allows for both "yes" and "no" answers.

89. C

This question asks whether the information in one or both statements is sufficient to find a specific value.

Since it's true that 1 raised to any power is always 1, if $a = 1$, then x could be any positive integer. And since it's true that anything raised to the power 0 equals 1, if $x = 0$, then a could be any number. And finally, since any negative number raised to an even exponent is positive, it could also be the case that -1^e (where e represents a positive even integer) is 1. So if $a^x = 1$, one of three things is true: a is 1; a is -1 and x is an even integer; x is 0.

Statement (1): This states that a is positive, but if x is 0, a could be any positive number. Insufficient.

Statement (2): If x is a positive integer, in order to satisfy $a^x = 1$, a must be equal to 1 or -1. If the value of x is an odd number, then if a is -1, $a^x = -1$, so a must be 1. However if x is an even number, then both $a = 1$ and $a = -1$ satisfy the equation $a^x = 1$. Insufficient.

Statements (1) and (2) taken together: Since statement (2) gives two possible values for a, 1 and -1, and (1) rules out $a = -1$, then $a = 1$.

The credited response is (C): When taken together, the information provided in the statements leads to a definite answer (for the record here, an absolute "no" in all possible circumstances), but when considered independently, each statement still allows for both "yes" and "no" answers.

90. A

This question asks whether the information in one or both statements is sufficient to find a specific value.

It is useful to first simplify the right side of the equation. The denominator $\left(\frac{2}{b}\right) + \left(\frac{4}{5b}\right)$ can be rewritten as $\left(\frac{10}{5b}\right) + \left(\frac{4}{5b}\right)$ or $\frac{14}{5b}$. So the entire right side of the equation can be written as $\frac{\left(\frac{3}{a}\right)}{\left(\frac{14}{5b}\right)}$. Simplified even further, that's:

$$\frac{\left(\frac{3}{a}\right)}{\left(\frac{5b}{14}\right)} = \frac{15b}{14a} \text{ or } \left(\frac{15}{14}\right)\times\left(\frac{b}{a}\right)$$

In order to evaluate that expression, you need a ratio $\frac{b}{a}$ or some variation thereof. Any statement or set of statements that allows us to determine such a ratio is sufficient.

Statement (1): If you have a single term with one variable on one side of the equation and a single term with the other variable on the other side of the equation, you can always express that as a variable:variable ratio. In other words, here we could simply divide each side by a to get $\frac{b}{a} = 4$. If you didn't know that, you could simply substitute $4a$ for b in the simplified equation. The value of R can be found: $R = \frac{(15b)}{(14a)} = \frac{(15 \times 4a)}{(14a)} = \frac{60}{14}$. Sufficient.

Statement (2): If you substitute $\frac{2}{3}$ for a, the numerator is $\frac{9}{2}$, or 4.5, with no way to evaluate the denominator. Or, you can actually substitute and see this play out: When $\frac{2}{3}$ is substituted for a in the simplified equation, $R = \frac{(15b)}{\left(14 \times \frac{2}{3}\right)} = \frac{(15b)}{\left(\frac{28}{3}\right)}$. Without additional information about the value of b, there is no way to determine the value of R. Insufficient.

The credited response is (A): Statement (1), taken independently, is sufficient to find the value in question, but statement (2) is not.

91. D

This question asks whether the information in one or both statements is sufficient to answer a yes or no question.

It is helpful to first note that $x^{-a} = \frac{1}{x^a}$. For instance, $3^{(-3)} = \frac{1}{3^3} = \frac{1}{27}$.

Statement (1): From this $n < 0$. Since the absolute value of n is a positive integer, $|n| \times n$ will yield a negative integer. Since when n is negative, 2^n will yield a positive fraction, which is greater than a negative integer, the inequality $|n| \times n < 2^n$ is true. Sufficient.

Statement (2): n is given here as a particular negative integer. By following the same logic as in (1), the inequality $|n| \times n < 2^n$ can be determined to be true. Sufficient.

Note, by the way, that if statement (1) is sufficient, that means that every negative value for n gives the same yes or no answer to the question, regardless of the value of x. So there is no way that statement (1) could be sufficient and statement (2) be insufficient.

The credited response is (D): Each statement, when considered independently, leads to an absolute answer in all circumstances (for the record here, both "yes").

92. B

This question asks whether the information in one or both statements is sufficient to answer a yes or no question.

Let's evaluate what we're asked for in terms of what we're given. The question, in brief: "Is $(b - a)$ a perfect square?"

Statement (1): This inequality can also be stated as $(b - a) > 21$. Looking at the original question, there are some values for $(b - a)$ such that $\sqrt{b - a}$ would be an integer. Take $(b - a) = 25$, for example: $25 > 21$ and $\sqrt{25}$ is 5, also an integer. However, if $(b - a) = 22$, then $\sqrt{22}$ is not an integer. Insufficient.

Statement (2): The equation given here is equivalent to $b = a^2 + a$. Then, $b - a = a^2$. So $\sqrt{b-a}$ is equal to $\sqrt{a^2}$, which is a, and it is given that a is an integer. Sufficient.

The credited response is (B): The information provided in statement (2) leads to a definite answer (for the record here, an absolute "yes" in all possible circumstances), but statement (1) allows for both "yes" and "no" answers.

93. B

This question asks whether the information in one or both statements is sufficient to answer a yes or no question.

Basically, the only information we're given is that $s < 0$, so s is negative. We're then asked whether t is positive.

Statement (1): Since it's given that s is negative, the value of t here could be 0. It could also be the case that t is positive, but $|s|$ is greater than t, so $(t + s)$ is negative, as in the example $t = 4$ and $s = -5$. It could also be the case that t is negative, as in the example $t = -2$ and $s = -5$. It is impossible from this information to determine which case is true. Insufficient.

Statement (2): Since s is negative (given) and $\frac{s}{t}$ is negative according to this statement, then t must be greater than 0. If $\frac{s}{t}$ is negative, s and t must have different signs; one is positive and the other negative. Since s is negative, t must be positive. Sufficient.

The credited response is (B): The information provided in statement (2) leads to a definite answer (for the record here, an absolute "yes" in all possible circumstances), but statement (1) allows for both "yes" and "no" answers.

94. B

This question asks whether the information in one or both statements is sufficient to find a specific value.

It will be helpful to first note that because a is directly proportional to e, which is in turn directly proportional to c, a is then directly proportional to c. To say that a is directly proportional to c is just to say that there is a constant k such that $ck = a$, or, perhaps more simply, that there is a fixed ratio between a and c. A statement, or set of statements, will be sufficient if and only if it determines that ratio.

Statement (1): From this, the proportional relationship between e and c can be determined. However, a is directly proportional to e, and nothing is said about that relationship; therefore, the value of a when $c = 3.0$ cannot be found. Insufficient.

Statement (2): This gives you the ratio you want. You don't need to actually calculate the value of a if $c = 3.0$. You just need to know that it's possible. Still not sure? Because a is directly proportional to c: $\frac{a}{c} = \frac{80}{6.0}$. Since the question asks for the value of a when $c = 3.0$, divide the numerator and denominator each by 2. $a = 40$. Or, if you're determined to cross multiply, substitute the given value for c: $\frac{a}{3.0} = \frac{80}{6.0}$. By cross multiplication, $6a = 240$. Therefore, $a = 40$. Sufficient.

The credited response is (B): Statement (2), taken independently, is sufficient to find the value in question, but statement (1) is not.

95. E

This question asks whether the information in one or both statements is sufficient to answer a yes or no question.

The best way to do this is probably to quickly head to the statements, picking numbers that meet the criteria given and plugging them in to test. If you're really observant, you might notice that you should focus on the relationship between m and n ($m > n$ or $m < n$), the difference between the two values (as that will affect the fractional relationship), and how each one's sign (positive or negative) will affect the fractional relationship. Use that knowledge to inform your number choices.

Statement (1): From this, n could be equal to -10. Then if $m = 12$, $\frac{(m-n)}{(m+n)} = \frac{(12+10)}{(12-10)}$, or 11, which is greater than 1. If $n = -10$ and $m = 2$, however, then $\frac{(m-n)}{(m+n)} = \frac{(2+10)}{(2-10)}$, or $-\frac{12}{8}$, which is less than 1. Insufficient.

Statement (2): From this, m could be equal to 8. Then if n = -6, $\frac{(m-n)}{(m+n)} = \frac{(8+6)}{(8-6)}$, or 7, which is greater than 1. If $m = 8$ and $n = 14$, however, $\frac{(m-n)}{(m+n)} = \frac{(8+14)}{(8-14)}$, or $-\frac{22}{6}$, which is less than 1. Insufficient.

Testing the statements together, we could use some previous examples:

$$n = -10;\ m = 12: \frac{(m-n)}{(m+n)} = \frac{(12+10)}{(12-10)},$$

or 11 > 1—Yes.

$$n = -10;\ m = 2: \frac{(m-n)}{(m+n)} = \frac{(2+10)}{(2-10)},$$

or $\frac{-12}{8} < 1$—No.

So it's clear that even both statements together aren't enough.

The credited response is (E): The information provided in the statements, taken independently or together, is insufficient; both "yes" and "no" answers are still possible (in other words, the answer is always "maybe").

96. D

This question asks whether the information in one or both statements is sufficient to find a specific value.

Let n represent the number of days before the new employee was hired, when the daily payroll was \$5,750 each day. Then 30 - n represents the number of days that the payroll was \$6,030 (\$5,750 + \$280) for each day. Then the average daily payroll would be equal to $\frac{[n(5,750)+(30-n)(6,030)]}{30}$.

Statement (1): From this, the payroll was \$5,750 for the first 10 days of the payroll cycle and \$6,030 for the remaining 20 days. Therefore, the average daily payroll for the cycle was equal to $\frac{[10(5,750)+20(6,030)]}{30}$, which can be determined. Sufficient.

Statement (2): Since the average daily payroll would have been \$5,750 through the first 20 days had the new employee been hired after the 20th day, the employee must have been hired during the first 20 days. Using this information, and letting n represent the number of days that the total daily payroll remained \$5,750, the average daily payroll for the first 20 days of the cycle can be represented by $\frac{[n(5,750)+(20-n)(5,890)]}{20}$. Solving the equation gives $n = 10$. Then by substituting 10 for n in the formula to find the average daily payroll for the entire 30-day cycle, as in (1), the average daily payroll can be determined. Sufficient.

The credited response is (D): Each statement, taken independently, is sufficient to find the value in question.

97. C

This question asks whether the information in one or both statements is sufficient to answer a yes or no question.

Statement (1): This does not provide any information about x or its relation to y. Insufficient.

Statement (2): y can be substituted for x in the inequality:

$\frac{1}{y} > \frac{y}{y^2+3}$ (Substitute y for x.)

$1 > \frac{y^2}{y^2+3}$ (Multiply both sides by y.)

When y is positive, this inequality will always hold true, since $y^2 + 3$ will always be greater than y^2. This means the term $\frac{y^2}{y^2+3}$ will be a fraction. However, in the case where $y <$ 0, when both sides are multiplied by y (as above), the inequality sign reverses, since the inequality is being multiplied by a negative number:

$\frac{1}{y} > \frac{y}{y^2+3}$ (Substitute y for x.)

$1 > \frac{y^2}{y^2+3}$ (Multiply both sides by y.)

The term $\frac{y^2}{y^2+3}$ would still be less than 1. Therefore, the inequality does not hold true when $y < 0$. Insufficient.

From (1) and (2) together. Since statement (2) implies that $\frac{1}{x} > \frac{y}{y^2+3}$ whenever $y > 0$, and statement (1) states that $y > 0$, these are sufficient together.

The credited response is (C): When taken together, the information provided in the statements leads to a definite answer (an absolute "yes"), but when considered independently, each statement still allows for both "yes" and "no" answers.

98. A

This question asks whether the information in one or both statements is sufficient to answer a yes or no question.

Note that when any number x is an integer, x^2 is also an integer, because the product of 2 integers (here, $x \times x$) is always an integer.

Statement (1): If $\sqrt{p}$ is an integer, then p is the square of an integer, and so is itself an integer. Sufficient.

Statement (2): The rule that if p is an integer, then p^2 is an integer does not logically imply that if p^2 is an integer, then p is an integer. If $p^2 = 4$, then $p = 2$, which is an integer. However, take the example $p^2 = 2$. Then $p = \sqrt{2}$, which is not an integer. Insufficient.

The credited response is (A): The information provided in statement (1) leads to a definite answer (for the record here, an absolute "yes" in all possible circumstances), but statement (2) allows for both "yes" and "no" answers.

99. B

This question asks whether the information in one or both statements is sufficient to answer a yes or no question.

Whenever the GMAT gives you a factorable expression, factor it.

$y^3 - y = y(y^2 - 1) = y(y - 1)(y + 1) = (y - 1) \times y \times (y + 1)$

So $y^3 - y$ is the product of three consecutive integers. Such a product will always be divisible by 4 if the least of the integers is even. It will not always be divisible by 4 if the least of the integers is odd.

Statement (1): Factoring this expression yields the expression $y(y + 1)$. This represents the product of two consecutive integers. It is given that this product is divisible by 10. Consider $y = 4$. Then $y(y + 1) = (4)(5) = 20$, which is divisible by 10 and $y^3 - y = 64 - 4 = 60$, which is divisible by 4. However, when $y = 10$, $y(y + 1) = (10)(11) = 110$, which is divisible by 10; but $y^3 - y = 1{,}000 - 10 =$

990, which is not divisible by 4. If this seems like casting about randomly for values, it isn't. You're trying to come up with an example such that $y - 1$ is odd, one of the terms y or $y + 1$ is a multiple of 5, and none of the three is a multiple of 4. Insufficient.

Statement (2): From this, y is an odd number. Therefore, $y - 1$ is even, and so is $y + 1$. So exactly two of the three terms in $y(y - 1)(y + 1)$ are even, which means that exactly two of the terms are divisible by 2. It follows that the if the product of the three terms were factored, there would be at least two factors of 2, and since the product of these 2 factors is 4, then 4 is a factor of $y(y - 1)(y + 1)$ and $y^3 - y$ is divisible by 4. Sufficient.

The credited response is (B): The information provided in statement (2) leads to a definite answer (for the record here, an absolute "yes" in all possible circumstances), but statement (1) allows for both "yes" and "no" answers.

100. B

This question asks whether the information in one or both statements is sufficient to find a specific value.

Statement (1): From this, n is 30 more than some multiple of 230. Do all such numbers have the same tens digit? No. $\frac{260}{230} = 1$ with a remainder of 30 (or 1 R30), $\frac{490}{230} = 2$ R30, and $\frac{720}{230} = 3$ R30. For each of these examples, the remainder is 30, but the tens digit has a different value. Insufficient.

Statement (2): From this, n is 30 more than some multiple of 200. This condition is only satisfied when $n = 230, 430, 630, 830$, and so on. Sufficient.

The credited response is (B): The information provided in statement (2) leads to a definite answer (for the record here, an absolute "yes" in all possible circumstances), but statement (1) allows for both "yes" and "no" answers.

101. A

This question asks whether the information in one or both statements is sufficient to answer a yes or no question.

If you're handy with weighted averages, you might recognize right away that if exactly 20% of the unreduced compensation from this contract was due to the last contract—the one that was reduced by 15% rather than by 10%—then Mrs. K's compensation for those three contracts would have been reduced by exactly 11%. If you're not that handy with weighted averages, they're not so important for the GMAT; just work with specific values given in the statements, keeping in mind that the greater the portion of the compensation reduced at 10%, the closer the average reduction will be to 10%.

Statement (1): Test the extremes this statement allows: Suppose that compensation for the three contracts was as low as possible: \$1,200, \$1,200, and \$550. This is a total of \$2,950. After reductions, she would be paid 0.9(1,200) + 0.9(1,200)+ 0.85(550), or \$2,627.50. The total, then, was reduced by \$322.50, which is less than 11% of \$2,950. The only way that you can change these figures is to make the largest of the three contracts larger still, but that will only bring the total percent reduction closer to 10%. Suppose that one of her first two contracts would have paid \$100,000 before the reduction. So instead of 100,000 + 1,200 + 550, or 101,750, she would receive 0.9(100,000) + 0.9(1,200) + 0.85(550), or 91,547.50. The total then was reduced by about \$10,202.50. This is almost exactly 10%. Sufficient.

Statement (2): This determines the compensation for the first late contract, but it does not give any information about the other two. Thus, it is not possible to determine the total amount of the original compensation, or the sum of the reductions. Insufficient.

The credited response is (A): The information provided in statement (1) leads to a definite answer (for the record here, an absolute "no" in all possible circumstances), but statement (2) allows for both "yes" and "no" answers.

102. D

This question asks whether the information in one or both statements is sufficient to answer a yes or no question.

The ratio $a{:}b$ is equivalent to $\frac{a}{b}$. So the question being asked is "Is $\frac{a}{b} > 5$?" or "Is $a > 5b$?"

Statement (1): This statement can be expressed as $a = 5b + 3$. For any value of b, $5b + 3 > 5b$; therefore, $a > 5b$. Dividing both sides of the inequality yields $\frac{a}{b} > 5$. Sufficient.

Statement (2): This statement can be expressed as the inequality $\frac{4a}{5b} > 4$. Multiplying both sides of the inequality by $5b$ yields $4a > 20b$, and dividing each side of that by 4 yields $a > 5b$. Sufficient.

The credited response is (D): Each statement, when considered independently, leads to an absolute answer in all circumstances (for the record here, both "yes").

103. D

This question asks whether the information in one or both statements is sufficient to find a specific value.

Something to consider before you start on the math: The only possible answers are (C) and (D). Obviously, if you have both parts of the diameter, you can add them to get 10, the diameter, so the answer can't be (E). But it can't be (A) or (B), either. Statements (1) and (2) give exactly the same sort of information: the length of one side of one of the smaller triangles. If statement (1) is sufficient, then so is statement (2).

It would help to know two geometry facts about this figure before turning to the statements. Realistically, if you didn't know these when you saw this problem, you wouldn't solve it in a time reasonable for the GMAT. First, if a triangle whose vertices are all on the circumference of a circle has one side that is a diameter of that circle, it's a right triangle. In this case, that means that XZ is the hypotenuse of a right triangle. Second, if you treat the hypotenuse of a right triangle as the base and draw an altitude to the opposite vertex, that altitude will divide the right triangle into two smaller right triangles, each of which is similar to the original right triangle and so each of which is similar to the other. Similar triangles are exactly the same shape, though they may be different sizes. Any two similar triangles share a common side:side:side ratio.

That means that the following ratios are all the same: $XY{:}YZ{:}(r+s)$, $4{:}r{:}YZ$, and $s{:}4{:}XY$.

Statement (1): If $r = 8$, then $s = 2$ in order to preserve the ratio $4{:}r = s{:}4$. Sufficient.

Statement (2): If $s = 2$, then $r = 8$ in order to preserve the ratio $4{:}r = s{:}4$. Sufficient.

The credited response is (D): Each statement, taken independently, is sufficient to find the value in question.

104. B

This question asks whether the information in one or both statements is sufficient to answer a yes or no question.

Note that if x does not have a factor n such that $1 < n < x$, x has no factors but 1 and x, and so x is a prime number. The question could more usefully be phrased "Is x non-prime?"

Also note that $n!$ ("n factorial") equals the product of all integers from 1 to n, inclusive. So $3! = (3)(2)(1) = 6$.

Statement (1): From this, $x > (3)(2)$, or $x > 6$. There are many possible values for x greater than 6 that are prime (7, 11, 13, 17, 19 . . .) and many that are not prime (10, 12, 14, 15, 16 . . .). There is not enough information to determine whether x is prime or not. In fact, any lower limit for x would be insufficient, since there is no greatest prime number and no greatest non-prime. This statement is not sufficient. Normally, when you see that statement (1) is insufficient, you can rule out (A) and (D). In this case, you can rule out (C) as well, because as soon as we turn to statement (2), we see that statement (1) must be true if statement (2) is true, so statement (1) adds nothing to statement (2).

Statement (2): This states that the possible values for x are $15! + 2$, $15! + 3$, $15! + 4$, . . . $15! + 15$. The critical insight here is that the sum of two multiples of any number n is itself a multiple of n. For instance, any two even numbers add to a third even number; any two multiples of 3 add to a third multiple of 3. So, the first possible value, $15! + 2$, has 2 as a factor, since 2 is a factor of 2 and of 15!. The second possible value, $15! + 3$, has 3 as a factor, since 3 is a factor of 3 and 15!. This pattern continues for all the possible values of x, up to $15! + 15$, which has a factor of 15. Therefore, each of these possible values of x has a factor n such that $1 < n < x$. Sufficient.

The credited response is (B): The information provided in statement (2) leads to a definite answer (for the record here, an absolute "yes" in all possible circumstances), but statement (1) allows for both "yes" and "no" answers.

105. C

This question asks whether the information in one or both statements is sufficient to answer a yes or no question.

Start with statement (2), because it looks much simpler to manage: Since any real number squared is positive, this can't possibly tell us whether p is negative. It does tell us that p has an absolute value of less than 1: $-1 < p < 1$. Insufficient.

Statement (1): If $p^3(1 - p^2)$, then one of p^3 or the expression $(1 - p^2)$ must be positive and the other negative. To test whether this implies a yes or no answer to the question "Is p a negative number?" see whether statement (1) is consistent with $p > 0$, with $p < 0$, or with both.

Is it possible that $p > 0$? Sure. If p is greater than 1, then $p^3 > 0$, and $(1 - p^2) < 0$. Is it possible that $p < 0$? If $-1 < p < 0$, then $p^3 < 0$, and $(1 - p^2) > 0$. In other words, if p is a negative fraction between -1 and 0, then a higher power will make the fraction smaller in absolute value, but since it's negative, it will actually be getting closer to zero (larger) as its absolute value gets smaller. You can see another advantage to starting with the easier statement here: Statement (2) drew our attention to the possibility that p might be a fraction, positive or negative. Insufficient.

Together the two statements are sufficient. From (1), $-1 < p < 0$ or $p > 1$. From (2) $-1 < p < 1$. The only overlap these inequalities have is $-1 < p < 0$. Therefore, p is negative.

The credited response is (C): When taken together, the information provided in the statements leads to a definite answer (for the record here, an absolute "yes" in all possible circumstances), but when consid-

ered independently, each statement still allows both "yes" and "no" answers.

106. B

This question asks whether the information in one or both statements is sufficient to find a specific value.

Statement (1): From this, the pool holds at least 3,700 gallons of water, but nothing about its maximum capacity is given or implied. Insufficient.

Statement (2): We'll show the math below, but it's best if you can answer this without doing all the computation. If 500 gallons represents $\frac{1}{9}$ of $\frac{3}{4}$ of the capacity, then you have an equation for the capacity. Let the maximum capacity of the Smiths' pool be represented by m, $500 = \left(\frac{1}{9}\right)\left(\frac{3}{4}\right)m$. Now don't bother solving.

If you want to walk through it a little more slowly:

The amount of water in the pool when it is $\frac{3}{4}$ full of water is $\left(\frac{3}{4}\right)m$.

When 500 gallons of water are added, the water volume is equal to $\left(\frac{3}{4}\right)m + 500$, which increases the previous volume $\left(\frac{3}{4}\right)m$ by $\frac{1}{9}$.

$$\left(\frac{3}{4}\right)m + 500 = \left(\frac{3}{4}\right)m + \left(\frac{1}{9}\right)\left(\frac{3}{4}\right)m$$

$$500 = \left(\frac{1}{9}\right)\left(\frac{3}{4}\right)m$$

Sufficient.

The credited response is (B): Statement (2), taken independently, is sufficient to find the value in question, but statement (1) is not.

107. E

This question asks whether the information in one or both statements is sufficient to find a specific value.

Statement (1) gives us the percentage decrease in the truck's price, but not the actual dollar figure and no information about the van. Insufficient.

Statement (2) gives us the percentage decrease in the van's price, but not the actual dollar figure and no information about the truck. Insufficient.

To compare the dollar decreases in price, we need to know or be able to calculate the original prices of the truck and the van. Since we're only given the percent decreases, the actual dollar amounts could be anything—$1,000, $20,000, $75,000, etc. Therefore, even both statements together are not sufficient to answer the question.

The credited response is (E): The information provided in the statements, taken independently or together, is insufficient; both "yes" and "no" answers are still possible (in other words, the answer is always "maybe").

108. D

This question asks whether the information in one or both statements is sufficient to find a specific value.

It's tempting to suppose that the answer must be (C)—that you must need two equations to determine the value of two variables. This is mistaken for two reasons: First, we don't need to solve for the value of two variables but for the value of an expression containing two variables. We may be able to solve for the value of $\frac{a}{3} - \frac{b}{3}$ without first solving for either a or b. Second, these two equations are not distinct. They contain exactly the same information.

Since $\frac{a}{3} - \frac{b}{3} = \frac{a-b}{3}$, the question really asks for the value of $a - b$.

Statement (1): This gives us the value $a - b$. Sufficient.

Statement (2): Since $\frac{a-b}{3}$ is equivalent to $\frac{a}{3} - \frac{b}{3}$, this equation can be rewritten as $\frac{a}{3} - \frac{b}{3} = 4$. Sufficient.

The credited response is (D): Each statement, taken independently, is sufficient to find the value in question.

109. D

This question asks whether the information in one or both statements is sufficient to find a specific value.

Statement (1): Since 3^3 has some constant number of factors, this answer is sufficient. You could figure out what that number of factors is, but it serves no purpose on the GMAT. Curious? $3^3 = 27$. The number 27 has 4 positive integer factors: 1, 3, 9, and 27, so k has 4 positive integer factors as well. Sufficient.

Statement (2): If $k = rs$, then the factor pairs of k are $(1 \times rs)$ and $(r \times s)$. Since r and s are prime, and therefore can't be broken down into smaller numbers, there are no other positive integer factors of k. The number k has 4 positive integer factors. If you're not comfortable with this theoretical approach, you could assign a couple of sets of prime values to r and s—say 3 and 5, or 2 and 7—then count the factors of the resulting product. Sufficient.

The credited response is (D): Each statement, taken independently, is sufficient to find the value in question.

110. B

This question asks whether the information in one or both statements is sufficient to find a specific value.

Statement (1): All this statement tells us is that the difference between length and width is 15; the rectangle could have a length of 20 and a width of 5, or a length of 510 and a width of 495, or anything else that fits $l - w = 15$. Since these rectangles would have very different perimeters, this statement alone is not sufficient to answer the question. Insufficient.

Statement (2): The perimeter of a rectangle with length l and width w is equivalent to $l + w + l + w$, or $2l + 2w$. Since we're given the equation $l + w = 35$, we can simply double it to $2l + 2w = 70$, which gives us the perimeter of the rectangle. Sufficient.

The credited response is (B): Statement (2), taken independently, is sufficient to find the value in question, but statement (1) is not.

111. E

This question asks whether the information in one or both statements is sufficient to find a specific value.

Statement (1): This statement gives us the difference between m and n, but it doesn't give any information on the actual scores of either student. All we know is that n is 7 greater than m, which doesn't allow us to determine anything about the class average. Insufficient.

Statement (2): This statement gives us the value of m, which tells us that Kevin scored 12% higher than the average. Since we're not told his actual score, we can't calculate the average. Insufficient.

Even when both statements are taken together, we can only determine that Kevin scored 12 percent above the average and Katherine scored 19 percent above the average. We can't actually calculate the average unless we know one or both of their scores, and we're not given that information.

Therefore, even statements (1) and (2) together are not sufficient to answer the question.

The credited response is (E): The statements don't provide sufficient information to find the value in question, not even when considered together.

112. C

This question asks whether the information in one or both statements is sufficient to find a specific value.

Statement (1) gives the value of *h*, which on its own tells us nothing about the value of *g*. Insufficient.

Statement (2) gives *g* in terms of *h*, which is not sufficient to answer the question. Insufficient.

However, combining the two statements allows us to substitute the value of *h* into the equation $g = \frac{h}{5.49}$, meaning that $g = \frac{11.83}{5.49}$. Therefore, both statements together are sufficient to answer the question.

The credited response is (C): Taken together, statements (1) and (2) are sufficient to find the value in question, but neither statement is sufficient when considered independently.

113. E

This question asks whether the information in one or both statements is sufficient to find a specific value.

Statement (1): The set in question contains three multiples of 9 (27, 36, and 45), so this statement is not sufficient to determine which number was selected.

Statement (2): The set in question contains three odd numbers (21, 27, and 45), so this statement alone is also not sufficient.

Combining both statements tells us that the number selected is both a multiple of 9 and an odd number. Since there are two numbers in the set that fit both of those conditions (27 and 45), both statements together are not sufficient to answer the question.

The credited response is (E): The statements don't provide sufficient information to find the value in question, not even when considered together.

114. C

This question asks whether the information in one or both statements is sufficient to answer a yes or no question.

Statement (1) tells us nothing about Becky and Chris, so it isn't sufficient to answer the question.

Statement (2) tells us nothing about Alan and Darla, so it isn't sufficient, either.

When both statements are combined, we can see that all four students are available to meet during the two-hour period from 1:00 p.m. to 3:00 p.m. This might be easier to realize if you sketch out a graphical representation. Clearly, both statements together are sufficient to answer the question.

The credited response is (C): When taken together, the information provided in the statements leads to a definite answer (for the record here, an absolute "yes" in all possible circumstances), but when considered independently, each statement still allows both "yes" and "no" answers.

115. A

This question asks whether the information in one or both statements is sufficient to find a specific value.

Statement (1): If $b = 5$, the original equation becomes $(2 \times 5)(a + 1) = 3$. Since this is a linear equation with a single variable, you can solve for *a*. You shouldn't take the time to, of course, but . . .

$$\begin{aligned} 10(a+1) &= 3 \\ 10a+10 &= 3 \\ 10a &= -7 \\ a &= -0.7 \end{aligned}$$

Statement (2): If $b^2 = 25$, then b could be equal to either 5 or -5. Do these two values for b yield the same value for a? We've calculated that $a = -0.7$ when $b = 5$, so we need to calculate the value of a when $b = -5$:

$$\begin{aligned} (2 \times -5)(a+1) &= 3 \\ -10(a+1) &= 3 \\ -10a-10 &= 3 \\ -10a &= 13 \\ a &= -1.3 \end{aligned}$$

Since $b = 5$ and $b = -5$ produce different values of a, statement (2) is not sufficient.

The credited response is (A): Statement (1), taken independently, is sufficient to find the value in question, but statement (2) is not.

116. E

This question asks whether the information in one or both statements is sufficient to find a specific value.

Statement (1): We're told how many total females went to the school, but that doesn't allows us to calculate how many of the new students were female, so this statement is not sufficient.

Statement (2): This statement gives the overall percentage of female students, but we can't assume that the percentage is the same for the group of new students. We have no way to calculate the percentage of new students that are female, so this statement is also not sufficient.

Together, statements (1) and (2) only allow us to calculate the total number of students at the school. Nothing in either statement or the problem leads us to the number of new female students, so statements (1) and (2) together are not sufficient to answer the question.

The credited response is (E): The statements don't provide sufficient information to find the value in question, not even when considered together.

117. B

This question asks whether the information in one or both statements is sufficient to find a specific value.

Statement (1): This statement can be written algebraically as $b = 2 + \frac{c}{2}$. You cannot convert this to a ratio, because the left side of the equation has two terms. This isn't obvious to many test takers, so you might try to simplify this statement further: If you divide both sides by c to find the value of $\frac{b}{c}$, the equation becomes $\frac{b}{c} = \frac{2}{c} + \frac{1}{2}$. Since this equation cannot be simplified further, statement (1) alone is not sufficient to answer the question. You might also realize this because you can come up with two sets of numbers that fit the condition $b = 2 + \frac{c}{2}$ but have different ratios. For example, $b = 5$ and $c = 6$ works, and the ratio of b to c is $\frac{5}{6}$. The equation is also satisfied if $b = 7$ and $c = 10$, which produces a ratio of $\frac{7}{10}$. Since $\frac{5}{6}$ and $\frac{7}{10}$ are different answers, we cannot find the ratio of b to c based on statement (1).

Statement (2): Here we have a ratio of $2b$ to $5c$. You can always move the coefficients—2 and 5 in this case—over to the other side of an equation. You needn't perform the computation, as long as you know it's possible. But here it is: $\frac{2b}{5c} = \frac{1}{2}$ can be rewritten as $\left(\frac{2}{5}\right)\left(\frac{b}{c}\right) = \frac{1}{2}$. If you then divide both sides by

$\left(\frac{2}{5}\right)$, you'd be left with $\frac{b}{c} = \frac{\frac{1}{2}}{\frac{2}{5}}$, or $\frac{b}{c} = \frac{5}{4}$.

Therefore, statement (2) alone is sufficient to answer the question.

The credited response is (B): Statement (2), taken independently, is sufficient to find the value in question, but statement (1) is not.

118. E

This question asks whether the information in one or both statements is sufficient to find a specific value.

Statement (1): This statement provides no information about profit during the fourth year, so it is not sufficient to answer the question.

Statement (2): This statement gives the relationship between profit during the third year and profit during the fourth year, but since we don't know the third year's profit, we can't use this to calculate the fourth year's profit.

Even taken together, the two statements only allow us to establish relationships among the three years' profits. We'd need to know the actual value of one of the three to calculate the fourth year's profit. Therefore, statements (1) and (2) together are not sufficient to answer the question.

Another way to come to that conclusion is to find two different answers that both satisfy all the stated conditions. For example, if Year 4 profit = \$20 million, then Year 3 profit = \$8 million and Year 5 profit = \$16 million. Or, if Year 4 profit = \$100 million, then Year 3 profit = \$92 million and Year 5 profit = \$184 million. Since multiple values work, the statements given are not sufficient to determine the answer.

The credited response is (E): The statements don't provide sufficient information to find the value in question, not even when considered together.

119. C

This question asks whether the information in one or both statements is sufficient to find a specific value.

Statement (1): This tells us that j is evenly divisible by 5, but we don't know anything about k. For example, if $j = 15$ and $k = 3$, then the remainder of $\frac{j+k}{5}$ is equal to 3. However, if $j = 15$ and $k = 10$, then the remainder of $\frac{j+k}{5}$ is equal to 0. Since this statement only gives information about j, it alone is not sufficient.

Statement (2): The same logic can be applied here to conclude that this statement isn't sufficient either. It tells us that k is divisible by 5, but we don't know about j. Insufficient.

When both statements are combined, it becomes clear that the remainder of $\frac{j+k}{5}$ must be 0. When j and k are both divisible by 5, their sum will always be divisible by 5 as well. To verify this, you could try it with any combination of numbers that satisfy both statements: 0 and 25, 35 and 10, 80 and −15, etc. Therefore, both statements together are sufficient to answer the question.

The credited response is (C): Taken together, Statements (1) and (2) are sufficient to find the value in question, but neither statement is sufficient when considered independently.

120. B

This question asks whether the information in one or both statements is sufficient to find a specific value.

Statement (1): This statement tells us that *m* and *n* have opposite signs; in other words, one is positive and one is negative. This is the case both in quadrant II (negative *x*, positive *y*) and in quadrant IV (positive *x*, negative *y*), so we can't determine the answer from this statement. All we know is that (*m*, *n*) does not lie in quadrants I or III, where coordinates are both positive and both negative, respectively. Insufficient.

Statement (2): This statement gives us the actual values for both coordinates, which allows us to plot the point (-4, 4) and determine that it lies in quadrant II. Therefore, Statement (2) alone is sufficient.

The credited response is (B): Statement (2), taken independently, is sufficient to find the value in question, but statement (1) is not.

121. D

This question asks whether the information in one or both statements is sufficient to find a specific value.

Statement (1): Multiplying both sides of this equation by p results in $24 = -3p$, which means that $p = \frac{24}{-3} = -8$. This statement is sufficient.

Statement (2): Combining like terms simplifies this equation to $4p + 6 = 3p - 2$, which in turn simplifies to $p = -8$. This statement is sufficient.

The credited response is (D): Each statement, taken independently, is sufficient to find the value in question.

122. E

This question asks whether the information in one or both statements is sufficient to answer a yes or no question.

Statement (1): The value of $(6)^2 + 1$ is 37, which is a prime number. However, if $n = 2$, $n^2 + 1$ is equal to 5, which is also a prime number. Therefore, *n* may or may not be equal 6; this statement alone is not sufficient.

Statement (2): Since there are plenty of other numbers greater than 2, this statement alone is not sufficient to answer the question.

When both statements are combined, $n = 6$ remains a possibility. However, *n* could also be equal to 10, since 10 is greater than 2 and $(10)^2 + 1 = 101$, which is prime. Since *n* could be either 6 or 10, statements (1) and (2) together are insufficient.

The credited response is (E): The information provided in the statements, taken independently or together, is insufficient; both "yes" and "no" answers are still possible (in other words, the answer is always "maybe").

123. C

This question asks whether the information in one or both statements is sufficient to find a specific value.

Statement (1): Knowing only the number of defect-free units does not allow us to determine the total number of units produced, so this statement alone is not sufficient.

Statement (2): We're given the percentage of defective units, but we'd need the number of defective units as well to calculate the total units produced. Insufficient.

If 20% of the units produced were defective, 80% of the units produced were nondefective. Statement (1) tells us that 16,000 nondefective units were produced, so 16,000 represents 80% of all units produced. From that point, we can set up a simple proportion to find that 100% of all units produced is equal to 20,000 units. Therefore, both statements together are sufficient.

The credited response is (C): Taken together, statements (1) and (2) are sufficient to find the value in question, but neither statement is sufficient when considered independently.

124. C

This question asks whether the information in one or both statements is sufficient to find a specific value.

Statement (1):

$1^3 = 1$

$2^3 = 8$

$3^3 = 27$

$4^3 = 64$

There are three positive integers k for which $k^3 < 60$: $k = 1$, $k = 2$, and $k = 3$ (the value of k^3 will be greater than 60 for all numbers 4 and higher). Since each of these three values is possible, this statement alone is not sufficient to find the value of k.

Statement (2): This statement tells us that k^3 is evenly divisible by 2, which means that k could be any even number, since $2^3 = 8$, $4^3 = 64$, $6^3 = 216$, and so on. This statement alone is also not sufficient.

However, combining both statements means that k must fit both conditions; that is, it must be 1, 2, or 3, and it must be even. Only one of those three numbers is even, so we know that k must be equal to 2. Therefore, both statements together are sufficient.

The credited response is (C): Taken together, statements (1) and (2) are sufficient to find the value in question, but neither statement is sufficient when considered independently.

125. A

This question asks whether the information in one or both statements is sufficient to answer a yes or no question.

Statement (1): The sum of the three interior angles of a triangle is 180 degrees, so if any two angles add to 90, the third angle (in this case, angle ABC) must be a 90-degree angle. This makes triangle ABC a right triangle with legs 3 and 4 and hypotenuse AC. Therefore, we can apply the Pythagorean theorem to calculate the length of AC:

$a^2 + b^2 = c^2$

$(3)^2 + (4)^2 = (AC)^2$

$25 = (AC)^2$

$AC = 5$

Statement (2): The fact that AC is the longest side of the triangle does not necessarily mean that $AC = 5$. The length of AC could be 4.8, 5.5, 6, or many other values. Therefore, statement (2) is not sufficient.

The credited response is (A): The information provided in statement (1) leads to a definite answer (for the record here, an absolute "yes" in all possible circumstances), but statement (2) allows for both "yes" and "no" answers.

126. C

This question asks whether the information in one or both statements is sufficient to answer a yes or no question.

Statement (1): There are plenty of sets of three integers that satisfy this condition, some of which are consecutive integers and some of which aren't. For example, $d = 4$, $e = 3$, and $f = 2$ works, but so does $d = 35$, $e = 25$, and $f = 15$. Therefore, this statement alone is not sufficient.

Statement (2): This statement mentions nothing about the value of e, so it alone is also insufficient.

However, both statements taken together are sufficient to prove that d, e, and f are consecutive integers. The difference between d and *f* is 2 (they're 2 numbers apart), and *e* is the same distance from both of them. Therefore, *e* must be halfway between the two, or one number away from each. If $d = 10$, then *f* must be 8 and *e* must be 9. No matter what integer value you choose for *d*, the three numbers will be consecutive. Another way to approach the problem is algebraically. Since $d - f = 2$, $d = f + 2$. We can substitute this value into the other equation ($d - e = e - f$) to get that $(f + 2) - e = e - f$, which simplifies to $2e - 2f = 2$ or $e - f = 1$. This means that *e* is greater than *f* by 1, so then *d* is greater than *e* by 1.

The credited response is (C): When taken together, the information provided in the statements leads to a definite answer (for the record here, an absolute "yes" in all possible circumstances), but when considered independently, each statement still allows both "yes" and "no" answers.

127. A

This question asks whether the information in one or both statements is sufficient to find a specific value.

Statement (1):

$0 + 1 = 1$

$0 - 1 = -1$

$0 \times 1 = 0$

$0 \div 1 = 0$

When the first number is 0 and the second number is 1, the only operation that produces an answer of −1 is subtraction. Therefore, this statement alone is sufficient.

Statement (2):

$1 + 0 = 1$

$1 - 0 = 1$

$1 \times 0 = 0$

$1 \div 0 =$ undefined

When the first number is 1 and the second number is 0, both addition and subtraction could produce an answer of 1. Therefore, Statement 2 alone is not sufficient.

The credited response is (A): Statement (1), taken independently, is sufficient to find the value in question, but statement (2) is not.

128. A

This question asks whether the information in one or both statements is sufficient to find a specific value.

Statement (1): This hardly looks sufficient at first glance, since it contains two variables, but as you simplify it, *b* disappears. This equation can be simplified to $2b - 2 = 2b - \frac{a}{3}$, which in turn becomes $-2 = -\frac{a}{3}$. We can then solve for *a* by multiplying both sides by -3, resulting in $6 = a$.

Statement (2): Solving this equation for *a* results in $a = b - 4$. This tells us that *a* is 4 less than *b*, but since we're given no information about *b*, we can't find the value of *a*. This statement alone is not sufficient. Therefore, statement (2) alone is not sufficient.*a*. This statement alone is not sufficient. Therefore, statement (2) alone is not sufficient.

The credited response is (A): Statement (1), taken independently, is sufficient to find the value in question, but statement (2) is not.

129. D

This question asks whether the information in one or both statements is sufficient to find a specific value.

Statement (1): Cross multiplying this proportion would allow us to solve for *m*, which is the number of pounds of barley in the bag. Since we know that $m + n = 5$ pounds, we can subtract from 5 to solve for the *n*, the number of pounds of oats. Sufficient.

Statement (2): Cross multiplying this proportion would allow us to solve for n, which is the number of pounds of oats in the bag. Sufficient.

The credited response is (D): Each statement, taken independently, is sufficient to find the value in question.

130. C

This question asks whether the information in one or both statements is sufficient to find a specific value.

Statement (1): There are three pairs of positive integers that multiply to 16: 16 × 1, 8 × 2, and 4 × 4. We can't determine which of these is the correct pair, or which of the numbers is m and which is n. Therefore, this statement alone is not sufficient.

Statement (2): There are an infinite number of possibilities for m and n given only that $m = n^3$. A few include $n = 1$ and $m = 1$, $n = 5$ and $m = 125$, and $n = 10$ and $m = 1{,}000$. Clearly, this statement alone is also not sufficient.

Of the three possible pairs in statement (1), though, only 8 and 2 satisfies the condition in statement (2): $8 = 2^3$. Furthermore, we know that m must be 8 and n must be 2, since $m = n^3$ and not the other way around. Therefore, both statements together are sufficient to answer the question.

The credited response is (C): Taken together, statements (1) and (2) are sufficient to find the value in question, but neither statement is sufficient when considered independently.

131. A

This question asks whether the information in one or both statements is sufficient to find a specific value.

Statement (1): This statement expressed algebraically is equivalent to $L - 6 = \frac{L}{2}$, where L is Lisa's current age. This can be simplified to $\frac{L}{2} - 6 = 0$, or $\frac{L}{2} = 6$, so $L = 12$. Another way to look at it is that based on the statement, 6 years represents half of Lisa's age, so Lisa's age must be 12. Sufficient.

Statement (2): This statement gives Lisa's age in terms of her brother Carl's age. Algebraically, it can be represented as $L + 8 = 2C$. Since we don't know anything about Carl's actual age, we can't use this information to calculate Lisa's age. Therefore, statement 2 alone is not sufficient.

The credited response is (A): Statement (1), taken independently, is sufficient to find the value in question, but statement (2) is not.

132. E

This question asks whether the information in one or both statements is sufficient to find a specific value.

Statement (1): The fact that $a^2 = b^2$ tells us that a and b must each be a square root, or a square root times –1. Either number could be any integer: the two numbers could be –2 and 2, 7 and 7, 13 and –13, etc. That is, the two will have the same absolute value, but not necessarily the same sign. Insufficient.

Statement (2): The fact that $\sqrt{b} = 2$ means that the value of b must be 4. However, this statement tells us absolutely nothing about the value of a, so it is not sufficient to determine the value of ab.

When both statements are used together, we know that $b = 4$ and $a^2 = b^2$. This means that $a^2 = 16$, but a could then be equal to either 4 or –4. Since the value of ab would be either –16 or 16, statements (1) and (2) together are not sufficient to answer the question.

The credited response is (E): The statements don't provide sufficient information to find the value in question, not even when considered together.

133. B

This question asks whether the information in one or both statements is sufficient to find a specific value.

Statement (1): This statement expresses the relationship between open odd-numbered lockers and open even-numbered lockers; we know that the former is 5 greater than the latter. However, we can't use this to determine the value of either. There could be 7 open odds and 2 open evens, or 39 open odds and 34 open evens. This statement alone is not sufficient.

Statement (2): Since the lockers are numbered 1–100, there are 50 odd-numbered lockers and 50 even-numbered lockers. This means that there are $\left(\frac{1}{5}\right)(50)$ or 10 open odd-numbered lockers and $\left(\frac{1}{10}\right)(50)$ or 5 open even-numbered lockers, so 15 lockers are currently open. Therefore, statement (2) alone is sufficient to answer the question, but statement (1) alone is not sufficient.

The credited response is (B): Statement (2), taken independently, is sufficient to find the value in question, but statement (1) is not.

134. A

This question asks whether the information in one or both statements is sufficient to find a specific value.

To determine the value of $2k$, determine the value of k. To determine the value of k, determine the value of the digits A, B, and C.

Statement (1): We know that the three digits are all nonzero integers, and that $A = 3B = 9C$. Through logic or experimentation, we can determine that C must be equal to 1, making B equal to 3 and A equal to 9. This is true because if C were any higher than 1, A (and, in some cases, B) would be a two-digit integer, and there's no way for a single digit of a number to be two digits long. Therefore, $A = 9$, $B = 3$, and $C = 1$, which gives us the value of k and allows us to calculate $2k$.

Statement (2): This answer seems attractive after statement (1), because it seems to give us the same information. In fact, though, it's much weaker. It's consistent with 931 but with many other values as well. This statement tells us that the ratio of A to B is the same as the ratio of B to C. There are numerous sets of three digits that fit this description, such as 124, 842, and 555, so this statement alone is not sufficient.

The credited response is (A): Statement (1), taken independently, is sufficient to find the value in question, but statement (2) is not.

135. E

This question asks whether the information in one or both statements is sufficient to find a specific value.

In order to answer the question, we need to know or be able to calculate two things: the volume of the water tower and the rate at which water is drained from it.

Statement (1): This statement allows us to calculate the area of the circular base, but we can't calculate the tower's volume without knowing the height. Additionally, nothing is mentioned about the rate of draining. Insufficient.

Statement (2): This statement gives us the rate of draining but tells us nothing about the tower's volume, so it is also not sufficient.

The two statements combined still don't give us the two things we need to know, since we still can't calculate the volume of the tower without its height. Therefore, statements (1) and (2) together are not sufficient to answer the question.

The credited response is (E): The statements don't provide sufficient information to find the value in question, not even when considered together.

136. A

This question asks whether the information in one or both statements is sufficient to answer a yes or no question.

Statement (1):

Simplify: $(x + 10) < 10 - x$

Transpose: $2x < 0$

Divide: $x < 0$

This statement is sufficient.

Statement (2): The fact that x is less than 3 does not help us determine whether x is positive. Possible values for x still include −12, 0, and 2. Therefore, Statement (2) alone is not sufficient.

The credited response is (A): The information provided in statement (1) leads to a definite answer (for the record here, an absolute "yes" in all possible circumstances), but statement (2) allows for both "yes" and "no" answers.

137. A

This question asks whether the information in one or both statements is sufficient to answer a yes or no question.

Statement (1): If $k^2 = 9$, the value of k can be either 3 or −3. Plugging either into the expression $\frac{k + 30}{k}$ gives an integer result, so this statement alone is sufficient to answer the question.

Statement (2): There are integers less than 5 that produce integer results when plugged into $\frac{k + 30}{k}$, such as 3: $\frac{3 + 30}{3} = \frac{33}{3} = 11$. However, there are also integers less than 5 that don't produce integer results, such as 4: $\frac{4 + 30}{4} = \frac{34}{4} = 8.5$. Since either is possible, this statement is not sufficient.

The credited response is (A): The information provided in statement (1) leads to a definite answer (for the record here, an absolute "yes" in all possible circumstances), but statement (2) allows for both "yes" and "no" answers.

138. E

This question asks whether the information in one or both statements is sufficient to find a specific value.

Statement (1): We can infer from this statement that *a* is greater than both *c* and *e*. This tells us nothing about the relative values of *c* and *e*, not to mention *b* and *d*, so we can't know which is the minimum. Insufficient.

Statement (2): This statement suffers from a similar problem; we're told *b* is greater than *d*, but what about *a*, *c*, and *e*? This only proves that the minimum can't be *b*; it could still be any of the other four values. Insufficient.

Even when both statements are taken together, we still know nothing about the relative values of *c*, *d*, and *e*. We know that *a* can't be the minimum (since it's greater than *c* and *e*) and *b* can't be the minimum (since it's greater than *d*), but any of the other three values could be. You could also reach this conclusion by picking different sets of values that fit both statements. If you did this, you'd find it possible to make *c*, *d*, or *e* the minimum under the right conditions. Statements (1) and (2) together are not sufficient to answer the question.

The credited response is (E): The statements don't provide sufficient information to find the value in question, not even when considered together.

139. C

This question asks whether the information in one or both statements is sufficient to find a specific value.

Statement (1): If k and p are consecutive even integers with a product of 48, then there are two possible pairs: One could be 6 and the other 8, or one could be −8 and the other −6. The value of $k + p$ is different in each case, so this statement alone is insufficient. Notice, by the way, that it is much easier to evaluate this informally. If you were to evaluate this formally, you would need to represent k as $p + 2$, plug that expression into the equation $kp = 48$ to get $p(p + 2) = 48$, and so on . . .

Statement (2): There are many positive numbers that multiply to 48, such as 48 and 1, 6 and 8, or 12 and 4. Since they have different sums, this statement alone is also not sufficient.

When we combine the two statements, however, we see that there is only one possible pair of numbers that fits all the conditions (multiply to 48, consecutive even integers, positive): 6 and 8. The sum of $k + p$ is the same whether $k = 6$ and $p = 8$, or vice versa. Therefore, both statements together are sufficient to answer the question.

The credited response is (C): Taken together, statements (1) and (2) are sufficient to find the value in question, but neither statement is sufficient when considered independently.

140. E

This question asks whether the information in one or both statements is sufficient to find a specific value.

The total amount that the auction house charges the seller can be represented as (percentage × selling price) + flat fee. We need to know or be able to calculate all three elements in order to find the dollar amount that the auction house charges Julie.

Statement (1): We're given the percentage, but not the selling price of the item or the flat fee. This statement is not sufficient.

Statement (2): We're given the flat fee, but not the percentage or the selling price. This statement is also not sufficient.

Even when both are combined, we know the percentage and the flat fee, but not the selling price of Julie's item. Since we need that piece of information to calculate how much she owes the auction house, statements (1) and (2) together are not sufficient to answer the question.

The credited response is (E): The statements don't provide sufficient information to find the value in question, not even when considered together.

141. A

This question asks whether the information in one or both statements is sufficient to find a specific value

Notice that you don't necessarily need to solve for the variables x and y in order to solve for the expression $x + y$.

Statement (1): This equation can be changed to $x + 2 + y = 5$, which in turn becomes $x + y = 3$. Clearly, this statement alone is sufficient.

Statement (2): If $(x + y)^2 = 9$, $x + y$ is equal to 3 or −3. Since either one is a possibility, this statement alone is not sufficient.

The credited response is (A): Statement (1), taken independently, is sufficient to find the value in question, but statement (2) is not.

142. D

This question asks whether the information in one or both statements is sufficient to find a specific value.

Statement (1): We know that Keith takes 90 minutes to paint the shelving working alone. Since this is twice as long as it takes the two working together, they can paint the shelving together in 45 minutes. This statement is sufficient.

Statement (2): If Samantha works at exactly the same rate as Keith, then the two working together should take exactly half as long as either one working alone. If this doesn't seem intuitive, you could solve algebraically. Keith paints $\frac{1}{90}$ of the shelving per minute, so Samantha paints $\frac{1}{90}$ of the shelving per minute, so together they paint $\frac{2}{90}$ or $\frac{1}{45}$ of the shelving per minute. Therefore, it takes them 45 minutes working together. You could also represent this as linear feet per minute rather than as jobs per minute.

The credited response is (D): Each statement, taken independently, is sufficient to find the value in question.

143. A

This question asks whether the information in one or both statements is sufficient to answer a yes or no question.

This question is equivalent to the question "Is *z* prime?" (Or, if you want to be precise, "Is *z* composite?") A statement or set of statements will be sufficient if and only if every number that it allows gives the same answer to that question, that is, only if every value is prime *or* every value is not prime.

Statement (1): The positive integers within this range are 24, 25, 26, 27, and 28. None of these are prime. All of these integers have more than two positive integer factors, so this statement is sufficient.

Statement (2): There are odd primes (numbers with only two positive integer factors), such as 17, but there are also odd numbers with more than two positive integer factors, such as 45. Since either could be true, this statement alone is not sufficient.

The credited response is (A): The information provided in statement (1) leads to a definite answer (for the record here, an absolute "yes" in all possible circumstances), but statement (2) allows for both "yes" and "no" answers.

144. E

This question asks whether the information in one or both statements is sufficient to answer a yes or no question.

Statement (1): This statement can be put in terms of g, resulting in $g > 10 - a$. It still tells us nothing about h, though, so it's not sufficient.

Statement (2): Similarly, we know from this statement that $h > 10 - a$, but we're given no information about g. It's also not sufficient.

Using both statements together, we know that $g > 10 - a$ and $h > 10 - a$. The fact that both g and h are greater than the same number tells us nothing about their relative values, however. To prove this, simply make up values. If $a = 6$, then $h > 4$ and $g > 4$. This leaves a lot of possibilities; h could be 8 and g could be 8, or h could be 101 and g could be 15. Therefore, statements (1) and (2) together are not sufficient to answer the question.

Remember, you cannot subtract inequalities so easily, since, in this case, what lives on the left side of each inequality can be anything above 10 to infinity. The subtraction of these figures results in different values depending on the ordering.

The credited response is (E): The information provided in the statements, taken independently or together, is insufficient; both "yes" and "no" answers are still possible (in other words, the answer is always "maybe").

145. A

This question asks whether the information in one or both statements is sufficient to answer a yes or no question.

Statement (1): The range of a set is the difference between the largest and smallest numbers. If the difference between k and n (two numbers in the set) is greater than 5, the range of the set is greater than 5. Whether n and k are the farthest apart or the closest together doesn't matter in deducing that the distance between the largest and smallest numbers must still be greater than 5. This statement is sufficient.

Statement (2): This statement tells us nothing about the range of the set or the difference between any of the numbers, so it is not sufficient.

The credited response is (A): The information provided in statement (1) leads to a definite answer (for the record here, an absolute "yes" in all possible circumstances), but statement (2) allows for both "yes" and "no" answers.

146. B

This question asks whether the information in one or both statements is sufficient to answer a yes or no question.

Translate the information in the question stem before moving on to the statements. If $a < 0.8b$, is $a < 50$?

Statement (1): This statement tells us that a is 20 less than b, and we already know that a is less than 80% of b. The values $a = 20$ and $b = 40$ fit these conditions, and a is less than 50. However, the values $a = 60$ and $b = 80$ also fit these conditions, and a is greater than 50. Since either is possible, this statement alone is insufficient.

Statement (2): Since a is less than 80% of b, and 80% of b is less than b, and b is less than 50, it follows that a must be less than 50. Sufficient.

Therefore, statement 2 alone is sufficient to answer the problem, but statement 1 alone is not sufficient.

The credited response is (B): The information provided in statement (2) leads to a definite answer (for the record here, an absolute "yes" in all possible circumstances), but statement (1) allows for both "yes" and "no" answers.

147. D

This question asks whether the information in one or both statements is sufficient to answer a yes or no question.

Statement (1): Any positive number raised to an odd power is positive, and any negative number raised to an odd power is negative. Therefore, if k^5 is positive, k must also be positive. Sufficient.

Statement (2): Dividing both sides of this equation by –3 results in $k > 0$ (don't forget to flip the sign), so k must be positive. Sufficient.

Each statement alone is sufficient to answer the question. You could check this by making up values for k. You'll find that for each statement, the inequality holds true if and only if k is positive.

The credited response is (D): Each statement, when considered independently, leads to an absolute answer in all circumstances (for the record here, both "yes").

148. C

This question asks whether the information in one or both statements is sufficient to find a specific value.

Statement (1): The only pairs of single-digit numbers in which one is the square of the other are 1 and 1, 2 and 4, and 3 and 9. We're told that the digits add to 6, so the pair must be 2 and 4. However, this means that t could be either 24 or 42, so this statement alone is not sufficient.

Statement (2): There are quite a few two-digit numbers greater than 30, so this statement alone is also not sufficient.

Both statements together, though, tell us that t is either 24 or 42 and that t is greater than 30. This allows us to determine that t is equal to 42. Therefore, both statements together are sufficient to answer the question.

The credited response is (C): Taken together, Statements (1) and (2) are sufficient to find the value in question, but neither statement is sufficient when considered independently.

149. E

This question asks whether the information in one or both statements is sufficient to answer a yes or no question.

Statement (1): Values of m and n that add to 7 include 3 and 4, which multiply to 12, and 2 and 5, which multiply to 10. Since mn could be either greater than 11 or less than 11, this statement is not sufficient.

Statement (2): Values of m and n that satisfy these two inequalities include $m = 5$ and $n = 4$, which multiply to 20, and $m = 3$ and $n = 2$, which multiply to 6. Again, we can't tell whether mn is less than 11 or not, so this statement is also not sufficient.

When both statements are combined, values of m and n must satisfy both inequalities *and* add to 7. One possibility is $m = 4$ and $n = 3$, which would make $mn = 12$. Another possibility is $m = 5$ and $n = 2$, which would make $mn = 10$. We still don't know whether mn is less than 11. Statements (1) and (2) together are not sufficient to answer the question.

The credited response is (E): The information provided in the statements, taken independently or together, is insufficient; both "yes" and "no" answers are still possible (in other words, the answer is always "maybe").

150. D

This question asks whether the information in one or both statements is sufficient to find a specific value.

Statement (1): The difference between October profit and September profit is equal to 10.3% - 9.8% = 0.5% of total sales. We're also told that the difference between October and September profit is equal to $19,600. We can calculate total sales per month by dividing $19,600 by 0.5%, or 0.005. Whatever that quotient is, multiply it by 10.3%, or 10.3, to get October's profit. Remember that we don't need to actually solve the problem. We just need to be certain that we can. If you're in the mood for some computation, $\frac{\$19{,}600}{0.005} =$ $3,920,000. Profit in October is 10.3% of this number. This statement is sufficient.

Statement (2): Since profit in September is 9.8% of total sales, we can calculate total sales by dividing $384,160 by 9.8%, or 0.098. Whatever that quotient is, multiply it by 10.3%, or 10.3, to get October's profit. If you're in the mood for some computation, you'll discover that $\frac{\$384{,}160}{0.098} = \$3{,}920{,}000$. This statement is sufficient.

The credited response is (D): Each statement, taken independently, is sufficient to find the value in question.

Chapter 3

Verbal

Section Overview

COMPOSITION OF THE VERBAL SECTION

In the Verbal section, you have 75 minutes to answer 41 Verbal questions in three formats: Critical Reasoning, Reading Comprehension, and Sentence Correction. These three types of questions are presented in no particular order throughout the Verbal section, so you never know what's coming next. Here's what you can expect to see:

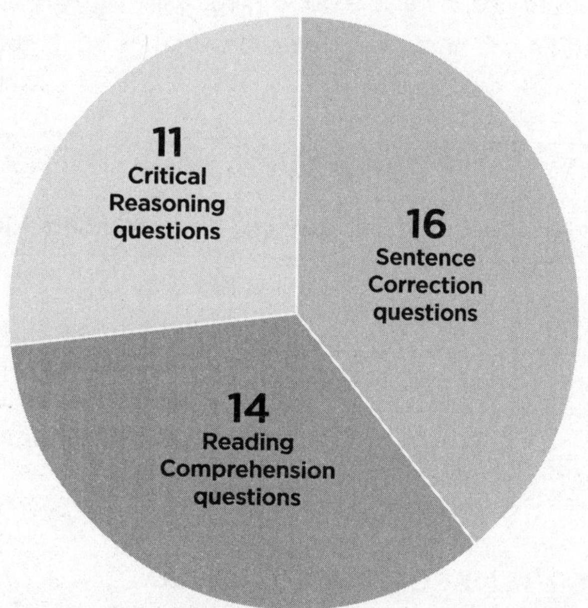

The Approximate Mix of Questions on the GMAT Verbal Section: 11 Critical Reasoning Questions, 14 Reading Comprehension Questions, and 16 Sentence Correction Questions

You may see more of one question type and fewer of another. Don't worry. It's likely just a slight difference in the types of "experimental" questions you get.

PACING ON THE VERBAL SECTION

For Critical Reasoning, you will want to read, understand, and select an answer for each question in about two minutes. Passages or arguments with less text may take less time, while complex arguments with more text may take slightly longer than two minutes.

The GMAT will also give you four Reading Comprehension passages. Two will likely be longer and have four questions each, and two will likely be shorter and have three questions each.

Sentence Correction questions should be tackled quickly and efficiently. Spending about one minute per question will allow you the time you'll need for longer Critical Reasoning and Reading Comprehension questions.

While it's far more important at first that you practice to build accuracy and mastery of the strategies, it's also a good idea to keep these timing recommendations in mind. Add more and more timed practice as you progress in your GMAT prep.

Verbal Section Timing	
Question Type	**Average Time You Should Spend**
Sentence Correction	1 minute per question
Critical Reasoning	2 minutes per question
Reading Comprehension	4 minutes per passage and a little less than 1.5 minutes per question

HOW THE VERBAL SECTION IS SCORED

Your GMAT score is not determined by the number of questions you answer correctly but rather by the difficulty level of the questions you answer correctly. When you begin a section, the computer

- assumes you have an average score (about 550), and
- gives you a medium-difficulty question. About half the people who take the test will get this question right, and half will get it wrong. What happens next depends on whether you answer the question correctly.

If you answer the question correctly,

- your score goes up, and
- you are given a more difficult question.

If you answer the question incorrectly,

- your score goes down, and
- you are given a less difficult question.

As you get questions right, the computer raises your score and gives you harder questions. If you feel like you're struggling at the end of the section, don't worry! Because the CAT adapts to find the outer edge of your abilities, the test will feel hard; it's designed to be difficult for everyone, even the highest scorers.

Critical Reasoning

PREVIEWING CRITICAL REASONING

Over 70 percent of Critical Reasoning questions are based on arguments, so understanding what they are and how they work will be of great help on Test Day.

An argument in Critical Reasoning means any piece of text with a clear point of view and statements that support that point of view. A statement such as "Susan should be elected board president" is not an argument—it's just an opinion. An argument must make some attempt to persuade. For instance, if the opinion statement above included a reason or two to support its point of view, then it would become a simple argument: "Susan should be elected board president because she has more experience than the other candidates." These main parts of the argument are referred to as the conclusion (the author's main point) and the evidence (the statements that support that point).

WHAT IS AN ASSUMPTION?

An assumption in the context of a GMAT argument is an unstated premise that an argument "depends" or "relies" on to allow a conclusion to hold true. Critical Reasoning questions that ask for an argument's assumption could be paraphrased as follows: "What important fact does the author of the argument take for granted but not directly state?" or "What else would need to be true in order for this argument to hold?" Identifying the central assumption is key to answering Critical Reasoning questions that involve arguments.

QUESTION FORMAT AND STRUCTURE

About 11 Critical Reasoning questions appear on the Verbal section of the GMAT. Critical Reasoning (CR) tests reasoning skills involved in making arguments, evaluating arguments, and formulating or evaluating a plan of action. These questions are based on materials from a variety of sources, though you will not need to be familiar with any subject matter beforehand.

The directions for Critical Reasoning questions are short and to the point. They look like this:

> **Directions:** Select the best answer choices given.

On the GMAT, in business school, and in your career, you'll need the ability to recognize and understand complex reasoning. It's not enough to sense whether an argument is strong or weak; you'll need to analyze precisely why it is so. This presumes a fundamental skill that's called on by nearly every Critical Reasoning question—the ability to isolate and identify the various components of any given argument.

Critical Reasoning Practice

1. Chemical pregnancy tests that measure the presence of human chorionic gonadotropin (HCG) sometimes exhibit a false negative, indicating that the woman is not pregnant when in fact she is; the tests can also give a false positive response, indicating that the woman is pregnant when she actually is not. Consumers should seek the pregnancy test with the lowest proportion of false negative results in order to most accurately detect pregnancy with an at-home test.

   The conclusion is most strongly supported by which of the following, if true?

   - O Some ultrasounds can detect pregnancy as early as one week into the gestation.
   - O Early symptoms of a pregnancy can include nausea, increased hunger, and disturbed sleep patterns.
   - O Prenatal medical supervision should begin as soon after conception as possible.
   - O All at-home pregnancy tests have the same rate of inconclusive test results.
   - O All at-home pregnancy tests produce the same proportion of false positive results.

2. While belly dancing is often marginalized within the dance world and not considered a valid art form, it is as much a valid art form as any dance, since it is performance centered with a repertoire of choreography and a rich history.

   The conclusion depends on which of the following assumptions?

   - O If people are willing to pay to see a dance performed, the dance should be considered an art form.
   - O Since belly dancing is performance centered, audiences usually enjoy the stories behind the dances as well as the dances themselves.
   - O If a dance does not have a rich history, it is not an art form.
   - O Any dance that is performance centered, with a repertoire of choreography and a rich history, is a valid art form.
   - O Since belly dancing has a repertoire of choreography, it can be taught easily.

3. More citizens of Alphaville tune in to nightly news programs than do citizens of Bentonville. Thus, citizens of Alphaville know more about global issues than do citizens of Bentonville.

   The conclusion is weakened by all of the following EXCEPT:

   - The population of Alphaville is 2,000,000; the population of Bentonville is 1,000,000.
   - Citizens of Bentonville are more likely to listen to news radio programs than are citizens of Alphaville.
   - Citizens of Alphaville generally put the television on as background noise during dinner and chores, while citizens of Bentonville never watch television unless they are paying full attention to it.
   - The nightly news programs in Alphaville are restricted to tabloid coverage of celebrities.
   - Citizens in Bentonville can view nightly news programs only by purchasing cable television access.

4. Purchasers of laptop computers generally do not use them often enough to justify the cost. Presumably, laptop computers are more expensive than desktop computers due to the laptop computers' portability. However, one survey showed that only 22% of laptop computer owners had used them outside the home in the past 30 days.

   The conclusion that purchasers of laptop computers do not use them often enough to justify the cost is most called into question by which of the following?

   - Some laptop computer owners do not like to take their laptops to school or work out of fear that the computers will be damaged or stolen.
   - Laptop computer owners sometimes overestimate how often they use their laptops outside the home.
   - Laptop computer owners often use their laptop computers in different locations around their own homes.
   - Laptop computer owners usually prefer to purchase computers that have wireless Internet capability, so the computers are more mobile.
   - Laptop computer owners who use their laptop computers outside the home tend to do so at least three times per week.

5. The Mabella temple in Italy was built at some point during the 1400s, but a more precise date has not been found in any records of the building. However, stonemasons of the period used distinctive methods of engraving cornerstones to mark their work, and the Mabella temple is marked by five different stonemasons who worked successively, indicating that construction of the temple was disrupted at various points. It is therefore likely that the temple was constructed between 1420 and 1430, when there was a series of stonemason labor stoppages in Italy.

   The theory that the Mabella temple was constructed between 1420 and 1430 is most supported by which of the following?

   - It is not unusual for several different stonemasons to work on the same building at various times.
   - Labor stoppages among stonemasons' unions were common in other parts of Europe during the 1300s and 1400s.
   - A master stonemason could be expected to lay up to 300 stones in a day.
   - Labor disturbances are the only reason that a stonemason would not work on the same project from start to finish.
   - Three of the five stonemasons who worked on the Mabella temple appear to have done so for only a short time.

6. Bob's Café, a busy restaurant, has decided to stop serving steak, which takes much longer to cook, and concentrate instead on poultry dishes. The management believes that this will allow servers to speed up customer turnover and therefore maximize profits by serving as many customers as possible at each meal.

   The Bob's Café management's plan to speed up customer turnover would be most undermined by which of the following?

   - Chicken takes only half as long to cook as steak in most instances.
   - Chicken is less expensive than steak for Bob's Café to purchase.
   - Chicken dishes can be sold for nearly as much as steak dishes.
   - The bistro next door to Bob's Café will continue to serve steak.
   - Customers who order chicken tend to order dessert much more frequently than do customers who order steak.

7. Assessing the potential earnings of tipped service employees can be difficult. Take as an example restaurant waiters: one might assume that the more customers a waiter has, the higher his earnings will be. But this fails to take into account the degree to which the service rendered might suffer when a waiter has so many customers that he cannot fully devote himself to the needs of any of them.

   The flaw in the example discussed in the argument relates to doubts about the accuracy of which of the following claims?

   - O The earnings of restaurant waiters are approximately the same as the earnings of other tipped service employees.
   - O Restaurant waiters' primary duty is to attend to the needs of their customers.
   - O The potential earnings of tipped service employees should be measured by examining average earnings rather than the earnings of specific individuals.
   - O A restaurant waiter's potential earnings depend on the quantity of customers he serves, not on the quality of service he renders.
   - O A restaurant waiter's earnings depend in part on how many customers he serves.

8. Freelance writers for *News Magazine* retain the copyrights to their articles. Joe, a freelance writer for *News Magazine*, has heard that *News Magazine* plans to assemble an online compilation of past issues. Joe believes that this will enable him to sell the copyrights to his *News Magazine* articles back to the magazine for use in the online compilation.

   Which of the following, if true, most calls into question the potential success of Joe's plan?

   - O Unlike *News Magazine*, most magazines automatically purchase the copyright to any articles that they accept from freelance writers.
   - O Under the federal tax code, copyrights are subject to amortization, and therefore the value of their basis declines over time.
   - O In Joe's full-time job, he is a computer programmer, not a writer.
   - O *News Magazine* owns the copyright to each issue of the magazine as a whole and can therefore republish those issues in any media without seeking any additional copyrights.
   - O News Magazine is considering moving into a weekly, rather than monthly, publication schedule.

9. Scientists believe that human heterosexual attraction can primarily be traced back to evolutionary drives. For instance, men are attracted to women with a waist to hip ratio of 0.7, clear skin, and large eyes, because these features signal youthfulness and reproductive viability.

   The scientists' belief described in the argument is most weakened by which of the following, if true?

   - Men are also attracted to women with high foreheads.
   - Scientists have observed that apes are more prone to mate with members of the opposite sex who display markers of fertility.
   - Women are typically attracted to men with square jaws and masculine features indicating high testosterone levels.
   - Some men prefer women with brown hair to women with black, blonde, or red hair.
   - Women with waists roughly the same size as their hips and women with a waist to hip ratio of 0.7 scored the same when rated by 1,000 heterosexual men in an anonymous study of attractiveness.

10. The school district's plan to build a new, expanded school building in Townsville is ridiculous. While there is enough money in the budget to pay for a larger building, there would be none left over to pay the salaries of additional teachers, so the additional new classrooms would sit empty and unused.

    The conclusion of the argument is most called into question by which of the following?

    - A larger school building will allow for expanded extracurricular facilities.
    - The new proposed school building would have space for nineteen more classrooms than does the current building.
    - Paying for the larger school building would force the school district to cut back its bus services.
    - The condition of a school building correlates with many other factors, including low dropout rates and high standardized test scores.
    - In the current school building, there is not space for all the classes, and many classes are held in portable trailers on the school grounds.

11. The average salary for a teacher who has been teaching for five years in the United States is $30,000 per year. Thus, a teacher who has been teaching for five years in the United States and makes $28,000 per year has received below-average raises, compared to the average teacher.

The reasoning in the argument demonstrates which of the following flaws?

- O Average salary does not take into account insurance benefits and vacation time.
- O Math and science teachers usually are paid slightly more than English teachers.
- O A salary of $28,000 is within the range of acceptable salaries for an experienced teacher.
- O Just because a raise is below average does not mean that the teacher's salary is not commensurate with the cost of living.
- O A conclusion about raises cannot be based on evidence that only addresses salary without regard for salary history.

12. In order for a union-organized workers' strike to succeed, the union must have the support of both the workers and members of the public. The employees of the Galt Hybrid Auto Plant support a strike, but the demand for hybrid autos is high, and the public will probably be opposed to the strike, as it will lead to a shortage of Galt autos. Therefore, ________.

Which of the following best completes the passage?

- O consumers will probably choose to buy cars from Galt's competitors in the event of a strike.
- O public support is not necessary for a successful union-organized strike.
- O a workers' strike at the Galt Hybrid Auto Plant would require the workers to withdraw their services in order to force the company to accede to the union's demands.
- O a union-organized workers' strike at the Galt Hybrid Auto Plant is unlikely to succeed.
- O Workers are unlikely to support a union-organized strike if the balance of public opinion is against the strike.

13. Some professional football players choose to diversify their training regimens by engaging in nontraditional conditioning activities like ballet, yoga, and Pilates, all of which promote flexibility and grace.

    All of the following provide reasons why professional football players might choose to participate in nontraditional conditioning activities EXCEPT:

    - Ballet's use of turnout strengthens small, injury-prone leg muscles in ways that traditional football strength training does not.
    - Ballet helps to increase the range of hip motion enjoyed by practitioners and can therefore decrease athletes' risk for groin strains.
    - Some dance movements echo the evasive maneuvers that football players employ on the field.
    - The enhanced flexibility enjoyed by practitioners of yoga and Pilates can reduce the stress that contact sports put on ligaments and tendons.
    - Like football players, ballet dancers have a high incidence of lower back and spinal injuries.

14. The average heart rates of a group of experienced runners and a group of novice runners were taken at various points throughout the day, and the scientists studying those heart rates were surprised to find that even though the experienced runners ran an average of 40% faster than the novice runners, their heart rates were 25% lower during peak exertion than were those of the novice runners.

    Which of the following best explains the scientists' findings?

    - Running generally places more stress on the cardiovascular system than does swimming or biking.
    - Experienced runners tend to enjoy more elevated levels of endorphins while running than do novice runners.
    - As runners gain experience, their hearts become strong enough that they don't have to exert themselves as much as novice runners, even when they outperform the less experienced runners.
    - All runners' average heart rates increase when they run in colder weather.
    - Runners whose goal is stress reduction tend to enjoy the activity more than do runners whose goal is weight loss.

15. During the busy holiday season, the Jones Toy Factory typically spends more money on maintaining its equipment and on safety precautions than it does when there is less demand for its products. Based on this information, there should be fewer employee injuries during the holidays.

    The conclusion of the argument is most called into question by which of the following facts about the Jones Toy Factory, if true?

    - Employees are eligible for production bonuses during the holiday season.
    - Temporary employees are often brought in to work in the factory during the holidays, but because of time limitations, they are rarely as well trained as the year-round employees.
    - Employees have greater job security during the holidays than they do during the rest of the year.
    - There is a cash prize each month for the division that has the best safety record.
    - The owners stay well-informed about new machinery that could be safer for factory workers, and they upgrade to that machinery whenever possible.

16. Recent U.S. legislation limiting the emissions permissible from automobiles will require auto manufacturers to incorporate new technology and more costly components into cars. This will drive up the price of cars, both at home and abroad. Therefore, the legislation will result in the loss of many export markets.

    The argument is most seriously weakened by which of the following?

    - Most of the countries to which U.S. automobiles are exported have recently enacted similar legislation limiting emissions.
    - Noncompliance with the new legislation can be punished with high fines.
    - Training factory workers to use the new technology required to manufacture compliant automobiles will be expensive and time-consuming.
    - Some automobile manufacturers will choose to relocate their plants to other countries that do not have stringent emissions standards.
    - Environmental groups have been leaning heavily on the auto industry to voluntarily institute such emissions standards.

17. Consumers formerly purchased designer clothing because designer clothing was of better workmanship and was made of higher-quality materials than was other clothing. However, with many high-end designers now producing low-cost capsule collections for mass-market retailers, a designer label is no longer a guarantee that the clothing will be of higher quality than similarly priced nondesigner clothing. Interestingly, however, designer clothing has become even more highly sought after in recent years.

    The paradox is best resolved by which of the following, if true?

    - Consumers believe that a designer label assures them that the clothing to which that label is affixed is as high in quality as any similarly priced nondesigner clothing.
    - Many consumers are concerned about the possibility of sweatshop labor playing a role in the production of designer clothing.
    - Successful designers sometimes license their names for use on collections that they actually play no role in creating.
    - The Internet makes it easier than ever for young designers to get exposure for their work and make a name for themselves.
    - Designer collections sold by mass-market retailers are often priced as reasonably as are similar nondesigner goods sold at the same stores.

18. Divers have discovered the wreckage of an unidentified ship about thirty miles from the shore near Boston. Scholars believe that the ship sank during a devastating hurricane that swept through the northeastern United States and down the coast in 1872, but there are no records of the ship available to confirm this hypothesis.

The scholars' hypothesis is most strongly supported by which of the following, if true?

- Among the cargo found on board the wreckage of the ship were several trunks of woodworking tools of a kind that were popular from about 1850 to 1890.
- Among the munitions discovered on board the wreckage were several trunks of guns of varieties that were popular in the late 1860s; no munitions manufactured subsequent to 1870 were discovered.
- It is widely accepted that Hurricane Bridie caused significant damage in the northeastern United States in 1872.
- Ceramics and pottery glazed in a style that was popular during the latter half of the 19th century were found among the wreckage of the ship, along with assorted items of cutlery.
- Divers found clay pipes in the cargo hold that were of a kind sold in tobacco shops in the early 1900s.

19. University professors are entitled to keep the royalties from any of their own faculty publications, although the university itself keeps the royalties from any patentable inventions that result from the professors' research. Thus, it is reasonable to conclude that university professors should be entitled to keep the royalties from any computer programs that they create based on their research.

Which of the following assumptions best supports the conclusion of the argument?

- Patents yield higher royalties than do faculty publications.
- University professors create more computer programs than patentable inventions.
- Universities receive more prestige from patentable inventions than from faculty publications.
- Most universities have found that computer programs based on professorial research are more profitable than are faculty publications.
- Under the standards by which royalties are awarded to university professors, computer programs based on faculty research are more analogous to faculty publications than to patentable inventions.

20. One function of highway engineers is to design traffic patterns that eliminate bottlenecks and delays. This also eliminates potholes and buckled asphalt, since bottlenecks and delays are often caused by potholes and buckled asphalt.

    The claim about the elimination of potholes and buckled asphalt assumes which of the following?

    - O All potholes and buckled asphalt cause bottlenecks and delays.
    - O Only highway engineers have the necessary skills to eliminate bottlenecks and delays.
    - O Municipal highway authorities are generally underfunded.
    - O One method for decreasing bottlenecks is synchronizing stoplights to stagger traffic appropriately.
    - O Highway engineers are not always successful in completely regulating the flow of traffic in urban areas.

21. At the Jones Thingamajig Factory, machinists are accustomed to working with Machine A. However, it has been reported that Machine B will allow the machinists, once trained, to work more quickly and with less possibility of muscle strain from repetitive motions. Therefore, replacing every Machine A in the Thingamajig Factory with a Machine B will immediately result in increased efficiency and higher profits for the factory.

    The conclusion is most called into question by which of the following?

    - O Machinists who are accustomed to both Machine A and Machine B have found that transitioning from Machine B to Machine A is more challenging than transitioning from Machine A to Machine B.
    - O Machine B is less expensive than Machine A and needs less maintenance.
    - O Most Thingamajig factories are transitioning to the use of Machine B.
    - O Training machinists accustomed to Machine A to use Machine B can be time-consuming and expensive.
    - O Inexperienced machinists can learn to use Machine B as easily as they can learn to use Machine A.

22. Metropolis-area dry cleaners have had a steady increase in business over the past year, and in order to take advantage of this trend and expand its market share, Neuman's Dry Cleaning is planning to expand its facilities to enable it to handle a higher volume of garments. Neuman's will maintain the same prices and weekly specials that it has employed for the past several years.

    The potential success of Neuman's plan to increase its market share is most called into question by which of the following, if true?

    - Neuman's share of the local dry cleaning market has declined over the past year, but its dry cleaning facilities are always at maximum capacity.
    - The average turnaround time to get a garment dry cleaned at Neuman's is slightly longer now than it was a year ago.
    - Most customers are not aware that Mr. Neuman sold his dry cleaning company to a franchise five years ago and no longer runs the facility himself.
    - Neuman's is one of the two most popular dry cleaners in Metropolis.
    - Despite a recent increase in advertising, Neuman's has been slightly less busy over the past six months than it was previously.

23. Eatco, a restaurant equipment supply firm, has decided to pay all of its salespeople on a commission structure rather than with the salaries that they previously received. Eatco executives have assured the sales staff that, with the busy holiday season coming up, the commission structure will either maintain or increase the salespeople's current pay.

    Which of the following could cause the assurances given by Eatco executives to the sales staff to be untrue?

    - A competing restaurant equipment supply firm also switches its salespeople over to a commission structure.
    - Some customers request items that are out of stock and have to be ordered.
    - The old salary structure did not include health insurance, but the commission structure provides salespeople with the option to subscribe to a cafeteria-style insurance plan.
    - Several new restaurants are opening in the area.
    - The Eatco executives decided to hire several new salespeople on the commission structure, in order to make sure that all customers are getting the best possible service.

24. Politician: Increasingly, citizens attempting to travel internationally are turned away at borders due to what are deemed suspicious travel documents. Some observers suggest that if any citizens of our country are denied entry at a border, we should retaliate by refusing to allow entrance at our borders to nationals of the denying country. However, if every country instituted this policy, soon international travel would be a thing of the past.

    Which of the following assumptions is necessary to the politician's argument?

    - There are no countries that currently retaliate against other countries that deny travelers entrance at their borders.
    - Retaliation against other countries with stringent border checks is never justified.
    - The border crossing difficulties of individual civilians are not appropriate subject matter for political action.
    - Every country will eventually deny entrance to at least one citizen of every other country.
    - Terrorism has increased the stringency of border-crossing regulations.

25. In an effort to lose body fat, Tom has decided to begin engaging in regular cardiovascular and muscle-building exercise. He plans to continue to eat only when hungry, as he does now. Although muscle gain may initially cause him to gain weight, it will also increase his metabolism, and he is confident that this will soon lead to a reduction in his overall body fat.

    If true, which of the following most calls into question the possible success of Tom's body fat reduction plan?

    - Increased cardiovascular exercise and a heightened metabolism due to muscle gain will cause Tom's appetite to increase significantly.
    - The weight of any body fat lost will be offset by the weight that Tom will gain in muscle.
    - Many people who plan to start a fitness program soon revert to their old habits.
    - Tom knows that he is likely to experience muscle soreness and fatigue when beginning a new fitness regimen.
    - Tom's plan for muscle-building exercise emphasizes his upper body instead of the major muscle groups in his lower body.

26. In one demonstration, a hypnotist will put his subject under and then tell her that she is deaf. He will then ask her if she can answer him, and the subject will reply, "No." One explanation that has been posited for this puzzling behavior is that the hypnotized subject has dissociated herself into different parts, and the part that responds to the hypnotist's question is separate from the part that is unable to hear.

    The explanation posited in the argument is most seriously called into question by which of the following queries?

    - Why doesn't the part of the subject that replies say, "Yes"?
    - Why is any explanation necessary for the phenomenon?
    - Why doesn't the subject question the suggestion that she is mute?
    - Why doesn't the explanation attempt to address the possibility that some subjects will behave differently?
    - Why don't some subjects dissociate themselves differently?

27. Homing pigeons released in unfamiliar territory will, within a short period of time, orient themselves to their location and find their way home. However, the time required for homing pigeons to get their bearings can be increased by plugging their nostrils.

    The phenomenon described in the argument is best explained by which of the following?

    - Homing pigeons have a more advanced sense of smell than do other birds.
    - The further from home a homing pigeon is released, the longer it takes the bird to get its bearings.
    - Male homing pigeons are more efficient at finding their bearings than are females.
    - Homing pigeons can find their bearings even in total darkness.
    - A homing pigeon's ability to home is guided by an olfactory map of its territory.

28. Maureen, a smoker, is a resident of the State of Wissesota. Wissesota has instituted a very high tax on cigarettes to discourage smoking. Maureen lives about 40 miles away from the neighboring State of Minconsin, a tobacco-growing state where cigarettes are tax-free. It is cheaper for Maureen to obtain her cigarettes in Minconsin than in Wissesota.

Which of the following, if true, supports the statements above?

- O Beer and wine are also cheaper in Minconsin than in Wissesota.
- O It is a violation of Wissesota state law for a resident of Wissesota to bring cigarettes purchased in another state across Wissesota state lines.
- O The cost of transporting cigarettes from Minconsin to Wissesota is less per pack than the sales tax on each pack of cigarettes purchased in Wissesota.
- O With gas prices at an all-time high, it is more expensive to drive to Minconsin to buy cigarettes than to pay the high cigarette tax in Wissesota.
- O Tobacco farming has been the linchpin of the Minconsin economy for decades.

29. Mayor: Downtown Rosco Lake is generally a clean area, but the Monday after the Fourth of July weekend, there was twice as much trash in the streets and parks as usual. Since downtown Rosco Lake is a major tourist destination on weekends, it must be the tourists who are littering.

The mayor's argument is most called into question by which of the following, if true?

- O Usually, community volunteers go through downtown on Monday mornings, picking up litter.
- O There is a correlation between tourist traffic and incidents of vandalism in many towns.
- O During the other weekends in July, there were no unusual amounts of litter.
- O The North Shore lakefront area in Rosco Lake is rarely visited by tourists and has almost no litter, compared to the South Shore, which is a touristy area and has lots of rubbish lying around.
- O The nearby town of Graylord was able to control its litter problem by instituting large fines that could be levied against litterers.

30. The proposed system of road improvements in Metropolis is fundamentally flawed, since the increased cost of gas and a highly efficient and functional public transportation are increasingly leading consumers to choose bus and train travel over driving. Therefore, the money that would be spent on road improvements should be redirected to further funding the operation of the public transportation system.

    The argument is most called into question by which of the following, if true?

    - Road improvements will create hundreds of new jobs in Metropolis.
    - Biking is both more economical and faster than driving within the city.
    - Buses also utilize the roads in Metropolis.
    - Commuting in trains and buses is more environmentally friendly than commuting in individual autos.
    - High tolls on the highways around Metropolis have led many commuters from the suburbs to favor the rail system over driving.

31. Restaurant service workers never want negative customer feedback to reflect poorly on them, so if such feedback is reported to management at all, it is generally minimized or twisted to preserve the worker's reputation. The restaurant manager therefore is generally less aware of any dissatisfied customers than are the service workers.

    On which of the following assumptions does the argument rely?

    - Restaurant service workers should resolve customer complaints whenever possible.
    - Restaurants should put in place incentive programs to encourage service workers to relay customer feedback more thoroughly.
    - Restaurant managers are generally more skilled at handling disgruntled customers than are service workers.
    - The only way that restaurant managers receive information about negative customer feedback is through the service workers.
    - Some restaurant service workers care more about good customer service than about the ways in which others perceive their job performance.

32. At human body temperature, the influenza virus can remain infectious for approximately one week. Because the virus becomes inactive in the human body after one week, an infected person cannot be held responsible for any transmission of the virus after that time has elapsed.

The conclusion is most weakened by which of the following, if true?

- The influenza virus is sometimes confused with the unrelated gastroenteritis.
- The influenza vaccine is highly effective in preventing transmission of the influenza virus.
- Because the influenza virus mutates, a vaccine that is effective in preventing transmission of the virus one year may be ineffective a year later.
- The influenza virus can remain infectious for longer than a week at temperatures below that of the human body.
- Generally, those most susceptible to life-threatening illness as a result of the influenza virus are children, the elderly, and those with compromised immune systems.

33. The profitability of a restaurant can be judged by neither the consistency of its overhead costs nor its daily receipts alone. Consistent overhead costs can be undercut by declining daily receipts, and high daily receipts may not signal significant profits if overhead costs increase. Both must be balanced in order to accurately evaluate how profitable a restaurant is.

The passage implies that the best indicator of a restaurant's profitability is the restaurant's

- consistent overhead costs balanced by high daily receipts.
- consistent overhead costs offset by declining daily receipts.
- increased overhead costs balanced by high daily receipts.
- decreased overhead costs offset by declining daily receipts.
- consistent daily receipts balanced by high overhead costs.

34. The coal mines at Newcastle were so rich that the coal mined there glutted the Scottish market, sending nationwide coal prices downward. To bolster coal prices, the Scottish Parliament offered mine owners who took 15% of the mine shafts out of production a direct subsidy payment, up to a certain maximum cap per mine. Scotland's subsidy program, though successful, was not a net burden on the budget.

Which of the following, if true, is the best explanation of the author's conclusion?

- O The nation lost tax revenues when lowered coal prices caused financial losses for mine owners.
- O The year that Scotland adopted this subsidy program, coal mining output in other parts of the UK fell 5%.
- O Available mine shaft area was 10% below its average level during the first year that Scotland adopted this subsidy program.
- O The maximum subsidy per mine caused subsidy payments per idle acre to be less for large mines than for smaller ones.
- O If mine owners took the subsidy, they found they could not put the idle mine land to any use.

35. Soldier: I am thinking of having my crew switch from Uzi submachine guns to Tommy guns.

Lieutenant: Why?

Soldier: Training new recruits on the Tommy would achieve a cost reduction of 9.9%.

Lieutenant: But that reason alone is not persuasive enough. We can instead recruit only people who already have experience in using the Uzi gun.

Which of the following, if true, most seriously undermines the lieutenant's objection to the replacement of Uzi submachine guns with Tommy guns?

- O All new enforcers in the syndicate must attend workshops on proper care and use of the Uzi gun in new situations.
- O Recruits, upon learning to use guns, change syndicates or become free-lancers more often.
- O Experienced users of the Uzi get much higher wages, as compared with enforcers who are inexperienced in gun use.
- O The average earnings of enforcers in the lieutenant's crew are below the average of enforcers in competing crews.
- O Jammed Tommy guns cost more to repair than Uzis.

36. Large-scale use of synthetic antibiotics has two extremely insidious consequences. First, antibodies that would naturally target the bacteria may also be killed off by the antibiotic. Second, the process often gives rise to strains of bacteria resistant to particular antibiotics because resistant strains have a better chance of surviving the antibiotic long enough to multiply.

    From this passage, it can be inferred that the effectiveness of large-scale use of synthetic antibiotics can be extended by which of the following, assuming each is feasible?

    - Using only antibiotics that are stable in the body
    - Regularly rotating the type of antibiotics used in the body
    - Constantly increasing the doses of antibiotics applied
    - Letting the body recuperate naturally
    - Attempting to increase the amount of blood in the body temporarily

37. Old, long-standing firms concentrate on protecting what they have already amassed. Consequently, they rarely innovate and often underestimate what consequences innovation by other companies will have. The best example of one such defensive strategy is the fact that ________.

    Which of the following best completes this passage?

    - electronics and mass-produced gears eliminated the traditional market for pocket watches, clearing the way for marketing them as elegant, old-fashioned luxury items.
    - an extremely popular prefabricated house was introduced by a company that, several years before, had failed miserably with its product line of glass houses.
    - a once-leading maker of buggy whips responds to the new availability of stick shifts by attempting to make better buggy whips.
    - smoking pipes, originally designed for use by typically older, more traditional smokers of tobacco, are now bought mostly by young smokers of scented or flavored herbal blends.
    - the psychiatrist who invented the anti-inhibition drug MDM did not mean for his product to be used by partygoers, who buy most of the drug now called "Ecstasy."

38. Two decades after the Dead Sea Barrier was built, none of the eight sea slug types indigenous to the Dead Sea was still growing adequately in the sea on one side of the barrier. Since the barrier reduced the annual range of salinity (percentage of salt) in the sea on one side of the barrier from 30% to 6%, scientists have hypothesized that sharply rising salinity must be involved in signaling the indigenous types of slugs to begin the growing cycle.

Which of the following statements, if true, would most strengthen the scientists' theory?

- The indigenous sea slug types could still grow only on one side of the barrier, where the yearly salinity range remained 30%.
- Before the barrier was constructed, the Dead Sea overflowed its shores yearly, creating salt licks that became key feeding spots for the indigenous types of sea slug.
- Before the barrier was built, the lowest recorded salinity of the Dead Sea was 16%, whereas after the barrier was built, the lowest recorded salinity of the Sea has been 25%.
- Nonindigenous types of sea slug, introduced into the Dead Sea after the barrier's construction, started competing with the declining indigenous sea slug types for salt.
- Of the sea slug types indigenous to the Dead Sea, six are not indigenous to any other sea in the Middle East.

39. At the Centers for Disease Control and Prevention, epidemiologists recently proved that sandwiches, even if left in refrigerators, can become infested with viruses that cause red plague and black plague in the stomach. They found that infestation usually occurs after sandwiches have been left for seven weeks. For that reason, people should discard leftover sandwiches at least once every seven weeks.

    Which of the following, if true, would most weaken the conclusion provided?

    - The epidemiologists could not understand why infestation happened only after sandwiches were left for seven weeks, and not before.
    - The epidemiologists did not research possible infestation of sandwiches by bacteria, bugs, and other pathogenic organisms.
    - The epidemiologists found that, in people who ate sandwiches infested with viruses that cause red plague and black plague, the infection rate for these plagues was no higher than among people who did not eat infested sandwiches.
    - The epidemiologists discovered that eaters who irradiated their sandwiches in a microwave thoroughly and sterilized the eating area were as likely to have infested sandwiches as were people who only dusted off their sandwiches.
    - The epidemiologists discovered that, for sandwiches left in the refrigerator for nine weeks, being left for longer durations did not correlate with a higher number of viruses being present.

40. Usually, clergy enter their vocation motivated by a desire to do charitable deeds and view as colleagues those with the same desire. Thus, whenever a clergy member gains prominence as a televangelist to the public, most other clergy members no longer view the televangelist as a true colleague.

    The explanation offered for the low opinion of televangelists held by clergy members assumes that:

    - achieving charitable deeds effectively cannot be done by one clergy member but instead depends on teamwork among a group of them.
    - clergy members are envious of televangelists' prominence and for this reason rarely view them as colleagues.
    - clergy members who have not done any charitable deeds may still become televangelists.
    - clergy members believe that prominent televangelists are not motivated by a desire to do charitable deeds.
    - the difficulty of religious charitable initiatives cannot be accurately estimated by those outside the clergy.

41. Due to rising travel costs, after today the Authoritarian Party plans to cut by half the number of voluntary fund-raising dinners it holds. However, the annual number of speeches, those speeches' quality, and the price for entry will remain unchanged. Political analysts predict that neither small nor large contributors will leave the party due to this plan.

    Which of the following, if true, gives the strongest evidence that the party's contributions may decline under the plan?

    - With rising travel costs, the average fund-raising dinner will cost one-third more to hold tomorrow than today.
    - Most of the party's small contributors do not care as much about fewer dinners than about a possible decline in the quality of the party's speeches.
    - Many party fund-raiser attendees would continue attending even if the prices rose.
    - Many paying attendees will continue to spend the same amount per dinner as in the past.
    - All other costs for the party are projected to remain unchanged.

42. New Rhode State is contemplating enacting an initiative to let senior citizens prepay their future nursing home care fees at today's price level. When the senior checks into any of New Rhode's state-operated public nursing homes, the initiative will pay the fees annually. To decrease their out-of-pocket costs for nursing home care, the mayor advises all seniors to pay into the initiative.

    Which of the following, if true, is the most appropriate reason NOT to pay into the initiative?

    - Seniors are not certain to which New Rhode State public nursing home they will go.
    - If the prepayment money is placed into an interest-bearing account today, the accumulated interest will exceed the total fees for any New Rhode State nursing home when the senior goes there.
    - It is projected that the annual cost of New Rhode State's nursing homes will grow at a faster rate than the annual cost-of-living increase.
    - Some large New Rhode State nursing homes are already considering large fees hikes for next year.
    - The prepayment initiative would not cover the cost of medical care and recreation for seniors.

43. It is true that it is illegal for American companies bidding to secure government contracts in foreign countries to bribe foreign officials. But if American companies do not bribe foreign officials, competitors from other countries will.

Which of the following is most similar to this argument's logical structure?

- O It is true that it is against American law to trade with Cuba. But if America wants to avoid an impoverished Cuba allying itself with a wealthier nation, some trade must be permitted.
- O It is true that it is illegal in all Asian countries to bribe government officials. But there is a long-standing tradition of bribery in many Asian countries.
- O It is true that it permissible in Texlahoma to shoot intruders who invade one's home and appear intent on robbing or hurting residents. But if the facts of this case are understood, it will be clearly seen that the defendant, a battered woman, did not actually believe that her drunken husband was a burglar.
- O It is true that it is against college basketball regulations to take performance-enhancing drugs. But if our team doesn't take such drugs, our big rivals will.
- O It is true that it is against the law to draft misleading financial statements. But there have been many accountants who disobeyed this law.

44. A Tyrannia government official: Many foreign tourists who have not yet visited our lovely country believe its "open air" lead plumbing system is inadequate. These tourists are wrong, as is obvious from the fact that for every one of the last 20 years, my country spent more money than any other nation for each mile of plumbing pipe improvements by adding even more lead.

Which of the following, if true, most seriously undermines the reasoning in the official's argument?

- Compared to several other countries, Tyrannia's expenditures on improving its pipes have grown more slowly over the last 20 years.
- Sufficiency of a country's plumbing system is less important to the average tourist than are cheap hostels.
- Over the last 20 years, many regular tourists stopped coming to Tyrannia, but just about as many new tourists started coming.
- Generally, the number of miles of pipes in any country depends on both its population and topography.
- The only nations that must spend large amounts of money on plumbing repair are those whose plumbing systems are inadequate.

45. A gallery was presented a coin, allegedly from Rome circa the second century BCE but without documentation. It is possible that the coin is a genuine antique, despite its lack of documentation, if it was newly excavated or held by a private owner. However, an ancient artifact should have uneven erosion, whereas this coin has the even exterior routinely created by the acid bath commonly employed by art forgers to duplicate an eroded artifact. Therefore, the coin is probably forged.

Which of the following, if true, most seriously weakens the argument?

- Legitimate dealers can purchase newly excavated antiquities only with verified export documentation from their country of origin.
- The coin's image and other features of the coin's appearance demonstrate all the most common features of Roman coins of the second century BCE.
- At one time, the acid bath that forgers currently use was used by antiquities sellers and collectors to modify the splotchy look of true ancient artifacts.
- Forgers have no way to replicate the patchy erosion common to ancient artifacts convincingly, according to officials.
- An allegedly Roman artifact with an even surface, similar to that of the coin being offered to the gallery, was newly shown to be forged.

46. That mammals first came to Europe less than 15 million years ago, through what is now Egypt, into West Europe was an accepted tenet of paleontology. But paleontologists now theorize that mammals came to East Europe first, after migrating across modern-day Asia, and then spread westward, based on later excavation of mammal remains in East Europe dating from 27 million years ago.

    Which of the following, if it were discovered, would be pertinent evidence against the new theory provided?

    - Signs of use by mammals 14 million years ago were found in excavations near East Germany.
    - Some evidence of mammal occupation in West Europe areas predates any such evidence in areas in East Europe.
    - The oldest known West Europe mammal habitat has a cooler climate than the 27-million-year-old East European site.
    - The mammal habitat in East Europe that was used 27 million years ago was used continuously until 6 million years ago.
    - World sea levels lowered dramatically during the first Ice Age, between 11 million and 15 million years ago.

47. When bees build a new hive composed of hexagonal honeycomb "rooms," they must build precisely the correct number to house the population of bees that will immediately inhabit the new hive. If there are too few rooms, some younger bees would be displaced and would freeze or starve outside the hive. If there are too many rooms, some bees would instinctively fight to the death to conquer the extra space.

    Which of the following conclusions can correctly be inferred from these data?

    - From the bees' hive-building behavior, the number of rooms in the largest hive that a particular colony of bees could build can theoretically be determined.
    - Trees on which hives are built have no properties that can affect the number of rooms of the hive built on them.
    - Bees learn how many rooms can be built in a hive from experience.
    - Building too many rooms in the hive would kill bees more quickly than building too few.
    - Builder bees determine the number of rooms to be built by the chemical scent of individual resident bees.

48. A famous foreign dictator recently triumphed in a lawsuit against his booking agency, which, after failing to find him at either his palace or his castle, used a similar-looking impersonator to perform his rendition of a well-known trademark rant for a soft drink commercial. Due to the outcome of that suit, advertisers will stop hiring impersonators for commercials. Thus, ad costs will increase because famous dictators charge more than impersonators do.

This argument is flawed because it makes which of the following unwarranted assumptions?

- O Most listeners cannot distinguish whether a speech is being performed by a famous dictator or an impersonator.
- O Ads that use famous dictators are often more effective than those that use impersonators.
- O Some famous speeches' original versions cannot be licensed for commercial use.
- O Booking agencies will continue using impersonators in place of famous dictators.
- O Advertisers will want to use original speeches.

49. Fermilab estimates that actual UFO landings happen about every 122 years, and any interplanetary UFO must have the energy signature of a nuclear missile. When a fully automated artificial intelligence encounters unforeseen stimuli, its response is unpredictable.

Which of the following conclusions can most properly be drawn, if the statements provided are true?

- O The system would respond incorrectly 122 years after becoming operational, starting a war inadvertently.
- O The system would be destroyed by the energy an incoming UFO would generate in Earth's atmosphere.
- O It would be impossible for the system to distinguish the energy of a UFO landing from the launch of a nuclear weapon.
- O Whether the system would respond incorrectly to the energy of a UFO landing would depend on the location of the landing.
- O It is not certain what the system's response to the energy of a UFO landing would be, if its designers did not plan for such a contingency.

50. According to the "tragedy of the commons" theory, drinking wells owned communally (i.e., freely usable by the public) will be used less prudently than personal drinking wells. Each drinker has incentives to deplete communal wells, because the water used would go to the individual drinker, while the detriments of overused wells' reduced quality resulting from the depletion would be shared among all users. Yet a poll comparing 200 communal drinking wells with 400 personal drinking wells revealed that the communal wells were in better condition.

Which of the following, if true and understood by the drinkers, would best explain the poll's findings?

- O The full benefits and detriments of depleting personal drinking wells are borne by individual users.
- O When communal wells are overused, the depletion attributable to any one user is less noticeable than with personal wells.
- O A user may gain a competitive advantage by depleting communal drinking wells to produce healthier herds than other users.
- O If one user of communal wells depletes them even slightly, other users will probably follow that example to a greater degree, so that the cost to each user will exceed the gain.
- O More drinking wells are owned personally than are held in common.

51. Particular receptors prevent harm to the stomach from toxic food by commanding the blood cells around the stomach to attack foreign objects. This in some measure protects the stomach from poisons. An allergy attack occurs when the receptors react without cause to benign things, such as certain fruits or nuts.

Which of the following, if true, points to the most serious flaw in a plan to develop a drug that would prevent allergy attacks by blocking receipt of any commands sent by the receptors as mentioned in the passage?

- O How the body produces the receptors that activate allergy attacks is not yet known by scientists.
- O What makes one individual's receptors more easily activated than others' is not yet known by scientists.
- O Since extensive lead times are involved in both research and production of such drugs, years would pass before they are available.
- O The drug could not differentiate between signals triggered by fruits and nuts and those triggered by toxic food.
- O This drug could not alleviate an allergy attack that has already started, being only preventative.

52. Occasionally, pharmaceutical companies mark down the price of a new drug sold to pharmacies during a trial phase, when the drug is being marketed to buyers. Such trials often cause pharmacies to buy a huge amount of the drug. Nonetheless, the pharmaceutical companies could often profit more by not giving trials.

Which of the following, if true, most strongly supports the claim above about the pharmaceutical companies' profits?

- Generally, the quantity of markdown given by pharmaceutical companies to pharmacies is prudently calculated to be the least needed to attract buyers to the drug.
- For many drugs, the trial phase during which prices are lowered is about a month, which is not long enough for buyers to get used to the low price.
- The rationale of such trials is to keep the new drugs at the top of buyers' minds and appeal to buyers now using competing drugs.
- Pharmacies often amass in their storage rooms drugs bought at markdown during trials and then sell these drugs later at regular prices.
- If some pharmaceutical companies offer trials but other competing pharmaceutical companies do not, the companies that offer trials will lure buyers away from the other companies.

53. The greater a company's financial resources, the greater the salaries that will be paid to its employees; employees at larger companies must be compensated at an increased level. This idea establishes the basis for determining salaries and is demonstrated by the fact that ________.

Which of the following best completes the passage?

- the most dedicated entrepreneurs are different in that they often work for riskier ventures without worrying about the base salary
- "bulge bracket" companies set higher initial base salaries than do smaller start-up companies
- if the stock market is booming, the increases in compensation at government offices may not keep pace with cost-of-living increases
- in an international joint venture, similar jobs in the project often pay matching salaries, regardless of which company an employee works for
- salaries in well-funded start-up companies can be, on net, greater than those at larger blue-chip companies

54. Anti-cancer activist: Your tobacco megacorporation inserts a standard quantity of nicotine into every cigarette. This shows your intent to keep your buyers addicted, because nicotine is addictive.

Tobacco corporation PR spokesperson: The way that cigarettes are lovingly rolled in our state-of-the-art factory means each cigarette contains less nicotine than the tobacco leaf from which cigarette tobacco is made.

As a refutation of the activist's argument, the spokesperson's reply is flawed, because it ________.

- o does not mention the issue of whether this corporation's cigarettes are intentionally infused with enough nicotine to keep smokers addicted
- o presumes without reason that all raw tobacco leaf contains the same amount of nicotine
- o does not detail precisely how much nicotine the manufacturing process extracts
- o responds to the activist's claim as if the activist were talking about the effect of each individual cigarette, instead of the aggregate harm of cigarettes
- o without giving any factual support, simply contradicts the activist's claim

55. In the United States, landowners are effectively insured against natural disasters because the government subsidizes all land repairs by providing emergency relief after natural disasters. This "subsidy" is a partial cause of the high percentage of houses built on disaster-prone lands because it gives owners no financial incentive to research whether the land on which they build their houses is secure against disaster, argues an actuary. If owners were more selective, then potential house sites would need to be safe before being developed.

Which of the following, if true, most seriously weakens the actuary's argument?

- O The repair cost for natural disasters, adjusted for inflation, was lower before the government began subsidizing owners against natural disasters than it is now.
- O Before the government began subsidizing land repairs, natural disasters frequently struck settlements more often because confused and fearful builders incorrectly picked the nearby lands most prone to natural disasters.
- O A significant percentage of owners know that their lands are subsidized by the government, according to surveys.
- O There is a cap on the repair cost of any owner's land that the government will subsidize, but very few owners' lands are worth more than this limit.
- O The security of land against disasters depends on its history and the safety of surrounding lands.

56. To conserve rent money, the Last National Bank had planned to move its main office from New York City to Samoa, where rents are lower, and have employees commute daily from New York. The bank asked for volunteers from among its New York bankers to attempt the commute for three months and found that, for these months, these bankers' sales were higher than during most previous periods.

    Which of the following, if true, would dictate most powerfully against making the relocation permanent, based on the findings of the trial period?

    - The volunteers in the study were mostly from among the bank's most loyal and hardest-working junior ranks.
    - Even if there were no increases in relocated workers' sales revenues, the move would be cost-efficient based on the rent savings alone.
    - Competitor banks that had tried such a plan and succeeded were usually much smaller in terms of staff than the Last National Bank.
    - The relocated volunteers were provided with inexpensive technology that let them integrate their laptops with the bank's computer system.
    - Sales revenue increases of the magnitude of those achieved by the volunteers could be accomplished by other means that require less disruption.

57. Seller's commercial: "*Aviator Magazine* reported that our Deathtrap 3000 airplane has the fewest injuries per accident of airplanes in its class. This clearly proves that our Deathtrap 3000 is one of the safest airplanes around."

    Which of the following, if true, most seriously weakens the argument in the advertisement?

    - According to this *Aviator Magazine* report, a number of airplanes in other classes had more injuries per accident than the Deathtrap 3000.
    - In the last two years, the Deathtrap 3000 was the best-selling airplane in its class.
    - Aircraft of the class to which the Deathtrap 3000 belongs have a greater probability of being involved in accidents than do other types of airplanes.
    - The difference in the number of injuries per accident for the Deathtrap 3000, compared to other airplanes in its class, is significant.
    - *Aviator Magazine*'s report is published only once annually.

58. Public health advocate: It is generally true that medications that undergo extensive FDA Phase III clinical safety testing are much safer than less-researched drugs. It is also true that **whenever such trials are conducted, fewer people have experienced unexpected harmful side effects, thus reducing public health risks**. However, eliminating the requirement that even FDA-tested medications continue to include extensive warnings about individual risk factors would almost certainly harm rather than help public health. Consumers would tend to rely on the FDA's general certification of safety, and **if no longer encouraged to read about individual risks and drug interactions, many patients would suffer serious adverse reactions**.

The two bolded statements serve what purpose in the context of the public health advocate's argument?

- The first is a general pattern that the advocate accepts as true; the second is said to be a natural consequence that must follow if the general pattern applies.
- The first is a causal relationship that the advocate believes will happen again in the case at issue; the second admits a situation in which the relationship would not hold.
- The first describes a cause-and-effect relationship that the advocate believes will not hold in the case at issue; the second suggests a consideration that supports that belief.
- The first is proof that the advocate uses to support a prediction; the second states that prediction.
- The first acknowledges a consideration that weighs against the stance that the advocate supports; the second is that stance.

59. In the last decade, a series of mishaps in building and operating nuclear power plants caused a corresponding spike in claims against insurers that underwrite policies for power plants. As a result, insurance premiums mushroomed, making it more expensive to build and operate power plants. In turn, this forces owners of power plants now in service to squeeze more performance out of them.

Which of the following, if true, best supports the conclusion that the cost of nuclear power plants will continue to increase?

- O Insurance premiums for power plants will always be expensive because there are relatively few units over which insurers can spread the risk.
- O If power plants explode, they are abandoned, and the exact reason for the explosion often remains unknowable.
- O Power plants will break down more often as greater performance demands are placed on them.
- O No economy of scale is possible because power plants are built in tiny numbers.
- O Inefficiencies in production are unavoidable because nuclear power plants tend to have major components manufactured by unwieldy joint ventures among separate companies.

60. The much-documented optical illusion of height and width makes containers appear more voluminous the taller the containers are. Thus, an observer's approximation of the available volume in a short jar is certain to be less than that of the volume in a tall bottle.

The conclusion would be more properly drawn if it were specified that the __________.

- O bottle's volume is assumed to be less than the jar's
- O bottle's volume is assumed to be the same as the jar's
- O bottle's volume is assumed to be greater than the jar's
- O observer's approximation of volume available is assumed to be more exact with jars than with bottles
- O observer's approximation of volume available is assumed to be more exact with bottles than with jars

61. The wholesale cost of asbestos, used in the manufacture of fire-retardant asbestos shorts, has seen a significant reduction in the past year, unlike that of its substitute, raw wire mesh. Thus, while asbestos shorts stores' retail prices have yet to fall, they will certainly do so eventually.

Which of the following, if true, most weakens this argument?

- O The weaving costs for asbestos cloth rose in the past year.
- O The gross wholesale price for untreated asbestos is usually more than that of the same volume of untreated wire mesh.
- O The average store specializing in the retail sale of asbestos shorts has seen its operating costs remain unchanged in the past year.
- O Retail price changes always lag behind wholesale price changes.
- O Asbestos manufacturing costs increased in the past year.

62. Street crime can be averted through regulations mandating the lighting of streetlights during daytime. However, daytime visibility is worse in nations farther from the equator, so obviously such regulations would be more successful in averting crime there. Actually, the only nations that have adopted such regulations are farther from the equator than the continental United States is.

Which of the following conclusions could be most properly drawn from the information?

- O Bystanders in the continental United States who were near lit streetlights during the day would be just as likely to become victims of a crime as would bystanders who were not near lit streetlights.
- O Inadequate daytime visibility is the single most important factor in street crime in numerous nations that are located farther from the equator than is the continental United States.
- O In nations that have daytime streetlight regulations, the percentage of street crime that happens in the daytime is greater than in the continental United States.
- O Nations that have daytime streetlight regulations probably have fewer incidents of street crime annually than occur within the continental United States.
- O Daytime streetlight regulations would probably do less to avert street crime in the continental United States than they do in the nations that have the regulations.

63. Proponents of a major retailer's construction plan conclude that it will bring a net benefit to small businesses. They claim that because the government-subsidized construction will have "trickle-down" effects for small businesses, small businesses will gain overall.

Each of the following, if true, raises a concern in opposition to the conclusion above, EXCEPT:

- O Building efficient marketing campaigns is top priority for small businesses and would be abandoned by the big business, which does not care about efficiency.
- O Employees needed by small businesses would prefer to work for the major retailer.
- O Small businesses will win subcontracts to provide materials and products needed during construction of the retail store.
- O If government subsidies are given to the large retailer, there will be less money available for small business development.
- O Increased government debt needed to subsidize the plan will depress the local economy.

64. Books by new authors that are distributed by publishing houses have a much lower failure rate than books distributed in alternative ways, such as self-publishing or online distribution. Thus, distribution is a more important causative factor in whether a book sells or fails than are other factors such as the talent of the author, the quality of binding, or the editing of the book.

Which of the following, if true, most seriously weakens the argument?

- O Publishing houses are usually more willing than alternative sources to increase marketing of the book, as needed.
- O Over 80 percent of all new books fail to sell and are withdrawn within four months.
- O The editing of a book is a less important determinant of whether there will be a sequel in the long run than is the talent of the author.
- O The editing of new books is usually less formal than that of works by known authors.
- O Publishing houses base their decisions to distribute books on such factors as the characteristics of the author and quality of editing of the book.

65. Increases in levels of density-inducing electrolytes (D.I.E.) in the human heart increase toxicity by decreasing the body's natural ability to purge those extra toxins. Levels of D.I.E. in the hearts of some individuals may rise as a result of regular adherence to the all-lard diet.

Which of the following is a correct inference that can be drawn from the information provided?

- O Individuals who eat a low fat, lard-free diet face no risk of increasing D.I.E. in the bloodstream.
- O Individuals who do not eat lard regularly will have a lower risk of developing increased toxicity in their bloodstreams as they age.
- O Abstaining from lard altogether is the most effective method of lowering toxicity.
- O A rigorous diet of pure lard will increase toxins in the bloodstreams of some people.
- O Only abstaining from lard is necessary to lower toxicity levels in the bloodstreams of individuals of average weight.

66. On the outskirts of Beverly Hills, a cutting-edge laboratory was constructed to produce, in a completely controlled environment, cloned chickens for consumption. The one-acre lab is so efficient that it produces as many chickens as would 50 acres of chicken coops. However, its other expenditures are costlier, in particular, purchasing stem cells, so chicken cloned there costs five times as much as the cooped chicken now raised throughout the Midwest.

Which of the following, if true, best supports a projection that the referenced facility will be profitable?

- O Operating costs can be lowered by 20 percent when the laboratory technicians gain experience.
- O Midwestern chicken's cost per pound is already so low that it virtually cannot be further lowered.
- O Unlike cooped chickens, cloned chickens are fed a pure diet free of any growth hormones or antibiotics, and thus they can be sold for an exceptionally high price to buyers such as health-conscious dieters.
- O The market for chicken cloned in Beverly Hills is no more limited to the Beverly Hills region than the market for Midwestern chicken is to the Midwest, because chicken ships relatively well.
- O Due to cheaper stem cells and high meat prices, a second cloning laboratory is being constructed in Mexico.

67. Historically speaking, successful long-term investors have preferred mixed investment portfolios with lower overall risk to less diversified portfolios containing more high-risk investments. But recent research shows that the most profitable investors carry a higher percentage of risk in their portfolios. This illustrates that choosing to develop a higher-risk investment portfolio is a better investment decision than is choosing to maintain a mixed portfolio with lower risk.

    The conclusion of the argument relies upon which of the following assumptions?

    - O Mixed portfolios with lower risk do not provide significant return on investment.
    - O Investors may either develop more diversified, lower-risk portfolios or less diversified, higher-risk portfolios.
    - O The returns on investment achieved by the most profitable investors can be achieved just as readily by less profitable investors.
    - O The most profitable investors invest the majority of the portfolios in higher-risk positions.
    - O The most profitable investors make better investment decisions than do those who receive a more modest return on investment.

68. Surveillance cameras outfitted with the latest facial-recognition imaging, which guard the entrances of sensitive buildings by allowing passage only to employees whose photos are stored in the database, recognize faces not only through optical analysis of the general form but also of 108 other features, including bone width and skin texture. Even the best disguise makers cannot re-create all 108 features of the face accurately.

    Which of the following is a logical conclusion based on the passage?

    - O In the time the imaging technology takes to scan and verify faces, unauthorized people have time to gain entry, so the imaging technology is impractical for ordinary use.
    - O Surveillance cameras outfitted with the imaging technology will be installed in most military bases before long.
    - O No one can enter a building monitored by a surveillance camera with the imaging technology merely by virtue of skill at disguising the face.
    - O Facial-recognition technology was developed over many years of intensive research and trial.
    - O The technology often malfunctions, mistakenly restricting access even to authorized employees.

69. In free-trade countries such as the United States, even if there is a coal-supply disturbance that increases international coal prices, domestic coal prices will also affect whether such free-trade countries import some or none of their coal.

Assuming this statement about coal-supply disturbances is true, which of the following policies in a free-trade country is most likely to reduce long-term economic impacts of unexpected spikes in international coal prices on that country?

- o Importing a constant amount of coal annually
- o Building more coal-hauling ships
- o Ceasing diplomatic relations with coal-producing countries
- o Practicing conservation to reduce coal consumption
- o Producing less coal domestically

70. A dinghy rower crossing the lake approached a distance-marking buoy on the route that said "42" on the side facing him and "44" on the reverse. He thought the next buoy would show that he was exactly at the midpoint of the route. However, the next buoy actually said "41" facing him and "45" behind.

Which of the following, if true, would explain the paradox mentioned in the passage?

- o The second buoy's numbers were reversed.
- o The buoys' numbers are denominated in nautical miles instead of land miles.
- o The numbers facing him represent miles left to the end of the route, not miles from the beginning.
- o Between the two buoys the rower saw, one was missing.
- o Originally, the buoys had been built for use by sailboats, not rowboats.

71. To reduce auto emissions, a well-known environmentalist governor proposed a daily "carbon footprint tax" on SUVs but not on cleaner ethanol-powered subcompact cars. This will cause many SUV owners to trade in their polluting vehicles for ethanol cars, the governor reasons, because the annual tax on SUVs is more than enough to buy a new ethanol car.

    Which of the following statements, if true, provides the best evidence that the governor's reasoning is flawed?

    - Economists warn that Middle East instability will increase the cost of gasoline.
    - It is already more expensive for most people to drive SUVs than ethanol cars because the price of gasoline is already high.
    - Most ethanol car owners do not also own an SUV.
    - Some drivers who love their SUVs say they would rather harm the environment than switch to ethanol cars.
    - SUVs owned and driven by city residents make up 20 percent of the city's pollution, on average.

72. Seniors with close family ties are far more likely to die immediately after a large family gathering than immediately before, according to research studies. Experimenters concluded that the will to live can extend life, at least for short periods.

    Which of the following, if true, would most strengthen the experimenters' conclusion?

    - Seniors with close family ties are less likely to die immediately before or during a large family gathering than at any other time of the year.
    - Seniors with close family ties fear dying less than other seniors do.
    - Some seniors who have close family ties live much longer than the majority of seniors who do not.
    - Most seniors who attend family gatherings do so for somewhat different purposes than younger attendees.
    - The spring and fall, which have lower death rates for seniors, are the times when many families schedule large gatherings.

73. The futures market lets investors speculate on future products before they are produced. If a poor pork bellies supply is expected later, pork bellies futures prices rise; if a bountiful pork bellies supply is expected, pork bellies futures prices fall. This morning, swineologists predicted an influx of much-needed slop in the pigpen regions of the country starting tomorrow. Thus, since sufficient slop is essential for the survival of a strong current supply of fuller pork bellies, prices of pork bellies futures will decline dramatically today.

Which of the following, if true, most weakens the argument?

- Pigs that do not consume adequate slop during the critical growth stage will not produce a full, rich product.
- This fiscal year, pork bellies futures prices have varied more erratically than they did last year.
- The slop that swineologists predict for tomorrow is only expected to be distributed well outside the pigpen areas.
- Today, a press release by pork experts said that the foot-in-mouth disease decimating some of the pork bellies supply will spread widely before the start of the slaughtering season.
- Investors who speculate in pork bellies futures rarely take physical possession of the pork bellies they trade.

74. The powdered U.S. cocaine epidemic is still rampant and shows no signs of abating. Last year in the United States, the total quantity of powder cocaine bought by users has risen, even though there was a decrease in the number of adults who use it.

Each of the following, if true, could explain the simultaneous increase in cocaine sales and decrease in the number of adults who use the drug EXCEPT:

- O Last year, the number of men who began to use was higher than the number of women who quit using cocaine.
- O Last year, the number of teenage children who began using was higher than the number of adults who have quit using cocaine during the same period.
- O During the last year, the number of cocaine non-users who began using crack cocaine "rocks," made from powdered cocaine, was higher than the number of people who have quit using cocaine.
- O The people who continue to use consume more cocaine per capita than in past years.
- O Much of the cocaine brought into the United States by dealers was then smuggled into Canada for resale.

75. Commentator: The book *The Fall of Architecture* hypothesizes that modern American architects are less skillful than those of the past 100 years. The book's comparison of 50 old buildings to 50 modern ones clearly shows that none of the modern ones are designed as skillfully as the older ones, and thus the book's theory must be correct.

Which of the following points to the most serious logical flaw in the commentator's argument?

- O The buildings picked for comparison by the author could be those that most support his thesis.
- O There could be criteria besides the technical skill of the architects by which to evaluate a building.
- O The book's title may cause readers to believe its thesis is true, even before they read the comparison of buildings that justifies it.
- O The particular methods used by modern American architects could demand less skill than methods used by architects in other countries.
- O Readers unfamiliar with architectural criticism's terminology may remain unpersuaded by the book's comparison of the 100 buildings.

76. In the very recent past, the U.S. Army minimized body armor to keep wartime equipment costs to a minimum. The most secure armors are costly, so few soldiers were issued such armors. This election year, the armor selling best to the Army—the Chainmail 1200—is also the safest one, clearly demonstrating that the Army assigned a higher priority to safety than to cheap equipment costs.

Which of the following, if true, most seriously weakens the argument?

- The armor that sold best last year was not the safest available.
- No Army department has intentionally leaked the information that it was making safer armor a higher priority this year.
- This year's high armor prices topped those of the last two years, when the best armors saw weak sales.
- Due to the increase in raw materials cost, all types of armors cost more to produce this year than in any past year.
- Due to technological innovations as a result of massive profits, the safest armor available this year costs less than most others currently sold.

77. In the barren African desert, water is available at an oasis, but each person or pack animal's daily water consumption is strictly rationed. Travelers may take only enough drinking water for themselves and their animals for seven days. But trees grow along the oasis's rim in a narrow circle and also consume its water. Clearly, therefore, if the travelers cut down those trees, they will have more water for drinking.

Which of the following, if true, most seriously weakens the argument?

- Trees around the oasis's rim provide shade, and even protect the oasis from extreme loss of water through evaporation from the sun and wind.
- Frequent travelers who use the oasis will demand a larger drinking water supply before investing in the cost of cutting down the trees around the oasis.
- The species of trees on the rim of the oasis have evolved to grow only in soil where the roots are always wet.
- Even if the trees were cut down, the land around the oasis, on which they grow, is too rocky to have any other use.
- The rationing and designated use of drinking water is designed to let travelers and pack animals take enough water to get to the next oasis, without depleting it for other travelers.

78. A principle called "cost-plus" is used to calculate the price that Congress pays when buying standard toilet seats from long-standing suppliers. Cost-plus is a formula that adds to the prior year's price a certain percentage, based on current inflation rates, thus letting suppliers maintain profit margins.

    Which of the following, if true, is the strongest reason for criticism of the cost-plus pricing system as an economically sound method of paying government contractors?

    - The state may continue to pay for inefficient purchases made in the past.
    - The inflation rate has fluctuated greatly over the last decade.
    - The price will be determined largely by the cost of raw materials.
    - Many taxpayer groups are outraged at the sums the government spends on toilet seats.
    - Cost-plus is based on past, historical prices, so it might not encourage improvements in toilet seat design.

79. Temperature shifts can trend toward warming or cooling, based on a number of gravitational, seasonal, and human variables. These variables affect different ecosystems differently and thus should produce a random pattern in which some ecosystems warm while others cool. However, data gathered in a 1980s study show that the shifts occur in a definitely skewed pattern, with most areas' temperatures rising simultaneously.

    Which of the following, if true, forms the best basis for at least a partial explanation of the patterned changes recorded in the study?

    - Massive warming can result from widespread pollution in many countries.
    - Certain regions with specific geographical features respond in varying degrees to surrounding changes.
    - Some regions grow warmer due to increased volcanic activity in those regions.
    - In the 1990s and beyond, a period that was not as well documented, human pollution skewed the trend toward warming.
    - Regions that are geographically closest are most likely to be affected in similar ways.

80. News commentator: "Our police commissioner announced a plan to dismantle manned surveillance video cameras throughout the city, because most man-hours spent observing them end up wasted because no crimes are recorded. Most residents now have cell phones or access to public phones, so video cameras are no longer needed, says the police commissioner. However, the biggest risk of crime is in the Warehouse District, where there are not many residents or public phones, so some video cameras are still needed."

Which of the following, if true, most seriously weakens the argument?

- O It costs over $5 million annually for the city to pay police officers to monitor video cameras.
- O Warehouses have automatic motion-detecting video cameras, which send an alarm to the police department.
- O Due to most video cameras' limited scope and quality, the police will receive less information from video cameras than from phone calls.
- O The police department is much nearer to residential areas than to the warehouse areas.
- O An average of one in five public phones does not work.

81. High national inflation rates do not result in stagnation in the rate of economic growth. If they did, those nations that have the highest inflation rates should also demonstrate the lowest economic growth rates. In fact, if countries are ranked in order of inflation rate, with rate statistics adjusted so that nations are relatively comparable, no such correlation exists.

If the statements provided are true, which of the following must also be true?

- O Nations with high inflation rates tend to erect trade barriers.
- O It is impossible to compare economic growth rates meaningfully and reliably among countries.
- O Reducing national inflation rates through stricter government spending will not necessarily cause a lowering of that country's individual rate of economic growth.
- O If the nations were ranked in order of their population, the largest nations would usually display the highest figures in terms of both inflation and economic growth.
- O Nations with the highest inflation rates never have comparably high economic growth rates.

82. One beneficial plan for the problem of gridlocked vehicle traffic in major metropolitan areas such as New York City and Los Angeles is to provide rickshaw or bike-cart service for trips of 5 to 25 city blocks. Implementing this remedy would be far cheaper than building overpasses to circumvent problem areas, and it would also reduce the number of taxis clogging the roads.

Which of the following, if true, could supporters of the plan above most appropriately cite as evidence for the feasibility of their plan?

- O An effective rickshaw system would require major repair of potholes.
- O Half of all car trips in the country's most congested city cover distances of nine city blocks.
- O The majority of rural travelers taking car trips in rural areas are traveling distances of over 25 city blocks.
- O Many new buses are being imported in areas presently served by existing rickshaw services.
- O A large percentage of people driving in cities are tourists who have made long-distance trips into the cities.

83. Ever since Mayor May Knott's publicity campaign for New York City's new express subway service began last year, car traffic in the city's crowded uptown decreased 10 percent. In that same year, there was an equivalent increase in the number of people riding subways uptown. Clearly, the mayor's publicity campaign persuaded many people to ride subways rather than drive their cars.

Which of the following, if true, casts the most serious doubt on the passage's conclusion?

- O New car prices have risen about 12 percent over the last year.
- O The mayor commutes uptown to City Hall daily on the subway.
- O Over the last year, pothole repairs have closed many lanes on roads leading uptown, which were previously used by commuters.
- O The total number of subway trains that come uptown in the mornings has stayed exactly the same as it was one year ago.
- O Surveys reveal that city residents who had been riding available subways for years were no more satisfied with subway service than they were a year ago, before the publicity campaign began.

84. Loyal fans of the Arena Football League are awarded some free tickets for future games. Many sell their complimentary tickets to Scalper Inc. Scalper resells them to people at less than retail prices, resulting in even less ticket revenues than would otherwise be paid to the Arena Football League through normal ticket sales.

To stop the resale scalping of tickets, the Arena Football League should restrict the

- o number of tickets that any single fan may be given in any particular year.
- o use of complimentary tickets to fans and their immediate families.
- o days that tickets are good for to weekdays only.
- o time limit before the tickets expire.
- o types of games for which the tickets are valid.

85. An egomaniacal businessperson-turned-author wants to raise his latest book's sales, so he is renting a signing booth at a book convention. The book shows people how they can turn millions into billions by inheriting a successful family business. At the booth, people can buy the book, have it signed by a stand-in, and even buy more financial advice. The businessperson wants the maximum number possible of potential customers to come to his booth. His plan is to call his 30 apprentices and order each to talk to their 10 best friends personally and invite them to buy a copy at the booth.

Which of the following, if true, is the best indicator that the businessperson's plan will be effective in raising book sales?

- o Even before the businessperson's new products are completed, he routinely calls everyone in his organization and their friends to promote the products.
- o Many competitors offering similar get-rich-quick books will also be at the fair, with their own marketing plans.
- o When people see a booth crowded with visitors, they will come to see it, even if they know it is the obnoxious businessperson's.
- o The readers of the businessperson's prior books also tend to buy the books of other get-rich gurus.
- o This 17th book by the businessperson contains even less useful information than his prior 16.

86. Leaders of a rebel group fighting for democracy against the puppet government in Brokel-controlled Tolnya, which supplies oil to Brokelland, are debating other strategies to pressure Tolnya to accept the rebels' democratic demands. The primary tactic the rebel leaders are considering is to provoke a mass work strike on the farms of Eustacia, which supply food to Brokelland and are controlled by Brokelland.

    The answer to which of the following questions is LEAST directly relevant to Tolnya's rebel leaders' consideration of whether attempting a strike in Eustacia will lead to acceptance of democracy for Tolnya?

    - Would work losses in Eustacia seriously affect Brokelland?
    - Can Eustacians easily buy food elsewhere?
    - Have other rebel groups won democratic reforms like the ones desired by Tolnya's rebels?
    - Have other rebel groups achieved their aims through similar strategies?
    - Do other dictatorships that control oil-rich republics also control agricultural republics?

87. Historically, churches that provided free aid to the poor relied primarily on donations from wealthier sponsors to do so. Almost all donors now are subject to the tax code, which effectively limits charitable contributions to churches so that the churches are only able to sustain regular operating expenses.

    Which conclusion is best supported by the statements provided?

    - Although technological innovations have made more cost-efficient aid available at a high cost, such investments are beyond the budget of churches.
    - If churches do not find some method of obtaining added money for aiding the poor, they must either deny some such aid or incur losses if they provide it.
    - Some potential donors' financial situations are such that it is advantageous to make some charitable contributions, but not to religious institutions.
    - If churches are able to provide aid at lower cost, the current tax laws will make it worthwhile for more people to make charitable contributions, thus providing *more* money for aid programs.
    - Government subsidies for churches, which historically provided some funding for church aid programs, are being reduced.

88. Thousands of people work at McDonut's, an inexpensive fast-food restaurant chain, which pays most employees minimum wage. Even though new laws forced an increase in the minimum wage, and thus substantially raised McDonut's labor costs, the chain's profits also rose substantially.

Which of the following, if true, most helps to resolve the apparent paradox?

- Only a very small part of the 70 percent of operating expenses paid by McDonut's for employee compensation goes to pay managers.
- People who earn minimum wage, or who rely on the earnings of others who do, comprise most of the restaurant chain's customer base.
- Other expenses of McDonut's rose dramatically after the wage hike, for reasons unrelated to the minimum wage raise.
- McDonut's decided to increase wages for managerial employees who were making slightly more than minimum wage simultaneously with the minimum wage increase.
- Cashiers and cooks, who are usually paid minimum wage, comprise most of the staff at McDonut's.

89. A vicious cycle ensues when students cheat on exams. Grade inflation drives schools to raise standards, which increases the pressure on noncheating students. In turn, this drives even more students to start cheating on exams.

The vicious cycle described could NOT result unless which of the following were true?

- When standards rise, they tend to give students an incentive to try raising their grades honestly.
- The ways to expel cheaters and counteract grade inflation are achievable through various means, but some single out innocent students, and effectiveness rates fluctuate yearly.
- When schools set grading standards to evaluate student performance, they do not adequately allow for cheating by some percentage of students.
- No regular cheaters will be discouraged from cheating by a lowering of the standards, unless stronger penalties are also added.
- All students will begin cheating when the standards reach the same level.

90. The State of Illisota is considering a 60% increase in the current per-gallon tax on gas in order to raise revenue to support the state's faltering public transportation system. The Illisota Secretary of Transportation claims that this will increase the tax revenue available to fund the public transportation system by at least 60%.

The Secretary of Transportation's claim depends on which of the following assumptions?

- O The annual budget requirements for the public transportation system will not increase.
- O The number of regular gas buyers in Illisota will increase.
- O The percentage of Illisota's traffic that comes from long-distance trips, as opposed to short commutes, will not change.
- O The number of commuters who use public transportation in Illisota will not decline.
- O A significant number of drivers will not switch to using public transportation to minimize their gas purchases.

91. If the main avenues around midtown tourist attractions were restricted to public buses and only those private rickshaws equipped with GPS maps, most private rickshaw traffic would be rerouted onto side streets. This reduction in the density of private rickshaw traffic would reduce the danger of crashes around tourist attractions.

The conclusion drawn in the first sentence depends on which of the following assumptions?

- O Most of the drivers of private rickshaws will find side streets as convenient as main streets.
- O Most of the side streets are too narrow to accommodate public buses.
- O The majority of private rickshaws using main streets are not equipped with GPS maps.
- O Public buses are more likely to crash than private rickshaws.
- O A decreased likelihood of crashes will ultimately result in more public bus traffic.

92. For years, Tyrannia has supplied itself with enough beans and lard by keeping demand below average. However, consumption of lard per capita is approaching average levels as Tyrannia's income per capita is approaching the average, and producing one pound of lard requires multiple pounds of beans. Therefore, if income per capita keeps increasing while bean production cannot grow, Tyrannia will need to import beans, lard, or both.

    Which of the following is an assumption on which the argument depends?

    - There will be no sizeable decrease in Tyrannia's aggregate land allocated to growing beans.
    - As incomes have grown, Tyrannia's population has stayed practically unchanged.
    - In Tyrannia, consumption of lard per capita is practically equal across all income levels.
    - The price of neither lard nor beans is subject to controls by Tyrannia's government.
    - Tyrannian people who increase consumption of lard will not drastically reduce consumption of beans.

93. When poor people rely on public assistance year after year, they forget the skills required to obtain a job. Thus, policy specialists recommend such people be given at least a few hours of paid work weekly. To receive public assistance from the government, people must not have worked in the past year.

    These statements, if true, sustain which of the following conclusions?

    - Government rules for public assistance run counter to efforts to employ people.
    - Putting those on public assistance into a permanent full-time labor program is the only answer to the problem of lost work skills.
    - By working a paid job for at least a few hours a week, poor people can pay their expenses.
    - Poor people will not be required to work a regular job through the eventual development of automation.
    - Poor people cannot survive on governmental public assistance benefits alone.

94. A-Co. produces and distributes the same widgets as B-Co. At both, employee salaries represent 60 percent of manufacturing costs. A-Co. seeks a competitive advantage with respect to B-Co. Thus, to gain advantage, A-Co. should lower salaries.

Which of the following, if true, would most weaken this argument?

- Since widget manufacturers produce only a few high-tech widgets annually, they cannot receive volume discounts from suppliers.
- Lowering salaries would demoralize employees and reduce their work quality, and the lowered quality would cause lower sales.
- Last year, B-Co. took away 25 percent of A-Co.'s clientele.
- After considering average bonuses and other cash awards, in fact, A-Co. pays its workers about 10 percent more than B-Co. pays its workers.
- Many widget plant workers live in regions where the widget plant is the only industry.

95. A proposed new regulation would mandate that all new houses and apartments come with window guards, which prevent small children from climbing through windows. However, a landlord argues that because over 95 percent of babies headed toward windows are stopped by family members without incurring serious injuries, residential window guards will reduce losses only slightly, at most.

Which of the following, if true, would most seriously weaken the argument?

- Most parents have not been formally trained on how to catch a baby.
- As new homes are only a handful of existing housing, the regulation will have an extremely small area of effectiveness.
- Installation of window guards in new residential buildings costs much less than smoke detectors.
- In the locale where the regulation was proposed, the average time required to respond to a falling baby is lower than the national average.
- The greatest harm from lack of window guards results when no family member is present.

96. At last week's conference on global climate change, most member nations favored laws governing the quality of emissions, whether or not specific areas could be shown to have been affected by a particular effluent.

To avoid undue restrictions, what must, of course, be proven is that ________.

- any uniform international regulations adopted at this conference will probably be put on a fast track for approval in members' legislatures.
- any substance made subject to these regulations actually causes environmental harm.
- the countries that advocate for more regulation are the ones with the smallest manufacturing base.
- all of any given pollutant that is to be regulated actually stays in the air, without immediately decaying into harmless elements.
- the global warming that has already taken place is reversible.

97. The treatment for obesity avoids some future medical costs by preventing diabetes and heart attacks. Yet the money saved totals just 20 percent of the expense of treating all obese patients. Thus, no economic justification exists for preventive treatment of obesity.

Which of the following, if true, most undermines the conclusion of the argument?

- The numerous deaths from diabetes and heart attack caused by untreated obesity result in only minor medical costs but huge economic losses of other kinds.
- Experts predict that prices for preventive treatment will remain the same during the next 30 years.
- Heart attacks have a much higher mortality rate than complications arising from diabetes.
- Efficient prevention presupposes early diagnoses, and initiatives to encourage them are expensive.
- The net savings in medical costs created by some preventive medical care is less than net losses attributable to some other care of this sort.

98. Since the passenger moped industry was opened to free competition in 1980, traffic congestion in the country's increasingly crowded streets has grown an average of 7 percent annually. To reduce congestion, more of the express lanes in the most crowded cities' busiest streets should be reserved for high-capacity, double-decker mopeds.

Which of the following, if true, casts the most doubt on the effectiveness of the proposed solution?

- O In the most crowded streets in the country, it was found that the major causes of traffic were rainy weather and shoddy open-toe sandals.
- O Since 1980, the number of mopeds on city streets has increased by more than 7 percent.
- O In the most crowded streets in the country, more than 60 percent of the express lanes are left for use only by high-capacity mopeds.
- O A small Alaskan town doubled its allocation of mopeds to express lanes and reported a decrease of 50 percent in the amount of traffic.
- O Since 1980, the average length of delay in traffic in the most crowded streets in the country has doubled.

99. A wholesaler of furniture found that it had great success at boosting profits by offering its retail outlets a bulk discount on each item if an outlet's order for winter quarter was at least 30 percent higher than its last winter quarter order. Many retailers were eligible for the discount. Sales volume grew enough to generate profits, even at the discounted price. The wholesaler plans to offer a similar promotion this spring and hopes for increased profits again.

Which of the following, if true, indicates the greatest flaw in the premise of repeating the promotion this spring?

- O Most retailers buy no more inventory for the spring quarter than for the winter quarter.
- O The wholesaler will hire more successful sales representatives to make calls and publicize the promotion to local retailers.
- O The retailers whose purchases were exceptionally low last year are the ones most likely to participate in the promotion.
- O The retailers who bought the discounted furniture were not obligated to pass the savings along to their buyers.
- O Buying more furniture in the winter to get the discount left many retailers with excess inventory for the spring quarter.

100. In an experiment, the experimental group, consisting of 50 percent of the participants, watched large amounts of a popular "shock-talk" show. Subsequently, this group exhibited greater stupidity than the other 50 percent of participants, the control group, who did not watch the talk show. The precipitous decline in intelligent behavior was attributed to the host's dull commentary, which is one of the show's main features.

Which of the following, if true, would best support the conclusion that some feature of the talk show was responsible for the experimental results?

- O Most TV watchers do not watch as much of this talk show as the experimental group did.
- O The host's dull commentary is a component of almost all talk shows, some of which TV viewers cannot avoid seeing.
- O The Federal Communications Commission recently ruled that the length of the show watched by the experimental group was safe.
- O Before conducting the experiment, the researchers found the two groups of participants equal in intelligence.
- O Another experiment, in which participants watched a tremendous amount of the same show, had no control group.

Answers and explanations begin on the next page.

Answer Key

CRITICAL REASONING PRACTICE

1. E
2. D
3. E
4. C
5. D
6. E
7. D
8. D
9. E
10. E
11. E
12. D
13. E
14. C
15. B
16. A
17. A
18. B
19. E
20. A
21. D
22. E
23. E
24. D
25. A
26. A
27. E
28. C
29. C
30. C
31. D
32. D
33. A
34. A
35. C
36. B
37. C
38. A
39. C
40. D
41. D
42. B
43. D
44. E
45. C
46. B
47. A
48. E
49. E
50. D
51. D
52. D
53. B
54. A
55. B
56. A
57. C
58. C
59. C
60. B
61. A
62. E
63. C
64. E
65. D
66. C
67. E
68. C
69. D
70. C
71. B
72. A
73. D
74. A
75. A
76. E
77. A
78. A
79. A
80. B
81. C
82. B
83. C
84. B
85. C
86. E
87. B
88. B
89. C
90. E
91. C
92. E
93. A
94. B
95. E
96. B
97. A
98. A
99. E
100. D

Answers and Explanations

CRITICAL REASONING PRACTICE

1. E

The question presents information about both false negative and false positive pregnancy test results, but concludes that the consumer need only take into account false negatives when choosing a test. Why aren't false positives an issue for concern? If all at-home pregnancy tests have the same likelihood of producing false positives, then the conclusion that the decision to purchase a test should be based on false negatives is reinforced. Answer choice (E) is correct.

2. D

The conclusion of this argument is that belly dancing is a valid art form, because it is performance centered and has a repertoire of choreography and a rich history. In order for that evidence to support the conclusion, we have to link the new term in the conclusion—that belly dancing is a "valid art form"—to the evidence—that it is performance centered and has a repertoire of choreography and a rich history. So the necessary assumption here is that any dance that is performance centered and has a repertoire of choreography and a rich history is a valid art form. That's choice (D).

3. E

This question's conclusion demonstrates faulty logic; the number of people who turn on news programs is not, by itself, enough to show how many people are knowledgeable about global issues. Four of the answer choices expose problems with this logic, while the correct one does not. Choice (E) is correct; while it does help explain why more people in Alphaville would tune in to the news than in Bentonville, it does not weaken the conclusion.

4. C

This question concludes that laptop owners do not use them enough to justify the cost, and it presumes that the higher cost is based on "portability." However, the evidence only addresses "portability" as it applies to using the computers outside the home. But "portability" can have a broader definition: What about moving around to different parts of one's own home? Choice (C) is correct: if people are willing to pay more for laptop computers for the convenience of being able to use them in different locations around the house, the conclusion that the computers' portability is not utilized often enough to justify the cost is weakened.

5. D

Several GMAT CR questions will ask the test taker to strengthen an argument or plan. A valid strengthener need not prove an argument or sell us 100% on a plan; it must only make the conclusion more likely or the plan more viable.

The most common ways to strengthen an argument or a plan include bolstering the central assumption, ruling out alternative possibilities, and supporting causality.

This passage's conclusion is that the number of different stonemasons involved in the temple indicates that it was built during the ten-year period when there were numerous stonemason strikes. However, that claim is weak without further information to connect the numerous different stonemasons to a labor issue. The correct answer eliminates other possibilities while reinforcing the connection between the succession of different stonemasons and the labor stoppages. Choice (D) is correct, because it provides a strong link between the evidence and the conclusion.

6. E

The test taker should note here that, although the plan that management has come up with is intended to maximize profits, the question only asks what would undermine the attempts to speed customer turnover. If chicken cooks faster than steak, only serving chicken might get customers through their entrées more quickly. But if they add an additional course, that might actually make their meal last longer than steak alone would have. Choice (E) is correct: if ordering chicken encourages people to order dessert as well, meals could end up taking longer than they would if the customers had gotten steak.

7. D

The argument challenges the assumption that a waiter's earnings depend on how many customers he has by pointing out that a waiter can have too many customers, which would cause a decline in the quality of service. The point of the argument, then, is that quality of service plays a role in the earnings of tipped employees. Since the question is looking for a claim with which the author of the argument would disagree, the correct answer will be a statement that is at odds with the idea that both quantity of customers and quality of service have an impact on a waiter's earnings. So, choice (D) is correct.

8. D

Joe's plan is based on the fact that he owns the copyright to the articles that he has sold to *News Magazine* and his assumption that, if the magazine is planning to reissue archived issues of the magazine in an online database, it would need to clear copyright ownership with the writers of the articles in those issues. But if *News Magazine* retains the copyrights on the compiled issues, it can republish those issues without seeking additional clearance. Choice (D) is correct.

9. E

This stimulus presents the theory that heterosexual attraction has a biological basis, and it supports that theory with evidence about the physical traits that cause men to find women attractive. Since the reader is asked to weaken the scientists' theory, the best way to do so is to show that the physical traits described are not necessary in order for a woman to successfully attract a mate. Choice (E) is correct. If women who do not possess a desirable evolutionary marker are still able to attract mates, then it becomes less likely that such markers are a driving force in attraction.

10. E

The argument here states that there would not be enough money to hire teachers to fill the new classrooms. It assumes that the new school will have space for classes that do not yet exist. One way to weaken this conclusion is to bring in evidence that there are already enough teachers and classes to fill the new building; that way, salaries for new teachers would not be an issue. Choice (E) is the correct response. If the school already has enough teachers to fill the new classrooms, additional salaries are no longer a consideration.

11. E

The argument reaches a conclusion about average raises based on average salary, which is not the same thing. In order for any conclusions to be reached about how teachers' raises measure up, the evidence would have to address the amount or percentage of the average raise, not just the average salary. Answer choice (E) summarizes this and is the credited choice.

12. D

In "Complete the Passage" questions, do just that: finish the passage by selecting an answer choice that is absolutely true and appropriate in scope. It's a good idea to paraphrase the argument or statements in questions of this type.

This question asks for a conclusion based on the facts presented; the correct conclusion must take into account the information in the passage without bringing in any outside considerations. Here, the passage states that there are two components for a successful strike: workers' support and public opinion. The Galt Hybrid Auto Factory workers support a strike, but it is unlikely that the public will support a strike. Therefore, one can conclude that the strike is likely to fail. Choice (D) is correct.

13. E

This question asks the reader to identify the one statement that does NOT provide a reason for football players to practice ballet, yoga, or Pilates. The four incorrect answers all discuss some benefit to the "nontraditional conditioning activities": flexibility, muscle strengthening, increased range of motion, etc. Why would a football player NOT want to practice one of these "nontraditional" activities, then? What if those activities put the same kinds of strain on the body as football, without providing any apparent protection from potential injuries? Choice (E) is correct. If ballet dancers tend to injure themselves in the same way that football players do, then it is likely that ballet does not provide any increased protection from those injuries and could instead exacerbate them.

14. C

Explain questions ask test takers to resolve an apparent inconsistency or leap in logic. The statements in these questions do not contain a complete argument, only a set of statements (often somewhat contradictory ones). The correct answer offers an explanation of how two seemingly contradictory statements offered actually can work together.

This question presents a set of seemingly contradictory circumstances. The correct answer will reconcile those circumstances, explaining why the experienced runners are faster while simultaneously exerting less cardiovascular effort. Choice (C) is correct. If experienced runners can run faster than novices while not putting as much stress on their hearts, the scientists' findings are explained.

15. B

This question's conclusion, that more money spent on safety and maintenance means fewer accidents, can be weakened by bringing in nonmonetary factors that could influence safety. Choice (B) is correct. Temporary employees who are not trained properly could have accidents that regular employees would not, which might be enough to counter any increased safety from the investment in precautions.

16. A

This question's conclusion—that the emissions standards legislation will result in the loss of many export markets for cars—rests on the assumption that the U.S. cars will become too expensive to be competitive in those markets.

However, if other countries have recently enacted similar legislation, then the costs of domestic automobiles in those markets are likely to increase as well, which would allow the U.S. exports to raise their prices without becoming too expensive to sell. Choice (A) is a match for this prediction.

17. A

This question presents a paradox: designers no longer create only high-end clothing; they now produce cheaper items as well, and therefore a designer label no longer automatically connotes high quality. Yet designer clothes are more popular than ever. Why? One possibility is that consumers, when faced with the choice between two garments of similar price—one with a designer label and the other without, will purchase the designer garment, assuming that it is guaranteed to be at least as good as the nondesigner garment. Choice (A) is correct. Consumers may not be able to rely on a designer label as an indication that the garment is of higher quality than other clothes, but if they still feel that a designer label indicates that the clothing is at least as good as any similarly priced clothes, that would motivate them to purchase the designer goods.

18. B

This question asks the reader to support the scholars' conclusion that the ship was sunk in 1872. The correct answer will provide evidence that the ship sailed prior to the hurricane in 1872, and not after that date. That's choice (B). Munitions from prior to the hurricane, but not after it, support the theory that the ship was sunk in the hurricane.

19. E

The conclusion of this question states that professors should keep the royalties from the computer programs that they create. Computer programs are never addressed in the evidence; however, faculty publications and patentable inventions are. The correct assumption must bridge the gap between publications and inventions on one side, and computer programs on the other. That's choice (E).

20. A

This question concludes that eliminating bottlenecks and delays will also eliminate potholes and buckled asphalt. This conclusion is based on the faulty assumption that just because some bottlenecks and delays are caused by potholes and buckled asphalt, all potholes and buckled asphalt cause delays. (A) is correct.

21. D

This question asks the reader to weaken the conclusion, which is that switching over to Machine B will result in immediate increases in efficiency and profits. A word like "immediately" should attract the reader's attention: the correct weakener doesn't have to make it less likely that the switch will increase efficiency and profits; it just needs to make it less likely that such an increase will be immediate, especially since the evidence used the disclaimer "once trained." Choice (D) is correct. If it is time-consuming and expensive to retrain the machinists, Machine B might be beneficial in the long run, but the cost of retraining makes it unlikely that the increases in efficiency and profits will be immediate.

22. E

Neuman's plan is to expand its facilities so it can handle more business. Evidence that Neuman's can expect continued success in the newly expanded facilities will support that plan, while evidence that Neuman's will see a decline in business will suggest that the plan will fail. Choice (E) matches this prediction.

23. E

The Eatco executives have assured the sales staff that they will continue to make at least as much money on the commission structure as they did on salary. However, commission depends on each salesperson maximizing his or her own sales. Look for an answer choice that challenges each employee's ability to do so. That's (E). Since commission depends on each salesperson maximizing his or her own sales, if Eatco hired new salespeople, the commissions received by current sales staff could decline.

24. D

The politician concludes that, if every country retaliated against every other country that denied entrance to the first country's citizens, soon no one would be able to travel internationally. In order for this extreme conclusion to be true, it would have to be true that every country would deny entrance to someone from every other country. If even one country maintained friendly borders with the politician's country, international travel would technically continue to exist. Choice (D) matches this prediction.

25. A

This question asks the reader to identify a possible weakness in the argument and point it out by pinpointing a situation that would bring that weakness into focus. Here, the weakness is Tom's lack of an eating plan. His intention to continue eating only when hungry depends on his appetite staying consistent; if his appetite increases, and he continues to eat when he's hungry, he may take on enough calories to counterbalance the calories he uses through exercise as well as any increase in his metabolism. Choice (A) matches this prediction.

26. A

The most common ways to undermine an argument or a plan include attacking the central assumption, calling attention to alternative possibilities, and reversing causality.

This question asks the reader to identify the weakness in the argument, as demonstrated by the answer choice queries. Here, the explanation posited is that the subject has one portion of herself that cannot hear and a different portion that answers the question. However, if the portion that answers the question is separate, shouldn't it respond to the hypnotist by affirming that it can, in fact, hear? (A) is correct.

27. E

Here, the homing pigeons' homing ability is described, along with the increased difficulty that the pigeons face when their nostrils are blocked. Why would plugged nostrils make it harder to home? Choice (E) is correct: it provides a link between a homing pigeon's sense of smell and its homing ability, which explains why plugging the pigeons' nostrils impedes their quick return.

28. C

If it is cheaper for Maureen to buy her cigarettes from 40 miles away, in Minconsin, than it is for her to pay the high cigarette tax in Wissesota, then the cost of transporting the cigarettes from Minconsin to Wissesota must be less per pack than the Wissesota tax. Choice (C) is correct. if it was NOT cheaper to transport the cigarettes from Minconsin to Wissesota than to pay the tax in Wissesota, then it would be cheaper for Maureen to obtain her cigarettes in Wissesota, which would contradict the last line of the passage.

29. C

The mayor's conclusion in this question is supported by evidence about only one occurrence of the littering to which he refers. This is a weakness in the argument; it leaves the argument open to being called into question by evidence that the one instance of littering was an exception, rather than the rule. That's choice (C). If there were several other weekends on which trash was not a problem, then maybe the Fourth of July weekend was an aberration, and the tourists are not litterers.

30. C

The argument claims that increasingly, people commute via trains and buses more so than by car, so instead of being spent on road improvements, the funds in question should be redirected to public transportation. However, it overlooks the fact that buses travel on roads, so road improvements will also benefit the public transportation system. Choice (C) is correct.

31. D

This question presents the conclusion that restaurant managers are not as well-informed about negative customer feedback as the service workers are, because the service workers often do not pass on such feedback truthfully. This conclusion would not necessarily be true, however, if managers had other ways of obtaining feedback from customers. (D) is correct.

32. D

Simply stated, the argument claims that since the flu virus is only infectious in the human body *at body temperature* for one week, an infectious person *can't be held responsible* for transmission after more than one week. There is a gap between the evidence's statement, which specifies the body temperature in which the virus remains infectious for a week, and the conclusion, which is drawn without regard to that idea about temperature. Weaken the argument by attacking that gap. (D) is correct: If the virus can survive longer at lower temperatures—for instance, at room temperature on doorknobs or furniture surfaces—then transmissions after more than a week could still be traced back to the original infected person.

33. A

The argument discusses two conditions, both of which must be simultaneously fulfilled in order to indicate that a restaurant is profitable: consistent overhead costs and high daily receipts. This question's difficulty lies mostly in the similarity of the answer choices; the reader should approach the answers with a prediction already in mind in order to cut through any potential confusion from the answers. (A) is correct.

34. A

To raise prices lowered by overproduction of coal, the government paid subsidies to mine owners who stopped using 15% of their mines. According to the author, these subsidies did not lose the government money.

What would explain how this did not cost the government money? (A) is correct. If the resulting higher product prices turned many unprofitable mines into profitable ones, the increased tax revenues could have exceeded subsidies paid.

35. C

In this atypical Weaken question, make sure to focus on the right element: the lieutenant's final conclusion. It's a good idea to paraphrase the argument to be sure you've comprehended it:

To reduce training costs for new recruits in his crew, a soldier proposes replacing Uzis with user-friendly Tommy guns. His lieutenant objects, instead suggesting hiring experienced Uzi users, implying that this will save even more money.

What point weakens the lieutenant's argument? Notice that the soldier proposes a change to reduce training costs, and the lieutenant counters with a plan to avoid any training costs. For both, the issue is cost cutting. (C) is correct. If experienced Uzi users cost more, then the cost of hiring them may exceed saved training costs, which hurts the lieutenant's argument.

36. B

Facts: Antibiotics have two "insidious" (bad) effects that undermine their effectiveness when used constantly: (1) They kill some good antibodies, and (2) they lead to antibiotic-resistant strains of bacteria. The task: Find what would make antibiotics effective longer. (B) is the credited response. This reduces effect #2; since bacteria are resistant to *one* kind of antibiotic, "rotating" (changing) the kind of antibiotic should kill off any strain resistant to a particular antibiotic before that resistance has a chance to become a problem.

37. C

Old companies protect their existing products, so they rarely innovate and often underestimate competitors' innovations.

Which scenario demonstrates this (a defensive strategy undertaken by an old company)? Choice (C): A maker of horsewhips trying to improve its existing product, without realizing that cars will make horses and whips obsolete, is indeed an example of a defensive strategy by a conservative company.

38. A

After a barrier was built, the range of saltiness on one side narrowed, and native slugs stopped growing normally. Scientists guess the lower salinity caused the slugs to grow more slowly.

What supports this proposed causal relationship? Choice (A): In experiments, to test causation and eliminate alternative causes, there should ideally be a "control" group (one not affected by the thing studied) and only one variable (here, salinity). If one side of the barrier has unchanged yearly salinity range, and slugs there grow normally, this helps eliminate alternative causes.

39. C

Researchers found that, after leftover sandwiches are left for seven weeks, they may become infested with viruses. Thus, the scientists concluded sandwiches should be discarded every seven weeks.

What information weakens the argument? The argument's underlying assumption is that those not discarding their old sandwiches may catch plague as a result of the viruses. This confusing choice means that people who eat infested sandwiches do not catch plague more often than those who do not eat them (i.e., sandwiches infested with viruses do not cause plague).

40. D

People become clergy because they are motivated to do charitable deeds, and they see other clerics with similar motives as colleagues. When a cleric becomes a televangelist, other clerics stop seeing him as a colleague.

What assumption is necessary [for clerics] to conclude that televangelists are not colleagues [motivated by charity]? Choice (D) is the credited response. If clergy consider charitably motivated clerics as colleagues but do not consider televangelists as such, they must assume televangelists are not charitably motivated.

41. D

Due to rising travel costs, a political party plans to halve the number of fund-raising dinners, though the entrance price and the quality/quantity of speeches will not change (i.e., double the number of speeches per dinner). Analysts conclude that this will not drive away large or small party contributors.

The question asks us to find an answer that suggests total donations *will* fall. So which choice would suggest a decline in total donations? (D): The statements say there will be no reduction in the *number of speeches* or *cost per attendee*; it doesn't mention *how* attendees are charged. If attendees pay the same amount per dinner—but they're hearing twice as many speeches now (to account for the 50% reduction in the *number* of dinners)—they're getting more bang for their buck, but the party is missing out on half of the contributions dinner tickets bring in.

42. B

A state initiative lets senior citizens reduce their future nursing home fees by prepaying now at today's rates, which lets them enter any state-run nursing home when needed.

What would make participating in the initiative a bad deal? (B) is correct. The initiative should save seniors money. One alternative is investing money to earn interest. If investing now will generate enough money later to cover any fee, and more, then senior citizens make/keep more money by investing rather than prepaying.

43. D

The passage presents a rule: that it's illegal for American bidders for foreign government contracts to bribe foreign officials. That truth, however, is followed by what will happen if American bidders follow the rule: if they don't bribe, competitors from other countries *will* (and it is possible that those other countries might then win the bids).

The task here is to find a set of considerations that is logically similar. (D) is correct.

44. E

An official, when told his country's plumbing pipes are "inadequate" for tourists, rebutted by saying the country has spent more per mile on improvements (specifically, adding more lead) than has any other country. The problem: We don't know what makes tourists claim the system is "inadequate." If it's simply because lead is bad, then adding more lead won't help; similarly, if the "open air" system is inherently bad, then improvements to that type of system still won't help, either. Or perhaps the system was in such bad disrepair that many years of substantial investment will be needed to bring it just barely up to par.

What weakens the argument? (E). If the only reason countries must spend massive amounts to "improve" pipes is that they started from an inadequate level and must catch up, then Tyrannia's spending may not improve pipes' quality beyond the bare minimum.

45. C

The genuineness of an undocumented coin, allegedly from second-century BCE Rome, is at issue. While most antiques' exteriors are patchy from erosion, this one looks evenly eroded, which is common in fakes. Thus, the coin is probably forged.

What undermines this conclusion? (C) is correct. The only evidence of forgery is even erosion, suggesting that artificial means were used to forge the coin's ancient appearance. Yet if past owners once used similar acid baths to even out the appearance of real antiques, then there is no basis to conclude this coin is forged.

46. B

Argument: Before, researchers thought mammals came to West Europe first, 15 million years ago. Yet after finding mammal remains in East Europe that predate these (at 27 million years ago), researchers now theorize mammals first arrived in East Europe.

Which proves mammals first arrived in West Europe? If Western fossil records are older than any Eastern ones, then mammals were in the West before the East, contradicting the theory. (B) is correct.

47. A

Bees building hives must build exactly enough rooms. If they build too few, some are left homeless and die; if they build too many, some bees kill each other fighting for the extra space.

(A) is correct, though somewhat convoluted. If you cannot understand an answer choice, you cannot eliminate it, so use process of elimination on the others and guess between remaining possibilities if necessary. This choice correctly identifies the conclusion that if you watch enough bees, then in theory, you could see the largest hive ever built and know that is the maximum possible size.

48. E

Just because this question uses the word "flaw," don't be mislead into thinking it's a Flaw question. It's asking for an assumption and is an Assumption question.

A famous dictator won a suit against an ad agency for having impersonators deliver his famous speech in commercials. Thus, ad costs will rise because famous dictators charge more than impersonators.

(E) is correct. Otherwise, without demand for original speeches, agencies could hire unknown impersonators for less money.

49. E

This one's tough. Take it one piece at a time and paraphrase: A UFO landing happens every 122 years *on average*, and *if* it does, it *may* seem like a hostile nuclear missile to an artificial intelligence-controlled nuclear missile system. An AI's reaction to unforeseen events (like a UFO) is *not* predictable.

If an AI controlled our nuclear missile defenses, what result can we *definitely* predict? Remember, the passage talks mostly about possible outcomes, but you need a certain outcome. Assume a UFO landing is unforeseen. (E) matches our prediction. Since basically all the passage's statements speak of possibilities rather than certainties, no certain conclusion follows logically. So just don't put all your eggs in one bomb shelter.

50. D

Theoretically, public wells will be overused more than private wells, because each user gains the full benefit, but faces only part of the cost/harm. Contrary to this theory, a poll comparing communal versus personal wells found the communal ones were in better condition.

Choice (D) is correct. Overuse would be discouraged if users knew that if they overused, others would follow their lead and use even more, thus leaving less for them.

51. D

In this argument, receptors signal stomach blood cells to attack toxins, partly preventing poisoning. Yet those receptors can also react to harmless foods, triggering allergy attacks. A drug to block the receptors is being considered.

What makes this plan to block all such receptors (allergen-induced and non-allergen-induced) seem like a bad idea? (D) is correct. The receptors do good when they react properly but cause harm when they overreact. The drug would block receptors completely, stopping the defensive action as well as the allergy.

52. D

During trial phases, pharmaceutical companies mark down prices and boost the amount of drugs sold to reseller pharmacies. However, pharmaceutical companies might make more without trials.

Why might trials lower pharmaceutical companies' profits? (D) is correct. If pharmacies buy so much that they cannot sell the drug during the trial but store it and sell it after the promotional period at the regular price, these sales compete with pharmaceutical companies' regular sales of the drug, possibly causing more losses than any profits from promotional sales or new customers.

53. B

This argument has an underlying principle: the larger the company, the larger the salaries it pays. What example demonstrates this principle? (B) is the credited response. "Bulge bracket" firms are larger than "smaller" start-ups, so they pay higher salaries, in accordance with the passage's principle.

54. A

Argument: An anti-tobacco activist argues that because nicotine is addictive and a tobacco company adds precise nicotine doses to its cigarettes, the company wants to keep customers addicted. The tobacco company's PR spokesperson replies that manufacturing causes the finished cigarettes to have less nicotine than raw tobacco.

Why does the PR spokesperson's counterargument not respond directly to the activist's argument? (A) is correct. The flaw in the PR person's response is that it doesn't address the accusation of the anti-cancer activist; instead, it compares cigarettes to raw tobacco, an issue irrelevant to the criticism leveled.

55. B

According to the actuary, government natural disaster relief encourages people to build homes on disaster-prone land because the relief subsidizes land repairs; without relief programs, builders would evaluate the land's risk more carefully.

What undermines the argument by suggesting that the subsidy DOESN'T encourage people to build on disaster-prone land? (B) is the correct answer. If the government began subsidizing to prevent confused, panicked people from wildly picking nearby unsafe lands, then the program is not all bad.

56. A

A bank plans to save on rent by moving its office to Samoa. Before doing this, it recruited volunteers for a three-month daily commute test, which found these volunteers' performance improved, too.

What flaw in the test makes it unreliable? One flaw could be an unrepresentative sample, which is the case here in (A). If those tested were volunteers who were far above average anyway, their high achievement is not representative of the bank's average workers.

57. C

Argument: An independent report found a certain airplane "has the fewest injuries *per accident* of *airplanes in its class*." Afterward, ads claim the airplane is one of the *safest* airplanes *around*. Question: What weakens the claim? The report's finding means that if the airplane does crash, fewer passengers get hurt than when other airplanes crash, *in that class* of aircraft. The ad claims the airplane is "one of the safest," implying in *any* class (or compared to *all* airplane types). (C) is correct. The report found the airplane the best in its class, yet if that class itself is a more dangerous class of airplanes (e.g., the "exploding gas tank" class), then this airplane may not be the safest airplane around.

58. C

Bolded statement questions ask test takers to articulate the particular function of one or two bolded statements, or their relationship to one another, in an argument or set of statements. To nail these rare and advanced questions, get comfortable paraphrasing arguments—breaking them down into components and identifying the roles of statements within them.

Generally, it's argued, FDA testing historically produced safer drugs. It is also true that **when drugs were tested, side effects were rarer, and public health improved**. But this will no longer be true if another policy— requiring fewer warnings on tested drugs—is applied simultaneously. This is because **users would assume the drug is safe in all cases and ignore their individualized risk factors**. (C) is correct. Phrase #1 gives a generally true causal relationship (FDA testing produces safer drugs), but this relationship will not occur in a particular case where another variable is changed (i.e., if testing results in fewer required warnings). Phrase #2 explains that the usual effects (safer drugs) will not apply in such circumstances because of a reason (i.e., because people will stop thinking about individual risks).

59. C

After nuclear power plant accidents triggered claims against nuclear insurers, insurers raised insurance premium prices. Now, new plants cost more to build, and existing plants must perform more. The cost of nuclear plants will increase more.

What added logical step is needed to get from the passage's details to the argument (that costs will keep rising)? This is an unusual phrasing of a more familiar question type, but it's essentially a strengthen/support question; we want something "taken with the information above" that would "best support" the conclusion. Remember, the conclusion in the question is that costs will *continue* rising, not just that they are high. (C) is correct. The passage says old power plants are forced to work harder. If we add the details that increased workload causes increased breakdowns, then there will be increasing costs to maintain existing plants as well as to build new ones. More frequent repair costs may further increase the cost of insurance.

60. B

An optical illusion makes shorter containers seem less voluminous than taller ones. Thus, an observer's estimate of volume is less for a short jar than for a tall bottle. The assumption of the argument is (B), that both containers are of similar volume.

61. A

Since the wholesale cost of raw material (asbestos) used in a finished product (asbestos shorts) fell, retail prices for the end product must fall soon. What fact undermines this argument? To get there, ask what assumption was necessary for the argument, then attack that assumption. (A) is correct. It undermines the argument by negating a necessary assumption. If the cost of weaving the raw material rose, this may prevent retail price decreases.

62. E

Laws requiring lit streetlights in daytime are more effective in preventing crime in nations with lower daytime visibility, which are located farther from the equator than the United States is. In fact, only nations farther from the equator than the United States is have such laws.

What conclusion is possible? (E). Daytime streetlights work best against crime in nations with bad lighting. Bad lighting only happens in nations farther from the equator than the United States is. Thus, lighting does not work as well in the United States as it does in other, more distant nations.

63. C

This question argues that small businesses will benefit from government-subsidized construction of a major retailer. From the choices, we need to determine which one would NOT weaken this conclusion. (C) is correct. If small businesses profit from being subcontractors, the small businesses benefit.

64. E

When books are distributed by publishing houses, the failure rate is lower than when books are distributed by other means. Thus, the most important component of books' success is the distribution source. (E) undermines the argument. If publishing houses consider other factors, like writing and editing, in deciding whether to distribute the book, then the most important component of success may not be distribution.

65. D

The question asks you to draw an "inference" or to "infer" something. Such questions demand that you make a logical conclusion based on the data given in the passage. Sentence 1 means humans—implying ALL humans—are poisoned by higher levels of D.I.E. Sentence 2 says "some" people increase D.I.E. levels by eating lard (pure fat). Thus, only "some" people who eat lard face increased toxic D.I.E. Answer choice (D) is correct.

66. C

A cloned chicken from a lab in Beverly Hills costs five times more than a chicken raised in a coop in the Midwest.

The correct answer is one that makes cloned chicken profitable. That's choice (C). The huge price gap basically means cloned chicken (and thus chicken-cloning labs) cannot compete with Midwestern cooped chicken on the basis of price. You need an alternate basis. If healthy eaters value cloned chickens' absence of chemicals and will pay exceptionally high prices for such chicken, then the cloned chickens can be sold to them for higher prices, meaning profits for the lab.

67. E

The arguer here concludes that it is a better investment decision to choose a higher-risk portfolio with less diversity than it is to choose a lower-risk portfolio with more diversity. She does so by pointing to research that shows the most profitable investors make this decision. The assumption? That the most profitable investors must necessarily make better investment decisions than do those less profitable. Answer choice (E) is correct.

68. C

Face-recognizing cameras restrict access to authorized people. They detect so many features that disguise makers can't duplicate them all. What conclusion follows? If such cameras scan more features than disguises can copy, then no disguise can fool them. That's answer choice (C).

69. D

International coal prices rise when a disturbance in international coal supply occurs; in this event, free-trade countries experience a rise in domestic coal prices, even if they do not import any coal. Now determine which policy would minimize the effects of foreign price increases. Answer choice (D) is correct.

70. C

Answer choice (C) explains why the second buoy doesn't indicate the midpoint and instead says 41/45. The rower assumed the number facing him is the distance traveled from the start and the reverse is the distance remaining to the end. Actually, they represent the opposite: The second buoy says he has 41 miles to the end and has traveled 45.

71. B

The environmentalist governor reasons that if we tax polluting SUVs daily or enough that the annual cost would be more than enough to buy an environmentally friendly ethanol car, then many SUV drivers will switch to ethanol cars.

There's a flaw in the governor's reasoning. The governor assumes drivers react primarily to monetary incentives. If SUV drivers are already willing to pay more to drive their vehicles, then they may not switch to ethanol despite the cost. Answer choice (B) is correct.

72. A

Using studies that show seniors with close family ties tend to die immediately after a major family gathering, rather than immediately before, experimenters conclude that the will to live can extend life, at least for a short period of time. Find the choice that supports that. It's answer choice (A). The argument is that the will to live to see family keeps seniors alive *through* gatherings. The experiment's scope is limited to gatherings. It is open to the criticism in choice (E). Choice A's evidence rules out that alternate cause by expanding the scope to the entire year, thus strengthening the argument.

73. D

Product futures rise when a small supply is expected and fall on predictions of larger supplies. Today's prediction says the pigpens will receive necessary slop, so pork bellies futures will fall today.

Answer choice (D) correctly undermines the argument. The argument is based on food supply, which is one factor pushing futures prices down. However, if swine flu or some other plague counteracts this, prices may not fall. This statement weakens the argument.

74. A

Which choice would NOT explain the paradox of why quantity rose while the number of buyers fell? To answer paradox questions (where two facts at first seem contradictory), look at EXACTLY what the question/passage talks about and what it does not. Here, we are talking about adults (not children), Americans (not foreigners), and cocaine powder (not other forms or drugs). Any answer dealing with the topics in parentheses could explain the paradox by introducing new information. Answer choice (A) is the odd man out. If more women started using than men stopped, then the number of adult users would be higher, since men and women are both adults. This would not explain the paradox.

75. A

A book compares 50 modern buildings with 50 old ones, and on that basis it argues that modern American architects lack the skills of earlier American architects. The commentator agrees, adding that the modern buildings shown in the book are truly not as good as the older ones.

What is the logical flaw in the commentator's argument? The argument is founded on comparing two sampled sets of buildings, but the samples may not be representative of all buildings and architectural skill. For example, perhaps the author picked 50 bad modern buildings and 50 great old ones to support his argument. Choice (A) is correct.

76. E

Argument: Since the best armor is costly, the Army bought little of it in previous years. This year, the Army bought mostly the best. Thus, the Army reset its priorities, from cost to safety. What undermines this argument? Look for a choice suggesting that price remains the Army's top priority. Choice (E) matches that prediction. If the best armors are also cheapest, then the Army's purchasing them may be motivated by continued frugality, not safety.

77. A

The water in a desert oasis is scarce and rationed for each traveler. But trees on the oasis's rim use up some water. Therefore, clearly, if the travelers cut down those trees, they will have more water. Choice (A) undermines the argument. If trees protect the oasis from evaporation, removing the trees may not result in more water.

78. A

On toilet seat sales, Congress calculates price as past price plus a percentage increase based on inflation. Your task is to find the best criticism of this formula. Choice (A) fits. The price is last year's price plus inflation adjustments; if past years' prices were excessive, then all later years' prices will include that waste.

79. A

Here's the argument, in sum: Climate change can have many causes, human and natural. We expect a random pattern, in which some regions warm and others cool. Yet 1980s data show a pattern in which most places got warmer in concert.

Let's rephrase the question: Which bit of information would BEST explain what caused the nonrandom pattern?

Choice (A) provides a human variable that explains widespread warming in the time period in which the study was conducted. The key word in answer (A) is "widespread." The other examples are either irrelevant or outside the scope of the argument.

80. B

Some manned video cameras remain necessary to fight crime, even though residents can report crimes by cell phone or pay phone, because the Warehouse District has high crime but few residents or phones to report crime. Choice (B) seriously weakens the argument. If the warehouses have automatic video cameras that will detect a prowler's movements and call the police, then *manned* cameras (and witnesses, phones, etc.) are unnecessary.

81. C

In this argument, data indicate there is no correlation (matching relationship) between nations' inflation and economic growth rates. Choice (C) is a valid inference. Since there is no correlation between inflation and economic growth, reducing inflation by curbing government spending won't correlate slow economic growth.

82. B

The plan (argument) is to reduce car traffic in big cities by replacing cars with rickshaws (bicycle-drawn carts) for medium-distance trips. You must pick facts best supporting this plan. The plan will work better if people opt for rickshaws instead of cars, if many trips are medium distance, and if the plan is cheap/easy, etc. Choice (B) is the credited answer. If most trips are medium distance, then the plan would help many people, which makes it more effective. Therefore, this evidence supports the plan most effectively and could be cited as evidence for feasibility of the plan.

83. C

After some advertising, car use dropped 10 percent, and subway train riding increased 10 percent, so the advertisements must have worked. Choice (C) casts the most serious doubt on the passage's conclusion. Since road closings made driving more difficult, maybe the shift away from cars was caused partly or fully by this, instead of by the publicity campaign. This reasoning—considering alternate causes—is a commonly tested idea.

84. B

A team wants to keep giving loyal customers free tickets, but it wants to discourage resale through scalpers. What would discourage resale? Remember, the team also wants to keep intended recipients happy by not reducing the usefulness of legitimate tickets. Choice (B) is correct. By restricting the use of the complimentary tickets to fans and families, the league discourages the purchase of scalped complimentary tickets by those who aren't supposed to use them.

85. C

Argument: An author is renting a booth at a book convention. He wants to raise book sales and believes the best plan is to attract as many browsers as possible to the booth. To find bodies, he tells his salespeople to personally invite their friends to visit. Choice (C) would work. If just having a crowded booth will attract more browsers who might not otherwise come, then telling friends to come (or any tactic that draws initial visitors) is likely to increase attendance, which presumably will increase sales.

86. E

Pro-democracy rebels in Brokel-controlled Tolnya (which provides Brokelland with oil) are debating whether they can pressure Brokelland to grant Tolnya democracy by causing farmers' strikes in Eustacia (another Brokel-controlled region that provides the Brokellanders with food). Which fact is LEAST relevant to the strike's effectiveness? Whether other countries control both oil- and food-producing areas does not predict this plan's outcome, and answer choice (E) is correct.

87. B

Before, churches gave free aid to the poor, using leftover money from rich sponsors' contributions. Now, for tax reasons, rich sponsors' contributions are limited to operating expenses only. What conclusion follows? The one in choice (B). The passage says that prior funding for free aid is now limited. Thus, it follows that churches either must save money by denying aid or give aid at their own expense.

88. B

A minimum wage payer's expenses increased when the minimum wage was increased by law. Paradoxically, profits also increased. What fact would explain the paradox? Choice (B) resolves the mystery. If McDonut's customers are mainly minimum wage earners, then their increased earnings may have let them buy more at McDonut's, with increased sales offsetting increased salary expenses.

89. C

A self-perpetuating problem happens when some students cheat, making schools raise standards, making more students cheat to meet them. Choice (C) is a necessary assumption. If the standards were set to allow some margin for cheating, they would not skyrocket when some cheating occurs, thus breaking the cycle.

90. E

The Secretary of Transportation concludes that a 60% tax increase will lead to a 60% increase in revenues from that tax. In order for that to be true, the total gallons of gas taxed must not decrease. If, however, commuters were to decide that the gas tax made driving too expensive and switched over to public transportation instead, the number of gallons of gas purchased would decline, and the tax revenue would not increase as expected. Choice (E) is correct.

91. C

Only private buses and public rickshaws with GPS maps will be allowed to use main streets around tourist attractions, resulting in fewer crashes around attractions. Choice (C) is the credited answer. Consider the reverse: If most of these private rickshaws had GPS maps, they would still be allowed to use main streets, which would not reduce traffic/collisions. Negating this assumption would undermine the argument, so the conclusion depends on this assumption.

92. E

A country formerly self-reliant in producing beans and lard (pig fat) will soon have to import beans and/or lard, because (1) people are getting richer, (2) per-person lard consumption grows with income, (3) producing one pound of lard requires several pounds of beans, and (4) bean farmland cannot increase. Choice (E) is correct. If people who start eating lard simultaneously cut down on eating beans, there may be no shortage of beans.

93. A

Unemployed people on welfare lose job skills. Experts recommend part-time jobs. Yet the government pays welfare only to the unemployed. (A) is supported and is the correct answer. If people want to collect welfare, they must remain unemployed, thus losing skills.

94. B

Two identical companies make identical products and pay identical salaries. A-Co., wanting a business advantage, proposes cutting salaries. Which choice weakens the reasoning for cutting salaries? Answer choice (B) weakens the argument. If low salaries produce less sales revenues, then that loss would reduce the savings from salary cuts.

95. E

Requiring window guards in new homes will not reduce losses much because over 95 percent of falling babies are caught by family. Which choice suggests the window guards *are* a good idea? Choice (E) is the correct answer. This statement seriously weakens the argument. The most harm happens when family members are *not* home to catch falling babies.

96. B

Which factor among the answer choices would help prove the fairness of new laws (the new laws aren't excessive)? Choice (B) is the credited answer. If regulations are limited to known harmful effluents, then harmless effluents are not regulated unnecessarily.

97. A

Preventively treating obesity is not cheaper because the cost to treat all obese people is much more than the cost of treating the diabetes and heart attacks that obesity causes.

Choice (A) suggests that there *is* an economic incentive for treating obesity, thus undermining the conclusion. The argument's flaw is that it compares only the cost of prevention to the cost of treating these diseases. This choice adds that, though these diseases do not incur greater *medical* costs than the cost of prevention, there are major *economic costs,* meaning that the treatment can be economically justified.

98. A

To reduce traffic delay in the busiest streets, more express lanes should go to high-capacity mopeds. Which choice suggests that these lanes should not be dedicated exclusively to high-capacity mopeds? Choice (A) is the credited answer. It casts doubt on the effectiveness of this solution. If the effects are caused by factors not affected by express lanes (e.g., weather and defective equipment), then changing the number of lanes may have little effect.

99. E

In the winter quarter, a wholesaler made profits by offering its retailers a discount if their order that quarter exceeded last winter's order significantly. Many retailers participated. This spring quarter, the wholesaler plans to offer the same promotion. Why might offering the promotion again now (one season later) not work? Answer choice (E) is correct. If retailers stocked up on inventory last quarter to get the discount and still have not sold it, they will not buy again so soon.

100. D

An experimental group watched large amounts of a show and exhibited decreased intelligence; the control group did not watch and showed no decrease. Thus, it is argued that a component of the show—dull commentary—must have caused this. Answer choice (D) supports the conclusion. Eliminating an alternate cause for the difference (that the control group started out smarter than the experimental group) strengthens the argument.

Reading Comprehension

PREVIEWING READING COMPREHENSION

GMAT Reading Comprehension is designed to test your critical reading skills. Among other things, it tests whether you can do the following:

- Summarize the main idea of a passage.
- Understand logical relationships between facts and concepts.
- Make inferences based on information in a text.
- Analyze the logical structure of a passage.
- Deduce the author's tone and attitude about a topic from the text.

Note that none of these objectives relies on anything other than your ability to understand and apply ideas found in the passage. Familiarity with the subject matter is not required. Reading Comprehension is a research task—everything you need is right there in front of you.

Many Reading Comp questions contain wrong answer choices based on information that is actually true but not mentioned in the passage. Be careful not to let your prior knowledge influence your answer.

QUESTION FORMAT AND STRUCTURE

The directions for Reading Comprehension questions look like this:

> **Directions:** The questions in this group are based on the content of a passage. After reading the passage, choose the best answer to each question. Base your answers only on the basis of what is stated or implied in the text.

You will see four Reading Comprehension passages—most likely two shorter passages with 3 questions each and two longer passages with 4 questions each, for a total of approximately 14 questions. However, as is usual for the computer-adaptive GMAT, you will see only one question at a time on the screen, and you will have to answer each question before you can see the next question. The passage will appear on the left side of the screen. It will remain there until you've answered all of the questions that relate to it. If the text is longer than the available space, you'll be given a scroll bar to move through it. Plan to take no longer than 4 minutes to read and make notes on the passage and a little less than 1.5 minutes to answer each question associated with the passage.

Reading Comprehension Practice

PASSAGE I

Historically, consumers have tended to purchase new technologies that they consider to be a good value. Price and quality of the product have long outweighed its design or emotional appeal. Within the last decade, however, analysts have noticed that consumers more frequently purchase an item based on its aesthetic quality or emotional appeal, even if it is not the best value.

Apple computers, for example, have risen to the top of the PC market. Many researchers attribute this product's success to its emotional impact, including its packaging and design. Even Apple cords and chargers have a sleek appearance, and the computer monitors have smooth edges that can give the home office the feel of an art studio. Such details are the keys to Apple's success. Even though Apple must charge higher prices to give its products an element of luxury, consumers are willing to pay the price.

Because consumers are paying more to purchase Apple computers, the company can use its large profits to continue adding expensive details to its products. Other computer makers might have to take a more economical approach because their profit margins are lower. However, the recent trend has shown that saving a few dollars by skimping on details may not be worth the cost.

1. The passage is primarily intended to do which of the following?
   - O Compare and contrast different types of PC computers
   - O Define the concept of emotional appeal
   - O Explain the pros and cons of a current marketing trend
   - O Offer an example of how emotional appeal is important in the current technology market
   - O Argue in favor of greater regulation within the technology industry

2. According to the passage, today's consumers are less concerned with value and more concerned with which of the following?
   - O Price and packaging
   - O A product's longevity
   - O The product's brand name
   - O Previous experience with the product
   - O Design and emotional impact

3. According to the passage, which of the following factors contribute to Apple's emotional impact?
   - O Its value
   - O Its large consumer base
   - O Its price
   - O Its packaging and design
   - O Its economical approach

4. The author of the passage implies which of the following about computer makers who take a more economical approach to their design?
   - O They will attract a wider consumer base.
   - O They will attract a consumer who appreciates luxury.
   - O They will have a higher profit margin.
   - O They may ultimately be unsuccessful in today's market.
   - O They will have more consumer loyalty.

5. The ability of Apple to use its profits to continue adding expensive details to its products is similar to
   - O the ability of a jeweler to sell more luxurious items.
   - O the ability of a local storeowner to cooperate with a global business.
   - O the ability of a wealthy person to invest more money and, in turn, earn more money from that investment.
   - O the ability of a car salesperson to make money from year-end sales.
   - O the ability of a multinational business to capitalize on foreign connections.

6. Which of the following statements best describes the role of the second paragraph within the overall passage?
   - O It provides an example of the trend mentioned in the first paragraph.
   - O It compares two different types of marketing approaches.
   - O It defines an abstract concept mentioned in the opening paragraph.
   - O It offers an extended analogy to clarify the relationship between two dissimilar things.
   - O It refutes the idea that emotional appeal is important in today's technology market.

PASSAGE II

Harvard professor Theodore Levitt is first credited with using the term "globalization" to refer to the global streamlining of economic, cultural, religious, and social systems. The concept of globalization has been popular with economists since the early 1980s, but it was not until the mid-1990s that it became a part of public consciousness. The primary effects of globalization are recognizable in the emergence of worldwide production markets, the realization of a global economy based on the freedom of exchange of goods and capital, and the creation of an international government that regulates the business relationships among nations and safeguards rights related to social and economic globalization, among others. Public attitudes toward these effects are divided.

Supporters of globalization maintain that free trade boosts the economy and that it increases opportunity among developing nations by improving civil liberties and leading to a more efficient allocation of resources. In general, supporters claim that free trade leads to higher employment rates, greater output, and a higher standard of living, including a higher level of material wealth. Critics of globalization are primarily concerned with damage caused by perceived unsustainable environmental practices and with perceived human costs, including injustice, inequality, and the decline of traditional cultural values. The critics of globalization point out that globalization is a process mediated by corporate—and not human—interests, so while corporations might benefit economically from being globally connected, these relationships do not have an overall positive impact on the world's people and its environment. Critics point out that the poor and working classes in particular do not benefit from such global connectedness, and the health of the environment is in decline because globalization encourages unsustainable production practices.

7. The primary purpose of this passage is to
   - define the concept of globalization and offer a specific example of how it works.
   - explain the causes and effects of globalization.
   - explain what globalization is and contrast two primary attitudes toward it.
   - argue that globalization has more negative than positive effects.
   - discuss the historical development of global markets.

8. It can be inferred from the passage that critics of globalization believe that if globalization were a process mediated by human interests,
   - the economic benefits would surpass what has been achieved so far.
   - more attention would be given to underprivileged communities and environmental issues.
   - the overall impact on the world's people would be negative.
   - opportunities among developing countries would decrease.
   - free trade would boost employment rates.

9. The passage suggests which of the following about the relationship between globalization and a free-trade economy?
   - Globalization fosters a free-trade economy.
   - Globalization inhibits a free-trade economy.
   - Globalization has little impact on a free-trade economy.
   - Globalization promotes a free-trade economy, but only for developing countries.
   - Globalization is the result of a free-trade economy.

10. The author of the passage mentions all of the following as effects of globalization EXCEPT:
    - increased opportunity for developing nations
    - free exchange of goods and capital
    - a more healthy environment
    - the creation of an international government
    - the emergence of worldwide production markets

11. In the first sentence of the second paragraph, the author of the passage cites "improving civil liberties" and "a more efficient allocation of resources" in order to
    - offer details that help define an abstract idea.
    - offer examples that show how globalization increases opportunity for developing nations.
    - set up a contrast between these details and the negative aspects of increased globalization.
    - offer examples of globalization's pros and cons.
    - introduce the main idea of the second paragraph.

PASSAGE III

Farming practices in the United States have changed since the days of the traditional family farm. The term "agribusiness" refers to the many businesses associated with modern farming, including machinery, retail sales, and marketing goods. Agribusiness is often contrasted with the family farm and associated with the practice of corporate farming, in which the business and corporate aspects of producing food have become more important than the service benefits of buying from a small producer.

At the beginning of the 20th century, family farms produced less food per acre than they do today. The U.S. Department of Agriculture reports that 98 percent of all farms in the United States today are family farms, but large-scale corporate farms supply 14 percent of the country's total agricultural output. Family farms have historically thrived because smaller production enables farmers to develop close relationships with their customers and then produce goods that satisfy those needs. Operating a smaller farm also enables farmers to collect and understand information that relates to that land's unique productivity.

However, operating a large farm has proven to be beneficial in its business aspects. Larger farms are able to bargain more effectively than smaller farms and to sustain themselves better financially through less productive seasons. Large farms are also able to develop corporate partnerships more readily than smaller farms, so they often have a technological advantage. The development of agribusiness has further benefited large farms because it has fostered the growth of agricultural research departments and associated academic disciplines. This information can, in turn, allow farmers to make business decisions based on proven research. Despite the greater productivity of large farms, many buyers fear that the personal service and individual attention they receive from owners of small farms will soon be lost.

12. Which of the following statements best summarizes the main idea of this passage?
    - O Agribusiness protects family farms from future economic crises.
    - O Large farms have a technological advantage because they are able to develop corporate partnerships.
    - O Family farms are less productive than large farms.
    - O Large farms are on the decline because agribusiness is starting to regulate farm size.
    - O Agribusiness benefits large farms but may reduce the amount of personal service that these farms can offer.

13. The passage implies that family farms, compared to large-scale corporate farms,
    - O have higher profit margins.
    - O are more likely to develop corporate relationships.
    - O contribute less per farm to the country's total agricultural output.
    - O contribute more to the international economy.
    - O require more work per acre.

14. The tone of this passage suggests that the rise of agribusiness makes the author of this passage most likely feel which of the following?
    - O Angry that large farms are destroying the traditional family farm structure
    - O Enthusiastic about the future of agribusiness
    - O Accepting of agribusiness but willing to acknowledge its consequences for small farms
    - O Sad that small farms are not as productive as they used to be
    - O Hopeful that small farms will become more business minded

15. The passage does NOT cite which of the following as a benefit of large-scale farming?
    - O A technological advantage due to corporate partnerships
    - O Greater bargaining power
    - O More environmentally sustainable farming practices
    - O More financial stability
    - O Greater productivity

16. The author mentions that the rise of agribusiness has prompted some buyers to fear that
    - O farms will not be able to sustain themselves through less productive seasons.
    - O many seasonal workers will lose their jobs.
    - O farms will produce less food per acre per day.
    - O the cost of farm equipment will rise.
    - O personal service and individual attention will decline.

PASSAGE IV

Collecting garbage, particularly recyclables, is an undervalued profession. Because our society does not appreciate the work of people who recycle our trash, the environment will continue to suffer, as will the people who work within this profession. One problem within the recycling profession is that collectors are not paid well enough for the work that they do to protect the future of our environment. Public opinion of recycling collectors continues to be low, as people think little of the items that they discard and, in turn, think little of those who come to take away their trash.

In order to reverse public opinion and to duly compensate those who work within the recycling profession, I would like to suggest a solution to the problems associated with the job of collecting and processing recyclable trash. I propose that local governments assess fines on people who do not recycle their trash and use the revenue to pay better salaries to those who work within recycling facilities. In this way, the fines would encourage people to take responsibility for their trash by sorting out the recyclable items and would promote a more positive opinion of people who work within the recycling industry. Furthermore, the revenue gained from the fines would help recycling collectors make more money and associate a monetary reward with the work that they do to safeguard the environment.

People might object to the extra money being paid to recycling collectors, primarily because the common opinion is that collecting trash does not require very much skill. People might also object to the fines penalizing them financially for not recycling their trash. Those who do not recycle might not value the activity and could become upset if they have to pay a fine for not doing something they don't agree with. Recycling collection does, in fact, require several different skills, and those skills should be rewarded because recycling will benefit the entire community. Maybe recycling collectors do not have the kind of skills that will save a sick patient or repair a broken vehicle, but their skills will preserve the quality of the water that we drink and keep clean the air that we breathe. Their work today will be greatly appreciated in the future.

Besides requiring several different skills, recycling can also be dangerous work, and people who work within the recycling profession should be compensated for the risks that they take. Recycling glass, for instance, requires workers to throw bottles into a grinder that breaks the glass into small pieces that can be processed and reused. This work is dangerous, as small pieces of glass could easily cut exposed skin or be inhaled. Workers must wear face masks, respirators, and thick gloves while they are processing glass for recycling. Workers are also routinely exposed to sharp objects and dangerous machines that compress recyclable material such as cardboard and aluminum cans.

Low wages prevent the recycling profession from retaining skilled workers. This problem adds to the danger of the job because when experienced workers leave to take higher-paying jobs, the inexperienced workers are left to operate dangerous machinery. If local communities were to fine people who do not recycle, the extra money could be paid to those who work in recycling facilities, hopefully encouraging them to remain within the recycling industry instead of seeking out other better-paying jobs.

Even if local communities start levying fines on people who do not recycle, there is no guarantee that everyone will begin to recycle. Some people will choose to pay the fine. Nonetheless, a financial penalty associated with not recycling will either help workers occupationally, because people will take more responsibility for their own recycling, or it will help them financially by contributing to the salaries of the workers who do the job.

17. The primary suggestion that the author of this passage argues in support of is

- O increasing the number of recycling facilities so that more workers have jobs.
- O fining those who do not recycle in order to pay recycling collectors more for their work.
- O increasing safety standards at recycling facilities to reduce the dangers that workers face.
- O having more formal training at recycling facilities for inexperienced workers.
- O reducing the amount of trash people generate so that fewer workers are needed.

18. The author of this passage implies that all of the following are true about the recycling industry EXCEPT:
   - Better pay for recycling collectors will help to increase public opinion of the profession.
   - Those who process recycling deserve to be financially compensated in accordance with risks that they take at work.
   - The importance of recycling is often overlooked because its results are long-term rather than immediate.
   - The recycling industry must hire unskilled workers because skilled workers are taking better-paying jobs elsewhere.
   - At some point in the future, laws will inevitably require people to recycle, so they should start recycling now when there is no penalty for choosing not to do so.

19. Which of the following details is mentioned in the passage as an example of opposition that people might have to the author's idea that revenue from fines should be paid to recycling workers?
   - People are opposed to the idea of the fines because they think that other issues, such as gun control, are more important.
   - People oppose the idea of fines because they believe that the fines are unconstitutional.
   - People believe that the revenue earned from the fines should be spent building newer recycling facilities instead of paying workers more money.
   - People object to the fines because they believe that the revenue will not encourage workers to do a better job.
   - People might not want the revenue from the fines to pay workers that they view as unskilled.

PASSAGE V

Recent studies on gecko footpads have determined that Van der Walls forces are what hold geckos to a wide variety of surfaces, enabling them to climb vertically on featureless walls and to walk upside down on ceilings. Van der Walls interactions, which are often referred to as noncovalent or intermolecular forces, occur between the minuscule setae that cover a gecko's toes. These interactions rely on the attractive and repulsive components of intermolecular forces, which involve electrostatic interactions between charges, polarization, and dispersion.

Van der Walls forces act between stable molecules and are weak compared to the forces involved in chemical bonding; however, they are strong enough to allow a gecko to cling to a vertical glass surface with only one toe. The forces contributing to the dispersion component of the intermolecular forces at work in a gecko's setae are called London dispersion forces, named after physicist Fritz London. London dispersion forces develop between transient multipoles in molecules that do not have permanent multipole moments. As electron density moves about a molecule, an uneven distribution will occur, creating a temporary multipole, which can interact with other nearby multipoles. In this way, a gecko's setae allow the gecko to adhere to slick surfaces. As an additional physiological benefit, a gecko's setae are self-cleaning and can slough off any dirt within a few steps, allowing optimal adhesion.

20. It can be inferred from the passage that since London dispersion forces are at work in a gecko's setae, then
    - O chemical bonds are also present.
    - O a self-cleaning mechanism is also present.
    - O the molecules in a gecko's setae do not have permanent multipole moments.
    - O Fritz London's dispersion force theory is proven correct.
    - O London dispersion forces are at work in the setae of other animals as well.

21. It can be inferred from the passage that which of the following would diminish a gecko's ability to adhere to a surface?
    - O The presence of a centripetal force
    - O The presence of chemical bonds in addition to intermolecular forces
    - O The presence of dirt on a surface or on the gecko's toes
    - O The presence of transient multipoles
    - O The presence of electrostatic interactions between charges

22. If it were found that another animal could walk upside down on a ceiling, which of the following would be necessary to explain that Van der Walls forces were responsible for this ability?
    - o Evidence proving that the other animal is a close relative of the gecko
    - o Evidence that the other animal has setae that contain chemical bonds
    - o Evidence that the other animal also possesses a self-cleaning ability similar to the gecko's
    - o Evidence to show that it is also able to cling to a vertical glass surface with only one toe
    - o Evidence that the other animal's setae work through the interaction of intermolecular forces

23. Which of the following, if true, would most seriously undermine the idea that Van der Walls forces are what hold geckos to a wide variety of surfaces?
    - o Chemical bonds are found to be weaker than Van der Walls forces.
    - o The setae of geckos are found not to contain intermolecular forces.
    - o Other animals lacking setae are also able to walk on ceilings.
    - o Geckos can more easily adhere to smooth surfaces than they can to rough surfaces.
    - o The self-cleaning ability of a gecko's setae is overestimated.

24. According to the passage, what creates the uneven distribution of charge necessary for London dispersion forces to work?
    - o The presence of chemical bonds
    - o The cleanliness of a surface
    - o A pressure gradient resulting from the difference in two surfaces
    - o The movement of electron density throughout a molecule
    - o Gravitational forces

25. The author of this passage most likely states that geckos can "cling to a vertical glass surface with only one toe" in order to
    - o demonstrate the strength of van der Walls forces by offering an example.
    - o provide evidence for the idea that Van der Walls forces are weaker than chemical bonds.
    - o discredit the idea that London dispersion forces are at work in a gecko's setae.
    - o highlight an instance when a temporary multipole may not be interacting with other nearby multipoles.
    - o offer an example of how chemical bonding works.

PASSAGE VI

When it was published in 1962, Rachel Carson's *Silent Spring* called attention to the use of pesticides and pollution of the environment. Carson's book is credited with facilitating a 1972 ban on agricultural use of the pesticide DDT in the United States and with launching the environmental movement in the western United States. Her study revealed the negative effects of pesticides on birds, in particular, and accused the chemical industry of misinforming the public about the effects of pesticides on humans and the environment. DDT had originally been used to control mosquitoes and the spread of malaria, and by the time of Carson's book, DDT was being produced in large quantities and sprayed indiscriminately as an agricultural insecticide. Carson proposed a more natural approach to pest control as an alternative to DDT, but chemical and agribusiness firms criticized her ideas as naive and impractical.

Carson's work was not advocating a ban on or a complete halt to the use of pesticides, but rather encouraging more responsible use of them in light of her findings that the chemicals could impact an entire ecosystem. Even before the book was published, it was strongly opposed by leading chemical manufacturers, who claimed that DDT was necessary to combat harmful disease-carrying insects. As it turned out, DDT was never banned for anti-malaria use, and Carson even granted in her book that chemical agents could have some benefits in the realm of pest control as long as they were used as sparingly as possible. Before writing *Silent Spring*, Carson was known for her writing on natural history, and she had not previously been considered a social critic. Carson was criticized for not being a scientist; nonetheless, her work had a tremendous impact. Given the state of public knowledge about chemical science at the time of the book's release, *Silent Spring* did a great deal to educate its readers about the ways in which toxins could accumulate in the environment, and it prompted the public to call for a change.

26. Based on the passage's discussion of Carson's book, which of the following arguments did the book most likely NOT include?
   - An argument in support of using pesticides sparingly
   - An argument in support of natural alternatives to DDT
   - An argument encouraging responsible pesticide use
   - An argument in support of banning pesticide use
   - An argument aimed at promoting a desired change

27. The passage implies that *Silent Spring* enabled Carson to establish a reputation as
   - a scientist.
   - a radical environmentalist.
   - a social critic.
   - a troublemaker.
   - a political activist.

28. According to the passage, an important outcome of Carson's book was that
   - DDT was banned for agricultural purposes but not for malaria control.
   - chemical companies lost revenue as a result of the book's publication.
   - birds were able to proliferate in areas where they were once endangered.
   - the research was not well received within the scientific community.
   - newer research has since disproved many of Carson's findings.

29. This passage is chiefly concerned with
   - explaining a book's impact.
   - evaluating a book's research base.
   - contrasting a book's subject matter with previous findings.
   - reporting the results of a newly released study.
   - criticizing an author's methods.

PASSAGE VII

University students entering the relatively new discipline of cinema studies may be surprised to learn that film history itself, with its seemingly immutable timelines and suppositions, has always been in a state of flux. This is a direct result of the constant unearthing and restoration of early film. The frequent revisions of Albert Denison's benchmark text, *Pictures That Move: Development of Film* (the revision process having been dubbed "film developing" by film buffs) attest to the uncertainty of constructing a definitive history of an art form when so much of the art itself has been unseen since its creation.

For example, when Denison's book was first published in 1951, he gave but one brief mention to the legendary Ford Mace in his discussion of silent film comedy; conventional wisdom at the time held that Mace (who passed away in 1915 and whose films had seemed to disappear with him) was merely a second-string imitator of Chaplin. It wasn't until 1973, when a number of Mace's original films were found, restored, and screened publicly for the first time in nearly 60 years, that historians discovered not only that Mace had preceded Chaplin—he had himself originated the costume and mannerisms of "The Little Tramp"—but also that Chaplin had copied Mace's work after the latter's untimely death.

In the early 1970s, significant numbers of lost silent films came to light and seemed to undermine most of Denison's theories on the development of narrative cinema. Changing attitudes and social mores had also rendered many of his observations on contemporary cinema (contemporary for 1951, that is) obsolete and woefully inadequate, and Denison increasingly found himself called to task by irate students and film buffs. At first, his response was to write testy letters to critics, complaining bitterly that he had done the best he could with what he had at the time, and stating (in one oft-quoted passage from a letter to New Yorker critic Pauline Kael), "I'm like a paleontologist who has to construct an entire dinosaur from a femur, a couple of ribs, and part of a skull . . . cut me some slack, please?" But then, spurred on by the critics and faced with the prospect of his book going out of print, Denison hit upon the idea of creating a foundation that would exist solely to update his book. Drawing on the contributions of academics, students, film buffs, and collectors worldwide, the Film Development Foundation, now in its 35th year, issues annual revisions of Denison's text—still a perennial on film history course reading lists—and has inspired a generation of film preservationists and archaeologists, all of whom hope to rise to the challenge of challenging Denison and associates' venerable text . . . and winning a lucrative foundation scholarship award if they make a discovery that can, indeed, "rewrite history."

30. The term "film developing" (line 8) refers to
   - screening old movies on the anniversary of their first screening.
   - the examination and research of historical films.
   - the revisionist nature of film history due to constant rediscoveries of lost films.
   - the loss of historical film discoveries to studios that fail to pay old nitrate vault bills.
   - the obstacles involved in knowing when information might lose validity.

31. Of the following, which is the best example of a situation comparable to the challenge faced by the paleontologist mentioned in line 35?
   - A doctor trying to X-ray a bone with an X-ray machine
   - An actor with a wealth of material prepared for an audition
   - An overview of a director for whom only 2 films, out of 50, have survived
   - A student documenting the publishing history of a famous English literature professor from a respected university
   - A bird building a nest in a tree

32. What tone toward Albert Denison does the passage's author take?
   - Earned admiration
   - Educated acquittal
   - Cautious exploration
   - Ardent disapproval
   - Unabashed praise

33. Which of the following statements best exemplifies Denison's view of film history?
   - One's cinematic historical research is either right or wrong.
   - Film history has been rewritten a few times because of new discoveries, but no new discoveries are expected.
   - Film history is a costly study permitted only to the most bourgeois in society.
   - Film historians have not tried hard enough to properly research cinema's past.
   - Film history is a fluid matter, constantly evolving due to new discoveries.

34. "Conventional wisdom," as used in lines 14–15, refers to the idea that
    - o Ford Mace was an imitator, not an innovator.
    - o Ford Mace's films were hard to find because he was not well liked when he was alive.
    - o Ford Mace was an innovator, not an imitator.
    - o the understanding of film history was in no way changed by the discovery of Mace's films.
    - o the later works of Ford Mace paled in comparison to his early films.

35. The passage suggests that Albert Denison regarded his critics' complaints as
    - o trite quips of the pretentious elite.
    - o valueless and overly disparaging.
    - o intelligible gems that validated his existence.
    - o kind in nature.
    - o ultimately worthy of consideration.

PASSAGE VIII

A quantum computer operates on a principle similar to that of a classical computer: an array of "switches" are each either "on" or "off." How then could a quantum computer perform a complex calculation in seconds when a classical computer would take years to solve the same problem? The answer lies in the bizarre physics of the subatomic world as defined by quantum mechanics, in which an atom may exist in a state of superposition, in which, in effect, it exists in two states at once. Thus, the "switch" in a quantum computer, unlike the electronic switch in a classical computer, is not just "on" or "off" but could also be both at the same time.

Some quantum computers use the charge of electrons in a helium atom as the computational "switch." Others use trapped ions. But the most "typical" quantum computer makes use of the spin state of the electron in a hydrogen atom. A spin-based quantum computer would consist of a number of "contained" hydrogen atoms as well as the means of control—in other words, the device that would contain the atom, read its spin as either "spin up" or "spin down," and also be able to change its spin. Each atom and its "containment field" are defined as one computational unit, a qubit, or quantum bit.

The quantum computer owes a debt to a man who may have doubted the possibility of its existence, the physicist Erwin Schrödinger. Studying the atomic decay of radioactive particles on a quantum level, Schrödinger proclaimed something must be wrong with the mathematics. The calculations seemed to suggest that two answers were possible at any given time, the superposition that is the basis of quantum computation. To show the absurdity of this outcome, Schrödinger created a thought experiment. Imagine a cat that is in a box and cannot be observed. Also in the box is a syringe of poison which will be injected into the cat, causing the feline to die. The trigger for the syringe is the same process of atomic decay that Schrödinger had been calculating. A scientist uses the math of quantum physics to determine at what point the syringe is activated and the cat dies. What the scientist discovers, however, is that, according to the mathematics, at any given point the cat is both alive and dead. Schrödinger had no idea that he had just designed the world's first quantum computer.

36. Which of the following does the passage suggest would be the most likely task performed by a series of qubits?
   - Calculating a complex equation
   - Controlling the spin of a number of hydrogen atoms
   - Administering medication automatically through a syringe-like device
   - Forming a network that can trap and contain a single hydrogen atom
   - Making calculations regarding the atomic decay of radioactive particles

37. It can be inferred that the author states that the quantum computer owes a debt to Schrödinger because
   - Schrödinger demonstrated that a quantum computer was possible.
   - Schrödinger pointed out a fundamental flaw in the mathematics of quantum mechanics.
   - Schrödinger inadvertently alerted others to a typical task that a quantum computer could be used for: controlling feline populations.
   - Schrödinger developed several principles regarding atomic decay that are used in quantum computational devices.
   - Schrödinger crafted an effective illustration of the phenomenon of superposition.

38. Which of the following is the most likely reason that the author places the word "typical" in quotes (line 14) ?
   - The spin-based quantum computer is actually not as common as computers based on ions or electron charge.
   - The characterization of the computer as typical comes from a quote by Schrödinger.
   - The spin-based quantum computer uses a process more exotic than the switches used in computers based on ions or electron charge.
   - The author wants to emphasize the notion that quantum computers may someday become standard and commonplace.
   - A quantum computer is such an innovative and unconventional computational device that it is really anything but typical.

39. Which of the following reasons does the author give for why the spin-based quantum computer is more "typical" than computers based on ions or electron charge?
   - It measures a simpler characteristic of the electron.
   - Hydrogen atoms are the only ones that exhibit spin, and they are much easier to control.
   - Because hydrogen is so abundant, a spin-based quantum computer would be resource efficient.
   - It is easier to change the spin of an atom than it is to change its charge.
   - None of the above—the author does not give a reason.

PASSAGE IX

Dams built by beavers are seemingly complex and massive undertakings. How do the animals accomplish this? Perhaps it's because beavers consistently display five major and unwavering concerns when building a dam: Will it be strong? Will it discourage predators? Is it the correct height? Is there a source of constant running water? Is there a dependable food source nearby? These considerations are crucial to the building of a proper dam, and dams with these characteristics result in the plushest lodges and the most successful colonies. Beavers are known as industrious, tireless workers, and new reports indicate beavers are also possessed of an evolutionary tool that aids in the effective construction of dams, namely a gland that secretes a substance that tests the durability of wood.

The five characteristics of successful beaver dams have long been thought to be the result of experiential behavior; that is, the beavers learn building techniques from elders within a colony, much as a cougar cub is taught to hunt by a parent. These beaver dam considerations are each vital to the survival of a colony. If any one of these characteristics is not present, then the entire colony suffers and is unlikely to survive. For example, a food source is useless if a dam is of insufficient height to prevent the beavers from drowning if the water level rises too high during a rainstorm.

Much like beavers, birds exhibit similar concerns when building nests, and these concerns are commutual in nature. They seek out locations based on rigid criteria designed to optimize chances for survival, and the successful implementation of each consideration in the construction of a nest strengthens and complements every other characteristic. North American songbirds build simple open-cup nests, sturdy enough to support several chicks, in high areas away from snakes; hummingbirds seek proximity to running water and build nests concealed in tree limbs at a height that enables them to easily observe food sources. The height also serves to limit contact with potential predators while providing offspring a desirable platform for their first attempts at flight. Each characteristic of a good nest—and a good nest builder—helps to ensure the survival of the species. In the case of birds, most of this nest-building behavior appears to be instinctive.

With the recent discovery of the beavers' "wood-test" gland, it now appears that some of their skill in dam building may also be instinctive, as opposed to learned, behavior. Beavers have been observed to "hug" a tree before cutting it down; it has now been determined that they have glands in their forearms that secrete an enzyme that causes a slight reddish discoloration in dead or dying wood that has begun to rot. If the wood turns red, the beaver abandons the tree and moves on in search of better lumber.

40. The author suggests that, unlike the learned behaviors that go into making a dam, the instinctual aspect of the beaver gland introduces
   - o another experiential tool that only the wisest beavers possess.
   - o a scientifically proven distinction that makes the beaver better than humankind at detecting viable lumber.
   - o an evolutionary chemical tool that does not have an experiential value.
   - o a change in the way dams will be built in the future.
   - o a replacement for the five considerations that beavers put into their dam building.

41. Of the following, which does the passage suggest is the job of the beaver's "wood-test" gland?
   - o To determine the usefulness of a tree
   - o To check the water for rough currents
   - o To allow for the detection of a good lodge area, replete with all the necessities
   - o To alert the beaver that a predator is near
   - o To determine the value of many trees at once

42. The passage implies that the behavior exhibited by a bird building a nest fulfills the same function toward survival as which of the following?
   - o A cougar cub learning from a parent
   - o A beaver swimming against a rough current
   - o A beaver foraging for food in the woods
   - o A beaver exhibiting the five major concerns for building a successful dam
   - o A beaver using its "wood-test" gland

43. According to the passage, beavers build the best dams possible when
   - o they observe and mimic the nest-building behaviors of birds.
   - o their dams exhibit five specific characteristics.
   - o they work alone, as other beavers only provide distraction.
   - o it rains heavily to provide a wealth of water.
   - o they have been well fed.

44. The passage states detailed concerns of nest-building birds in order to demonstrate
   - o why birds have survived as a species for so long.
   - o that baby birds love the nests into which they are born.
   - o that birds have instincts that place them in a variety of locations.
   - o that birds have exactly the same concerns as beavers when building nests.
   - o the commutual nature of these requirements.

PASSAGE X

It has been long been assumed that strictures of the bile duct are the result of poor dietary habits and alcohol abuse, especially if such degradation has occurred over a period of ten or more years. Recent studies have shown, however, that bile duct strictures are most often an unfortunate consequence of certain types of surgery, the body's reaction to invasive procedures. These strictures occur when the liver produces an excess of bile, which then becomes stuck in the ducts and crystallizes. It is believed that the use of general anesthetics halts the ducts' natural motion of undulation, allowing the excess bile to build up. It has further been hypothesized that, strangely, the type of surgery performed has a causal effect on where the stricture occurs within the duct system.

These new ideas could have a profound impact on the diagnosis of strictures, especially since the medications generally given to surgical patients mask the obvious warning signs of bile duct strictures. In previous times, those suffering from such strictures would exhibit telltale symptoms, an oozing of pus from the pores of the chest, a dark discoloration of the urine and saliva. But the prevalent use of multivitamins and antibiotics keeps these symptoms hidden in patients, giving doctors no external indications of a problem in the bile duct system.

Doctors have had to resort to other methods of detection, primarily biopsy through either traditional means or endoscopy. However, even microendoscopy is enough of an invasive technique that the procedure itself could provoke the same reaction that may cause bile duct strictures. Newer, noninvasive technologies such as MRI (magnetic resonance imaging) or ultrasound could, thus, prove to be beneficial. Still, even these techniques are not useful unless the approximate location of the stricture is known. Without some empirical evidence of where the blockage is occurring or some theory that could successfully pinpoint its locale, an ultrasound scan could be a quixotic endeavor.

45. The author's primary purpose in this passage is to

- promote diagnosis of strictures by examination of secretions and excretions.
- show how and why certain new theories may be useful.
- expound upon the differences between invasive and noninvasive diagnostic techniques.
- illustrate the process used in the development of a hypothesis.
- counter assertions made by the mainstream medical community.

46. According to the passage, bile crystallizes within the bile duct system as a result of

- an excessive buildup of bile in the ducts.
- the long-term effects of alcohol poisoning.
- overuse of multivitamins and antibiotic medications.
- a rhythmic and surging motion of the ducts, caused by anesthesia.
- processes that cannot be observed by any known diagnostic technique.

47. It can be inferred from the passage that a doctor who wishes to detect the presence of a bile duct stricture within a patient would have the most success by performing which of these procedures?

- Having the patient fill out a questionnaire about the patient's diet and habits over the previous ten years
- Allowing the patient to undergo certain surgical techniques but without the use of anesthetic
- Pinpointing certain areas of the duct system based on the patient's history of surgery and then conducting ultrasound scans
- Considering the patient's entire medical history with a focus on the types of medications the patient has taken
- Examining the patient's urine and saliva and taking samples from the patient's pores

48. According to the passage, which of the following would lead to the easiest detection of possible bile duct strictures?

- Knowledge of a patient's history of alcoholism
- Knowledge of a patient's history of surgery
- Microendoscopic examination of the bile duct system
- The presence of dark, discolored urine and saliva
- An ultrasound scan of the entire bile duct system

49. If correct, which of the theoretical ideas mentioned in the first paragraph would be most helpful to a doctor performing an ultrasound scan to detect bile duct strictures?

- The theory that particular types of surgery cause strictures in particular areas of the duct system
- The theory that lifestyle choices and diet contribute to the development of strictures
- The theory that the use of anesthetics promotes the buildup of excess bile in the ducts
- The theory that bile duct strictures are provoked by invasive procedures such as surgery
- The theory that extra bile becomes crystallized in the duct system and causes blockage

50. The author implies that a successful scan of bile ducts in an attempt to diagnose strictures would be helped by which of the following?

I. How invasive or noninvasive the detection procedure is
II. Whether the area searched is found through direct observation or theoretical prediction
III. Whether the patient has had a type of surgery that corresponds to a location within the duct system

- I only
- II only
- III only
- I and II
- I and III

PASSAGE XI

One of the aims of public education is, ostensibly, to provide equal opportunity to the children of all citizens in order to "level the playing field" and erase class and cultural distinctions. A more just and democratic society is the hope upon which the creation of public school education is based. However, in practice, the quality of public school education often differs. We find that lower socioeconomic classes are not afforded the same opportunities and that members of society still have varying degrees of access to educational opportunities. The relation of quality public education to the upward social mobility and economic status of one's parents is still an issue.

Unfortunately, even with the good intentions of public education, serious inequities occur in minority and low-income areas. In many cases, this is due to another economic inequity, namely, the divergence in property tax revenues available for funding schools. Lower-income areas have a weaker tax base, which yields fewer funds, and thus the schools tend to be underfunded. Some would say that students in lower-income areas are poorly behaved and as a result do not deserve better opportunities. Our findings blame the opportunities for the behavior. With less money for books and educational supplies, the schools in poor neighborhoods are unable to stay current on ever changing historical topics and methodologies in teaching, which often results in students learning outdated subject matter in an outdated manner. As a result, schools in poor neighborhoods always underperform public schools in wealthier neighborhoods. This system perpetuates the inequality of educational opportunity and, thus, upward mobility. Forced busing initiatives were introduced as an attempt to address some of these concerns, albeit more from a racial (desegregation) motivation than an economic one, but they only served to make poorer students feel like outcasts going to school in richer neighborhoods. And in this situation, the attempt to bridge the inequality gap only served to raise the dropout rate for students from poorer neighborhoods, who would rather not go to school than try to learn in a socially intimidating atmosphere.

It is true that without the state providing education, children's access to education would be wholly dependent on the economic status of their parents, and upward mobility would be nearly impossible for children of lower classes to obtain. The necessity of public education is markedly important, because without it the character of the populace would suffer from extreme divisions between haves and have-nots, which would ultimately lead to social instability. However, to simply view it as an educational ideal in utopian terms, without taking into account that serious inequities in the system must be addressed, is naive.

51. Based on the passage, "an educational ideal in utopian terms" (lines 48–49) overlooks which of the following in regard to the value of public education?
    - Most of the students get free financial aid when they apply for colleges.
    - There are flaws inherent in a system that displays disparaging inequality for some members of society.
    - Overall, a study of how many people benefit from public education has not been done.
    - There are positives for children of wealthy parents.
    - With less money for books and educational supplies, the schools in poor neighborhoods produce students with lower self-esteem.

52. The passage is primarily concerned with presenting the idea that
    - the more children are born, the more funds have to be put into public education.
    - as long as there is some form of public education, then society will function properly.
    - lower socioeconomic classes are not afforded the same educational opportunities as members of higher socioeconomic classes.
    - forced busing allowed students from poorer neighborhoods to go to schools in wealthier neighborhoods.
    - public education is incredibly important.

53. Society may have the best intentions for maintaining a public educational system, but unfortunately, based on the passage, society mistakenly assumes that
    - the system is in danger of collapse in low-income neighborhoods.
    - the system is only useful to poorly behaved children.
    - the system only benefits the wealthy.
    - the system is going to change radically in the future.
    - the system equally benefits all who participate.

54. Of the following, which would most likely lead to "social instability" as referenced in lines 47–48?

- Free entrance into private schools for those of lower socioeconomic backgrounds
- The complete absence of any public education
- An increased dropout rate at private schools in rich areas
- Giving grants to children who perform well under dire conditions
- Donating books to schools in poor neighborhoods

55. Which of the following can most reasonably be inferred about lower-income families in low-income neighborhoods?

- They have the same number of students in schools as other socioeconomic groups.
- They are often unfairly harassed by their landlords.
- They often do not reap the intended benefits of public school education.
- Where their public education is lacking, their tax benefits make up the difference.
- They pursue worse job opportunities than others do.

PASSAGE XII

In the 1850s, several literary critics began to propose that the plays generally ascribed to Shakespeare had, in fact, been written by Sir Francis Bacon and that Shakespeare had made no real contribution to the composition of the plays he later became renowned for. Modern scholarship, however, tends to dismiss any role that Bacon may have played in inspiring and informing Shakespeare, considering the notion that Bacon penned the plays himself as the babble of misguided zealots and, further, blasphemy.

This controversial thesis has recently gained new ground, though, with the publication of Gail Gross's fascinating new book, *The Magus and the Bard*. The crux of Gross's argument concerns the fact that there is a distinct alchemical thought recurrent in Shakespeare's writing and that, even though the Hermetic practices central to alchemy may have been known to Shakespeare, Bacon was undeniably well versed in them and had written extensively on the subject in numerous essays, whose phrasings are remarkably similar to those found in plays such as *Romeo and Juliet*.

In fact, as Gross lays out her case for Bacon's authorship, she devotes a large portion of it to an intricate analysis of this most popular work of the Shakespearean canon. Gross contends that the union of Romeo and Juliet, two star-crossed lovers from feuding families, is symbolic of the alchemical formula for what is known as the *prima materia*, a union of opposites with transformational potential. In alchemy, this process is achieved through the use of the "universal solvent" mercury. In the play, the lovers' tragic end comes about after Romeo's friend Mercutio is slain. Alchemically, mercury is considered both male and female in its character, while the character of Mercutio is often portrayed as androgynous. The end result of the alchemical formula is that most pure of all elements, gold, and in the epilogue of Romeo and Juliet, Gross notes, the formerly feuding families decide to erect a memorial to the lovers "in pure gold."

What Gross's argument lacks in persuasiveness, it makes up for in minutiae. An entire chapter explores the possible meaning of Juliet's age (14 years) in alchemical terms and the significance of her birthday's coincidence with the feast of Lammas. Another chapter discusses the relationship of the name Romeo to Sirius, the "dog star."

Unfortunately, in the final analysis, instead of cogently making her case for Bacon's having been responsible for the alchemical imagery in Shakespeare's plays and thus having been the actual author of them, Gross spends the last chapters of the book railing against what she calls "Shakespeare apologists," stating that they have developed such admiration for their own imaginings of who Shakespeare was that they have lost sight of the man himself and are unable to realize that Shakespeare was not sufficiently educated to have included such profound and esoteric ideas in his plays. Apparently, only Sir Francis Bacon could have done so.

56. How would those described as "Shakespeare apologists" be most likely to explain the theories concerning Bacon that were popular in the mid-nineteenth century?

- o Those who believed Bacon wrote all of Shakespeare's plays were misguided, the victims of a delusion brought about by a too intensive focus on Bacon's alchemical works.
- o Those who believed Bacon wrote all of Shakespeare's plays did not recognize how much of a genius Shakespeare truly was.
- o Those who believed Bacon wrote all of Shakespeare's plays had come to the realization that Bacon was the only man intelligent enough to have written plays with such deep meaning.
- o Those who believed Bacon wrote all of Shakespeare's plays have undermined the stability of Shakespearean scholarship and caused many rifts between those who study Shakespeare's plays.
- o Those who believed Bacon wrote all of Shakespeare's plays have since apologized to the more devoted scholars and devotees of Shakespeare.

57. The author's main point in writing this passage is to

- o examine the merits of both sides of a current debate in literature.
- o review the argument of a new book on the works of Shakespeare.
- o analyze the position of those referred to as "Shakespeare apologists."
- o lend support to a controversial view of Shakespearean authorship.
- o promote further study of Bacon's alchemical works.

58. It can be inferred that the author of *The Magus and the Bard* would agree with which of the following statements about *Romeo and Juliet*?
   - o Most of the phrasings in *Romeo and Juliet* are identical to those found in the writings of Bacon.
   - o Though Romeo and Juliet were in opposition to each other, they were both actually very similar in character.
   - o The end of the feud between the families of Romeo and Juliet is symbolic of the transformational power of the *prima materia.*
   - o The character of Mercutio should be portrayed as strong and manly in accord with the alchemical symbolism of the play.
   - o The theme of *Romeo and Juliet* reflects alchemical thinking, but the details of the play merely serve the story line and have little meaning.

59. The author points to all of the following as possible instances of alchemical symbolism in *Romeo and Juliet* EXCEPT:
   - o portrayals of Mercutio's sexuality
   - o the statue erected in Romeo and Juliet's honor
   - o Romeo's name
   - o the characters' use of mercury
   - o Romeo and Juliet's feuding families

60. It can be determined from the passage that certain scholars in the nineteenth century believed that
   - o Shakespeare was not the author of the plays credited to him.
   - o Bacon had been falsely accused of plagiarism.
   - o Shakespeare had needed the help of other writers when composing his plays.
   - o Bacon had provided the thematic and symbolic core of Shakespeare's works.
   - o Shakespeare had had no direct ties to Bacon.

PASSAGE XIII

A new theory indicates that truffles may thrive in areas rich in marmot dung. This contrasts with the theory generally held by truffle enthusiasts, which specifies that truffles only proliferate in areas of moist dirt and darkness. New evidence has found that wherever a truffle patch has been discovered, marmot droppings were found in close proximity.

This recently established theory is of substantial value and could yield useful results in its pragmatic application. All of the truffles found during the great fungal flourishes were a result of turning over damp muddy fields to expose colonies of truffles growing in the dark. Granted that this simplistic search method uncovered pounds of truffles each year, many truffles have grown (and rotted) before being found. Also, countless muddy fields have been ripped up only to yield no results.

The great difficulty in discovering truffles comes from how little people actually know about what spurs their growth. Other than requiring moist soil and having a proclivity for dark, not much has been determined. Current approaches, which combine the fungus-smelling noses of truffle-hounds and the bare hands of intuitive forgers digging through the damp dark ground, attest to the primitive nature of traditional truffle-hunting techniques. Some technologically minded truffle hunters have gone into probable patches with X-ray–like devices that have aided in the detection of some truffles, but not much thought has gone into the biochemical properties of truffle-rich fields. Without this understanding, people tend to rely on random searches in areas of past truffle finds. To increase their likelihood of locating new truffle source areas, hunters must consider additional causal relationships with environmental and biochemical conditions that appear to have the ability to promote truffle growth and incorporate these data into models that will suggest new likely truffle fields.

These new models will encompass the traditional empirical observations of areas rich in truffles. The truffle hunter uses these observations (i.e., damp soil, low light, etc.) as a foundation, since these are demonstrated environmental requirements for truffle growth, and then adds newly discovered biochemical data (for example, the apparent causal relationship between marmot dung and truffle proliferation) in order to focus the search area and increase the likelihood of truffle hunt success.

61. The passage supports which of the following claims regarding truffle field sightings?
    - Recent sightings of truffle fields are going unreported, as truffle hunters do not wish to reveal their findings to competitors.
    - Future sightings of truffle fields will likely be due to new biochemical information regarding the presence of marmot dung in a field sample.
    - Many fear that truffles are growing less in the current environment and that the great fungal flourishes are purely a thing of the past.
    - Truffle hunters are split on the issue of whether or not the truffle-hounds are as useful in the fields as they used to be.
    - Many truffle fields have already been found and excavated thanks to the new theory.

62. Which of the following makes truffle fields so hard to find?
    - The size of the marmot dung makes it an easy target to miss.
    - The excavating during the great fungal flourishes ruined many truffle fields and killed several varieties of truffles.
    - It is easy to mistake wild mushrooms for truffles in the dark.
    - People know little about what makes truffles grow and the environments in which they proliferate.
    - The X-ray-like devices that are used in the detection of truffles are exorbitantly priced.

63. It can be inferred that marmot droppings connect to empirical data in which of the following ways?
    - They allow for samples to be tested biologically, and the results, if used in conjunction with observed data, will prove useful for truffle-finding analysis.
    - They prove that truffles are dependent upon them as a very specific fertilizer.
    - They, in fact, do not connect to empirical data and are a time waster for hard-working truffle hunters.
    - They are factors in disproving that the truffle-hounds are useful tools and thus allow for new theories to be placed into practice.
    - They are a much slower and less useful indication system than the technologically superior X-ray-like devices.

64. The passage suggests that in order to focus the search area and increase the likelihood of truffle hunt success, one must depend on which of the following?

    I. The biochemical testing devices being properly coded and showing a correct feedback result in determining the nature of the dung tested

    II. An increased understanding of the dampness, moisture, and other demonstrated environmental requirements of truffles rather than an awareness of the biochemical results of the marmot dung

    III. The security of knowing the marmot dung being tested has not been mishandled or labeled incorrectly

    - II only
    - I only
    - I, II, and III
    - II and III
    - I and III

65. This passage's main goal is to
    - support a rebellion against new theories.
    - discuss the significance of a new theory.
    - argue the points of two disparate systems.
    - give historical examples that brought about a new theory.
    - disagree with the ideology of a hypothetical discussion.

66. According to the passage, the theory generally held by truffle enthusiasts specifies that truffles only grow
    - in areas of moist dirt and darkness.
    - in fields wherever marmot droppings are found.
    - under the force of X-ray–like devices.
    - in dry fields.
    - under water.

PASSAGE XIV

During the summer of 1946, two large abstract paintings sold for $150,000 at Agatha & Agatha's Auction House. Manhattanites desirous of social pride outbid each other for these two prize canvases replete with black lines, green triangles, and purple circles. Winners Adam Ovariano and his wife Teresa hired professionals to asymmetrically mount the massive pieces onto the mantle above their fireplace. The couple loved how their ownership of the paintings made them the envy of all. Sixteen years later on January 26, 1962, Adam and Teresa's first and only child, James Ovariano, was born. Before he could even speak, he would look up from his baby building blocks to the paintings and scowl. In 2007, James Ovariano sold the paintings at only a fraction of the 1946 price.

Now in 2007, 45-year-old James Ovariano keeps up a wonderful sociological blog called "Ovariano's Tomorrow" in which he details his concerns regarding his family's classist past. He rejects their values, arguing that in the earlier part of the twentieth century, large, expensive art denoted class and wealth. James writes: "In the twenty-first century, I think that people are growing more impressed with love. Compassion is our strongest commodity." This new take on love and money is spreading across the Internet with such slogans as "Love is Ovariano you need."

James's blog painfully accounts many times when his parents could have donated thousands to charities with humanitarian causes, but instead opted to buy expensive things. He feels that their consumer decisions were motivated by societal pressure. In his parents' environment, the more you had, the more everyone thought of you. James feels that society now has less interest in praising individuals for lavish purchases. He urges his readership: "Items are getting smaller and more convenient. Information that once occupied an entire storage room now fits on a drive the size of three fingers." James believes that big collectibles have lost value due to their wasteful grandiosity in a world that, he insists, is becoming less materialistic and more maternal.

Another blogger, known only as Captain CapitalYay, disputes James's assertion that society is interested in love. CapitalYay feels that the decrease in the size of technological items is only a sign of the growing population. He or she, as CapitalYay's sex is unknown, commented on James's blog:

"Cities are crowded and land is limited. Things are smaller because there is less space. Less is not more, less is less." This explanation, however, does not consider the example of people's actions. When James's childhood home was in danger of foreclosure, he auctioned off those two "prized" paintings but this time got only $40,000 from the Manhattanites, instead of the original $150,000. Desperate to keep his family home, James set up a virtual donation booth on his blog. Readers could click on a "donate now" button to save the home. People were quick to join the cause, citing the fact that the blog and its author had brought them much love, joy, and insight. In record time, $200,000 was donated from his adoring fan base, proving in James's eyes that love is worth much more than garish, oversized belongings.

67. What would Captain CapitalYay most likely cite as a reason for the falling value of large art items?
   - o People have stopped having strong feelings when they looked at big paintings.
   - o The population has exploded in recent times, leading to people having less space and less need for large goods as a result.
   - o The value fell because people became less interested in themselves as individuals and more interested in the good of society.
   - o Art students started failing classes, and it became increasingly difficult for them to churn out quality works.
   - o The IRS stopped allowing tax deductions for wealthy patrons of auction houses, causing demand for art to go down.

68. James Ovariano discusses all of the following as reasons for large artwork going out of fashion EXCEPT:
   - o the world becoming less materialistic.
   - o the world becoming more maternal.
   - o rejection of a classist past.
   - o the decrease in the size of technological items.
   - o people becoming more impressed by love.

69. The main goal of this passage is to
   - o discuss the daily newspaper from a new sociological stance.
   - o show the main arguments from a blog.
   - o compare and contrast two views on art.
   - o disprove a commonly held assumption about the value of art.
   - o raise funds for research in an underappreciated social field.

70. One can infer from the passage that which of the following ideas was true of Manhattanites when the twenty-first century began?
   - Most Manhattanites had less money to spend at auctions.
   - Manhattanites had trouble finding artists to paint large canvases.
   - Manhattanites participated in competitive bidding on large artwork less in the twenty-first century than they had in the twentieth.
   - Manhattanites had to spend more time on finding professionals to mount paintings.
   - Manhattanites became more dependent on their jobs for money as their trust funds became depleted.

71. One can infer from the passage that the fiscal value of large works of art in the twentieth century was estimated based on
   - the social pride of acquisition.
   - the signature of the artist on the painting.
   - what the outbid Manhattanites said when they lost the auction.
   - what the Ovarianos' other paintings were worth.
   - the amount of time it took the artist to paint the paintings.

PASSAGE XV

Thanks to wireless Internet access, mobile email devices, and cellular phones, employees never need to be out of touch with their superiors. This technology also allows an increasing number of companies to hire employees to work remotely, in a different city or even a different country from the one in which the home office is located. By using technology to keep in touch, employers are able to tap into a much larger pool of talent; workers who refuse to relocate for a job can now be recruited to take a position remotely.

However, there can also be disadvantages to this kind of virtual workplace. Employees may be under-managed, leading to problems that are not caught until it is too late to fix them. And it's crucial that companies look for self-motivated workers, since employees won't have an office environment or coworkers on-site to draw energy and inspiration from. It's also critical that both employees and supervisors be aware of the potential for breaches of new technology etiquette. Nuances of communication that are clearly communicated in person can be misunderstood or missed completely via instant messaging or phone calls. Despite these challenges, though, a company that is able to handle the potential pitfalls of remote hiring and supervision will reap significant benefits in employee recruiting and retention.

72. The problem described in lines 18–20 is most clearly illustrated by which of the following?
    - o A supervisor is unable to reach his remote employee by phone or email for days at a time.
    - o A supervisor finds that a remote employee is not sufficiently motivated to do the volume and quality of work required.
    - o A supervisor does not discover problems in a remote employee's work until it is too late to correct those problems.
    - o A supervisor makes a sarcastic statement over the phone, and it is taken at face value and thus misunderstood by the remote employee to whom he is speaking.
    - o A supervisor is unable to find appropriate employees in his geographic area.

73. All of the following are mentioned in the passage as potential pitfalls of remote hiring and supervision EXCEPT:
   - O Employees may be more easily headhunted by recruiters for competing companies when they are not present in the home office.
   - O Employees will not have coworkers around them for motivation.
   - O Employees may misconstrue communications by instant messaging.
   - O An employee may make mistakes that are not caught in as timely a manner as they might be in a more traditional workplace.
   - O Supervisors may miss a nuance in a phone conversation.

74. The information in the passage most clearly implies which of the following about employee recruiting?
   - O Employees are often willing to work for a lower salary in exchange for the convenience of working from home.
   - O Some employers find that they can hire more qualified candidates by looking outside of the company's immediate geographical area.
   - O Employers will not be successful in recruiting remote employees unless they offer "perks" not seen in normal workplaces.
   - O Employees are often happier working from home than they are working in a traditional office.
   - O The role of technology in remote employee recruiting is negligible.

75. The main purpose of the passage is to
   - O explain how to utilize a business model.
   - O discuss the pros and cons of a business practice.
   - O evaluate the outcome of a company's new approach to hiring.
   - O advocate an approach to employee retention.
   - O recommend against adopting a business model.

PASSAGE XVI

Prior to the mid-nineteenth century, women's involvement in social justice issues was largely limited to movements promoting abolition and temperance and societies intended to benefit the poor. However, around the time of the American Civil War, women began organizing to address more specifically feminist concerns. In 1848, at the first Women's Rights Convention, Elizabeth Cady Stanton read her Declaration of Sentiments, in which she called for legal reforms in marriage, inheritance, and suffrage laws. Stanton and her friend Susan B. Anthony spent the next fifty years working tirelessly for political, educational, and social changes.

Among the causes for which Stanton, Anthony, and their contemporaries labored were equal education, more control over working women's wages, and the right to vote. Their interests were broad; feminists of the period even briefly took up the cause of dress reform, trying to convert women to wearing the split skirts known as "bloomers" for reasons of health, comfort, and mobility. However, faced with public derision and fearful that the negative attention would spill over onto other women's issues like suffrage and property laws, most feminists abandoned bloomers.

Women continued through the latter part of the nineteenth century to campaign for their rights through print journals and speeches. Although most of the members of this first wave of American feminism did not live to see women finally receive the right to vote in 1920, their work laid the foundation for women's participation in all realms of public life.

76. The passage suggests which of the following about the feminist campaign for dress reform?

- O Opponents of women's dress reform considered bloomers to be unfeminine and unattractive.
- O The dress reform movement eventually failed because, although bloomers were initially very popular with many women, they became less so over time.
- O One advantage of wearing bloomers was that they did not require a corset and were therefore more beneficial to women's health.
- O Some feminists considered the dress reform issue to be less important than the suffrage movement.
- O Dress reform became a major issue once more in the twentieth century.

77. The author of the passage probably describes the dress reform effort in order to

- show one of the failures of the early feminist movement.
- demonstrate how varied the issues addressed by early American feminists were.
- provide an example of one of the major successes achieved by early American feminists.
- show a contrast between pre- and post–Civil War feminism.
- clarify the author's position on the ultimate futility of feminist struggles prior to the twentieth century.

78. According to the passage, the feminist movement during the latter part of the nineteenth century was interested in all of the following EXCEPT:

- Reforming marriage laws
- Obtaining women's right to vote
- Gaining more control over women's wages
- Allowing women to buy and sell property
- Dress reform

79. The organization of the first paragraph of the passage is best described by which of the following?

- A historical backdrop is provided, a contrasting development is presented, and then some specific details of that development are given.
- The author's viewpoint is stated, and an example is given to support that viewpoint.
- A statement is made, and then a counterclaim is made and supported.
- A historical period is summarized, and broad conclusions about it are drawn.
- A statement about a political trend is made and then rebutted.

80. The passage suggests that a woman involved in social reform prior to the mid-nineteenth century would be most likely to work for which of the following causes?

- Promoting women's right to inherit property
- Obtaining universal suffrage
- Supporting freedom for slaves
- Increasing women's access to education
- Showing that women should have the same property rights as men

81. The author's purpose in writing the passage is to

- compare the political contributions of two famous feminists.
- describe early developments in the American feminist movement.
- support a thesis about the role played by women in the political development of early America.
- provide biographical information about famous American women.
- explain the shortcomings in current views of the roles of women in post–Civil War America.

PASSAGE XVII

Many observers believe that middle-class Americans are dogged by debt as a result of their own extravagant spending on luxury items. However, new research indicates that this is untrue. Harvard professor Elizabeth Warren demonstrates in her books, *The Fragile Middle Class* and *The Two-Income Trap*, that American families today have only about half as much discretionary income as their parents did, after paying for increasingly expensive basics like housing and health care. For instance, although nearly half of the money that the average American spends on food goes toward dining outside the home, most Americans still spend only 10 percent of their incomes on food. This is a drastic reduction from the 20 percent that they spent in the 1970s.

Skeptics of Warren's theory point to the rise in household incomes since the 1970s, but this is in many ways an illusion. Take as an example the "average" dual-income, two-child family; having two wage earners means that their household income is about 75 percent higher than it would have been in the 1970s, but this is largely the result of the wife working outside the home, which also necessitates fixed expenditures, like day care and a second car, that would have been unnecessary to the same family a generation ago.

One reason that Americans appear to be spending more on items like electronics and clothing is that the prices of many consumer goods have gone down. Adjusted for inflation, the costs of some common items, like refrigerators and televisions, have decreased over 50 percent since the 1970s. This allows middle-class Americans to achieve a higher standard of living than their parents, even as a much smaller percentage of their income is being spent on discretionary items.

However, this higher standard of living masks the real culprit behind the financial squeeze faced by the average American: skyrocketing costs for housing, health care, and education. Between 2000 and 2006, household incomes stagnated, while housing costs increased by 32 percent. Middle-class financial anxiety isn't the product of too many lattes and designer shoes; it is the result of increased costs for the cornerstones of modern life.

82. Which of the following is most analogous to the change in the financial circumstances of the average middle-class American family from the 1970s to today, as described in the passage?

- A company has a 60 percent decrease in profits over a year due to higher staffing costs.
- A company has a 60 percent decrease in profits over a year but compensates for the losses by moving to a less expensive office space.
- A company has a 40 percent increase in net income from sales over one year but in the same period has a 90 percent increase in rent on its office space, leaving it with a lower profit than in the previous year.
- A company has a 60 percent increase in profits over one year and chooses to reinvest that additional money by purchasing the office space it had previously rented.
- A company's profits remain roughly the same from one year to the next, because although its net income from sales was lower than expected, the proceeds of a sale of real estate assets were an unexpected boon.

83. According to the passage, since the 1970s the fixed expenditures of middle-class Americans

- have expanded to include costs like student loan debt that were not generally included in the budgets of families in the 1970s.
- have become more manageable due to an increase in average household incomes that can be attributed to the addition of a second wage earner in most families.
- have increased at a greater rate than the average household income.
- have become a smaller percentage of total household expenditures compared to housing costs for families living at or below the poverty line.
- Have become less of a burden on the household income than the costs of food and clothing.

84. The passage implies which of the following about dual-income, two-child middle-class families?

- They would have fewer expenses if the wife did not work outside the home.
- They should reduce their expenditures on luxury items in order to eliminate their consumer debt.
- Expenditures for college education often mean that these families need to take out a second mortgage on their homes.
- They spend more of their household income on food than on medical care.
- They have a lower standard of living than did families in the 1970s.

85. It is reasonable to infer from the passage that "discretionary" purchases

- account for a larger percentage of the average middle-class family's expenditures than they did a generation ago.
- make up an increasing percentage of a family's expenses as its household income increases.
- are things like health insurance, day care, and automobile expenses.
- are not critical to a family's well-being and can be eliminated when necessary.
- include consumer electronics like television sets.

86. The organization of the passage can best be described by which of the following?

- A thesis is stated, an example is cited in support of the thesis, and a counterexample is cited and then rebutted.
- A researcher's methodologies are explored, statistics are debunked, and then a counterclaim is established.
- A problem is examined, two possible solutions are discussed and then rebutted, and a third solution is advocated.
- A possible explanation for a problem is presented, the explanation is debunked with examples and statistics, and an opposing explanation is presented.
- A claim is made about a problem, examples of the problem are given, and then a solution is discussed and ultimately advocated.

87. The author's main purpose in writing the passage is to

- discuss a problem that has been resolved.
- rebut a popular view.
- suggest a solution to a problem.
- question research methods.
- discredit experts.

PASSAGE XVIII

Along with posing significant risks to humans, the threat of global warming is ominous for various animal species. Particularly in colder climates, the impact of global warming could be catastrophic to some animals. One species in particular has been garnering attention recently: the polar bear. Polar bears are threatened by global warming in several ways. For instance, changes in seasonal snow or rain patterns could have a detrimental effect on the seal population, and since polar bears' primary food source is seals taken at the edge of sea ice, a reduced seal population could lead to a polar bear famine. Another danger for the bears is the retreat of the sea ice, which can force bears onto land earlier in the year, before they have hunted enough to build up sufficient fat stores for the summer. Sea ice retreat can also force bears to swim farther to get to land, causing exhaustion and sometimes resulting in death by drowning. Finally, increasing temperatures could impact polar bear denning by causing snow dens to collapse or melt completely, which could have negative implications for polar bear reproduction and survival. Although proposals have recently been made to list polar bears as a "threatened species," such protective measures will do little to help the bears if global warming continues unabated.

88. The passage suggests which of the following about polar bear denning?
    - O It is dependent on the consistency of the sea ice.
    - O It can force the bears onto land earlier in the year.
    - O It plays a role in polar bear reproduction.
    - O It assists in the bears' hunting.
    - O It helps the bears build up sufficient fat stores to survive the summer.

89. According to the passage, bears depend on which of the following in the summer?
    - O Denning in a cold climate
    - O Fat stores built up through hunting
    - O Hunting seals at the edge of sea ice
    - O Living on land away from sea ice
    - O Increasingly warm temperatures

90. It can be inferred from the passage that which of the following would increase the chances of polar bear survival?
   - O A reduction in the amount of emissions produced by cars and trucks
   - O An increased effort to recycle more plastic products
   - O More publicity about the dangers of global warming
   - O A moratorium on hunting polar bears
   - O Conservation efforts directed at reducing the impact of global warming on the seal population

91. Which of the following can be inferred about the attention being paid to the potential dangers of global warming to polar bears?
   - O It has resulted in increased efforts to reduce air pollution.
   - O It will not change the current political climate in regard to global warming.
   - O It has increased recently.
   - O It has not been as significant as the media coverage given to the dangers faced by seals.
   - O It threatens to overshadow the attention paid to the impact of global warming on animals that live in warmer climates.

92. The organization of the passage is best described by which of the following?
   - O A problem is presented, and two possible solutions are evaluated.
   - O Opposing viewpoints on a topic are explained and then reconciled.
   - O An issue is presented, examples of the issue are addressed, and then possible future developments are mentioned.
   - O A theory is presented, counterexamples are described, and then the author's opposing theory is stated.
   - O A problem is presented, a solution is mentioned, and then an opposing view is described.

93. Which of the following, if true, would best support the author's contention that a reduction in the seal population would have a detrimental effect on the polar bear population?
   - O A parasitic outbreak that caused a 25 percent reduction in the seal population ten years ago was followed, one year later, by a famine among the polar bears that resulted in a 20 percent drop in the polar bear population.
   - O Seals and polar bears have both been known to feed on capelin, a cold-water fish.
   - O Brown bears depend on fish and mammals as food sources.
   - O Polar bears have been known to eat each other when food is scarce.
   - O The only predator of polar bears is humans.

PASSAGE XIX

The cosmetics industry has traditionally struggled to obtain satisfactory intellectual property protection in a field where counterfeits and knockoffs abound. Trademark law may protect the advertising, name, and trade dress, but it does not address the product itself. Patent law rarely covers makeup, hair and body products, or fragrance. And traditionally, copyright has been applicable only to text or artwork on the packaging, not to the substance within the package. Considering the vast resources that go into developing and marketing a product, the level of protection provided seems deficient.

One product over which litigation has become increasingly common is perfume. Some believe that a perfume is a work of art and should be protected under the same standards that apply to literature, music, and sculpture. However, those who favor protection only for a perfume's scent, as opposed to the formula from which it is made, or who advocate no intellectual property protection for perfumes at all, think that perfumes should not be compared to visual or auditory works of art and should instead be looked at as chemical compounds. One commentator has pointed out that copyright is traditionally applied to immaterial works, like the words of a book, as opposed to the paper on which the book is printed. This argument has some merit, but it becomes more muddled when perfume is compared instead to copyrightable works like sculpture, in which the physical embodiment is virtually impossible to separate from the artistic expression.

Companies producing and distributing perfume knockoffs typically market their products so as to stay just on the right side of the law, while associating themselves as closely with the famous original products as possible. They achieve this through using product names and packaging that imitate those of the original scent. By cutting through the technicalities that such companies use to maintain the legality of their efforts and addressing the fundamental intentions and effects produced by their actions, courts can provide greater protection for the intensive investment that developing companies make to bring a successful product to the marketplace. This approach seems preferable to the potential chaos of attempting to extend copyright protection to works perceived by olfactory means.

94. According to the passage, which of the following is true of copyright protection?
   - It frequently extends not only to the artwork and text of cosmetics packaging but to the product itself.
   - It is only applicable to immaterial works, like words on the pages of a book.
   - It is the most promising form of protection for the scents and chemical compositions of perfume.
   - It is merely a technicality with which manufacturers of knockoff scents have no trouble dealing.
   - It is sometimes applicable to works in which the physical embodiment is virtually impossible to separate from the artistic expression.

95. With which of the following statements about the current state of intellectual property protection for perfumes would the author be most likely to agree?
   - Perfumes should be protected as works of art, just like literature, music, and sculpture.
   - Perfumes should be protected as chemical compositions.
   - Perfumes are not currently receiving sufficient intellectual property protection.
   - Perfumes are receiving too much intellectual property protection, at the cost of clarity in the law.
   - Perfumes are not appropriate subject matter for copyright, trademark, or patent protection.

96. Which of the following is an assumption underlying the author's recommendation for intellectual property protection for perfumes?
   - Courts will continue to extend intellectual property protection to perfumes.
   - There is no legal way to protect perfumes outside of intellectual property law.
   - Knockoffs of famous perfumes always infringe on the originals.
   - Critics are correct in likening perfumes to words on a page, rather than to sculptures.
   - Consumers are interested in purchasing knockoff perfumes.

97. The primary purpose of the second paragraph is to do which of the following?
   - Advocate a particular solution to the debate over the copyrightability of perfume.
   - Present some background information on the field of intellectual property law.
   - Describe recent judicial decisions dealing with the copyrightability of perfume.
   - Summarize the debate over the copyrightability of perfume.
   - Present a counterexample to the position described in the first paragraph.

98. The author's purpose in writing the passage is to
   - discuss whether patent protection is appropriate for perfume compositions.
   - evaluate several current legal issues facing the cosmetics industry and advocate for greater intellectual property protectivism.
   - explain the problems facing intellectual property protection for perfumes and suggest one possible solution.
   - criticize the current state of intellectual property law as it is applied to trademarking olfactory works.
   - advocate for copyright protection for both the scents and compositions of perfumes.

99. The passage suggests which of the following about knockoff perfumes?
   - They should be banned entirely, due to their infringement on the intellectual property rights of the developers of the original fragrances.
   - They are made of lower-quality ingredients than the scents on which they are based.
   - They are always made from the same formula as the scents on which they are based.
   - They are marketed so as to adhere to the letter of the law, if not the spirit.
   - They pose a danger to the economic survival of major cosmetics companies.

100. Which of the following can be inferred from the passage about the author's opinion of intellectual property protection for perfumes?
   - It is most achievable through trademark and copyright protection for the fragrances' packages and names.
   - It is nearly impossible to extend any protection to the cosmetics industry to help prevent knockoff versions of scents from being marketed.
   - It is not a desirable goal, since any kind of intellectual property protection for perfumes would lead to chaos.
   - In recent years there has been almost no litigation on the subject.
   - It should only apply to perfumes that are widely considered works of art.

Answers and explanations begin on the next page.

Answer Key

READING COMPREHENSION PRACTICE

1. D
2. E
3. D
4. D
5. C
6. A
7. C
8. B
9. A
10. C
11. B
12. E
13. C
14. C
15. C
16. E
17. B
18. E
19. E
20. C
21. C
22. E
23. B
24. D
25. A
26. D
27. C
28. A
29. A
30. C
31. C
32. A
33. E
34. A
35. E
36. A
37. E
38. E
39. E
40. C
41. A
42. D
43. B
44. E
45. B
46. A
47. C
48. D
49. A
50. C
51. B
52. C
53. E
54. B
55. C
56. B
57. B
58. C
59. D
60. A
61. B
62. D
63. A
64. E
65. B
66. A
67. B
68. D
69. B
70. C
71. A
72. D
73. A
74. B
75. B
76. D
77. B
78. D
79. A
80. C
81. B
82. C
83. C
84. A
85. E
86. D
87. B
88. C
89. B
90. E
91. C
92. C
93. A
94. E
95. C
96. A
97. D
98. C
99. D
100. A

Answers and Explanations

READING COMPREHENSION PRACTICE

Passage I

1. D

This question tests your ability to determine the primary intent of the passage. The last sentence of the first paragraph states that "analysts have noticed that consumers more frequently purchase an item based on its aesthetic quality or emotional appeal, even if it is not the best value." (D) is the credited response. The second paragraph offers an example of this concept by explaining how Apple computers have emotional appeal.

2. E

This question asks you to identify a supporting detail. Because the question uses the phrase "according to the passage," be sure that you can find text within the passage that directly supports your answer choice. Line 4 begins a contrast "within the last decade" to what consumers have "historically" done. So look for today's consumers after line 4: They "more frequently purchase an item based on its aesthetic quality or emotional appeal, even if it is not the best value." Choice (E) is correct.

3. D

This passage tests your ability to identify supporting details. Because the question uses the phrase "according to the passage," be sure that your answer choice is supported by the text. Paragraph 2 mentions that researchers attribute Apple's success "to its emotional impact, including its packaging and design." Choice (D) is correct.

4. D

This question tests your ability to make an inference based on what is stated in the passage. Look for an answer choice that is supported in the text but not stated outright.

The passage's first paragraph mentions that consumers are now *less* likely to consider a product's value, which means that consumers are not as interested as they used to be in purchasing economical products. The final paragraph mentions that some computer makers might have to take a "more economical approach" because their profit margins are lower, but the final sentence of the passage says that this approach "may not be worth the cost." These statements imply that economical designs will ultimately be unsuccessful in today's market. Choice (D) is correct.

5. C

This type of question tests your ability to apply a reasoning concept that the passage employs to a situation that is logically similar but contextually unrelated to the passage. This particular question is asking you to apply what you know about how Apple uses its profits to another scenario. In order to do so, you need to identify the nature of how the process works for Apple. Based on the passage, it is evident that a circular relationship exists for Apple, in that the company's profits can be used to add expensive details so that the company earns more profit, and so on. Choice (C) is correct.

6. A

This question tests your ability to determine how a portion of the passage functions within the overall passage. Notice that the first paragraph sets up a discussion of a particular trend and the second paragraph offers an example of how Apple illustrates that trend. Choice (A) is correct.

Passage II

7. C

This question tests your ability to identify the main purpose of the passage. Ask yourself, "What is the author of this passage trying to do?" The answer to this question should begin with a verb—the primary action undertaken by the author throughout the passage. Notice that the first paragraph in this passage introduces the idea of globalization and lists several effects of globalization. The final sentence in the first paragraph mentions that "public attitudes toward these effects are divided." The remainder of the passage focuses on why people might support or criticize globalization. Choice (C) is correct.

8. B

An inference is something that is supported by the passage, but not usually stated outright. In paragraph 2, the author mentions that "the critics . . . point out that globalization is a process mediated by corporate—and not human—interests, so while corporations might benefit economically from being globally connected, these relationships do not have an overall positive impact on the world's people and its environment."

This statement contrasts corporate with human mediation and implies that the corporate aspects of globalization do not allow it to have an overall positive impact on people and the environment. It can be inferred, then, that if globalization were mediated by human instead of corporate interests, the opposite could occur. Choice (B) is correct.

9. A

The word "suggests" in the question offers a clue that the answer to this question is implied rather than stated directly in the passage. Paragraph 1 lists "the realization of a global economy based on the freedom of exchange of goods and capital" as one of globalization's primary effects, and paragraph 2 says that "supporters of globalization maintain that free trade boosts the economy and that it increases opportunity among developing nations by improving civil liberties and leading to a more efficient allocation of resources." These details suggest that globalization promotes, or fosters, a free-trade economy. Choice (A) is correct .

10. C

This question tests your ability to identify supporting details mentioned within the text. Be careful to note that this is an "EXCEPT" question, so the best answer choice will be the only one *not* directly supported by the text. The passage does *not* mention that globalization is related to a more healthy environment. This is the only answer choice that is not directly supported by a detail mentioned within the text, so answer choice (C) is correct.

11. B

This question tests your ability to determine why the author of the passage uses the particular details quoted in the question text. In questions like this one, don't focus on *what* is mentioned but instead on *why* it is mentioned. The question tells us that the quoted material can be found in the first sentence of the second paragraph, so make sure to refer to the surrounding sentences in order to determine the context. Choice (B) is correct. Because the word "by" precedes the quoted portions of this sentence, it is apparent that the author cites these details as examples of how globalization increases opportunity for developing nations.

Passage III

12. E

This question tests your ability to identify the passage's main idea. The main idea is the topic that guides the discussion, or the author's main point. In this passage, the first paragraph introduces the main idea and the passage's key themes. The final sentence of the first paragraph states, "Agribusiness is often contrasted with the family farm and associated with the practice of corporate farming." Notice that the second paragraph focuses on small farms, and the final paragraph contrasts the corporate farm with small farms. Answer choice (E) best summarizes these key themes.

13. C

This passage tests your ability to make an inference based on what is said in the passage. Look to the text for your answer to this question; notice that paragraph 2 mentions, "The U.S. Department of Agriculture reports that 98 percent of all farms in the United States today are family farms, but large-scale corporate farms supply 14 percent of the country's total agricultural output." This detail reveals that each corporate farm produces proportionally more of the country's total agricultural output. By reverse reasoning, you can infer that family farms contribute less per farm to the country's total agricultural output than do corporate farms. Choice (C) is correct.

14. C

This question tests your ability to determine the passage's tone. The tone of a passage indicates a general attitude or view of the author, and it will usually reveal what the writer may be thinking or feeling about the issue. Look for areas where a writer inserts his or her own opinion or look for particular words or phrases that may indicate an author's feeling about the issue. In this passage, the writer offers unbiased information about how agribusiness has affected small and corporate farms. The passage's final claim, that "despite the greater productivity of large farms, many buyers fear that the personal service and individual attention they receive from owners of small farms will soon be lost," suggests that the author is willing to acknowledge the ways in which agribusiness benefits large farms but has its drawbacks in the area of customer service. Choice (C) is correct.

15. C

This question tests your ability to identify supporting details as they are stated in the passage. The word "cite" in the question text prompts you to look directly to the passage for the correct answer.

Because this is a "NOT" question, narrow down your answer choices by eliminating each choice that you can find directly in the text. Choice (C) is correct. The passage does not state that large farms have more environmentally sustainable farming practices.

16. E

This question tests your ability to identify a supporting detail. Because the question says that the author "mentions" this detail, look for direct support from the passage in order to choose the correct answer. The final sentence of the passage mentions a fear, saying, "Despite the greater productivity of large farms, many buyers fear that the personal service and individual attention they receive from owners of small farms will soon be lost." Answer choice (E) summarizes this point.

Passage IV

17. B

This question tests your ability to determine the main idea expressed in the overall passage. The word "primary" in the question should lead you to recognize that this is a main idea question. Notice that the first paragraph introduces the problems associated with the recycling industry, and the second paragraph offers a solution to this problem. The remainder of the passage offers ideas in support of this solution. The correct answer choice will then summarize the solution that the author recommends. That's choice (B).

18. E

This question tests your ability to determine what the passage implies about the recycling industry. Inference questions such as this one ask us to identify what can be inferred, or concluded, based on the details offered in the passage. The inferences themselves are usually not stated in the passage but rather are based on the information the passage presents. Choice (E) is correct. There is no basis for this inference in the passage, so it *is* the credited response to this "EXCEPT" inference question. The author of this passage does not state or imply that future laws will inevitably require people to recycle. The passage instead argues that local communities should adopt such laws to protect recycling workers.

19. E

This question asks you to choose the answer that is best supported by "details . . . mentioned in the passage." Eliminate choices that you do not find mentioned directly in the text. Notice that paragraph 3 mentions several reasons why people "object to the extra money being paid to recycling workers." The correct answer, choice (E), is supported by details found in this paragraph. The author of the passage states directly in lines 26–27, "because the common opinion is that collecting trash does not require very much skill."

Passage V

20. C

This question tests your ability to make an inference based on what is stated in the passage. The trick in a tough passage like this is to avoid getting caught up in the scientific jargon; you can earn these points without fully grasping the science.

Notice that the second paragraph discusses how London dispersion forces work, saying that "London dispersion forces develop between transient multipoles in molecules that do not have permanent multipole moments." Therefore, it can be inferred that since London dispersion forces are at work in the setae of geckos, then the molecules in a gecko's setae do not have permanent multipole moments. Choice (C) is correct.

21. C

This question tests your ability to make an inference based on what is stated in the passage. The final sentence states that "a gecko's setae are self-cleaning and can slough off any dirt within a few steps, allowing optimal adhesion." By reverse reasoning, it can be inferred that the presence of dirt would diminish a gecko's ability to adhere to a surface. Choice (C) is correct.

22. E

This question tests your ability to apply a concept that relates the gecko to another animal. The first sentence of the passage states that Van der Walls forces enable geckos to walk upside down on ceilings. Therefore, if it could be explained that Van der Walls forces enabled another animal to do this, then the same assumptions about how Van der Walls forces work would also apply to that animal's ability. Since Van der Walls rely on "the attractive and repulsive components of intermolecular forces" for the gecko, the Van der Walls forces that allowed another animal to adhere to a ceiling would have to rely on intermolecular force as well. Choice (E) is correct.

23. B

This question tests your ability to determine how additional information would affect the logical structure of this passage. The passage explains how intermolecular forces are essential to the functioning of Van der Walls forces, so if it were found that the setae of geckos did not contain intermolecular forces, the idea that Van der Walls forces hold geckos to a variety of surfaces would be invalid. Choice (B) is correct.

24. D

This question tests your ability to identify a supporting detail stated in the text. The phrase "according to the passage" should prompt you to look directly to the passage for your answer. Eliminate any answer choices that you can not find support for in the text. London dispersion forces are described starting at line 20: "As electron density moves about a molecule, an uneven distribution will occur, creating a temporary multipole, which can interact with other nearby multipoles." Choice (D) is correct.

25. A

This question tests your ability to determine how particular details contribute to the logical structure of the passage. Notice that the first sentence in paragraph 2 states that "Van der Walls forces act between stable molecules and are weak compared to the forces involved in chemical bonding; however, they are strong enough to allow a gecko to cling to a vertical glass surface with only one toe." So they're relatively weak in terms of bonds, but strong enough to accomplish the geckos' feat. Use these details to locate the correct answer, choice (A).

Passage VI

26. D

This question tests your ability to infer what type of argument Carson most likely did NOT include in her book. You must read the passage carefully in order to find the correct answer to this question. Because this is an inference question, you will find textual support for the valid inferences, but they may not be stated directly. Once you find support for a particular choice, eliminate it to narrow down your possible options.

Choice (D) is correct. This directly contradicts a point made about the book in the passage, so it *is* the credited response to this inference "NOT" question. The passage states that "Carson's work was not advocating a ban on or complete halt to the use of pesticides." This sentence offers examples of two arguments that Carson was likely to exclude from her book. Because Carson's *work* was not advocating a total ban on the use of pesticides, it is likely that her *book* did not include an argument in support of banning pesticide use.

27. C

This question tests your ability to make an inference based on what is stated in the text. The word "implies" should prompt you to approach this question as an inference question. The correct answer choice will be supported by the passage, but it is likely that you will have to take the logic of what is stated a step further than the actual text.

Paragraph 2 discusses Carson's reputation, saying that "Before writing *Silent Spring*, Carson was known for her writing on natural history, and she had not previously been considered a social critic." This sentence implies that she was not considered a social critic before she wrote the book, but after its publication, she was. Choice (C) is correct.

28. A

This question tests your ability to identify supporting details stated within the passage. The phrase "according to the passage" in the question text should prompt you to eliminate any answer choice that you cannot find direct support for within the text.

The first paragraph says that "Carson's book is credited with facilitating a 1972 ban on agricultural use of the pesticide DDT in the United States," and the second paragraph clarifies this claim by saying that: "As it turned out, DDT was never banned for anti-malaria use." Taken together, these details could be summarized by the statement that DDT was banned for agricultural purposes but not for malaria control. Choice (A) is correct.

29. A

This question tests your ability to identify the primary concern, or purpose, of this passage. Each of the answer choices begins with a verb, so a good way to approach this type of question is to ask yourself: "What does this passage do?" The answer will lead you toward the action that the passage undertakes.

Notice that the opening sentence establishes the focus of this passage on Rachel Carson's *Silent Spring*. Throughout the first and second paragraphs, several consequences of the book are mentioned and explained. Even though the passage does several things, it is chiefly concerned with explaining the impact, or consequences, of Carson's book. Choice (A) is correct.

Passage VII

30. C

In order to answer this question, one must first look for the term "film developing" in the passage. It is stated in lines 6–11 that "revisions . . . (the revision process having been dubbed 'film developing' by film buffs) attest to the uncertainty of constructing a definitive history of an art form when so much of the art itself has been unseen since its creation." The author uses the term, common among film enthusiasts, to familiarize the reader with the jargon of the culture, as well as teach its meaning to better make the point that the revision process in film history is a constant one. Choice (C) is correct.

31. C

This question asks that one apply an understanding of a situation. Look at the third paragraph around line 35 (both above and below the line) where Denison compares himself to "a paleontologist who has to construct an entire dinosaur from a femur, a couple of ribs, and part of a skull." What does this mean? Denison is explaining that being 100 percent correct without all the relevant information is impossible. The same is true in trying to do a career overview of a director for whom only a handful of films have survived. It is an impossibly hard situation to discuss a history of which most facts have been lost. Choice (C) is correct.

32. A

The tone and sentiment of the author are conveyed by the language and structure of the passage. The passage presents a well-balanced discussion of Albert Denison's trials and tribulations in his pursuit of studying film history. One almost imagines, especially when looking at lines 35–37—"'I'm like a paleontologist who has to construct an entire dinosaur from a femur, a couple of ribs, and part of a skull . . . cut me some slack, please?'"—in which Denison is allowed an amusing yet sympathetic quote, that the author of this piece may have once been a student of Denison's. As such the content's tone is of earned admiration, and choice (A) is correct.

33. E

In order to answer this question, look especially at the first and last paragraphs of the passage. Through Denison's words and actions, one can infer that his ultimate view of film history is that it is constantly changing in response to new discoveries. Denison found that the best way to handle the vast number of unanswered questions regarding cinema studies is to accept that the field's history is changing and to enlist film buffs to present their continued findings, thus resulting in a present account that most accurately reflects the past. Choice (E) is correct.

34. A

In order to best answer this question, one must look for how the term "conventional wisdom" is used in the passage. *Conventional wisdom* suggests a manner in which people typically think of something. People used to think that Ford Mace was merely an imitator. It was only with time and new discoveries that people came to view him as an innovator. One can therefore infer that according to the conventional wisdom of the time, Ford Mace was an imitator, not an innovator. Choice (A) is correct.

35. E

In order to answer this question, look at how Denison felt toward his critics at first, but also understand what he did with their criticism. Look at the last paragraph where it states in lines 31–32, "At first, his response was to write testy letters to critics," which indicates that Denison was initially annoyed with the critics, but through his actions one can infer that ultimately he considered their criticism useful. Faced with his book going out of print, Denison started a foundation to constantly update it; because of the critics, he accepted that film history is a living and changing course of study. Choice (E) is correct.

Passage VIII

36. A

First, you must understand what a qubit is. The passage defines it as a computational unit, an atom along with the device that controls it and reads it. You must see that it is one of the "switches" that a computer runs on and that "a series of qubits" is the same as the "array of 'switches'" mentioned in the first sentence of the first paragraph. Shortly after that sentence, the answer is given: A quantum computer could perform a complex calculation in seconds. Choice (A) is correct.

37. E

This question may be somewhat difficult—you need to determine why the author uses the example of Schrödinger or why he says that the quantum computer owes a debt to Schrödinger. Consider, however, that the main similarity between the information in the first two paragraphs and that in the last two is that all focus on the importance of the phenomenon of superposition. In the first two paragraphs, it is the basis of quantum computing. In the last two paragraphs, it is something that Schrödinger thinks is an error in the math—something he resists and then constructs an interesting example of in an attempt to show its absurdity. Choice (E) is correct.

38. E

This question has more to do with the author's style than anything else. However, you can use your understanding of the passage to eliminate most of the choices. With questions such as these, consider first: Why do authors put words in quotation marks? Unless the author is actually quoting another source, the most likely reason is that the author is showing that the word doesn't quite mean what it says—its literal definition doesn't convey the full weight of its meaning in the passage. As you evaluate the choices, consider this common usage of quotes. Choice (E) is correct.

39. E

This question relates to the information in the second paragraph, in which three models of a quantum computer are discussed and one of them is described in detail. The question asks why the computer based on the spin of hydrogen electrons would be more typical than the other two.

Does the author make a comparison among the different types of quantum computers? No. Choice (E) is correct.

Passage IX

40. C

To best answer this question, read the third and fourth paragraphs in which the author details how instinct and learned behaviors differ. Then, go back to the last sentence of the first paragraph where it mentions: "beavers are also possessed of an evolutionary tool that aids in the effective construction of dams." This means that the "wood-test" gland is a feature that is biological, not experiential. Beavers are born with this unique tool that allows them to differentiate wood. Choice (C) is correct.

41. A

This question is best answered by looking at the passage. Find what the passage says about the use of the beaver's special evolutionary tool known as a "wood-test gland" and make an inference from that information. In this passage, it is clearly stated in lines 45–49 that "Beavers have been observed to 'hug' a tree before cutting it down; it has now been determined that they have glands in their forearms that secrete an enzyme that causes a slight reddish discoloration in dead or dying wood that has begun to rot." This means that a beaver, one tree at a time, uses its glandular secretion to determine whether the tree is a viable source of wood. Choice (A) is correct.

42. D

In order to answer this question, make an inference based on the stated information. Look at the first sentence of the third paragraph: "Much like beavers, birds exhibit similar concerns when building nests, and these concerns are commutual in nature." This sentence compares the ways that birds build their nests to the ways that beavers build their dams. Now, if one then looks back to the first paragraph where it mentions that "beavers consistently display five major and unwavering concerns when building a dam," then one can infer that birds, being similar, would display the same major concerns when constructing their nests. Choice (D) is correct.

43. B

In order to answer this question, look for information in the passage. Lines 2 and 3 state, "beavers consistently display five major and unwavering concerns when building a dam," which introduces the five characteristics of a successful dam. One can then infer that the best dams exist when these five characteristics are exhibited. Choice (B) is correct.

44. E

To answer this question, look at the third paragraph where birds are discussed. In the first sentence, it is stated that their concerns are "commutual in nature," which means that there is interdependency within the structure of their nest building. The key point is that every part of their building affects another part and so on. So all of the details regarding how the birds build their nests are described in order to demonstrate the importance of a commutual system. That's choice (E).

Passage X

45. B

When answering certain questions, you must often weigh those verbs that are too general against those that are too specific. With a question such as this, which simply asks about the author's primary purpose, it is usually best to stick with more general answer choices. A choice that refers to only one aspect of the passage, something that is perhaps discussed in only one paragraph, would not be broad enough to represent the author's overall purpose. Although it is general, choice (B) encapsulates the author's purpose in writing this passage. The author is trying to show how some new theories about what causes bile duct strictures could be useful in the detection of these strictures.

46. A

This question is straightforward, requiring literal comprehension of what is directly stated in the passage. Refer to the first paragraph, in which the crystallization of bile is discussed, and find the sentence that explains why this phenomenon occurs: "These strictures occur when the liver produces an excess of bile, which then becomes stuck in the ducts and crystallizes." It couldn't be much simpler than that: there is an excess of bile and it gets stuck. Choice (A) is correct.

47. C

For this question, link the theories mentioned in the first paragraph with the rest of the information in the passage concerning diagnostic procedures to make the required inference. What the first paragraph states is that (a) bile duct strictures may be an aftereffect of surgery, (b) perhaps caused by the use of anesthetic, and (c) the location of a stricture may correspond to what type of surgery is performed. Now, use the information about the various diagnostic procedures to see which one would be successful in light of the theory. Choice (C) is correct.

48. D

This question requires comprehension of content stated in the passage: Of all the diagnostic methods, which one would be the easiest? Two phrases in the second paragraph point out which diagnostic method is the easiest: "obvious warning signs" and "telltale symptoms." Both of these refer to checking for oozing pus and discolored urine or saliva—obviously, the presence of these would make diagnosis of strictures quite easy. Choice (D) matches this prediction.

49. A

This question relates to the most important point the author makes in this passage: that a certain theory about bile duct stricture formation may be combined with a diagnostic procedure such as ultrasound scans to bring success to the discovery of strictures. Realizing the drawbacks of the various diagnostic procedures, you can come to the conclusion that the ultrasound or MRI is best, provided that a more specific location of a possible stricture is known. So, which theory gives information about the specificity of a stricture location? Choice (A) is correct.

50. C

This question relates to the main implication that the author makes in the passage, that one of the new theories can be used in combination with certain diagnostic techniques to greatly improve the detection of bile duct strictures. The author has tried to show the relevance of the theory that certain types of surgery cause strictures in certain parts of the duct system and that such a correspondence would allow a doctor to pinpoint the possible area of a stricture. Only III—answer choice (C)—is correct.

Passage XI

51. B

This question asks the reader to go to the line with the cited phrase and interpret it. The last line of the last paragraph states: "However, to simply view it as an educational ideal in utopian terms, without taking into account that serious inequities in the system must be addressed, is naive." This sentence clearly states that utopian terms are naive; therefore, an explanation of the opposite view would yield what is lacking in a utopian view. According to this passage, the flaw in this system is that it displays a disparaging amount of inequity to those of lower socioeconomic status. Answer choice (B) is correct.

52. C

In order to answer this question, take into account the whole passage. The first paragraph presents the point of public education, to "level the playing field," but then contrasts it with the reality in practice. The second paragraph is a detailed account of the inequities faced by children from areas of lower socioeconomic status as they attempt to gain an education in the poorly funded public schools of their neighborhoods. In the final paragraph, the author recognizes the need for public education but continues to argue that the system is seriously flawed. Answer choice (C) is correct.

53. E

One should look to the passage as a whole to answer this question. In the first paragraph, the author establishes that the aim of public education is being missed. Then, in the last paragraph, the author describes those with utopian beliefs regarding education as being "naive" (line 50). Hence, a mistaken society feels that public education equally benefits all who participate. That's choice (E).

54. B

This question is best answered by carefully reviewing the lines cited in context. The term "social instability" in lines 47–48 of the passage implies that society would fall and be unable to function. The author argues that the flaws in the educational system prevent children from lower-income families from getting a fair education. So if one applies this logic and looks at the last paragraph, it becomes evident that the words "the necessity of public education is markedly important, because without it . . . the populace would suffer from extreme divisions between haves and have-nots, which would ultimately lead to social instability" (lines 44–48) declare the social value of the system, even if it is flawed. Choice (B) is correct.

55. C

To answer this question, look at the arguments made by the passage. Every paragraph details the lack of equality in public education as experienced by those from low-income families. So the logical inference in this case points to the statement that lower-income children do not reap the intended benefits of the public school system. Choice (C) is correct.

Passage XII

56. B

First, find where in the passage the Shakespeare apologists are mentioned—it is in the last paragraph. Here, the author states that Gross speaks against the apologists, saying that "they have developed such admiration for their own imaginings of who Shakespeare was" that they overlook the fact that Shakespeare was not educated. It can be assumed, therefore, that they believe Shakespeare was smarter than his lack of education would indicate. Also, since the question refers to the ideas of nineteenth-century scholars, refer again to the first paragraph. These scholars did not think Shakespeare wrote *any* of his plays; furthermore, the first paragraph states that modern scholars view such ideas as misguided, fanatical, even blasphemous. Correct answer choice (B) matches the prediction that the nineteenth-century scholars were incorrect in their view of Shakespeare's ability or intelligence.

57. B

Though several of these answer choices may seem plausible, consider what the topic of each paragraph is and, further, how the author introduces the ideas of the passage. Does the author agree with the thesis about Shakespeare authorship? Does he present a counterargument, disputing the findings of those who believe Bacon wrote the plays? He does not. Instead, the author merely presents the ideas of a new book on the subject; the passage is more like a book review than an attempt to persuade the reader or to compare and contrast opposing views. Choice (B) is correct.

58. C

The author states many viewpoints of Gail Gross, and the majority of them are in the third paragraph, so focus your attention there. As this question is an inference question that refers to many of the details of Gross's argument, pay close attention to what the passage actually states and how closely the answer choices correspond to the passage. Choice (C) is correct.

59. D

This question is detail oriented, as are most questions that use "EXCEPT." Essentially, you need to find instances in the passage in which the author points out four of these answer choices *or* determine which one is NOT pointed out. Choice (D) is correct. Though the author mentions the alchemical importance of mercury, he does not state that the element is used in the play or specifically referred to in the play, only that the character Mercutio's name may be derived from the word *mercury*.

60. A

Where in the passage does the author mention nineteenth-century scholars? You might attempt to simply scan the passage for any dates, and what you may find is "1850" in the first sentence. It is here that the author states the thesis of these scholars. They proposed that the plays ascribed to (credited to) Shakespeare had been "written by Sir Francis Bacon and that Shakespeare had made no real contribution to the composition of the plays." Choice (A) is correct.

Passage XIII

61. B

This question is best answered by finding appropriate information within the passage. One should read the claims and think about whether or not they are supported by evidence in the passage. Look at how the passage is structured. The first paragraph reveals a new theory in contrast to an old method. The second paragraph details that the theory is of substantial value and has pragmatic worth in the face of old methodology. The third paragraph details how little people have known about what spurs truffle growth and discusses technological changes that may aid in new discoveries. And the final paragraph discusses how the new model of biochemical observations could increase the likelihood of finding truffles. Choice (B) is correct.

62. D

This question is best answered by taking into consideration what the passage states about the difficulty of finding truffles and our knowledge of the fungus. Look at each paragraph in the passage and decide what would make the truffle fields hard to find. Correct answer choice (D) is stated directly in the third paragraph: Our "great difficulty in discovering truffles comes from how little people actually know about what spurs their growth."

63. A

In order to answer this question, look at the first paragraph and then compare it with the third and fourth paragraphs. In the first paragraph, the theory regarding marmot droppings is established, and empirical uses are considered in the third. As far as the empirical data are concerned, the fourth paragraph says they will be of practical use in finding truffles. Choice (A) is correct.

64. E

For this question, look at the three answers provided to see which idea(s) best match the examples in the passage. Point I is discussed within the last paragraph. Point III takes into account the importance of point I. If the testing and biochemical results from the marmot dung are deemed important, it is logical to infer that the sample being tested has to be properly handled. Point II is correct in suggesting the significance of empirical data, but it totally discounts the important of the new theory that is the main point of this passage. Answer choice (E), I and III, is correct.

65. B

This question is most concerned with one's understanding of the passage as a whole. It requires one to figure out the main goal or purpose of the passage. If you look at the first paragraph, you will note that it explains the pragmatic significance of a new theory regarding the appearance of marmot dung at places of truffle growth. The rest of the passage elaborates upon how this new theory will improve old methods and inform advances in the hunt for truffles. Choice (B) is a match for this prediction.

66. A

This question requires that you look in the passage for stated information. The new theory differs from what truffle enthusiasts have generally regarded as true. If you look at lines 2–4, which state, "This contrasts with the theory generally held by truffle enthusiasts, which specifies that truffles only proliferate in areas of moist dirt and darkness," you will find the answer—choice (A).

Passage XIV

67. B

To learn how Captain CapitalYay would view the falling value of large art items, go to the fourth paragraph where his or her ideas are presented. CapitalYay argues with James Ovariano's assertion that people are becoming more loving and losing the need to outdo each other with large purchases. CapitalYay writes in lines 43–44, "Cities are crowded and land is limited. Things are smaller because there is less space." It is clear that CapitalYay believes a change in available space, not emotions, is responsible for people's actions. Choice (B) is correct.

68. D

One can answer this question by finding examples in the passage where James Ovariano states why he thinks that large artwork has gone out of fashion. Look to each answer provided and see what lines of the passage contain it. Through this process of elimination, you can find the choice Ovariano does NOT cite as a possibility. That's (D). Ovariano mentions that items are getting smaller in lines 32–33, but he does not expressly mention this as the reason for large artwork going out of fashion. Instead, he feels that as large items have gone out of style, small ones have replaced them. He does not see small items as a reason but as a result.

69. B

One can infer the author's intention by looking at the way the passage is structured. The first paragraph sets up the situation and history of the Ovarianos's purchase of the two paintings, and it contrasts their passion for the artwork with their young son's view. Then the author introduces their son, James Ovariano, as an adult with a blog about his social values regarding his parent's "classist past" and the way he believes things have changed for the better with the decreasing value of large art items. The majority of the passage is about James Ovariano's "wonderful sociological blog," and the author only discusses his detractor, Captain CapitalYay, in order to present a contrast in opinions. Choice (B) is correct.

70. C

An inference about Manhattanites' actions throughout the years can be made by looking at their actions as described in the first paragraph, where in "1946, two large abstract paintings sold for $150,000," and "Manhattanites desirous of social pride outbid each other." These two sentences show both the social and economic value of the artwork to Manhattanites in 1946. One can then look to both the last lines of the first paragraph and lines 46–48 in the last paragraph to see that the paintings sold for only $40,000 to Manhattanites in the twenty-first century. With these data, one can infer that Manhattanites now express less demand for big works of art. Choice (C) is correct.

71. A

You can draw an inference from the stated information. The passage states that "during the summer of 1946, two large abstract paintings sold for $150,000," and that "Manhattanites desirous of social pride outbid each other." Then the paragraph further details how the winners were "the envy of all." With this information, you can infer that the people outbidding each other were doing so in order to advance their social pride by acquiring an artwork that someone else did not have. Choice (A) is a match.

Passage XV

72. D

This question requires that you apply the potential problem described in the passage to a more concrete scenario. The potential problem identified is one in which a conversational nuance is lost due to the remote nature of the communication. Choice (D) is a solid match. Misconstruing sarcasm as sincerity would be an example of missing a conversational nuance.

73. A

This question asks for what is NOT stated in the passage; therefore, the four uncredited answers will all be things that ARE stated in the passage, and you should use process of elimination to find the one answer that is not mentioned. Here, the potential problems are mentioned in the second paragraph, so look there for the uncredited answers. Choice (A) is correct. Nowhere in the passage are headhunters for competing companies discussed.

74. B

This question asks you what is implied in the passage; therefore, the correct answer will be something that is not explicitly stated but that is closely related to the information in the passage. Be careful not to stray too far from what is stated in the passage. Answer choice (B) is correct. The passage states that employers are able to tap into a larger pool of talent using remote hiring and that the remote employees sometimes work in different cities or even countries from the home office.

75. B

This question asks you to identify the main idea of the passage. To do so, it is important to keep the author's tone in mind. The author is primarily objective, with some cautious optimism about the potential benefits of remote hiring and supervision. Choice (B) is correct.

Passage XVI

76. D

This question asks for what the passage "suggests," which means that it is an inference question and the correct answer will be implied by the text, not expressly stated. With any inference question, the key is to stay very close to the stated information instead of bringing in outside knowledge or conjectures. Answer choice (D) is correct. Since feminists chose to abandon the dress reform movement out of fear that the negative attention it attracted would harm other reform efforts like suffrage, one can infer that at least some feminists prioritized suffrage over dress reform.

77. B

This question asks for the role of a detail in the passage. Context is key here; the sentence in which dress reform is first mentioned begins with the phrase "their interests were broad," indicating that feminists were working to achieve change in different arenas. Therefore, the detail probably supports that perspective. Answer choice (B) matches this prediction.

78. D

This question asks for what is stated in the passage; because it says "EXCEPT," the correct answer will be the one that is NOT found in the passage. The question must therefore be approached by comparing each answer choice to the passage and eliminating the ones that are mentioned, leaving the one that is not as the correct answer. Answer choice (D) is correct; the ability to buy and sell property is never mentioned in the passage as a right for which feminists worked.

79. A

This question asks for the organization of a paragraph within a passage. It's important to keep in mind the overall purpose of the passage when evaluating it. The passage as a whole does not advocate any particular view; it is simply descriptive, and therefore the role of the first paragraph within that description should be examined. Choice (A) is correct. Pre-nineteenth-century women's activism is briefly addressed, and then the changes in that activism are mentioned and supported with details.

80. C

This question asks for an inference about women's social activism prior to the mid-nineteenth century; since it is an inference question, the correct answer will not be explicitly stated, but will be supported by the text. Here, women's movements prior to the mid-nineteenth century are briefly addressed in the first sentence, which says that they were largely limited to "abolition and temperance and societies intended to benefit the poor." Choice (C) is correct.

81. B

This question asks for the author's primary purpose in writing the passage; it is important, when answering a question like this, to be aware of the author's tone. Is the author advocating a particular view? Here, the author's tone is detached and informative, and no specific opinions—hers or anyone else's—are offered. Choice (B) is correct. The passage is descriptive in tone, and it addresses developments in the first wave of American feminism.

Passage XVII

82. C

In order to answer an application question, paraphrase the events in the passage in an abstract fashion and then apply that abstraction to other specific circumstances. Here, the average American family is described as having a higher household income now than in the 1970s but also as facing higher fixed expenditures, leaving it with less discretionary income than families had a generation ago. The "profits" in the answer choices are analogous to household incomes. Choice (C) is correct.

83. C

This question begins with the phrase "according to the passage," so the correct answer will be something that the author has expressly stated. "Fixed expenditures" are discussed near the end of the second paragraph; the author says that increases in those expenditures have outpaced increases in average household income. Choice (C) is the credited response.

84. A

This question asks what the passage implies; therefore, it is an inference question, and the correct answer will be close to the text but not explicitly stated. Dual-income, two-child families are discussed in the second paragraph, where the second sentence says that with women working outside the home, middle-class families face expenditures like child care and a second car that would not have been an issue in the 1970s. That's a match for choice (A).

85. E

Since this question asks what can be inferred from the passage, the correct answer will not be explicitly stated but will remain close to the text of the passage. In the third paragraph, the author describes how, although discretionary purchases make up a smaller portion of the average household budget, families enjoy a higher standard of living now than their parents did, in part because of the lower costs of some consumer goods. Examples given in this paragraph include refrigerators and television sets. Choice (E) is correct.

86. D

The organization of this passage is best described as follows: A popular view of a problem is presented and is then rejected; two paragraphs of examples and statistics are presented to support the author's rejection of the popular view; and then in the last paragraph, the real cause of the problem is explained and the author's main point is stated. No solutions are ever presented for the problem. Choice (D) is correct.

87. B

This question asks for the author's main purpose in writing the passage; it's important to keep the entire passage in mind, not just a portion of it. It's also important to have a clear idea of the passage's structure. Here, the author presents a viewpoint, rebuts it, and then provides statistics and counterexamples supporting her conclusion. Answer choice (B) is correct.

Passage XVIII

88. C

This question asks for an inference about polar bear denning, which is discussed in the second-to-last sentence of the passage. Regarding denning, the author says that if the dens collapse or melt, there could be "negative implications for polar bear reproduction and survival." Based on this statement, it is reasonable to infer that denning plays a role in polar bear reproduction. That's choice (C).

89. B

This question asks for a detail that is expressly stated in the passage. In the sixth sentence, the author mentions summer and describes the danger that retreating sea ice will force bears onto land before they have built up sufficient fat stores. Therefore, the correct answer is a paraphrase of this detail, choice (B).

90. E

This question asks for an inference based on information in the passage. The key here is to stay close to the text and not bring in any outside information. Choice (E) is correct. The passage mentions that global warming puts seals in danger, which cuts into the bears' primary food source. Conservation efforts to boost the seal population will give the bears a more plentiful food source.

91. C

As with any inference question, the key here is to look for something that must be true based on the statements made but that is not explicitly stated by the author. The public response to the dangers faced by polar bears as a result of global warming is discussed at the beginning and end of the paragraph; in sentence 3, polar bears are said to have been "garnering attention recently," and in the last sentence, the author says that "proposals have recently been made" to place the bears on a threatened species list. Therefore, one can infer that polar bears have gotten increased attention recently. Answer choice (C) is correct.

92. C

This question asks for the overall structure of the passage. The main difficulty here is that the entire passage is one paragraph, so it can be more challenging to map out the organization than if several paragraphs had been used to present the same information. Answer choice (C) is correct. The author presents an issue (polar bears face increased danger from global warming), develops it with examples of ways that global warming could harm polar bears, and then predicts that there could be dire consequences in the future if global warming continues unabated.

93. A

This question asks for evidence to strengthen a point made by the author. The author claims that, since seals are the primary food source for polar bears, a reduction in the seal population would cause the bears to starve. Evidence showing that something similar had happened in the past would support the idea that polar bears are dependent on seals. Choice (A) is correct.

Passage XIX

94. E

This question asks what is true "according to the passage," so the correct answer will be something that is expressly stated in the text. The author's main focus on copyright protection is in the second paragraph. Choice (E) is correct. In the last sentence of the second paragraph, the author refers to sculpture as an example of copyrightable work in which the physical embodiment is virtually impossible to separate from the artistic expression.

95. C

The author's viewpoint is expressed at the end of the first and last paragraphs; she classifies current levels of protection as "deficient," and proposes a way in which courts can extend protection to perfumes without entering into confusing copyright territory. Therefore, the author is likely to agree with a statement reflecting the idea that greater intellectual property protection for perfumes would be desirable. Answer choice (C) is correct.

96. A

The author's conclusion is the recommendation that protection be extended further to the names and packages of perfumes, presumably remedying the "deficiency" to which she referred in the first paragraph. This recommendation, however, is based on the notion that courts will extend intellectual property protection to perfumes in future cases—that the question is not a matter of whether that protection will be available, but rather the degree to which it is available and the exact subject matter protected. Answer choice (A) is correct.

97. D

Since the question asks for the primary purpose of the second paragraph, it is important to keep the entire paragraph in mind, instead of focusing on any one part of it. It's also important to be mindful of the role that the paragraph plays in the larger framework of the passage as a whole. Here, the author presents a problem, summarizes the debate relating to that problem, and then suggests one possible solution to the problem. That's choice (D).

98. C

Because the passage's tone is generally academic, the reader must seek contextual clues about the author's purpose in writing. At the end of the first paragraph, the author states that the current level of intellectual property protection for cosmetic products seems "deficient," and in the last sentence, she says that it is "preferable" to extend protection to the names and packages of perfumes, rather than copyrighting scents. (C) is the credited response.

99. D

Knockoff perfumes are discussed in the first and last paragraphs; in the last paragraph, the author discusses how knockoff manufacturers stay "just on the right side of the law" and the need for judges to "cut through the technicalities that such companies use to maintain the legality of their efforts." Therefore, you can infer that knockoffs are created to abide by the law while coming as close as possible to infringing upon the intellectual property of the creators of the original scents. Answer choice (D) is correct.

100. A

This question asks you to make an inference about the author's opinion of intellectual property protection for perfumes. However, since that is the topic of the entire passage, it's almost impossible to predict what the correct inference will be. Therefore, the best way to approach this question is to evaluate each answer choice in turn. Choice (A) is correct. In the first paragraph, the author describes the functions of trademark and copyright law as applied to cosmetics: they can protect the name, advertising, and packaging of the products. And in the last paragraph, the author states that the best course of action for protecting perfumes is to protect their packaging and names from knockoff producers and distributors. Therefore, it is reasonable to infer that the author believes that trademark and copyright protection are the best course of action for extending intellectual property protection to perfumes.

Sentence Correction

PREVIEWING SENTENCE CORRECTION

Sentence Correction questions cover a range of grammatical errors, some of which are obscure enough that even good writers commit them. However, you don't have to be a grammar expert to do well on this section. All you need is a strategy and some knowledge about what does—and does not—constitute good GMAT grammar.

Another key element in GMAT Sentence Correction is style, or what the directions for this question type refer to as "effectiveness of expression." The GMAT is looking for English that is clear and exact and without awkwardness, ambiguity, or redundancy.

Each Sentence Correction sentence will contain an underlined portion and ask you which of the choices best fits in place of that underlined portion. Answer choice (A) will always repeat exactly that underlined part of the sentence. So, choice (A) is correct when there's no error. Recognizing this pattern means that you never need to spend any time reading choice (A) once you've read the original sentence. Given the statistically random distribution of correct answers across the five choices, you can anticipate that choice (A)—the sentence is correct as written—will be correct approximately 20 percent of the time.

QUESTION FORMAT AND STRUCTURE

The GMAT Verbal Reasoning section includes about 16 Sentence Correction questions, which are mixed in with Critical Reasoning and Reading Comprehension.

The directions for Sentence Correction questions look like this:

> **Directions:** Each Sentence Correction question presents a sentence, part or all of which is underlined. Below each sentence you will find five ways to phrase the underlined portion. The first answer choice repeats the original version, while the other four choices are different. If the original seems best, choose the first answer choice. If not, choose one of the revisions.
>
> In choosing an answer, follow the norms of standard written English: grammar, word choice, and sentence construction. Choose the answer

that produces the most effective sentence, aiming to eliminate awkwardness, ambiguity, redundancy, and grammatical error.

Sentence Correction tests your command of standard written English—the rather formal language that is used in textbooks and scholarly periodicals. It's the language that's used to convey complex information precisely, as opposed to the casual language that we use for everyday communication. The good news is that you do not need to know every grammar rule for these questions. Errors reflecting certain rules show up repeatedly on the GMAT. Focus on mastering these commonly tested rules—that's how to get the biggest bang for your study-time buck.

Sentence Correction Practice

1. Scientists claim that the fossilized remains of ancient ancestors of the modern North American brown bear found in Alberta and estimated at 25,000 years old offer the solution to a genealogical mystery regarding the bear's early migration through Beringia into the northernmost parts of Canada.
   - O at 25,000 years old offer the solution to
   - O as being 25,000 years old offers resolution to
   - O that it is 25,000 years old offers the solution to what was
   - O to be 25,000 years old offer the solution to
   - O as 25,000 years old offers the solution to what was

2. The mid-twentieth century hosted the emergence of the Information Age, with radical inventions and innovations facilitating the spread of information, creating new industries, and revolutionized the way people worldwide live, work, and interact.
   - O revolutionized
   - O it revolutionized
   - O revolutionizing
   - O would revolutionize
   - O it had revolutionized

3. Beyond the current sales slump the auto manufacturer experiences, its long-term success depends on if it can reduce production costs and improve fuel economy for its existing lines of popular vehicles.
   - O if it can reduce production costs and improve
   - O its capacity for reducing production costs and improving
   - O whether it can reduce production costs and improve
   - O whether or not it has the ability to reduce production costs and improve
   - O the capacity for it to reduce production costs and improve

4. A debt ratio of 30 percent of gross domestic product is even so much that the strongest national economies incur, and then only as a means to finance short-term undertakings of national or international prominence.

- O even so much that
- O even as much that
- O even so much as
- O so much as even
- O as much as even

5. The company announced Friday that sales increased by 11.3 percent in 2007, while prices remained constant when it might have been expected for them to fall.

- O it might have been expected for them to fall
- O they might have been expected to fall
- O it might have been expected that they should fall
- O their fall might have been expected
- O there might have been an expectation they would fall

6. Even though Walt Whitman's *Leaves of Grass* received a lukewarm reception in his native United States, it gained such international acclaim, it became a classical work almost overnight.

- O it gained such international acclaim, it became a classical
- O it gained such international acclaim that it became a classic
- O so acclaimed internationally it gained as to become a classic
- O such was the international acclaim it gained, it became a classical
- O there was so much international acclamation that it became a classical

7. Attempts to balance the distribution of campaign funds available to legitimate political candidates, a contemporary goal of election reformers in several states, has not notably diminished the disparities persisting between the best and worst fundraisers.

- O has not notably diminished the disparities persisting
- O has not been notable in diminishing the disparities that persist
- O has not made a notable diminution in the disparities that persist
- O have not notably diminished the disparities that persist
- O have not been notable in a diminution of the disparities persisting

8. Health officials involved in the diagnosis and treatment of methicillin-resistant *Staphylococcus aureus* (MRSA) have found the cases of infection are difficult to diagnose, highly contagious, and are resistant to treatment.
   - o the cases of infection are difficult to diagnose, highly contagious, and are
   - o cases of infection to be difficult to diagnose, highly contagious, and are
   - o that cases of infection are difficult to diagnose, highly contagious, and
   - o cases of infection are difficult to diagnose and highly contagious, and they are
   - o that cases of infection are difficult to diagnose and highly contagious, and they are

9. While wealthier individuals can afford to buy their own homes, many poorer people are finding that the expense affiliated with purchasing a home and with the maintenance and improvement of interior and exterior areas are restrictive.
   - o expense affiliated with
   - o expenses affiliated with
   - o expenses deriving from
   - o expense of
   - o expenses of

10. Dark matter, which accounts for most of the mass in the observable universe, thought to contain yet undiscovered elementary particles.
    - o thought to contain
    - o some think it to contain
    - o some think it contains
    - o is thought to contain
    - o it is thought that it contains

11. Six captive-born Vancouver Island marmots were successfully released into their native habitat last month, and brought to 35 the population count of animals in the wild.
    - o and brought
    - o bringing
    - o and brings
    - o and it brings
    - o and it brought

12. The printing press, which Johannes Gutenberg developed in the mid-fifteenth century, shortened from months to days the necessary time of publishing a book.
    - from months to days the necessary time of publishing a book
    - the time being necessary to publish a book, from months to days
    - the time being necessary to publish a book, months to days
    - the time needed to publish a book from months to days
    - from months to days, the time needed for the publishing of a book

13. Some pathologists claim that the relatively low recent number of medical visits statewide provides evidence that the state will escape the influenza epidemic that many had anticipated earlier this year and instead enjoy a considerably mild flu season.
    - that the state will escape the influenza epidemic that many had anticipated earlier this year and instead enjoy
    - in the state to escape the influenza epidemic, what many anticipated earlier this year, instead to enjoy
    - in the state's ability to escape the influenza epidemic, something earlier this year many had anticipated, and rather to enjoy
    - in the state to escape the influenza epidemic many were anticipating earlier this year, and instead to enjoy
    - that the state will escape the influenza epidemic that was anticipated earlier this year by many, with it instead enjoying

14. To Henry David Thoreau, harmony with nature was his ideal a century and a half before it became popular to be an environmentalist, and he retained his fascination with and respect for nature as essential elements of his lifestyle until his death.
    - To Henry David Thoreau, harmony with nature was his ideal a century and a half before it became popular to be an environmentalist
    - For Henry David Thoreau, a century and a half before it became popular to be an environmentalist, harmony with nature was his ideal
    - Henry David Thoreau idealized harmony with nature a century and a half before to be an environmentalist became popular
    - A century and a half before it became popular to be an environmentalist, Henry David Thoreau idealized harmony with nature
    - A century and a half before it became popular being an environmentalist, harmony with nature was ideal to Henry David Thoreau

15. By developing industry-leading technology including computers, media players, cellular phones, and devising creative and memorable marketing campaigns, Techno Inc. has become one of the most successful purveyors of technology in the world.

   - cellular phones, and devising
   - cellular phones, and by devising
   - and cellular phones, devising
   - and cellular phones, and devising
   - and cellular phones, and by devising

16. Her financial planner recommended that Susan should consolidate high-interest loans, unnecessary credit cards should be closed, and budget her monthly finances.

   - should consolidate high-interest loans, unnecessary credit cards should be closed, and budget her monthly finances
   - should consolidate high-interest loans, unnecessary credit cards should be closed, and her monthly finances should be budgeted
   - should consolidate high-interest loans, unnecessary credit cards should be closed, and to budget her monthly finances
   - consolidate high-interest loans, close unnecessary credit cards, and her monthly finances budgeted
   - consolidate high-interest loans, close unnecessary credit cards, and budget her monthly finances

17. Many start-up companies offer stock option incentives that allow an employee with inadequate disposable income for independent financial investment to be able to invest in company stock and apportion pretax income to pay for the investment.

- O incentives that allow an employee with inadequate disposable income for independent financial investment to be able to invest in company stock and apportion
- O incentives that allow an employee with inadequate disposable income for independent financial investment to invest in company stock and apportion
- O incentives; that allows an employee with inadequate disposable income for independent financial investment to invest in company stock, to apportion
- O incentives, which allows an employee with inadequate disposable income for independent financial investment to invest in company stock, apportioning
- O incentives, which allow an employee with inadequate disposable income for independent financial investment to be able to invest in company stock, apportioning

18. That many individuals were not vaccinated against the virus before its resurgence cannot plausibly be argued that it is their fault: researcher Sam Daniels, one of the leading experts on the virus, reported a quarter-century ago that the virus was effectively contained and that no action beyond education was necessary.

- O That many individuals were not vaccinated against the virus before its resurgence cannot plausibly be argued that it is their fault
- O That many individuals were not vaccinated against the virus before its resurgence cannot plausibly be argued to be at fault
- O It cannot plausibly be argued that it is the fault of individuals who were not vaccinated against the virus before its resurgence
- O It cannot plausibly be argued that individuals are at fault for not receiving vaccination against the virus before its resurgence
- O The fact that individuals are at fault for not receiving vaccination against the virus before its resurgence cannot plausibly be argued

19. The Christmas holiday brought a brief respite to opposing armies during World War I in that an unofficial cease-fire spread along the Western Front on Christmas Eve, 1914.

- o armies during World War I in that an unofficial cease-fire spread along the Western Front on Christmas Eve, 1914
- o armies during World War I, spreading an unofficial cease-fire along the Western Front on Christmas Eve, 1914
- o armies during World War I when they spread an unofficial cease-fire along the Western Front on Christmas Eve, 1914
- o armies during World War I, for an unofficial cease-fire spread along the Western Front on Christmas Eve, 1914
- o armies during World War I by the spread of an unofficial cease-fire along the Western Front on Christmas Eve, 1914

20. While all businesses face similar fiscal concerns, labor market conditions and the size of the company significantly affects cost basis and profit margin, as well as the style of management.

- o all businesses face similar fiscal concerns, labor market conditions and the size of the company significantly affects
- o each business faces a similar fiscal concern, their labor market conditions and size of the company significantly affect
- o all businesses face a similar fiscal concern; their labor market conditions and company size significantly affects
- o each business faces similar fiscal concerns, labor market conditions and the size of each company significantly affects
- o all businesses face similar fiscal concerns, labor market conditions and the size of each company significantly affect

21. Current tax law requires anyone who earns a profit on an investment that was held less than a year pay tax at ordinary income rates on such investments.

- o pay
- o will also pay
- o to pay
- o must pay
- o must then pay

22. In an attempt to reclaim the tax money unjustly collected by the king's men, Robin Hood suggested planting in the entourage's path a rebel disguised as a damsel in distress to serve as a distraction, so that it halts the caravan and allowing the rebels to access the king's gold.
   - o to serve as a distraction, so that it halts
   - o to serve like a distraction so as to halt
   - o to serve as a distraction, halting
   - o serving as a distraction, halting
   - o serving like a distraction, halt

23. After they surveyed the shattered glass, metal shrapnel, and scattered personal effects, the insurance adjusters did not dispute whether the damage was the tornado that swept through the area early Tuesday morning.
   - o did not dispute whether the damage was
   - o have no dispute over whether the damage was
   - o had not disputed whether the damage was
   - o have no dispute over whether the damage was the result of
   - o did not dispute that the damage was the result of

24. Prompted by observations of seemingly related species in neighboring locales that he made during his five-year voyage around the world on the HMS *Beagle*, Charles Darwin conceived his theory of natural selection in which all species evolved over time from a single ancestor or very few common ancestors.
   - o in which all species evolved over time from a single ancestor or very few common ancestors
   - o in which all species evolve from a single ancestor or very few common ancestors over time
   - o whereby over time all species evolve from a single ancestor or very few common ancestors
   - o whereby all species have evolved over time from a single ancestor or very few common ancestors
   - o whereby all species evolved over time from a single ancestor or very few common ancestors

25. Increasingly in recent times, environmentalists, economists, and politicians are touting research as a means to better fuels progressively and encouraging investment in "green" technologies.
    - o to better fuels progressively and encouraging
    - o to better progressive fuels and encouraging
    - o of better fuels progressively and encourage
    - o of better progressive fuels and encourage
    - o for better progressive fuels and the encouragement of

26. Since 1975, the proportion of white males in executive positions at Fortune 500 companies have consistently declined, while the percentages of women and ethnic minorities who hold such positions have grown.
    - o have consistently declined, while the percentages of women and ethnic minorities who hold such positions have grown
    - o have consistently declined, while women and ethnic minorities holding such positions have increased in percentage
    - o declined consistently, while there was an increase in the percentage of women and ethnic minorities holding such positions
    - o has consistently declined, while the percentages of women and ethnic minorities holding such positions have grown
    - o has consistently declined, while those of women and ethnic minorities who hold such positions grew

27. A fifty-year accord signed in 1994 by the United States, Canada, and Mexico dictated the reduction of tariffs that member nations had been permitted to levy on imports from other member nations.
    - o dictated the reduction of tariffs that member nations had been permitted to levy
    - o dictated the tariff reduction that member nations had been levying
    - o dictates the tariff reduction member nations were permitted to levy
    - o dictated the reduction of tariffs that member nations are permitted to levy
    - o dictates the reduction of tariffs permitted for levying by member nations

28. Ordinances prohibiting alcohol consumption and limiting noise levels on municipal beaches have been passed in several cities throughout the state; the concern of beachfront businesses is whether students on spring break will continue to vacation in our state and patronize our beaches after their restrictions are enacted.

- O whether students on spring break will continue to vacation in our state and patronize our beaches after their restrictions are
- O whether students on spring break will continue to vacation in our state to patronize one once their restrictions are
- O whether students on spring break will continue to vacation in our state to patronize our beaches once the cities' restrictions have been
- O if students on spring break will continue to vacation in our state and patronize our beaches once the cities' restrictions are
- O if students on spring break will continue to vacation in our state to patronize one after the cities' restrictions have been

29. The phrase "urban gentrification" is a phenomenon in which individuals and private entities, rather than the government, are entrusted to improve the aesthetics of a neighborhood.

- O is a phenomenon in which individuals and private entities, rather than the government, are entrusted to improve
- O refers to a phenomenon in which individuals and private entities, rather than the government, are entrusted to improve
- O is a phenomenon entrusting individuals and private entities, rather than the government, to improve
- O refers to a phenomenon entrusting individuals and private entities, but not the government, to improve
- O has reference to the phenomenon entrusting individuals and private entities, instead of the government, to improve

30. The only feasible way to eradicate fruit blight is if the infected and nearby plants are quickly destroyed before it spreads when resident insect eggs hatch.

- O if the infected and nearby plants are quickly destroyed before it spreads when resident insect eggs hatch
- O to immediately destroy all infected and nearby plants before it spreads when resident insect eggs hatch
- O for them to be destroyed immediately before it spreads when resident insect eggs hatch
- O if they are quickly destroyed before resident insect eggs hatch to spread it
- O to destroy them immediately before it spreads when resident insect eggs hatch

31. In contrast to traditional banks, the venture capital seeker is not required to have two or more years of operational history to receive funding.

- O the venture capital seeker is not required to have
- O with venture capital seeking there is no requirement of
- O venture capital seekers are not required to have
- O for the venture capital seeker there is no requirement of
- O venture capital firms do not require a funding seeker to have

32. Unlike math or science, there is an incapacity on the part of most people to acknowledge the severity of their language deficiencies.

- O Unlike math or science, there is an incapacity on the part of many people to acknowledge the severity of their language deficiencies.
- O Unlike math or science, which they acknowledge are weak, many people are unable to acknowledge that they have language deficiencies.
- O Unlike math or science, language brings out an incapacity in many people to acknowledge that they are deficient.
- O Many people, able to acknowledge weaknesses in math or science, are unable to acknowledge their language deficiencies.
- O Many people have an incapacity to acknowledge deficiencies in language while able to acknowledge their weaknesses in math or science.

33. NASA recently published a report cautioning that many of the space debris to which satellites and space-faring vessels are exposed pose a significant risk of damaging or destroying satellites and vessels in instances of accidental impact.

- o many of the space debris to which satellites and space-faring vessels are exposed pose
- o many of the space debris that satellites and space-faring vessels are exposed to poses
- o many of the debris that is in space and that satellites and space-faring vessels are exposed to pose
- o much of the debris that is in space and satellites and space-faring vessels are exposed to poses
- o much of the space debris to which satellites and space-faring vessels are exposed poses

34. The resurgence of interest in sixteenth-century art, or a "Renaissance renaissance," can increase prevailing prices in the art market enough to suppress short-term demand for period pieces, stimulate trader speculation that may cause market weakness in certain regions of the United States and destabilization in international markets.

- o to suppress short-term demand for period pieces, stimulate
- o that the short-term demand for period pieces is suppressed, stimulate
- o that it suppresses the short-term demand for period pieces, stimulate
- o that the short-term demand for period pieces is suppressed and stimulate
- o to suppress the short-term demand for period pieces and stimulate

35. The satellite's observations indicated a smaller relative radius of Pluto, which decreases to eight the total number of bodies recognized as planets orbiting the sun.

- o which decreases to eight the total number of bodies recognized as planets orbiting
- o decreasing to eight the total number of bodies recognized as planets orbiting
- o which decreases to eight the total number of bodies recognized as planets in orbit around
- o decreasing to eight the total number of bodies recognized as planets to orbit
- o which decreases to eight the total number of bodies recognized as planets that orbit

36. An African scribe and mathematician, <u>the first computation of pi was made by Ahmes without benefit of the abacus or calculator</u>.

- o the first computation of pi was made by Ahmes without benefit of the abacus or calculator
- o without the benefits of the abacus or calculator, the first computation of pi was made by Ahmes
- o Ahmes made the first computation of pi without the benefit of the abacus or calculator
- o there was made, without the benefit of the abacus or calculator, the first computation of pi by Ahmes
- o was Ahmes, who, without benefit of the abacus or calculator, made the first computation of pi

37. Increasing malpractice costs and legal fees threaten to erode the financial viability of the medical profession, a vocation <u>that once generated more profit than any other vocation</u> in the country.

- o that once generated more profit than any other vocation
- o that had once generated more profit than had any other vocation
- o that once generated more profit those had
- o once generating more profit than those did
- o once generating more profit than those were

38. Not since medieval times had France refurbished <u>so many historical structures at once as they had after</u> World War II.

- o so many historical structures at once as they had after
- o at once as many historical structures as
- o at once as many historical structures that there were with
- o as many historical structures at once as it refurbished after
- o so many historical structures at once that refurbished them after

39. Residents of the heritage district have explored winding streets and saw cottages nestled on the sidewalks, whose shingled roofs cluster together like beads on a string.
   - saw cottages nestled on the sidewalks, whose shingled roofs cluster
   - saw cottages nestled on the sidewalks, whose shingled roofs were clustering
   - saw cottages nestled on the sidewalks, with shingled roofs clustering
   - seen cottages nestled on the sidewalks, with shingled roofs clustered
   - seen cottages nestled on the sidewalks, whose shingled roofs have clustered

40. Montmartre is a hill in northern Paris renowned for its white-domed Basilica of the Sacre Coeur and an artistic community made famous by Pablo Picasso and Vincent van Gogh, two artists who built studios near the church and used them as residences.
   - who built studios near the church and used them as
   - who, building studios near the church, used them like
   - who, when they had built studios near the church, used them like
   - who had built studios near the church, using them to be
   - building studios near the church and using them as

41. The new "reality shows" enable television stations to garner high ratings without the costly requirements of writer compensation and utilization of demanding actors by traditional television show formats.
   - requirements of writer compensation and utilization of demanding actors by traditional television show formats
   - requirements by traditional television show formats of utilization of demanding actors and writer compensation
   - requirements for utilization of demanding actors and writer compensation of traditional television show formats
   - utilization of demanding actors and writer compensation that is required by traditional television show formats
   - writer compensation and utilization of demanding actors that are required by traditional television show formats

42. In order to raise attendance, the Museum Board has lowered admission prices; museum tickets have been priced to move and they are.
   - have been priced to move and they are
   - are priced to move, and they have
   - are priced to move, and they do
   - are being priced to move, and have
   - had been priced to move, and they have

43. A new board bylaw mandates that corporate financial statements be audited each month.
   - mandates that corporate financial statements be audited
   - mandates corporate financial statements to be audited
   - mandates that corporate financial statements will be audited
   - has a mandate for audited corporate financial statements
   - has a mandate to audit the corporate financial statements

44. The compost heap is not a lifeless mound in which organic waste sits and decomposes; rather an energetic "disposal system" that actively breaks down the waste material.
   - decomposes; rather
   - decomposes, but rather
   - decomposes; but rather that of
   - decomposes; but that of
   - decomposes; it is that of

45. Although the lobbyists sought a reduction in the minimum wage, state legislators have proposed the wages of experienced employees be raised and that the economic effects be monitored.
   - the wages of experienced employees be raised and that the economic effects
   - that wages of experienced employees should be raised, with the results being
   - the raising of wages for experienced employees and the economic effects to be
   - wages raised of experienced employees, with its results
   - that the wages of experienced employees be raised and the economic effects

46. The Eco Team is evaluating soil samples to determine whether microbes can be deployed to reduce toxic waste levels.
   - o to determine whether microbes can be deployed to reduce
   - o to determine whether microbes can be deployed as help to reduce
   - o to see if microbes can be deployed for reducing
   - o that see if microbes are able to be deployed in reducing
   - o that see whether microbes are able to be deployed for help in reducing

47. Unlike the American Kennel Club, which controlled the world of dog shows over the last decade, the Westminster Kennel Club created no new dog show competitions and generated only a smattering of new breeds.
   - o the American Kennel Club, which controlled
   - o the American Kennel Club the control of which
   - o the American Kennel Club, who controlled
   - o the American Kennel Club's control of
   - o the American Kennel Club controlling

48. The housing prices in various counties, some of them at significant rates, are increasing just as the interest rates are, yet being still low enough to avoid an inflationary effect.
   - o The housing prices in various counties, some of them at significant rates, are increasing just as the interest rates are, yet being
   - o Both interest rates and housing prices of various counties are increasing, some at significant rates, but they are
   - o Although like the interest rates the housing prices are increasing, some of them at significant rates, yet
   - o As the interest rates, the housing prices are increasing, some of them at significant rates, but they are
   - o The housing prices of various counties are increasing like the interest rates, some of which at significant rates are increasing but

49. The renowned Masai warriors of Kenya are among the world's tallest people, with an average height over six feet, several inches taller than in most other countries of the world.
   - o taller than in
   - o taller than that of
   - o and taller than that of
   - o which is taller than in
   - o which is taller than it is in

50. Le Caramelize, the transformation of the surface of crème brûlée, a process in which molecules of sugar and oxygen react releasing volatile chemicals that have produced the unique nutty flavor and brown color.

- o a process in which molecules of sugar and oxygen react releasing volatile chemicals that have produced
- o a process where molecules in sugar and oxygen are reacting to release the volatile chemicals that are producing
- o a process in which molecules of sugar and oxygen react and which releases the volatile chemicals that are produced
- o is a process in which molecules of oxygen and sugar react to release the volatile chemicals that produce
- o is a process where molecules of oxygen and sugar are reacting and release the volatile chemicals producing

51. Leonardo da Vinci, in his drawings, publishing them with his scientific findings, leveraged his artistic ability and his grasp of anatomical principles.

- o Leonardo da Vinci, in his drawings, publishing them with his scientific findings,
- o In his drawings, publishing them with his scientific findings, Leonardo da Vinci
- o In his drawings, which he published with his scientific findings, Leonardo da Vinci
- o Published with his scientific findings, Leonardo da Vinci, in his drawings
- o Leonardo da Vinci, in his drawings, published them with his scientific findings and

52. At the finish line, vibrant banners were held by throngs of supporters who had been recruited to assist either in congratulating the exultant winners or in encouraging the weary stragglers.

- o in congratulating the exultant winners or in encouraging the weary stragglers
- o in congratulating the exultant winners and to encourage the weary stragglers
- o in congratulating the exultant winners, and encouraging the weary stragglers
- o to congratulate exultant winners or to encourage weary stragglers
- o to congratulate exultant winners or encouraging weary stragglers

53. In his commentary, the journalist distinguished student rebellions, which may be raucous without their being driven by activism, from authentic political protest.

- student rebellions, which may be raucous without their being driven by activism, from authentic political protest
- student rebellions, perhaps raucous without being driven by activism, and authentic political protest
- between student rebellions, which may be raucous without being driven by activism, and authentic political protest
- between student rebellions, perhaps raucous without being driven by activism, from authentic political protest
- authentic political protest and student rebellions, which may be raucous without being driven by activism

54. One of the most important decisions for most people experiencing being relocated for work is if to purchase a home immediately.

- being relocated for work is if to purchase
- being relocated for work is whether they should be purchasing
- being relocated for work is whether or not they purchase
- relocation for work is if to purchase
- relocation for work is whether to purchase

55. Filmed in Brooklyn, the producer and director of *It's Time for a Change* were two young activists, Abner Macon, and Aaron Louis, who would later establish a reputation as a community organizer.

- Filmed in Brooklyn, the producer and director of *It's Time for a Change* were two young activists, Abner Macon, and Aaron Louis, who would later establish a reputation as a community organizer.
- Filmed in Brooklyn, two young activists, Abner Macon and Aaron Louis, who would later establish a reputation as a community organizer, were the producer and director of *It's Time for a Change*.
- Filmed in Brooklyn, *It's Time for a Change* was directed and produced by two young activists, Aaron Louis, who would later establish a reputation as a community organizer, and Abner Macon.
- *It's Time for a Change* was owned and edited by two young activists, Abner Macon and Aaron Louis, who would later establish a reputation as a community organizer, and filmed in Brooklyn.
- The producer and director being two young young activists, Abner Macon and Aaron Louis, who would later establish a reputation as a community organizer, *It's Time for a Change* was published in Brooklyn.

56. In July 2000, *Self-Portrait*, Frida Kahlo's early representation of herself sold for $5.1 million and it was the highest price ever paid for a work by a female artist at auction.

- o herself sold for $5.1 million and it was
- o herself, which sold for $5.1 million, was
- o herself, was sold for $5.1 million,
- o herself was sold for $5.1 million, being
- o herself, sold for $5.1 million, and was

57. The Finance Committee's decrease in fees paid on deferred tuition payments to the school is both an acknowledgment of students' current financial burdens and an effort to ease them in the future.

- o decrease in fees paid on deferred tuition payments to the school is both an acknowledgment of students' current financial burdens and an effort
- o decrease in fees paid on deferred tuition payments to the school is an acknowledgment both of students' current financial burdens as well as an effort
- o decrease in fees paid on deferred tuition payments to the school both acknowledge current financial burdens and attempt
- o decreasing fees paid on deferred tuition payments to the school is an acknowledgment both of current financial burdens and an effort
- o decreasing fees paid on deferred tuition payments to the school both acknowledge current financial burdens as well as attempt

58. The researcher's hypothesis of there being different emotions associated with different hormones in the body has not yet been proven.

- o of there being different emotions associated with different hormones in the body has not yet been proven
- o of different emotions that are associated with different hormones in the body has not yet been proven
- o that different emotions are associated with different hormones has not yet been proven
- o which is that there are different emotions associated with different hormones has not yet been proven
- o which has not yet been proven is that there are different emotions associated with different hormones

59. Out of America's obsession with all things pet related have grown a market for human-inspired accessories and accoutrements that are bringing forth rhinestone-studded collars, cashmere dog sweaters, and canopied pet beds.

- o things pet related have grown a market for human-inspired accessories and accoutrements that are bringing
- o things pet related has grown a market for human-inspired accessories and accoutrements that is bringing
- o things that are pet related has grown a market for human-inspired accessories and accoutrements that bring
- o pet-related things have grown a market for human-inspired accessories and accoutrements that are bringing
- o pet-related things has grown a market for human-inspired accessories and accoutrements that bring

60. A new book on the impact of church ministry reveals positive effects of global outreach activities, including improvement in the standard of living, greater availability of food, digging deep water wells, and a decline in child mortality rates.

- o digging deep water wells
- o the digging of deep water wells
- o dug deep water wells
- o deep water wells dug
- o deep water wells that were dug

61. Doctors in rural areas lack adequate transportation to such a significant degree as to make it difficult to distribute them throughout a countryside becoming increasingly populated with people fleeing the urban lifestyle.

- o lack adequate transportation to such a significant degree as to make it difficult to distribute them throughout a countryside becoming
- o lack adequate transportation to a significant enough degree as to make it difficult to distribute themselves throughout a countryside that becomes
- o lack of adequate transportation is so large as to be difficult to distribute them throughout a countryside that becomes
- o are lacking so much in adequate transportation as to be difficult to distribute throughout a countryside becoming
- o are so lacking in adequate transportation that they find it difficult to distribute themselves throughout a countryside becoming

62. The decision by one of the nation's prominent universities to grant an additional $1 billion in financial aid to low-income students could mean reduced lending to needy students and increasing the availability of scholarships from donors to supply the funds.

   - o increasing the availability
   - o the increasing availability
   - o increased availability
   - o the availability increased
   - o the availability increasing

63. Sociologists estimate that the annual cost to the region of unemployment in lost productivity and trade revenues is more than $10 billion per year.

   - o the annual cost to the region of unemployment in lost productivity and trade revenues is more than $10 billion per year
   - o the annual cost of unemployment to the region is more than $10 billion per year because of lost productivity and trade revenues
   - o unemployment costs the region more than $10 billion per year in lost productivity and trade revenues
   - o $10 billion per year in lost productivity and trade revenues is the annual cost to the region of unemployment
   - o lost productivity and trade revenues cost the region at least $10 billion per year because of unemployment

64. In Venice, Italy, a larger percentage of tax revenue is spent on protecting their infrastructure from high water than is spent on road maintenance in Los Angeles, California.

- In Venice, Italy, a larger percentage of tax revenue is spent on protecting their infrastructure from high water than is spent on road maintenance in Los Angeles, California.
- In Venice, Italy, they spend a larger percentage of tax revenue on protecting their infrastructure from high water than Los Angeles, California, does on road maintenance.
- A larger percentage of Venice, Italy's, tax revenue is spent on protecting their infrastructure from high water than Los Angeles, California, spends on road maintenance.
- Venice, Italy, spends a larger percentage of its tax revenue protecting its infrastructure from high water than the road maintenance spending of Los Angeles, California.
- Venice, Italy, spends a larger percentage of its tax revenue on protecting its infrastructure from high water than Los Angeles, California, does on road maintenance.

65. Stephen Gaskin, viewed community, as a few other 1960s commune founders, like a structured family arrangement rather than a loosely knit community based on convenience.

- Stephen Gaskin, viewed community, as a few other 1960s commune founders, like a structured family arrangement rather than
- As did a few other 1960s commune founders, Stephen Gaskin viewed community to be a structured family arrangement rather than viewing it as
- Stephen Gaskin viewed community to be a structured family arrangement, like a fewer other 1960s commune founders, rather than viewing it as
- Community to Stephen Gaskin, like other 1960s commune founders, was viewed as a structured family arrangement rather than
- Stephen Gaskin, like a few other 1960s commune founders, viewed community as a structured family arrangement rather than

66. Forest rangers expect that the replanting of redwoods in the eastern Sierras would succeed if the activity of the brushfires in that region is less numerous than one fire for every 5,000 acres.

- O would succeed if the activity of the brushfires in that region is less numerous than
- O would succeed provided the activity of the brushfires in that region is less than
- O should succeed if the brushfire activity in that region was less than
- O will succeed if the activity of the brushfires in that region is less than
- O will succeed if the brushfire activity in that region were less numerous than

67. Found on several Indonesian islands, Komodo dragons dominate their habitat and grow to lengths of up to 10 feet, running swiftly enough that deer and wild boar serve as its primary live prey.

- O Komodo dragons dominate their habitat and grow to lengths of up to 10 feet, running swiftly enough
- O Komodo dragons dominate their habitat and grow to lengths of up to 10 feet, and with such swift running
- O Komodo dragons dominate their habitat and grow to lengths of up to 10 feet, they run swiftly enough
- O the Komodo dragon dominates its habitat, growing to lengths of up to 10 feet and running so swiftly
- O the Komodo dragon dominates its habitat, grows to lengths of up to 10 feet, and it runs swiftly enough

68. Because of rapid technology breakthroughs in the last 20 years, many people that might have at one time suffered as new employees from lack of remote access, multiple computer viruses, or technical glitches now enjoy flawless wireless access as veteran workers.

- O that might have at one time suffered as new employees
- O who might once have suffered as new employees
- O that as new employees might once have suffered
- O who, as new employees, might have at one time suffered
- O who, when they were new employees, might at one time have suffered

69. Cioppino is a rich seafood stew developed in Italy by Genoan fishermen who migrated to California in the mid-1800s; the dish is essentially a regional fish soup to which has been added shellfish, fresh tomatoes, wine sauce, and other savory ingredients.

- o to which has been added shellfish, fresh tomatoes, wine sauce, and other savory ingredients
- o added to which is shellfish, fresh tomatoes, wine sauce, and other savory ingredients
- o to which shellfish, fresh tomatoes, wine sauce, and other savory ingredients have been added
- o with shellfish, fresh tomatoes, wine sauce, and other savory ingredients having been added to it
- o and, in addition, shellfish, fresh tomatoes, wine sauce, and other savory ingredients are added

70. Many sociologists contend that homelessness is caused by decreasing wages, as well as dwindling availability of affordable housing, a lack of family support, and a decline in health care coverage.

- o decreasing wages, as well as dwindling availability of affordable housing
- o a decrease in wages and in availability of affordable housing
- o a decreasing of wages, along with availability of affordable housing
- o wages being decreased, along with availability of affordable housing
- o wages and availability of affordable housing being decreased, with

71. Although the term "diva" is often used to describe an extremely demanding and temperamental person, in the operatic world, it is anyone who is the principal female lead of the opera.

- o it is anyone who is
- o it is a person
- o they are women who are
- o it refers to someone who is
- o it is in reference to human beings

72. Spanning three generations, the corporate chieftain commenced his career in an obscure internship as a systems processor and culminated in the most prestigious award that the industry associations could bestow.

- O corporate chieftain commenced his career in an obscure internship as
- O corporate chieftain's career commenced in an obscure internship as
- O corporate chieftain had commenced his career with the obscure internship of being
- O corporate chieftain commenced his career with the obscure internship of being
- O career of the corporate chieftain has commenced with an obscure internship of

73. The Pulitzer Prize–winning author is the kind of writer who receives critical acclaim while living, only strengthens after death, and forever retains its place in American literature always.

- O only strengthens after death, and forever retains its place in American literature always
- O whose reputation strengthens after death and forever retains its place in American literature always
- O and whose reputation only strengthens after death and forever retains its place in American literature
- O who strengthens in reputation after death and who retained its place in American literature again always
- O then has strengthened in reputation after death and always retained its place in American literature

74. The rate at which the high school courses—reading, math, and writing—proceeds were dictated from the proficiency that students achieved early in their elementary school years.

- O proceeds were dictated from
- O proceeds were dictated because of
- O proceeds were dictated through
- O proceed was dictated by
- O proceed was dictated as a result of

75. Many domestic cats, like domestic dogs, have owners who care for their pets in several ways such as taking them for walks, exercising them regularly and to give them space to play, and making sure that they are fed properly.
   - exercising them regularly and to give
   - exercising them regularly and giving
   - to exercise them regularly and to giving
   - to exercise them regularly giving
   - to exercise it regularly and giving

76. A recent press release announced that the numbers of teenagers driving without a license decreased by more than a 5 percent decline in the past three years but failed to explain why more than 10 percent of teenagers were driving without a license in the first place.
   - numbers of teenagers driving without a license decreased by more than a 5 percent decline
   - numbers of teenagers driving without a license decreased by more than 5 percent
   - numbers of teenagers driving without a license were lowered by more than 5 percent
   - number of teenagers driving without a license decreased by more than 5 percent
   - number of teenagers driving without a license was lowered by more than a 5 percent decline

77. At the beginning of the war, leaders decided how the enemies would be punished, offered moral support to their followers, and granted favors or special privileges to loyal troops and faithful servants in the surrounding area.
   - and granted favors or special privileges to loyal troops and faithful servants in the surrounding area
   - and granting favors or special privileges to loyal troops and faithful servants in the surrounding area
   - and granted favors or special privileges as they were concerned with being related to surrounding loyal troops and faithful servants
   - which also were granted favors or special privileges because of being loyal troops and faithful servants in the surrounding area
   - the granting to loyal troops and faithful servants in the surrounding area of favors or special privileges

78. Tired after the long and arduous race over North America's highest mountain, it was determined by the ultra-runner that he needed a long rest.

- o it was determined by the ultra-runner that he needed a long rest
- o the determination was made that the ultra-runner needed a long rest
- o the ultra-runner determined that he needed a long rest
- o a long rest was needed by the determined ultra-runner
- o a long rest had been determined as needed by the ultra-runner

79. The declining of values of stock shares for several agricultural businesses has provided an additional reason for local farmers to invest their money in a variety of markets.

- o The declining of values
- o Declining values
- o The declining value
- o Since the declining value
- o Because of the declining values

80. The variety of Europe's landscape becomes apparent as a person travels along its scenic byways that vary in terrain from steep mountain passes in the Alps or cobbled roads through wineries in northern Italy.

- o or
- o to
- o with
- o among
- o and additionally

81. The rising cost of tuition might deter students from applying to graduate school; students may, for example, choose to join the workforce and earn a paycheck instead of taking out student loans.

- o school; students may, for example, choose
- o school, for example, students choose
- o school, like students may choose
- o school, such as students choosing
- o school; which may, as an example, result in choosing

82. Besides being a jazzy tune that the musician himself wrote in 1918, Muggs Daley's hit song "Moonshining" was also recorded by many other bands in the 1970s, showing the song's timeless appeal.

- o Besides being a jazzy tune that the musician himself wrote
- o Besides a jazzy tune with the musician himself writing it
- o Except a jazzy tune being written by the musician himself
- o Besides the instance of a jazzy tune that the musician himself wrote
- o Besides the fact of a jazzy tune with the musician writing himself

83. At the time of its building by the neighborhood committee, the public recreation area was clean and safe; a type of community bond developed between those who used the space regularly with those who lived in nearby houses.

- o between those who used the space regularly with those who lived in nearby houses
- o between those who used the space regularly and those who lived in nearby houses
- o between those using the space regularly with those living in nearby houses
- o among those who used the space regularly and those who lived in nearby houses
- o among those who used the space regularly with those who lived in nearby houses

84. The piano, one of the most commonly played instruments, produces deep and complex sounds, every sound a small component of its acoustic production.

- o every sound a small component of its
- o all the sounds a small component of their
- o all the sounds a small component of its
- o each sound a small component of their
- o every sound a small component of their

85. Rising commercial real estate rates, a gauge that brokers use to determine the strength of the housing market, is likely to deter many new homeowners from buying houses this spring.

- O a gauge that brokers use to determine the strength of the housing market, is
- O that brokers use as a gauge to determine the strength of the housing market, is
- O a gauge used by brokers in determining the strength of the housing market, is
- O that is used by brokers as a determining factor of the strength of the housing market, are
- O a gauge that brokers use to determine the strength of the housing market, are

86. At the costume party, my sister Jenna confused her date for the evening as another man who wore the same costume.

- O her date for the evening as another man who wore the same costume
- O her date for the evening with another man who wore the same costume
- O for the evening her date to another man wearing the same costume
- O her date as it was evening with another man wearing the same costume
- O for the evening her date as being another man who wore the same costume

87. However a minimal role in causing air pollution, trash pollutes both land and sea, creates problems in wildlife habitats, and harms endangered species.

- O However
- O With
- O Being
- O Therefore accounting for
- O Despite playing

88. For many decades scientists have taught at universities, in part that the academic life fosters quality research and partly because academic colleagues inspire new ideas.

- O in part that the academic life fosters quality research
- O in part for the quality research that the academic life fosters
- O partly because of the academic life fostering quality research
- O partly because quality research should be fostered by the academic life
- O partly because the academic life fosters quality research

89. Unlike Simpson, the music of Melody Hawthorne is deep, full, and complex—given to blues-inspired riffs as well as to soul-shaking sounds.

- O Unlike Simpson, the music of Melody Hawthorne
- O Unlike Simpson, Melody Hawthorne's music
- O Unlike Simpson's, Melody Hawthorne's music
- O Differing from Simpson, Melody Hawthorne's music
- O Differing as Simpson the music of Melody Hawthorne

90. The Tough Road Tire Service has for decades run a business with the goals of improving customer satisfaction and decreasing the amount of time it takes to fix a tire.

- O goals of improving customer satisfaction and decreasing
- O goals of the improving of customer satisfaction and to decrease
- O goals of the improvement of customer satisfaction and decreasing
- O goals of which is the improving of customer satisfaction and decreasing
- O goals to improve customer satisfaction and decreasing

91. California is one of the few U.S. states that still has a significant porpoise population, and where this marine animal remains close to the shore.

- O that still has a significant porpoise population, and where
- O that still has a significant porpoise population, where
- O that still has a significant population of porpoises, and where
- O where the population of porpoises is still significant;
- O where there is still a significant population of porpoises and where

92. In response to the recent uprising in the city, residents quickly claimed that their trust in the mayor and the local government is being undermined by reports of political irresponsibility.

- O In response to the recent uprising in the city, residents quickly claimed that
- O Responding to the recent uprising in the city, residents quickly made the claim about
- O When responding to the recent uprising in the city, residents quickly make the claim about
- O As a response to the recent uprising in the city, residents quickly made the claim about
- O Responding to the recent uprising in the city, residents quickly claim that

93. Global market researchers have claimed that the recent increase in gasoline prices so that they were the highest price in five years foreshadows little relief from the ongoing petroleum crisis.

- so that they were the highest price in five years
- so that they were the highest five-year price
- to what should be the highest price in five years
- to a five-year high level
- to the highest price in five years

94. Abraham Lincoln's simple writing style and enduring themes—the spirit of the common man, the importance of hard work, and the necessity of cooperation—was as inspirational to his fellow citizens as it is to ours.

- was as inspirational to his fellow citizens as it is
- were as inspirational to his fellow citizens as they are
- has been as inspirational to his fellow citizens as they are
- had been as inspirational to his fellow citizens as it was
- have been as inspirational to his fellow citizens as

95. Unlike other birds, the geese migrated toward the far edge of Canada's rocky coast.

- Unlike other birds, the geese migrated
- Unlike other birds, the geese's migration was
- Just as other birds, the geese migrated
- As did other birds, the geese's migration was
- The geese's migration, as other birds', was

96. The report on pet abuse claims that even after several years, dogs and cats continue to remember some of the trauma of an abusive event happening when it was young.

- happening when it was young
- happening when young
- that happened when it was young
- that happened when they were young
- that has happened as each was young

97. A new employment analysis has revealed that within the last decade, more women had chosen child care programs rather than quit their jobs or take extended time off work after having a child.

- o had chosen child care programs rather than quit
- o had chosen to use child care programs instead of quitting
- o have chosen using child care programs instead of quitting
- o have chosen to use child care programs rather than quitting
- o have chosen to use child care programs rather than quit

98. The new law stipulates that an apartment rental company disclose to their tenants how far in advance they will require notice of an intent to vacate the property.

- o that an apartment rental company disclose to their tenants how far in advance they will require notice of an intent to vacate the property
- o an apartment rental company to disclose to their tenants how far in advance they will require notice of an intent to vacate the properties
- o that an apartment rental company disclose to its tenants how far in advance it will require notice of an intent to vacate a property
- o an apartment rental company should disclose to its tenants how far in advance it will require notice of an intent to vacate someone's property
- o that apartment rental companies disclose to tenants how far in advance notice of an intent to vacate a property is required

99. Unlike a socialized health care system, in which all patients are guaranteed treatment, individual responsibility is the basis of a private health care system.

- o individual responsibility is the basis of a private health care system
- o the basis of a private health care system is individual responsibility
- o the responsibility of the individual is what a private health care system is based on
- o the individual responsibility of a private care system is the basis
- o a private health care system is based on individual responsibility

100. Even though he decided to be a vegetarian as being a youth, Frank Whittle decided to start eating meat again when he was 65 years old.

- o as being a youth
- o while in youth
- o at the time of his being young
- o while being a youngster
- o as a youth

Answer Key

SENTENCE CORRECTION PRACTICE

1. D
2. C
3. C
4. E
5. B
6. B
7. D
8. C
9. B
10. D
11. B
12. D
13. A
14. D
15. E
16. E
17. B
18. D
19. D
20. E
21. C
22. C
23. E
24. D
25. B
26. D
27. D
28. C
29. B
30. B
31. E
32. D
33. E
34. E
35. B
36. C
37. A
38. D
39. D
40. A
41. E
42. C
43. A
44. B
45. E
46. A
47. A
48. B
49. B
50. D
51. C
52. A
53. C
54. E
55. C
56. C
57. A
58. C
59. B
60. B
61. E
62. C
63. C
64. E
65. E
66. D
67. D
68. B
69. C
70. B
71. D
72. B
73. C
74. D
75. B
76. D
77. A
78. C
79. C
80. B
81. A
82. A
83. B
84. A
85. E
86. B
87. E
88. E
89. C
90. A
91. E
92. E
93. E
94. B
95. A
96. D
97. E
98. C
99. E
100. E

Answers and Explanations

SENTENCE CORRECTION PRACTICE

1. D

Idiom is a concept that confuses many test takers. Idiom, simply stated, consists of properly worded phrases that are consistent with the usage that has come to be considered correct. In other words, it's just the way it is—like the preposition that properly follows a particular verb, as we see here. The proper idiom in this sentence is "estimated to be." When followed by a verb, "estimated" must be followed by that verb in the infinitive form, here "to be." No other form will do.

Another way to eliminate some choices here: the subject of the clause is "remains," which is plural. That means you'll need a plural verb form that agrees with the plural subject. Only (A) and (D) are in the right form, "offer," and only one uses the correct idiom.

2. C

This one's pretty straightforward. Whenever we see only one word underlined, our task is clear: check the form and choose the right variation. Upon inspection, we see that the underlined verb, "revolutionized," is the third and final item in a list: "facilitating," "creating," and . . . "revolutionized"? Look for the choice that's parallel to the first two. Choice (C), "revolutionizing," is properly parallel with "facilitating" and "creating."

3. C

This sentence and its variants test some very commonly confused words: "whether" and "if." "Whether" is appropriate when there are two alternatives (to do or not to do); "if" is preferred in hypothetical or conditional situations. The auto manufacturer's situation falls under the former category: Either it can do these things and it will succeed in the long term, or it can't and it won't. Therefore, we must use "whether." Keep in mind that it's not necessary to include the "or not" portion, as it is implied when "whether" is used. And always remember that concise sentences are preferable. Choice (C) is correct.

4. E

We've got idiom and modification issues in this sentence, so look for the version that contains the proper idiom—"as much as"—and a properly placed modifier—"even." Choice (E) corrects these errors.

5. B

As written, the underlined phrase is unnecessarily wordy. We can tighten it up by moving the more direct pronoun, "they" (the proper pronoun, which refers to "prices"), to the spot immediately before "might have been," where it should replace the ambiguous pronoun "it." Doing so also eliminates the need for the bumbling "for them" and clears up the idiom problem, leaving the correct "expected to fall." Choice (B) corrects all elements of the sentence.

6. B

The idiom being tested in this sentence is "so/such —(1)— that it —(2)—." In this case, only two choices contain the proper idiom, (B) and (E). But this question has another hidden giveaway. It's always wise to compare the choices, paying specific attention to the beginning and the end of each alternative. Doing so here yields "classic" versus "classical." Common sense tells us that a work can't logically become "classical" overnight;

"classical" usually refers to ancient Greece and Rome or to art and music inspired by that era.

Therefore, choose the only answer that contains both the proper idiom "so/such . . . acclaim that it became" and "classic" instead of "classical." Choice (B) is correct.

7. D

This question primarily tests subject-verb agreement, and it secondarily tests rhetorical skills. The subject of the sentence is "attempts," although the distance between the subject and the verb that must agree with that subject—filled with phrases that can easily distract many test takers—makes it easy to lose sight of the proper subject. "Attempts" is plural, so we need to change "has" (singular) to "have" (plural). This narrows the possible choices to (D) and (E).

With these two remaining choices, the more concise answer is preferred. That's (D).

8. C

Parallelism helps us tremendously here, but we also need to use a little bit of grammar logic to make sense of the rules governing this sentence. If we take the sentence at face value, then—simply stated—"officials . . . have found the cases." Were they lost? The phrasing isn't correct. We have to change it to "officials . . . have found that . . ." in order to clarify that officials aren't *actually* finding cases. That reduces the field to (C) and (E).

Now we can concentrate on parallelism. Both (C) and (E) read, "Officials . . . have found that cases . . . are . . ." "difficult to diagnose," "highly contagious," and "resistant to treatment," but only one lists the items the way they should be—parallel with one another. That's choice (C).

9. B

Here we must do two things: (1) check for number agreement of "expense" and (2) keep the two types of expenses that are stated in parallel form. Since there are, in fact, two different types of expenses, we have to use the plural "expenses." The plural "expenses" also agrees with the verb "are." And since the second group of expenses is introduced with the words "and with," we must do the same for the first in the underlined portion. (B) is correct.

10. D

Often on the GMAT, lengthy—and unnecessary—descriptive phrases are inserted to evaluate a test taker's ability to focus on the important stuff. Everything between the commas is supplementary, and the sentence becomes much easier to correct without it: "Dark matter . . . thought to contain . . . "

That isn't a complete thought. As stated, "thought" is a participle, which means the sentence is missing a verb. Let's add one. You should end up with answer choice (D).

11. B

When the *-ing* form of a verb is used to describe something, we call it a participle. As written, this sentence suggests that the marmots—the subject of the sentence—brought the population count to 35. (Think of it this way: "The marmots brought the population count to 35.") That clearly doesn't make any sense; it was the act of releasing them into the wild that brought the count to 35, so we need to use a different form, the participle. And using the participle form in this sense (as a description) means that we should not use the conjunction "and." Choice (B) is correct.

12. D

A supplementary descriptive phrase interrupts this sentence, and our task is much easier if we mentally remove that phrase. "The printing press . . . shortened . . ." is much easier to understand. Now we need to find the idiomatically correct and most concise variation of the underlined portion.

What, exactly, did the printing press shorten? The time needed to publish a book. The order of the sentence (as written) is awkward because another interjecting phrase interrupts the connection between the verb ("shorten") and its object ("the time"). Rearranging the order makes the relationship clearer and the sentence smoother. It also makes sense in a question with lengthy answer choices, such as this, to test the shortest answer choice first. (D) is correct.

13. A

A highly complicated structure makes this sentence tough to digest, but if we take it one step at a time, it's not so bad. A mental edit of the first non-underlined portion gives us: "[Some . . . claim that] . . . the . . . number . . . provides evidence . . ." Let's finish it up: "The number . . . provides evidence that the state will escape . . . and instead enjoy . . ." As written, this sentence is clear and concise as possible, and it's idiomatically correct. (A) is your answer.

14. D

This sentence is tough because it contains two complete thoughts ("independent clauses"), and the first one is structured awkwardly. There aren't any grammatical errors, per se, but there is significant grammatical inefficiency that we need to correct. Thoreau is the subject of the second clause, and he's vital in the first . . . so why not make him the subject of each? Answer choice (D) is correct.

15. E

Techno Inc. has done well. It has developed top technology (three types) and devised great marketing campaigns. We need to phrase this sentence so its accomplishments are clear. Choice (E) is the correct version, as it lists three examples of technological developments in parallel and then gives the second action in parallel with the first.

16. E

Since the financial planner made three recommendations to Susan, they need to be listed in parallel form. Susan should (1) consolidate high-interest loans, (2) close unnecessary credit cards, and (3) budget her monthly finances.

The only other concern is idiom. To complete "recommended that" properly—in the subjunctive form (wishes, commands, etc.)— the subject of the recommendation must follow, and then the recommended action must be stated as a present tense verb (without a preposition to introduce the verb). In this case: ". . . recommended that Susan consolidate . . . , close . . . , and budget" is correct. That's choice (E).

17. B

This one's challenging because there's a lot going on. To simplify, ask, "What do the stock option incentives do?" They allow employees . . . to (1) invest . . . and (2) apportion. In that simpler format, it's easier to see the error: To say that options "allow employees . . . to be able to" is redundant.

We also have to determine the pronoun: "which" or "that"? The description of the incentives provides a necessary definition of them; since it's required, we need the restrictive pronoun "that" instead of "which." Note also that the unrestrictive "which" must be preceded by a comma; the restrictive "that" does not. Choice (B) is correct.

18. D

The toughest element of this sentence is the degree to which the original is wrong. In the first half of the sentence (before the colon), the author's basically trying to say, "It's not fair to blame people for not getting vaccinated." Finding the correct subject in that clause is another tricky task.

In the credited choice, (D) "it" is the subject, and the verb is "cannot." The rest gets tacked on to the subject or the verb. The other answer choices are wordy or illogical (or both).

19. D

Both proper idiom and the logic of the sentence must guide our selection of the correct answer choice. We need to consider how the second portion of the sentence relates to the first portion: The second part describes how the Christmas holiday brought a respite to the opposing armies. Verbal clues help to clarify this as a cause-and-effect relationship. We're looking for a conjunction that works with this relationship. Choice (D) does that and is correct.

20. E

Our chief concern in this sentence is number agreement between our compound subject and our verb. "Labor market conditions and the size of the company" is plural; we need the plural form "affect." With that information alone, we can eliminate three choices, leaving us with only two to compare.

A quick comparison of the two choices that remain reveals that one begins with "each" and the other begins with "all." Since the intent of the sentence is to contrast the commonalities of all to the unique concerns of each, "all businesses" is appropriate here. Choice (E) is correct.

21. C

This question tests idiom exclusively, particularly idiom in the subjunctive mood (used with wishes, recommendations, suggestions, etc.). The subjunctive mood is just one of those grammar oddities you have to learn or refresh yourself on for the test, but luckily, there's not much of it to (re)commit to memory (and most of it is probably already familiar to you).

The proper phrase here is "requires . . . to pay." In the subjunctive mood, require must be followed by the infinitive form, here "to pay." That's choice (C).

22. C

The complex structure of this sentence should be adequately digested before attempting any corrections: "Robin Hood suggested planting . . . a rebel disguised . . ." Why would Robin Hood's men plant a disguised rebel in the path? "To serve . . ."

Next: Is the disguised rebel going to be serving *similar* to a distraction (use the word "like"), or will the disguised rebel *be* a distraction? He will *be* a distraction, of course, so "serve as a distraction" is right (in fact, idiom dictates "serve as" as the only correct option of the two alternatives).

Finally, let's check to make sure the two effects of the distraction are parallel in structure. Since we see "and allowing" in the non-underlined portion, we must use the form "halting" to parallel it in the underlined portion. Choice (C) is correct.

23. E

It is not logical that the damage "was" the tornado. The damage "was the result of" the tornado, so we're already down to two choices, and one of the two is excessively wordy and uses the wrong verb tense. Choice (E) is correct.

24. D

Before you get caught up in the distracting "in which" versus "whereby" debate, there's an easier way to burn through this question in no time flat: verb tense. According to Darwin's theory, is natural selection finished? No! Let's get rid of the simple past tense "evolved." And the simple present tense verb form, "evolve," suggests that the action is taking place only now. The sentence clarifies that species "evolve . . . from a single or a very few common ancestors," so this must this have begun in the past, certainly. So the corrected sentence must include the present perfect form "have evolved," which allows the action to start in the past and continue into the present, something Darwin would agree with.

You could have also used the misplaced "over time" modification to eliminate choices. What are "ancestors over time" (B), and how much is "over time all" (as in (C), which is missing commas)? These phrases don't make sense, so they can't be correct. And, for the record, both "in which" and "whereby" work in this sentence. Choice (D) is correct.

25. B

First, use the generally easier to fix parallelism error: What are the mentioned groups doing? They are (1) touting and (2) encouraging. Since we can't change "touting" (because it isn't underlined), we need "encouraging" to match. This reduces the field to (A) and (B).

Next, we must thoroughly understand the differences between adjectives and adverbs. "Progressively," like most words ending in *-ly*, is an adverb, and—as such—may describe a verb, an adjective, or another adverb. "Progressive," the adjective variant, can describe a noun or a pronoun. Surely the author didn't intend "to better" as a verb modified by "progressively"; that would be redundant. The author must have meant that the people mentioned see research "as a means to" progressive fuels that are better than previous fuels and, as a result, these people are touting the fuels as such and encouraging investment to further that end. Choice (B) is correct.

26. D

We have to check number agreement between subjects and verbs in this complex sentence construction. "The proportion" is singular, so the first "have" should be "has." "Percentages," however, is plural, so "have" in the second phrase is correct. The time frame for this sentence's context is noted with "since," so we know the clock is still ticking, so to speak, which makes the simple past tense verb forms "declined" and "grew" incorrect. Choice (D) is correct as written.

27. D

The accord was signed in 1994, so the past tense verb "dictated" correctly describes this past action. Since we're still in the 50-year period following the signing of the agreement, however, its effects continue into the present, affecting the tariffs now, so the correct construction should be "tariffs that member nations *are* permitted." And idiom dictates that the infinitive form follow: "permitted to levy."

Note that because the accord is still in effect, "dictates" would also be correct. However, the two answer choices that use "dictates" are flawed in other ways. Choice (D) is correct.

28. C

Many people confuse "whether" and "if," but there's a clear and easy way to keep it straight. "Whether [or not]" is used when there are only two alternatives—the "whether" and the "not." "If" is used with conditional or hypothetical situations. Here, students either will or won't continue to vacation in the state, so this is properly a "whether" situation. (Note that the "or not" can be implied rather than stated.)

Next, as written, "their" refers to the students, but the restrictions certainly don't belong to the spring breakers! "Their" can't be correct. And finally, looking at the remaining two "whether" choices, some ambiguous pronouns can help make the right answer more apparent. Choice (C) is the correct version of this sentence.

29. B

This phrase ("urban gentrification") isn't a phenomenon; it's a *term* that *refers to* a phenomenon. Technicality? Sure. Important? Absolutely. And the phrase "has reference to" in the final choice is archaic; it could be improved. Finally, the "phenomenon" isn't "entrusting"; it is merely a phenomenon and can't possibly take on an anthropomorphic task like "entrusting." We need to clarify who is doing the entrusting in the proper construction. Choice (B) is correct.

30. B

This question tests your ability to identify and correct a commonly misused phrase. Proper idiom for this construction is "the [only] way to eradicate . . . is to . . .," completing the phrase with an infinitive form verb. "If" is only correct in hypothetical situations, which this is not.

With this in mind, we're down to (B) and (E). We must make sure each pronoun in our choice has an unambiguous referent. Also, our selection should be active and concise and contain the proper logic. Here, we must accurately represent the relationship of hatching insect eggs to the spread of fruit blight. The hatching of eggs must lead to the spread of blight, so we need to clarify that in our answer. That means choice (B) is correct.

31. E

This is an easy question disguised as a tough one. Whenever an opening modifier is underlined in a sentence in GMAT Sentence Correction, it must refer to whatever immediately follows the comma. The same is true in reverse here. So what, we ask, can we contrast to "traditional banks"? Venture capital firms! Correct this comparison to find the right answer—choice (E).

32. D

Here we want an accurate comparison in active form. Three choices begin with the modifying phrase "unlike math or science." Of the options, "language" is the only valid comparison that can be made to "math or science." This eliminates two answer choices, (A) and (B). Next, tackle clumsy wording and passive voice to find the most concise answer, choice (D).

33. E

"Much" and "many" are commonly confused words. "Many" is right for countable quantities and is plural; "much" is correct when discussing unquantifiable amounts and is singular. So, one counts "many stars" but sees "much light." In other words, "many" tends to modify plural nouns and "much" singular ones.

Since "much" is singular, its verb should be, too ("poses"). But be careful: Even though "much" is singular, "satellites and space-faring vessels" is a compound—and therefore plural—noun, so "are exposed" is correct. Now choose the option that is clear, concise, and correct. Choice (E) is a match.

34. E

This sentence describes two separate (but equal) effects of a boom in Renaissance art, so they should be in parallel form. It increases prices enough both to suppress demand and to stimulate speculation. Note that the word "to" does not need to be repeated with a compound infinitive ("to" plus a verb), as it is understood. The conjunction "and" is necessary to show that the two effects are equal and separate. Separating them only by a comma would be incorrect because the second effect then appears to be a subset of the first, which is not true. Choice (E) is correct as written.

35. B

In this sentence, the pronoun "which" refers vaguely to everything in the preceding part of the sentence instead of referring to a specific noun, as it should. To create a phrase that can correctly modify the entire clause preceding it, you must use a participle, "decreasing." Also, "recognized as planets orbiting . . ." is idiomatic; it's consistent with standard English rules, whereas "recognized as planets to orbit" is not. Choice (B) is correct.

36. C

The introductory phrase "An African scribe and mathematician" cannot logically modify "the first computation of pi." And since we can't change the non-underlined portion, let's revise the sentence so that "Ahmes" immediately follows the introductory phrase to correct the error in modification *and* transform the sentence from the weaker passive voice ("was made") to the preferred active voice ("made").

Recognize the opening modifier quickly—a common GMAT tip-off—and remember that what follows the comma after that modifier must be the thing it modifies ("Ahmes"). Then skip to the only answer that correctly places "Ahmes" where he belongs—choice (C). Doing so will earn you quick GMAT points and help you bank extra time for tougher questions that follow.

37. A

The underlined portion is a relative clause that describes "a vocation"; the clause correctly uses the simple past tense, "generated." Choice (A) is correct.

38. D

This sentence compares the number of structures refurbished before and after World War II. For this type of comparison, the accepted standard English construction is "as many . . . as."

Next, because two different time periods are compared, the verbs must reflect the difference; the period before World War II requires the past perfect, "had refurbished," because past perfect expresses an idea that began *before* another specific time in the past. The period after World War II requires the simple past tense, "refurbished," since it is the period that is the later (more recent) of the two periods. (D) is correct.

39. D

The subject of the main clause, "residents," should be followed by two verbs of the same tense, namely "have explored" and "have seen." Note that the "have" in the second verb, however, is understood and does not need to be repeated.

Next, as the modifying clause is written, "whose shingled roofs" illogically modifies "sidewalks" rather than "cottages." Replacing the clause with the phrase "with shingled roofs clustered" corrects this error so that this portion's subject is "cottages." Choice (D) is correct.

40. A

The original sentence correctly uses the two verbs "built" and "used" in the simple past tense for action completed in the same time period (the past), and the construction "used them as residences" is consistent with standard rules of English. Choice (A) is correct as written.

41. E

The sentence confuses two constructions: "requirements of X" and "required by Y." The incorrect construction is "the requirements of X by Y." The most direct way to express the two prohibitive factors in traditional television show formats is "costly writer compensation and utilization of demanding actors" The two factors can then be modified by the clause "that are required by" as the best way to show their relationship to the traditional show formats. Choice (E) is correct.

42. C

In GMAT Sentence Correction questions, semicolons have only one job: to separate independent clauses. If the underlined section of an SC question comes after a semicolon, much of what comes before the semicolon can be disregarded. Certainly the meaning and logic of the first part are relevant, and pronouns in the second part may refer to nouns in the first part, and there are other connections, but your first focus should be on the independent clause in which the underlined section appears.

In this question, the first complete verb phrase after the semicolon is "have been priced to move." The second verb must be an extension of the first. The verb does not need to repeat the word "move" because it is understood from the first use. However, the second verb must be correctly conjugated with the understood "move." "They are move" is incorrect, so strike (A); "they have move" is incorrect, so strike (B), (D), and (E); "they do move" is correct, so the credited choice is (C).

43. A

When verbs such as "request," "require," "ask," or "mandate" are followed by a subordinate clause beginning with "that," the subjunctive mood is required. The subjunctive in these cases uses the base form of the verb "be." This sentence demonstrates the correct use of the subjunctive: "mandate that" is followed by the subjunctive "be audited." Choice (A) is correct.

44. B

The correct, parallel structure for the contrast in this sentence is "not X, but rather Y." So, "X" (lifeless mound) should be followed by "but rather Y" (an energetic "disposal system"). Also, a comma, not a semicolon, should separate the two parallel parts of the contrast. Using a semicolon results in a sentence fragment unless a subject and verb are provided in the construction. In a GMAT Sentence Correction question, a semicolon serves only one purpose: to separate two independent clauses, each with its own subject and verb. In (A), (C), and (D), the clause after the semicolon is not independent.

Choice (B) corrects the error in (A) by replacing the semicolon with a comma. It also uses the coordinating conjunction "not X, but rather Y." This requires that the X and Y parts be parallel. In this case, they are, so (B) looks good.

Choice (E) does fix the problem in choice (A); each of the clauses now has its own subject and its own verb. However, "that of" has no referent.

45. E

There are two acceptable idioms here: "proposed that X be Y" or "proposed X be Y." You should know that the first is more likely on the GMAT, but by no means is the second wrong.

Whichever idiom the credited response uses, it will have to use it consistently. The problem with choice (A) is that it uses both idioms. It's fine to write "proposed the wages be raised and the effects studied"; it's fine to write "proposed that the wages be raised and that the effects be studied"; it's even fine to write "proposed that the wages be raised and the effects studied," because the "that" and "be" are understood to be distributed. But you can't write "proposed the wages be raised and that effects be studied." You can't distribute the "that" and "be" backward.

Of the remaining choices, only choice (E) uses a correct form of the idiom.

46. A

This correctly written sentence clearly states the purpose of the evaluation, "to determine whether microbes can be deployed," and the purpose of the deployment, "to reduce toxic waste levels."

47. A

The original sentence correctly compares the American Kennel Club to the Westminster Kennel Club, committing no error of faulty comparison. Thus, the issue in this sentence concerns the use of essential and nonessential expressions. An essential expression is vital to the meaning of the sentence and requires no comma offset. Traditionally, the word "that" is used in such a case.

In contrast, a nonessential clause may contain useful information, but this information is not essential to the sentence. The term "which" is commonly reserved for such a case. When a clause is nonessential, commas are used to convey this fact to the reader; thus, the correct answer will include a comma before "which." Choice (A) is correct.

48. B

The first part of the original sentence intends to compare housing prices and interest rates. The comparison is most effective at the beginning of the sentence: "Like the interest rates, the housing prices . . ." (or something similar). This construction would lead the reader to expect the verb ("are increasing") immediately after the subject. The modifying phrase, "some of them at significant rates," is best placed after "increasing."

The entire construction "Like the interest rates, the housing prices . . . are increasing, some of them at significant rates," is a main clause and should be followed by a comma and then a coordinating conjunction (such as "yet" or "but") that introduces a second main clause. In order to make the sentence work, the second clause must have a subject and a verb, so "they are" should replace "being." Choice (B) is correct.

49. B

The correct comparative construction for this sentence is "X is taller than Y," with X and Y as parallel elements. The sentence attempts to compare "the average height" of the Masai with the average height of other countries of the world. However, it fails to complete the comparison because "average height . . . Masai" is not equivalent to "in most other countries of the world." In order to compare two logically equivalent elements while avoiding the wordy repetition of the phrase "of the average height," the pronoun "that" must be used in the second element.

50. D

This amalgamation of phrases and clauses results in a sentence fragment; there is no main verb. This problem is solved by inserting the verb "is": "Le Caramelize . . . is a process . . ."

The clause defining the process, "in which molecules of oxygen and sugar react," is clear and correct. However, the subsequent phrase, "releasing . . ." is not. A comma could be positioned between "react" and "releasing" in order to make "releasing . . ." a participial phrase that modifies the previous clause. Another solution would be to follow "react" with "to release" in order to show purpose. Choice (D) is correct.

51. C

This sentence loses its clarity and logical meaning because it awkwardly presents two phrases intended to modify "Leonardo da Vinci." In the original sentence, the modifiers create a choppy sentence that doesn't flow by creating too much separation between the subject, "Leonardo da Vinci," and the verb, "leveraged." In order to create a stronger main clause, unite the subject with the verb: Begin the sentence with "In his drawings" followed by the relative clause "which he published with his scientific findings." Choice (C) is correct.

52. A

This correct sentence uses parallel structure to explain that "supporters were recruited to assist either in congratulating . . . or in encouraging." The pair of correlative conjunctions, "either/or," is correctly used since each element is followed by a parallel grammatical form. "Either . . . or" always work together; "either" should only be followed by "or."

As well, the noun "assist" is correctly followed by "in congratulating" rather than by the infinitive " to congratulate."

To recap, choices (B) and (E) get the parallelism wrong, (C) uses "and" instead of "or" (so does (B)), and (D) gets the idiom wrong ("to assist . . . to congratulate"). The sentence is correct as written.

53. C

This sentence needs the correct idiomatic expression to contrast two situations. The journalist "distinguished between X (student rebellions) and Y (authentic political protest)." The clause that describes student rebellions ("which may . . .") should be as clear and concise as possible. The possessive "their" is awkward and should be omitted. Choice (C) is correct.

54. E

This sentence fails because of poor word choice: "experiencing being relocated" is awkward and wordy. The sentence does not need to show the process of "being relocated," since "experiencing" already contains the idea of process. To complete the sentence grammatically, "experiencing" should be followed by the noun "relocation." When only two alternatives are possible, to purchase or not to purchase, "whether" (or "whether or not") should be used rather than "if." Choice (E) is correct.

55. C

A modifying phrase must be placed near the word it modifies. Here, the incorrect placement of the phrase "filmed in Brooklyn" describes the "producer and director" when it should describe the film. The use of the singular "producer and director" is confusing:

Did one activist produce and the other direct? Or did they jointly produce and direct? It is also unclear which of the two activists is described in the clause beginning with "who." The credited choice (C).

56. C

Commas are the key to making this sentence clear. The modifying phrase "Frida Kahlo's earliest representation of herself" should be set off by commas because it describes the subject, "*Self-Portrait*." Without a comma after "herself," it is easy to mistake the modifying phrase for the subject of the sentence because the verb immediately follows it. Another comma is also needed after "million" once the unnecessary "and it was" is omitted. Once again, the comma sets off a long modifying phrase. Also, the preferred construction here is the passive voice: "The painting WAS sold for a certain amount," rather than "The painting SOLD for a certain amount," which is a colloquial English. Choice (C) is correct.

57. A

In a sentence this long and full of phrases, an analysis parallelism is needed to make it easier to understand. The correct parallel construction for this sentence is "both X (an acknowledgment . . .) and Y (an effort . . .)." Just as "both" is followed by an article and a noun, "and" should be followed by an article and a noun. Choice (A) is correct as written.

58. C

For clarity, a lengthy and confusing description like this one requires a relative clause, "the researcher's hypothesis that . . ." The subject-verb structure of the clause clearly identifies "the researcher's hypothesis." A series of phrases, on the other hand, provides neither the same clarity nor grammatical correctness. Choice (C) is correct.

59. B

It is difficult to identify the subject, "a market," in this sentence because of the inverted word order. Be alert to incorrect verb number and tense.

The plural verb "have grown" does not agree with "market," a singular noun. "Market" is also the subject of the second verb, which should be "is bringing" rather than "are bringing." The present progressive verb shows ongoing action, which is more appropriate than the present tense, "bring," in this context. Choice (B) is the credited response.

60. B

Each of the four positive effects, except the one included in the underlined portion, is given in noun form: "improvement," "availability," and "decline." "Digging" is a participle and thus not parallel to the other nouns; it can be transformed into a noun by adding the article "the." Choice (B) is correct.

61. E

The underlined portion is so awkward and wordy that it makes the whole sentence difficult to understand. The sentence discusses an ongoing situation (the countryside is "becoming . . ."), so the present progressive tense ("are lacking in") should be used in place of the present tense ("lack"). "Them" refers to the doctors and, as a referent to the same, should be replaced with "themselves." The long, awkward modifier "to such a large degree as to make it difficult" should be simplified and condensed. The standard English idiom "so X . . . that" can be joined with the progressive verb for greater clarity: "Doctors . . . are so lacking in adequate transportation *that* they find it difficult to distribute themselves . . ." Choice (E) corrects this sentence and is the credited response.

62. C

The sentence shows two results of a decision: "reduced lending" and "increasing the availability." Although "lending" and "increasing" may look similar because they are both formed from verbs and use the *-ing* ending, they do not have the same function. "Lending" is a gerund modified by the adjective "less." "Increasing" is a participle and introduces a phrase. "Increasing the availability" can be made parallel to the adjective-noun form by revising it to be a noun phrase, "increased availability." That's choice (C).

63. C

The awkward and wordy sequence of phrases makes the sentence very difficult to understand. To make the sentence more direct, make the subject and verb of the clause more clear. "Unemployment costs" makes the focus of the sentence immediate and clear—and the use of "costs" as a verb rather than a noun eliminates one of the prepositional phrases ("to the region") by requiring a direct object instead. "Annual" and "per year" are redundant in some of the choices. Choice (B) is correct.

64. E

The comparison between Venice and Los Angeles is not clear because it is not parallel. Making the comparison parallel eliminates the other problems, such as the use of a plural pronoun, "their," without a referent.

To be parallel, the comparison should be this: Venice, Italy, spends more X ("percentage of tax revenue") on Y ("protecting its infrastructure . . .") than Los Angeles, California, spends on Z ("road maintenance.") The grammatical structure is the same for both clauses: The city is the subject; "spends" and "does" ("spend" is understood) are the verbs. Choice (E) is correct.

65. E

"As" is a conjunction that can introduce a subordinate clause (a clause always has a subject and a verb); "like" is a preposition that may introduce a phrase (a phrase never has a subject and a verb). The phrase "like other 1960s commune founders" modifies Stephen Gaskin and should immediately follow his name.

Furthermore, the sentence should use the commonly accepted standard construction, "view X (community) *as* Y (a structured family arrangement)." Choice (E) corrects the errors.

66. D

The prediction uses the construction "if X (brushfire activity is less) happens, Y (replanting will succeed) will happen." The clause that discusses the outcome (the replanting will succeed) must use the future tense since the "if" clause uses the present tense. The conditional "would succeed" is incorrect.

Also, in this context, "activity" is not a quantity that can be counted, so it cannot be modified by "less numerous." "Less activity" is the correct term. Choice (D) is correct.

67. D

This sentence contains errors in pronoun agreement. The plural "Komodo dragons" and the referent "their" do not agree with the singular "its" in the non-underlined section of the sentence. Therefore, "Komodo dragons" must be replaced by the singular "Komodo dragon" and "their" by "its."

Next, the present participle form of a verb (*-ing*) is appropriate when the word or phrase is used as an adjective or in an adjectival phrase, so "growing" and "running" are preferable and appropriate since they refer to the Komodo dragon's domination of its habitat.

Finally, the phrase "running swiftly enough that" is not the correct idiom. The correct construction is "so X that Y," or "running so swiftly that deer . . ." Choice (D) is the correct response.

68. B

This sentence has an error in pronoun usage and parallelism errors. First, the pronoun "who," rather than "that," is the word that should be used to refer to people.

Parallel elements should be placed in the same order; the adverbs "once" and "now" should be placed before their verb phrases, "have suffered" and "now enjoy." The phrases "as new employees" and "as veteran workers" should be placed after their verb phrases.

As well, "once" is a better word choice than the wordy and ambiguous "at one time." Choice (B) is correct.

69. C

The sentence describes cioppino as "a regional fish soup" and then modifies that description by noting the addition of other ingredients. Since "ingredients" is a plural noun, a plural verb is required. The inverted order of the the verb phrase, "has been added," and subject, "shellfish . . . ingredients," is awkward and confusing. Answer choice (C) corrects the errors.

70. B

The sentence uses parallel structure to describe the causes of homelessness. Parallel noun phrases list two of the three causes: "lack of family support" and "decline in health care coverage." Thus, the first item in the series must also be written as a noun. "Decreasing" is a participle, whereas "a decrease" functions as a noun. For the sake of both clarity and conciseness, the issues of wages and availability of affordable housing should be combined into a single noun phrase: "a decrease in wages and in availability of affordable housing." Choice (B) is correct.

71. D

This sentence defines the term "diva." In the sentence, the pronoun "it" should refer to "the term." However, it seems illogically to refer to "anyone." So, the sentence reads as if "the term . . . is anyone who is the principle female lead . . .," which makes no sense.

The sentence should be reworded to make it clear that "diva" is a term used to describe a specific kind of person. Choice (D) is correct.

72. B

It was the corporate chieftain's career, not the chieftain himself, that "spanned three generations" and "culminated in the most prestigious award . . ." Therefore, the subject of the sentence must be "the corporate chieftain's career." Remember that an opening phrase like "spanning three generations" modifies the first noun that follows the comma (in this case "chieftain," when it should be modifying "career"). Choice (B) is correct.

73. C

Faulty parallelism in the relative clause ". . . who receives . . . strengthens . . . retains . . ." makes it unclear who or what is being described. The original clause begins by describing a type of author. In the sentence as written, with "who" as the subject, the phrases ". . . only strengthens . . ." and "retains its place . . ." illogically refer to the author. Logically, it must be the reputation that strengthens after the author's death. Choice (C) matches this logic.

74. D

There are several issues here. "Proceeds" and "were dictated from" have errors in agreement. "Proceeds" should be plural to agree with its subject "the high school courses." "Were dictated" should be singular to agree with its subject, "the rate." The idiom "dictated *by*" is used to express cause—not "dictated from," "dictated through," or "dictated as." Choice (D) is correct.

75. B

This question is testing your ability to construct a sentence that is grammatically parallel in form. The phrase "several ways such as" indicates that a list of actions will follow. When several items are joined in a series, as in this sentence, those items must be in the same grammatical format. Notice that the *-ing* verb forms "taking" and "making" are in a similar grammatical format. Likewise, the verb forms that further modify the walks should also be in the same grammatical form. Choice (B) is correct.

76. D

This question confuses the word "numbers" with the correct word "number" to refer to the specific quantity of teenagers cited in the press release. The sentence also contains a redundancy because the words "decreased" and "decline" are not both necessary, since they both convey essentially the same idea. The correct answer choice (D) corrects both of these errors.

77. A

This question tests your ability to choose a sentence construction that is grammatically parallel and free of wordiness or redundancy. The best answer choice will use clear and precise prose and have its verbs in the same format—don't get bogged down in the details but look for the basic sentence components. Notice that the sentence joins three verbs: "decided . . . offered . . . and granted." These verbs are in the same format, so parallelism is achieved in the sentence as written. Notice also that the original version of the sentence is the most clear and precise. Choice (A) is correct.

78. C

This question tests your ability to make sure that the introductory clause modifies the subject of this sentence's main clause. Also note that the main clause of this sentence is in the passive voice. Generally, the strongest sentences will be in the active voice and contain concrete subjects and action verbs. Choice (C) is correct.

79. C

This question tests your ability to choose a complete sentence that is free of wordiness and that contains a grammatically correct subject and verb. Always try to identify the subject of the sentence and the verb to make sure that they agree. Plural subjects should be paired with plural verbs; singular subjects should be paired with singular verbs. Even when you are confronted with a complex sentence, take the time to identify its most basic structure. Choice (C) is correct. The subject in this version of the sentence is clear and precise. The singular subject "value" also agrees with the sentence's verb "has."

80. B

This question tests your ability to choose the best word to complete an idiomatic expression. In order to compare things that "vary," the correct way to state the range is to say "from" one item "to" another. In this sentence, the items vary from "steep mountain passes" to "cobbled roads." The original sentence, with the prepositions "from" and "or," does not correctly employ the "from . . . to" idiom. The credited response is choice (B).

81. A

This question tests your ability to punctuate a sentence that makes a generalization and then offers a specific example. Notice that this sentence's independent clauses contain similar ideas—the second clause offers an example of the idea expressed in the first—so it is appropriate (and correct) to punctuate the sentence with a semicolon at the juncture of its two independent clauses. Choice (A) is correct. The semicolon correctly divides this sentence's two related independent clauses. Note that the portions of the sentence both preceding and following the semicolon can stand alone as separate units.

82. A

This question tests your ability to choose a concise sentence construction whose subject "hit song" is modified by the introductory phrase. Also pay attention to correct use of idiom; when used in this comparison, the word "besides" should be followed by a construction that can logically be compared to its parallel construction in the main clause. The correct version of the sentence compares two actions: Besides "being a jazzy tune," the song "was also recorded." Unless the word "being" follows the word "besides" in the opening clause, this comparison is not logical or grammatically parallel. Choice (A) is correct.

83. B

This question tests your ability to choose idiomatic expressions. The correct idiom is "between" one item "and" the other. This sentence is incorrect because it pairs "between" and "with," a construction that is nonsensical and grammatically incorrect. Choice (B) is correct.

84. A

This question is primarily testing your ability to choose elements that agree in case and number. The underlined portion of the sentence is a descriptive phrase, and the words "sound," "component," and "its" should all agree, as they do in the original sentence. Choice (A) is correct.

85. E

This question tests your ability to recognize and correct a subject-verb agreement error. Note that the subject of this sentence is the plural word "rates" but the sentence's verb "is" is a singular verb. The best answer choice will correct this error while maintaining a coherent organization of ideas within the appositive phrase describing "rates." Be wary when a lengthy phrase or clause increases the distance between subject and verb. Choice (E) is the credited response.

86. B

This question tests your ability to identify and correct an idiom error. The idiom in question involves the word "confused." It is possible to confuse one thing "with" another, but the original sentence incorrectly says that Jenna confused her date "as" another man. The correct answer choice will correct this error, and that's choice (B).

87. E

This question tests your ability to identify and correct an idiom error. The underlined word in this sentence must set up a logical relationship between the ideas that follow. Notice that the opening phrase should construct a relationship of opposition. The correct phrase will show that even though trash is not a large contributor to air pollution, it still pollutes in other ways. Choice (E) is correct.

88. E

This question tests your ability to choose a sentence structure that is grammatically parallel. Notice that the sentence gives two reasons why scientists have taught at universities. These reasons should be structured in the same grammatical format and both introduced by the word "partly" in order to achieve parallelism. Be careful to avoid wordiness and redundancy in your answer. Choice (E) corrects the sentence's errors.

89. C

This question tests your ability to choose the best form of comparison to describe the music of two different musicians. With any comparison question, make sure that two similar items are being compared. The credited choice will either compare the two musicians or their music. Choice (C) is correct. Simpson's music is being compared to Melody Hawthorne's music. This question is tricky because the opening phrase does not repeat the word "music" following the word "Simpson's." When two possessives match each other as they do here ("Simpson's" and "Hawthorne's"), it is not necessary to repeat the word "music" because the structure already implies the comparison.

90. A

Choice (A) is correct. Note that the company's goals are listed as "improving" one thing and "decreasing" another. These verb forms are in the same grammatical form, and they introduce the following goals, which are the nouns "customer satisfaction" and "the amount of time." This sentence achieves parallel structure and is otherwise grammatically correct.

91. E

This question is tests your ability to identify and correct an error in parallel structure. Note that this sentence describes two things that occur in the state of California. These two items must be listed in a similar grammatical format so that this sentence achieves parallelism. Choice (E) is the credited response. This sentence achieves parallel structure by placing the items that occur in California in the same grammatical format. The word "where" signals the two items, and the words that follow are also parallel.

92. E

This question is primarily testing your ability to identify and correct an error in verb tense. Notice that the sentence's independent clause contains a main clause and a subordinate clause. In order for this sentence to make sense chronologically, both of the verbs in these clauses need to be in the same tense. Choice (E) is correct. Notice that the verbs "claim" and "are being undermined" are both present tense verbs. This choice creates a sentence that is chronologically possible, and the introductory phrase correctly modifies the subject of the main clause, "residents."

93. E

This question contains a modification error. Notice that the word "increase" is a noun and therefore cannot be modified by the adverb "so that." A prepositional phrase can modify a noun, so an answer choice that contains a prepositional phrase will likely be the correct choice. Answer choice (E) is the credited response. This prepositional phrase correctly modified the noun "increase."

94. B

This question tests your ability to identify and correct agreement errors and verb tenses. Even though this sentence looks complex, do not forget to look at its most basic parts. The compound subject of this sentence is "writing style and enduring themes." This plural subject must be paired with plural verbs and plural pronouns throughout the sentence. Choice (B) corrects the sentence errors. The pronoun "they" refers to the "enduring themes" and is grammatically correct.

95. A

This question tests your ability to structure a comparison between two like things. The comparison must be made between two equal elements—it is possible to compare two kinds of birds, but it is not possible to compare a bird to an activity such as migration. The original sentence is clear, concise, and grammatically correct.

96. D

This question tests your ability to identify and correct a pronoun agreement error. The singular pronoun "it" incorrectly refers to its plural antecedent "dogs and cats." The phrasing of this sentence is awkward as well; the phrase "happening when it was young" would be clearer if it were written as a subordinate clause. Choice (D) corrects these errors and is the credited answer.

97. E

This question primarily tests your ability to construct a sentence with parallel grammatical construction. Note that the women are choosing one thing instead of another. These items need to be expressed in the same grammatical form.

This question is also testing your ability to choose the best verb forms for the multiple actions being described. The action that the women perform is one that started in the past ("within the last decade") but continues into the present ("take"). Therefore, it is best to use the present perfect tense "have chosen" instead of "had chosen." Choice (E) corrects the sentence and is the credited response.

98. C

This question tests your ability to recognize and correct an agreement error. The "apartment rental company" is a singular entity; therefore, the pronouns that refer to it must also be singular. Pronouns must agree with their antecedents (the nouns to which they refer) in gender, case, and number. Choice (C) is correct.

99. E

This question tests your ability to construct a logical contrast. In the question text, a "socialized health care system" is being contrasted with "individual responsibility." This contrast illogically pairs unlike entities. It would be better to contrast a "socialized health care system" with a "private health care system," so the correct answer will begin with a reference to this health care system. Choice (E) is the credited answer.

100. E

This question tests your ability to use the correct idiom to make a comparison between different stages of a person's life. The question compares Frank Whittle's habits "as a youth" (the correct idiomatic expression) to his habits as an adult. Choice (E) is correct: This expression is clear, concise, and idiomatically correct.

Chapter 4

Integrated Reasoning

Section Overview

The Integrated Reasoning section is the second section of the GMAT. It appears immediately after the AWA, and you'll have 30 minutes to complete the 12 questions it contains.

The Integrated Reasoning section consists of four question types. They are as follows:

- Multi-Source Reasoning questions provide given information in the form of text, charts, or tables spread across two or three tabbed pages. Some of the questions are traditional, 5-answer multiple choice, while others consist of three true/false-style statements that must all be answered correctly in order to receive credit for the question.
- Graphics Interpretation questions contain two statements that must be completed using drop-down menus. The statements pertain to a graph, chart, or other form of visual information.
- Table Analysis questions present information in the form of a sortable spreadsheet. Table Analysis questions feature the same question formats as Multi-Source Reasoning questions.
- Two-Part Analysis questions start out like an ordinary Quant or Verbal question, but instead of selecting one answer from five choices, you must select answers to two related questions from a common pool of six choices. The two answers can be the same.

With the exception of the occasional traditional multiple-choice question, every question in an Integrated Reasoning section requires two or three selections. There is no partial credit. Thus, getting two questions right and one question wrong on a three-part question in Table Analysis or Multi-Source Reasoning is exactly the same as getting all three questions wrong.

You'll receive your unofficial Integrated Reasoning score on Test Day. The Integrated Reasoning section has its own scoring scale, independent from the 200 to 800 scale. You'll receive a score from 1 through 8, in whole-point increments. A solid score in this section is 5, as this is the score at which you beat the median.

Integrated Reasoning	
Percentile	**Score**
92%	8
81%	7
67%	6
52%	5
37%	4
24%	3
12%	2
0%	1

Percentiles vs. Scaled Scores for the Integrated Reasoning Section

As of this writing, Integrated Reasoning is still a young section. As a result, business schools don't weigh it nearly as heavily as they do the total 200 to 800 score. You want to show schools that you're in the better half of the Integrated Reasoning field, but at the same time, an exceptional 200 to 800 score will do more for your application than will an exceptional Integrated Reasoning score, and you should prioritize your study time accordingly.

Unlike the Quantitative and Verbal sections of the GMAT, the Integrated Reasoning section isn't adaptive: You'll see a predetermined sequence of 12 questions no matter how many you get right and wrong as you go along. However, despite not being adaptive, the Integrated Reasoning section does not let test takers skip questions or return to previously answered questions. As a result, it's often advantageous to guess and abandon a hard question early in the section to ensure that no easy questions are left unanswered at the end of the section.

Practice begins on the next page.

Multi-Source Reasoning Practice

Memo 1	**Memo 2**	**Memo 3**

Memo from ***campaign manager*** *to campaign volunteers*

July 17, 8:36 am

As you know, next week is the first in a series of debates between our candidate and the opposition leader. Did we gather enough data yet about the audience makeup to know their political party affiliations ahead of time? Do we need to invite more local supporters to attend?

Memo 1	**Memo 2**	**Memo 3**

Memo from the ***volunteer coordinator*** *to the campaign manager, in response to campaign manager's July 17, 8:36 am message.*

July 17, 8:57 am

Already, we know there will be 500 invited audience members. We have data for approximately 300 of them who have already been invited, and currently we do not have a majority. The makeup of the remaining 200 is still being determined. There is about a 25% chance, given the usual distribution of political beliefs in this city, that a random audience member will be favorable to our position. (This does not necessarily mean that 50 of the remaining 200 will automatically support our side, but it's a ballpark estimate.) We can invite more local supporters to attend the debate to stack the remaining 200 in our favor (meaning a majority would support us), but we'd need more fliers to reach out to them. I estimate every 100 recruitment fliers will probably give us at least 1 extra local supporter in attendance. What is our total budget for more recruitment fliers?

Memo 1	**Memo 2**	**Memo 3**

Memo from ***campaign manager*** *to volunteer coordinator, in response to volunteer coordinator's July 17, 8:57 am message.*

July 17, 9:09 am

Our total budget for recruitment fliers is $5,000 for this month, but I'd like to save at least half of that money for the later debates. The fliers are typically 25 cents each to print. Make sure the audience for the debate is stacked in our favor, but do not go over budget.

1. Consider each of the following statements. Does the information in the three emails support the inference as stated?

Yes	No	
O	O	If the collected data show that so far, 100 out of the 300 attendees are supporters, then the volunteer coordinator can stay within budget and guarantee a majority.
O	O	Given the restrictions, the volunteer coordinator might be able to stack the debate in the campaign's favor.
O	O	The campaign manager is willing to exceed some of the budget restrictions to get more supporters at the debate.
O	O	The volunteer coordinator and the campaign manager disagree on the amount of money required to get a majority of supporters at the debate.

2. Consider each of the following statements. Does the information in the three emails support the inference as stated?

Yes	No	
O	O	The budget only allows for 20,000 fliers to be used in total.
O	O	There is a 75% chance that the volunteer coordinator will not be able to achieve a majority.
O	O	If each flier only costs 10 cents, the volunteer coordinator would be able to guarantee a stacked house and come in under budget.
O	O	If the remaining 200 attendees are all supporters, there is no need to make and distribute more fliers.

Message 1	Message 2	Message 3

Message sent from an attorney to his clients

12:34 pm: I just received good news from the opposing counsel. Steinholm Industries is willing to offer a settlement of $400,000. I know this is lower than we had hoped, but remember that it is common to begin settlement negotiations with a low offer. I believe that if we counter with an amount not in excess of $450,000, there is a good chance the offer will be accepted immediately, and you will still be receiving a settlement amount that is not less than 15% of what we had initially hoped for. Let me know at your earliest convenience what counteroffer you would like to make.

Message 1	**Message 2**	Message 3

Message sent from clients to their attorney, in response to the attorney's 12:34 pm message.

1:04 pm: We are pleased that they have opened settlement negotiations so that we can potentially avoid a trial. Their offer is too low, however, and we would like to ask for $500,000. We feel this is a stronger position to begin negotiations, though we do want to settle this matter quickly and efficiently. Please present our amount to the opposing counsel and let us know Steinholm Industries's response.

Message 1	Message 2	**Message 3**

Message sent from an attorney to her clients, in response to the clients' 1:04 pm message.

3:15 pm: The opposing counsel communicated your settlement demand to his client. However, Steinholm Industries responded by stating that $500,000 was "too high." They did express their interest in continuing negotiations in the hopes of avoiding trial and the accompanying media circus. If you agree not to speak to the media regarding this dispute, and ask for $440,000 in settlement monies, they will likely settle immediately.

3. Consider each of the following statements. Does the information of the three messages support the inference as stated?

Yes	No	
O	O	The original hoped for settlement amount was more than $550,000.
O	O	Steinholm Industries places a higher priority on the clients' relationship with the media than on the final settlement amount.
O	O	It is possible for both Steinholm Industries and the clients to negotiate a settlement that is not more or less than 15% of either's first offer.
O	O	The clients' attorney would accept a lower settlement amount than his clients would approve.

4. Consider each of the following statements. Does the information in the three messages support the inference as stated?

Yes	No	
O	O	Steinholm Industries will not settle the case without an agreement in place regarding the media.
O	O	The initial hoped for settlement was $530,000.
O	O	The clients' counsel has a vested interest in avoiding the media and settling the case quickly.
O	O	Both parties in this dispute share common ground.

Article 1	Article 2	Article 3

From a local Southern California newspaper

Typically, fewer people vote in local elections than in national ones, but participation can vary widely by state. A new poll has found that more people in California vote in local elections than do people in Nevada, Arizona, and New Mexico combined. This has been attributed to the high number of independent voters in our state, as well as the high enthusiasm for local elections. City councilman Brad Zellman was pleased to see such a high turnout at the recent city council election. "It's a unique opportunity for local citizens' votes to carry more weight than they would in big national elections, and it's great to have so much participation in these smaller campaigns statewide."

Article 1	Article 2	Article 3

Editorial from the Opinion section of a competing newspaper

The recent city council election has seen many a politico claim that the increased voter turnout is due to local citizens wanting to be a part of an election where their vote is proportionally more important. However, it is incorrect to suggest that voting in local elections somehow means your vote "counts more." True, local politicians make decisions that affect day-to-day operations of our cities, but national politicians make decisions that ultimately affect the outcomes of our lives. When you vote for national figures in larger elections, your vote matters more because you are voting for people who will ultimately have a bigger impact on your life long-term.

Article 1	Article 2	Article 3

Results from recent California elections

City councilman elections: 13,000 local votes cast (22% of the eligible population voted), 80% of citizens who voted were polled as "extremely satisfied" with the results.

District representative elections: 1.9 million votes cast (19% of the eligible population voted), 67% of citizens who voted were polled as "extremely satisfied" with the results.

5. Consider each of the following statements. Does the information in the articles support the inference as stated?

Yes	No	
O	O	Californians are more concerned with politics than are people in Nevada, Arizona, and New Mexico.
O	O	The "weight" Zellman describes refers to the scale of political decision making.
O	O	Local citizens are more satisfied by smaller elections than by larger ones.
O	O	Local politicians are likely to have more short-term impact on their constituents' lives than national politicians do.

6. In the recent election, if everyone who voted in the city councilman elections also voted in the district representative elections, how many of those voters were "extremely satisfied" with both elections?

   O Less than 7,000

   O Approximately 10,400

   O More than 1.3 million

   O It cannot be determined.

Answer Key

MULTI-SOURCE REASONING PRACTICE

1. NO, YES, NO, NO
2. NO, NO, YES, NO
3. NO, NO, YES, NO
4. NO, NO, NO, YES
5. NO, NO, NO, YES
6. D

Answers and Explanations

MULTI-SOURCE REASONING PRACTICE

1. NO, YES, NO, NO

If the collected data show that so far 100 out of the 300 attendees are supporters, then the volunteer coordinator can stay within budget and guarantee a majority.

The answer is No. If there are 100 supporters currently, and an estimated 50 more from the remaining 200, that is approximately 150/500. The campaign manager wants a stacked house, and so would need at least 101 more supporters to have a majority (since 251/500 is the smallest majority). To get 101 supporters, 10,100 fliers are needed to encourage their attendance. The campaign manager has stipulated that only $2,500 max can be used for fliers. At 25 cents each, that would only make 10,000 fliers—not enough to guarantee a majority.

Given the restrictions, the volunteer coordinator might be able to stack the debate in their favor.

The answer is Yes. The vaguely positive "might be able to" is key. It is still possible for the volunteer coordinator to stack the debate and stay under budget. For example, if there were 149 supporters currently, and an estimated 50 more from the remaining 200, then that would be 199/500 supporters, and only 52 more would be needed for a majority. 52 supporters would require 5,200 fliers to guarantee their attendance. Since we have a budget that allows for 10,000 fliers, it's possible for a majority to be obtained within the budget.

The campaign manager is willing to exceed some of the budget restrictions to get more supporters at the debate.

The answer is No. The campaign manager makes it clear in the final memo not to go over budget.

The volunteer coordinator and the campaign manager disagree on the amount of money required to get a majority of supporters at the debate.

The answer is No. There is nothing to support an inference that they disagree. With data lacking on the number of original supporters, it is simply unknown whether a majority can be gained within budget.

2. NO, NO, YES, NO

The budget only allows for 20,000 fliers to be used in total.

The answer is No. The fliers are 25 cents each, and the campaign manager stipulates that only $2,500 should be used, so the budget allows for $2,500/0.25 = 10,000 fliers.

There is a 75% chance that the volunteer coordinator will not be able to achieve a majority.

The answer is No. The 25% mentioned in the passage refers to the likelihood a random audience member would support the candidate. There is a 75% chance that a random audience member would NOT support the candidate, but that has nothing to do with the volunteer coordinator.

If each flier only costs 10 cents, the volunteer coordinator would be able to guarantee a stacked house and come in under budget.

The answer is Yes. If each flier costs 10 cents, that would make $2,500/0.10 = 25,000 fliers. That is enough to guarantee 250 volunteers. We know that so far fewer than 150 out of 300 are supporters (because Memo #2 says, "currently we do not have a majority"), and we do not know the makeup of the remaining 200. As long as there is at least 1 supporter already in the 300, which is implied by the passage, then there would be a majority.

If the remaining 200 attendees are all supporters, there is no need to make and distribute more fliers.

The answer is No. If 200/500 are guaranteed supporters, the only way there would be no need to make more fliers would be if at least 51 of the 300 for which data are available are supporters. That is information that is not provided by the passage.

3. NO, NO, YES, NO

The original hoped for settlement amount was more than $550,000.

The answer is No. In Message 1, the attorney states that a settlement of $450,000 would not be less than 15% of the original hoped for settlement. That means that $450,000 would need to be at least 85% of the hoped for settlement. However, 85% of $550,000 is $467,500, so $450,000 is too low—only about 81% of $550,000. A simpler way to think of this is that $450,000 × 1.15 = $517,000, which is lower than $550,000.

Steinholm Industries places a higher priority on the its relationship with the media than on the final settlement amount.

The answer is No. Although the final message indicates that Steinholm Industries is concerned about the media, there is nothing to indicate the media has a "higher priority" than the settlement.

It is possible for both Steinholm Industries and the clients to negotiate a settlement that is not more or less than 15% of either's first offer.

The answer is Yes. The first offer from Steinholm Industries is $400,000. The first offer from the clients was $500,000. Then 15% of $400,000 is $60,000, so an increase of 15% would be $460,000. Also, 15% of $500,000 is $75,000, so a decrease of 15% would be $425,000. There is a $35,000 overlap. A settlement anywhere between $425,000 and $460,000 would allow both sides to remain within 15% of their original offer.

The clients' attorney would accept a lower settlement amount than his clients would approve.

The answer is No. While the attorney does encourage his clients to make an offer less than $450,000, and the clients initially want to ask for $500,000, there is nothing to indicate that the attorney would "accept" any kind of settlement without his clients' approval.

4. NO, NO, NO, YES

Steinholm Industries will not settle the case without an agreement in place regarding the media.

The answer is No. This is too extreme. While Steinholm rejected the offer as "too high," there is nothing to indicate that Steinholm would not accept a more reasonable offer, even if it omitted a binding nondisclosure agreement regarding the media.

The initial hoped for settlement was $530,000.

The answer is No. In Message 1, the attorney states that a settlement of $450,000 would not be less than 15% of the original hoped for settlement, but he does not specifically say what that settlement amount was. It does not have to be $530,000.

The clients' counsel has a vested interest in avoiding the media and settling the case quickly.

The answer is No. A "vested interest" implies a personal stake in the outcome. There is nothing in the passage to suggest the attorney has any expectation of financial gain if the settlement occurs expeditiously.

Both parties in this dispute share common ground.

The answer is Yes. The passage states that both parties wish to "avoid trial."

5. NO, NO, NO, YES

Californians are more concerned with politics than are people in Nevada, Arizona, and New Mexico.

The answer is No. This argument falsely assumes that the percentage of people who vote in California is higher than in the other three states put together, based on the fact that the number of people who vote is greater in California. Percentages and actual numbers are entirely different concepts.

The "weight" Zellman describes refers to the scale of political decision making.

The answer is No. Zellman likely means that your vote carries "more weight" in local elections since "typically fewer people vote in local elections" according to Article 1. This is further established by Article 2, which begins with a refutation of Zellman and the idea that a vote in a local election "counts more."

Local citizens are more satisfied by smaller elections than by larger ones.

The answer is No. In Article 3, though a higher percentage of citizens were polled as "extremely satisfied" in the smaller "city councilman" elections, there is nothing to indicate that the size of the election was the cause of the satisfaction. The effectiveness of the political process itself could have been a factor, for example. There are not enough data to draw this type of conclusion.

Local politicians are likely to have more short-term impact on their constituents' lives than national politicians do.

The answer is Yes. This inference is supported by Article 2, which states that "local politicians make decisions that affect day-to-day operations of our cities." The author of the opinion journal then continues to develop the idea that national politicians have long-term impact, suggesting that local politicians have a shorter-term impact.

6. D

The correct answer is (D). Article 3 gives us the information we need. If 13,000 voted in the councilman elections, and 80% of those were satisfied, that is 10,400 people. Those 10,400 were then among the 1.9 million who voted in the representative elections, 67% of whom said they were "extremely satisfied" with this second election. There is no way to tell, however, how many of the 10,400 were among the 67%. It certainly could not be *more* than 10,400, but it could be all, a partial number, or none.

Practice begins on the next page.

Graphics Interpretation Practice

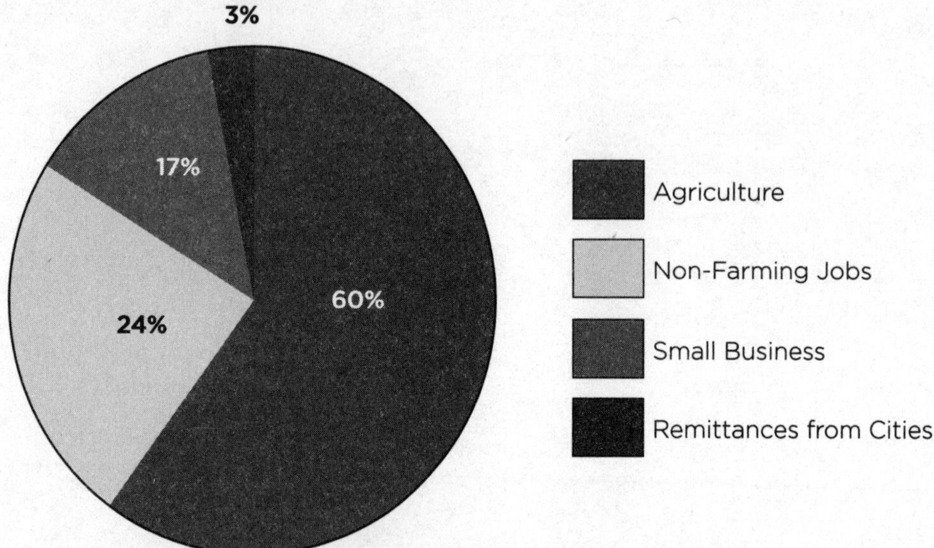

Rural Economy in Central America—2000

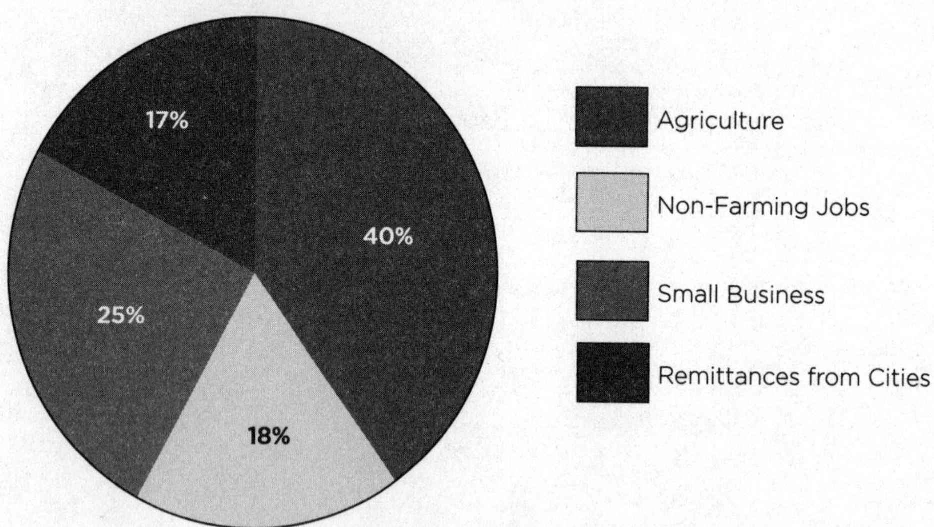

Rural Economy in Central America—2010

The above pie charts give the percentages of rural economic activity in a Central American country for the years 2000 and 2010.

1. The change in the overall earnings for non-farm jobs plus small businesses between 2000 and 2010 ________.

   - O is positive
   - O is negative
   - O is zero
   - O cannot be determined

2. The smallest proportional change in percentage between 2000 and 2010 in the segment of the rural economy taken up by a particular category was in ________.

   - O agriculture
   - O non-farm jobs
   - O small businesses
   - O remittances from cities

3. If the same rate of growth for remittances from cities as a proportion of the rural economy continues for the next 10 years, in 2020 we would expect it to occupy about ________ of the rural economy.

   - O 3
   - O 30
   - O 50
   - O 80

4. If, between 2010 and 2020, 20% of agriculture's portion of the rural economy is replaced by remittances from cities, and 15% of agriculture's portion of the rural economy is replaced non-farm jobs, then the largest sector of the rural economy in 2020 will be ________.

   - O agriculture
   - O non-farm jobs
   - O small businesses
   - O remittances from cities

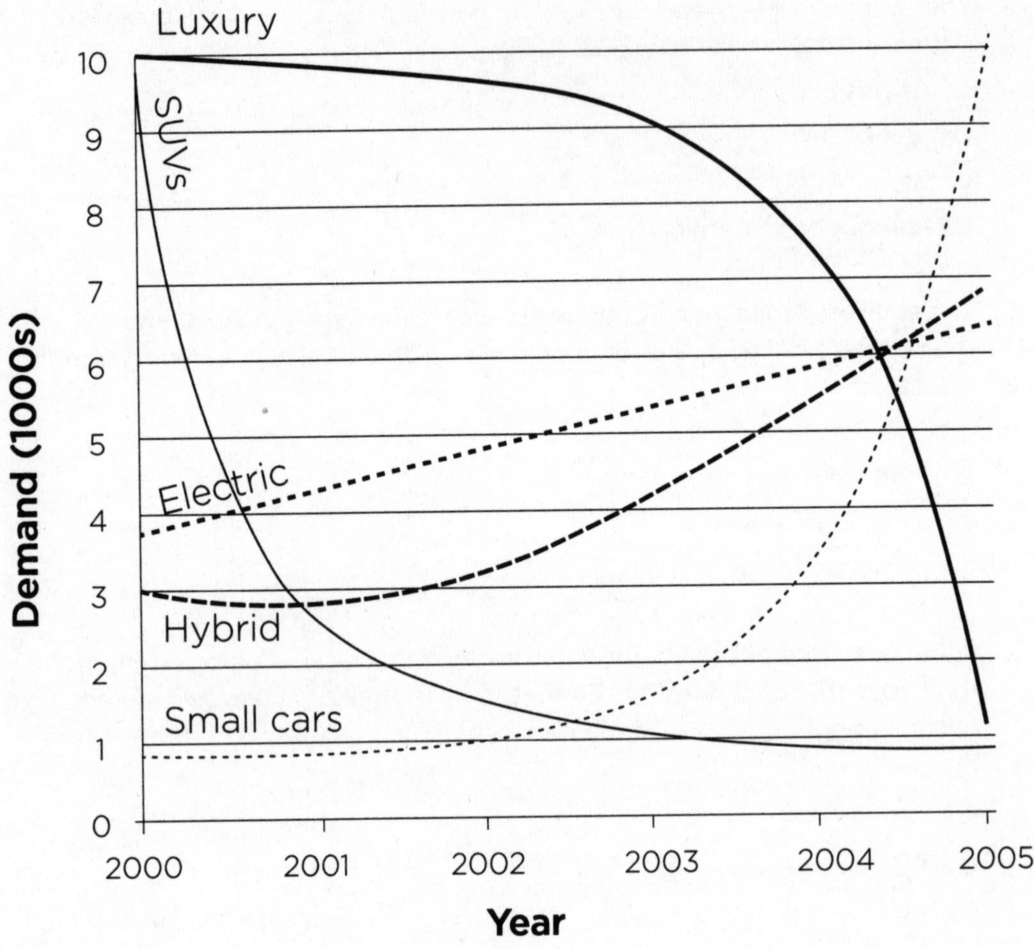

The above chart shows the annual demand for SUVs, electric cars, hybrid cars, and regular gasoline small cars over a five-year period.

5. The slope of the small car curve is ________ the slope of the electric car curve over this period.
   - O always greater than
   - O always less than
   - O equal to
   - O sometimes greater than and sometimes less than

6. The demand for hybrid cars is ________ each year during the entire five-year period.
   - O trending upward
   - O constant
   - O trending downward
   - O none of the above

7. The total demand for these cars was greatest in ________
   - O 2001
   - O 2002
   - O 2003
   - O 2004

8. The rate of change in demand for SUVs between each year during the period presented is ________.
   - O constantly declining
   - O constantly increasing
   - O constant
   - O alternately declining and increasing

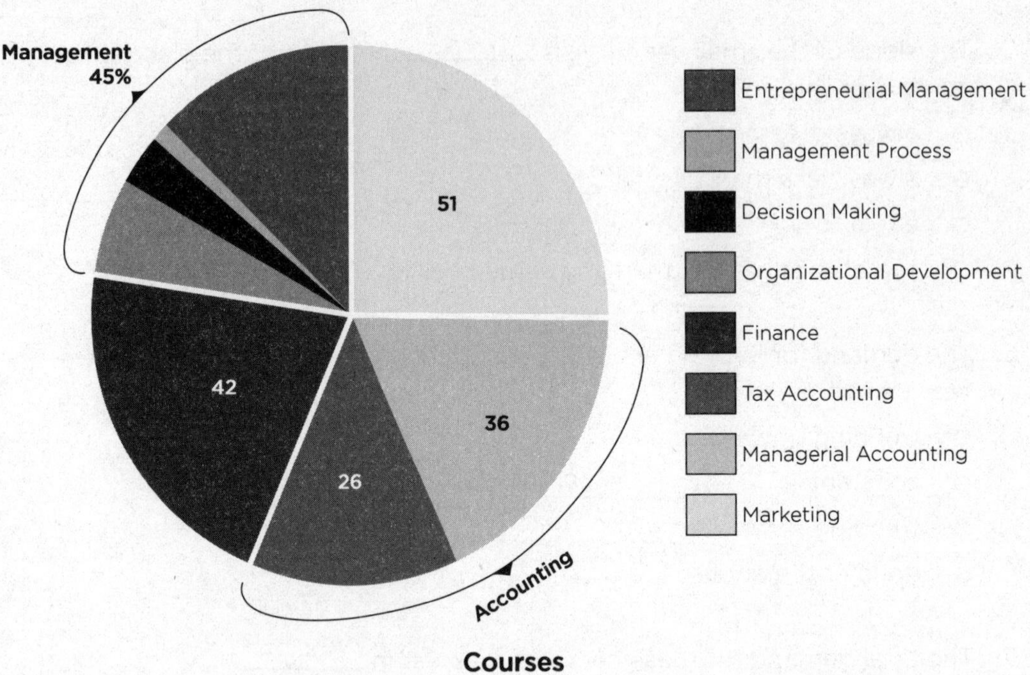

Courses

The above pie chart gives the number of course offerings in the business school in four subject areas—management, marketing, accounting, and finance—and some of their subareas.

9. ________ of total course offerings are in accounting.
   - O 13%
   - O 31%
   - O 36%
   - O 62%

10. If students take 6 courses a semester for 2 years (2 semesters per year), and in each semester must take courses from two subject areas, and in each year must take at least one course in each subject area, then a student could take at most ________ of the managerial accounting courses.
    - O 27.8%
    - O 29%
    - O 50%
    - O 55%

Answers and explanations begin on the next page.

Answer Key

GRAPHICS INTERPRETATION PRACTICE

1. D
2. B
3. D
4. A
5. D
6. D
7. D
8. A
9. B
10. C

Answers and Explanations

GRAPHICS INTERPRETATION PRACTICE

1. D

The correct answer choice is the fourth one, cannot be determined. Don't be tricked into just adding up the percentages. The charts give the relative portions of these four categories of rural economic activity, but nowhere are we told absolute amounts: What was the overall size of the economy in 2000 and in 2010? This value would be necessary to calculate overall earnings in these particular areas in 2000 versus in 2010. Since we don't know in which year the overall economy was larger, or whether the economy was the same size in both years, we cannot make this comparison.

2. B

The charts give percentages of rural economic activity. This question asks about percent change in those percentages.

The percentage of economic activity contributed by small businesses nearly doubled in these 10 years, for a percent change of nearly 100%.

The percentage of economic activity contributed by remittances increased nearly sixfold, for a percent change of around 467%.

So we can quickly eliminate those two. But the percentages of the economy attributed to agriculture and non-farm jobs both decreased by proportionally similar amounts. Which experienced the smaller percent change?

Non-farm jobs decreased by 6/24, or 25%.

Agriculture decreased by 20/60, or 1/3, or 33%.

Put in these terms, clearly non-farm jobs experienced a smaller percent change than agriculture, since 25% is less than 33%.

Select the second option: non-farm jobs.

3. D

What was the rate of growth for remittances from cities as a proportion of the economy between 2000 and 2010? Nearly 5 times, or 467%. What is 467% of 17? Around 79, so the fourth option, 80, is the correct answer.

1st option, 3: No, there's no reason to assume it will oscillate back to what it was in 2000. The question assumes the same rate of growth, not a reverse rate of growth.

2nd option, 30: No, don't just add another 14 to the percentages as we saw between 2000 and 2010. "The same rate of growth" is determined not by absolute numbers but rather by the *rate* of growth, which is nearly 600%.

3rd option, 50: No, this is what we would expect for small businesses, not for remittances from cities.

4. A

The key here is correctly understanding the question. Calculate 20% of agriculture's portion of the rural economy in 2010 as 40/5 = 8% of the overall economy. Likewise, 15% of agriculture's portion is 6% of the overall economy.

In other words, in 2020, remittances from cities will constitute 17% + 8% = 25% of the overall economy.

And non-farm jobs will constitute 18% + 6% = 24% of the overall economy.

Agriculture will constitute 40 - 8 - 6 = 26% of the overall economy.

And small businesses' percentage of all economic activity will remain at 25%.

So mark the first option correct: Agriculture would just barely remain the largest part of the economy.

5. D

The electric car demand curve is a straight line, which has constant slope of around 0.5.

The small car curve shown here has consistently positive slope, but at first it's very close to 0 and by the end it's much higher, closer to 7.

Even without doing any calculations, you can quickly visually determine that at first the electric car demand curve has greater slope, and then at some point around 2003, the slope of the small car curve becomes greater.

Select the final choice: sometimes greater than and sometimes less than.

6. D

From 2000 to 2001, the demand for hybrid cars went down. In every other year recorded here, the demand went up. Thus, it's not constant (since it changes), it's not always trending upward (increasing), and it's not always trending downward (decreasing)—select the final choice, none of the above.

7. D

Here, you can quickly sum the demand for each car in each of these years.

2001: Demand for all cars adds up to a little under 21.

2002: Demand adds up to around 19.

2003: Demand adds up to more than 21.

2004: Demand adds up to close to 23.

Select the last option, 2004.

8. A

The key here is understanding the term "rate of change." The curve for SUVs shows a negative slope throughout this 5-year period. In other words, the demand is always decreasing. But we are asked about the rate of that change: How fast is the demand decreasing? Between 2000 and 2001, demand declined very rapidly, meaning the change in demand was relatively large. Over the following years, demand continued to decline, but less and less rapidly. Thus, the rate of change is decreasing—it's becoming less and less negative.

9. B

The pie chart shows that there are two subareas for accounting: managerial accounting and tax accounting. Together, they account for 62 courses.

How many total courses are there? Add them up: 45 + 51 + 62 + 42 = 200.

Thus, the accounting courses are 62/200 = 31% of the total.

Select the second option, 31%.

Incorrect answer explanations:

13: No, this is the total percentage of courses offered in tax accounting, but there's another accounting subarea, managerial accounting.

36: No, this is the total number of courses offered in managerial accounting, but the question asks for the percentage of the total number of courses offered, not the absolute number.

62: No, this is the total number of courses offered in accounting, but the question asks for the percentage of the total number of courses offered, not the absolute number, and there are 200 total courses, not 100.

10. C

There are 36 total managerial accounting courses.

There are 4 total subject areas.

Each year, a student can take at most 9 of their 12 courses in a single subject area, since they also must take at least one course in every other subject area.

Thus, over two years, a student could take 18 of their 24 courses in managerial accounting, or 50% of the total managerial accounting courses. The third answer choice is correct.

Incorrect answer choice explanations:

27.8%: Note that the text under the pie chart specifies that there are 4 subject areas. Don't just count all 8 pieces of the pie as subject areas, which could lead you to think that a student could take at most 5 courses a year in managerial accounting.

29%: No, the question asks what percentage of managerial accounting courses could be taken, not what percentage of overall accounting courses.

55%: In order to take a course in every subject area each year, it's not possible to take 10 out of 12 courses per year in managerial accounting. That would only leave room for courses in 2 out of the 3 non-accounting subject areas.

Table Analysis Practice

Sort By | Select... ▼

Book Title	Publisher	Format	Retail Price	Retail Profit per Book	Highest Sales Ranking	Current Sales Ranking	Number of Weeks on Sales Charts	Total Sales to Date
Vehicular Homicide, She Wrote	J. Brint & Sons	Mass-market paperback	$6.99	$0.79	14	32	8	22,776
Cybil Crowley Chronicles, Part 34	J. Brint & Sons	Mass-market paperback	$7.99	$0.99	10	17	2	10,765
The Killer Wore Killing Clothes	Lone Tree Books	Mass-market paperback	$6.99	$1.39	14	35	15	156,711
"S" Is for Significant Stabbings	Tumbler Books	Mass-market paperback	$7.49	$1.47	18	18	1	5,677
Poison Was the Cure, Whereby "Cure" I Mean Murder Weapon	Lone Tree Books	Mass-market paperback	$7.99	$1.99	20	20	1	6,781
"S" Is for Significant Stabbings	Tumbler Books	Trade paper-back	$16.99	$2.19	23	29	10	54,332
Deadly Deathful Deadfalls	J. Brint & Sons	Mass-market paperback	$8.99	$2.29	15	29	6	33,221
Cybil Crowley Chronicles, Part 34	J. Brint & Sons	Trade paper-back	$13.99	$2.52	8	9	7	45,342
The Stocking Stalker	Tumbler Books	Mass-market paperback	$7.99	$2.63	4	4	3	33,476
Deadly Deathful Deadfalls	J. Brint & Sons	Trade paper-back	$18.99	$2.78	15	16	3	18,764
Cybil Crowley Chronicles, Part 34	J. Brint & Sons	Hardcover	$23.99	$2.99	22	25	2	8,766
Vehicular Homicide, She Wrote	J. Brint & Sons	Hardcover	$24.99	$3.01	27	31	3	14,577
The Stocking Stalker	Tumbler Books	Trade Paper-back	$14.99	$3.21	1	2	2	23,643
Text "M" for More Murders	J. Brint & Sons	Trade paper-back	$17.99	$3.51	5	5	4	45,656
The Killer Wore Killing Clothes	Lone Tree Books	Hardcover	$26.99	$3.52	43	49	4	23,224
Deadly Deathful Deadfalls	J. Brint & Sons	Hardcover	$27.99	$3.59	23	41	5	12,753
"S" Is for Significant Stabbings	Tumbler Books	Hardcover	$26.49	$3.99	32	40	10	33,554
The Stocking Stalker	Tumbler Books	Hardcover	$24.49	$4.27	3	3	2	43,764
Text "M" for More Murders	J. Brint & Sons	Hardcover	$25.99	$4.39	13	24	16	132,456
Poison Was the Cure, Whereby "Cure" I Mean Murder Weapon	Lone Tree Books	Hardcover	$26.99	$4.63	32	46	6	33,677

The table provided gives sales information about 20 mystery novels. For each book, the table describes the title, the publisher, the format in which the book was published, the retail price of the book, the retail profit from the book at that price, the highest weekly sales ranking the book received, the current sales ranking, the number of weeks the book has been on the sales charts, and the total book sales to date.

Sort By Format ▼

Book Title	Publisher	Format	Retail Price	Retail Profit Per Book	Highest Sales Ranking	Current Sales Ranking	Number of Weeks on Sales Charts	Total Sales to Date
Poison Was the Cure, Whereby "Cure" I Mean Murder Weapon	Lone Tree Books	Hardcover	$26.99	$4.63	32	46	6	33,677
Text "M" for More Murders	J. Brint & Sons	Hardcover	$25.99	$4.39	13	24	16	132,456
The Stocking Stalker	Tumbler Books	Hardcover	$24.49	$4.27	3	3	2	43,764
"S" Is for Significant Stabbings	Tumbler Books	Hardcover	$26.49	$3.99	32	40	10	33,554
Deadly Deathful Deadfalls	J. Brint & Sons	Hardcover	$27.99	$3.59	23	41	5	12,753
The Killer Wore Killing Clothes	Lone Tree Books	Hardcover	$26.99	$3.52	43	49	4	23,224
Vehicular Homicide, She Wrote	J. Brint & Sons	Hardcover	$24.99	$3.01	27	31	3	14,577
Cybil Crowley Chronicles, Part 34	J. Brint & Sons	Hardcover	$23.99	$2.99	22	25	2	8,766
The Stocking Stalker	Tumbler Books	Mass-market paperback	$7.99	$2.63	4	4	3	33,476
Deadly Deathful Deadfalls	J. Brint & Sons	Mass-market paperback	$8.99	$2.29	15	29	6	33,221
Poison Was the Cure, Whereby "Cure" I Mean Murder Weapon	Lone Tree Books	Mass-market paperback	$7.99	$1.99	20	20	1	6,781
"S" Is for Significant Stabbings	Tumbler Books	Mass-market paperback	$7.49	$1.47	18	18	1	5,677
The Killer Wore Killing Clothes	Lone Tree Books	Mass-market paperback	$6.99	$1.39	14	35	15	156,711
Cybil Crowley Chronicles, Part 34	J. Brint & Sons	Mass-market paperback	$7.99	$0.99	10	17	2	10,765
Vehicular Homicide, She Wrote	J. Brint & Sons	Mass-market paperback	$6.99	$0.79	14	32	8	22,776
Text "M" for More Murders	J. Brint & Sons	Trade paper-back	$17.99	$3.51	5	5	4	45,656
The Stocking Stalker	Tumbler Books	Trade Paper-back	$14.99	$3.21	1	2	2	23,643
Deadly Deathful Deadfalls	J. Brint & Sons	Trade paper-back	$18.99	$2.78	15	16	3	18,764
Cybil Crowley Chronicles, Part 34	J. Brint & Sons	Trade paper-back	$13.99	$2.52	8	9	7	45,342
"S" Is for Significant Stabbings	Tumbler Books	Trade paper-back	$16.99	$2.19	23	29	10	54,332

1. J. Brint & Sons has the highest retail profit per book in at least two formats.

   O True

   O False

Sort By Total Sales to Date ▾

Book Title	Publisher	Format	Retail Price	Retail Profit per Book	Highest Sales Ranking	Current Sales Ranking	Number of Weeks on Sales Charts	Total Sales to Date
The Killer Wore Killing Clothes	Lone Tree Books	Mass-market paperback	$6.99	$1.39	14	35	15	156,711
Text "M" for More Murders	J. Brint & Sons	Hardcover	$25.99	$4.39	13	24	16	132,456
"S" Is for Significant Stabbings	Tumbler Books	Trade paper-back	$16.99	$2.19	23	29	10	54,332
Text "M" for More Murders	J. Brint & Sons	Trade paper-back	$17.99	$3.51	5	5	4	45,656
Cybil Crowley Chronicles, Part 34	J. Brint & Sons	Trade paper-back	$13.99	$2.52	8	9	7	45,342
The Stocking Stalker	Tumbler Books	Hardcover	$24.49	$4.27	3	3	2	43,764
Poison Was the Cure, Whereby "Cure" I Mean Murder Weapon	Lone Tree Books	Hardcover	$26.99	$4.63	32	46	6	33,677
"S" Is for Significant Stabbings	Tumbler Books	Hardcover	$26.49	$3.99	32	40	10	33,554
The Stocking Stalker	Tumbler Books	Mass-market paperback	$7.99	$2.63	4	4	3	33,476
Deadly Deathful Deadfalls	J. Brint & Sons	Mass-market paperback	$8.99	$2.29	15	29	6	33,221
The Stocking Stalker	Tumbler Books	Trade Paper-back	$14.99	$3.21	1	2	2	23,643
The Killer Wore Killing Clothes	Lone Tree Books	Hardcover	$26.99	$3.52	43	49	4	23,224
Vehicular Homicide, She Wrote	J. Brint & Sons	Mass-market paperback	$6.99	$0.79	14	32	8	22776
Deadly Deathful Deadfalls	J. Brint & Sons	Trade paper-back	$18.99	$2.78	15	16	3	18764
Vehicular Homicide, She Wrote	J. Brint & Sons	Hardcover	$24.99	$3.01	27	31	3	14577
Deadly Deathful Deadfalls	J. Brint & Sons	Hardcover	$27.99	$3.59	23	41	5	12,753
Cybil Crowley Chronicles, Part 34	J. Brint & Sons	Mass-market paperback	$7.99	$0.99	10	17	2	10,765
Cybil Crowley Chronicles, Part 34	J. Brint & Sons	Hardcover	$23.99	$2.99	22	25	2	8,766
Poison Was the Cure, Whereby "Cure" I Mean Murder Weapon	Lone Tree Books	Mass-market paperback	$7.99	$1.99	20	20	1	6,781
"S" Is for Significant Stabbings	Tumbler Books	Mass-market paperback	$7.49	$1.47	18	18	1	5,677

2. Every publisher has had a book ranked in the top 10 in sales.

- ○ True
- ○ False

Sort By | Number of Weeks on Sales Chart ▼

Book Title	Publisher	Format	Retail Price	Retail Profit per Book	Highest Sales Ranking	Current Sales Ranking	Number of Weeks on Sales Charts	Total Sales to Date
Text "M" for More Murders	J. Brint & Sons	Hardcover	$25.99	$4.39	13	24	16	132,456
The Killer Wore Killing Clothes	Lone Tree Books	Mass-market paperback	$6.99	$1.39	14	35	15	156,711
"S" Is for Significant Stabbings	Tumbler Books	Trade paper-back	$16.99	$2.19	23	29	10	54,332
"S" Is for Significant Stabbings	Tumbler Books	Hardcover	$26.49	$3.99	32	40	10	33,554
Vehicular Homicide, She Wrote	J. Brint & Sons	Mass-market paperback	$6.99	$0.79	14	32	8	22,776
Cybil Crowley Chronicles, Part 34	J. Brint & Sons	Trade paper-back	$13.99	$2.52	8	9	7	45,342
Deadly Deathful Deadfalls	J. Brint & Sons	Mass-market paperback	$8.99	$2.29	15	29	6	33,221
Poison Was the Cure, Whereby "Cure" I Mean Murder Weapon	Lone Tree Books	Hardcover	$26.99	$4.63	32	46	6	33,677
Deadly Deathful Deadfalls	J. Brint & Sons	Hardcover	$27.99	$3.59	23	41	5	12,753
Text "M" for More Murders	J. Brint & Sons	Trade paper-back	$17.99	$3.51	5	5	4	45,656
The Killer Wore Killing Clothes	Lone Tree Books	Hardcover	$26.99	$3.52	43	49	4	23,224
The Stocking Stalker	Tumbler Books	Mass-market paperback	$7.99	$2.63	4	4	3	33,476
Deadly Deathful Deadfalls	J. Brint & Sons	Trade paper-back	$18.99	$2.78	15	16	3	18,764
Vehicular Homicide, She Wrote	J. Brint & Sons	Hardcover	$24.99	$3.01	27	31	3	14,577
Cybil Crowley Chronicles, Part 34	J. Brint & Sons	Mass-market paperback	$7.99	$0.99	10	17	2	10,765
Cybil Crowley Chronicles, Part 34	J. Brint & Sons	Hardcover	$23.99	$2.99	22	25	2	8,766
The Stocking Stalker	Tumbler Books	Trade Paper-back	$14.99	$3.21	1	2	2	23,643
The Stocking Stalker	Tumbler Books	Hardcover	$24.49	$4.27	3	3	2	43,764
"S" Is for Significant Stabbings	Tumbler Books	Mass-market paperback	$7.49	$1.47	18	18	1	5,677
Poison Was the Cure, Whereby "Cure" I Mean Murder Weapon	Lone Tree Books	Mass-market paperback	$7.99	$1.99	20	20	1	6,781

3. Every book with at least 10 weeks on the sales charts has sold at least 20,000 copies to date.

   O True

   O False

4. No title has had a higher retail profit total in any format than "The Killer Wore Killing Clothes" in mass-market paperback.

   O True

   O False

Sort By Select...

Name	Flat Rate (less than 2 pounds)	Rate 1st Pound	Rate, Subsequent Pounds	Pickups per Day	Weekend Pickups	On-Time Guarantee
Git-R-Gone	2.79	0.88	2	3	n	n
Next Day Jay	2.56	0.99	1.75	3	n	n
Rapid Riders	2.35	1.04	1.4	3	n	n
Zip Ship	2.45	1.05	1.5	2	n	n
Car-Go Shipping	2.66	1.19	1.5	2	n	n
PDQ Delivery	3.15	1.99	1.43	1	n	y
Caravan Sarah	3.87	1.85	2.25	1	n	y
Parcelmouth	1.75	0.79	1.11	1	n	y
Box Populi	1.88	0.65	1.45	2	n	y
Letter Fly	1.98	0.71	1.37	2	n	y
Packard's Packages	2.5	1.11	1.4	1	y	n
Tom Swift Delivery	2.47	1.33	1.2	2	y	n
Moto Go-To	2.43	1.15	1.42	2	y	n
The Tony Express	3.22	2	1.3	2	y	n
Psycho Cyclist Couriers	2.3	0.95	1.53	1	y	y
Speedy Fleet	2.58	0.85	1.9	2	y	y
Faster Masters	1.99	0.58	1.55	1	y	y
A.S.A.P.	3.23	0.75	2.55	1	y	y
Ad Astra	3.33	1.75	1.75	2	y	y
Courier & Drives	3.23	1.22	2.1	2	y	y

The table provided gives rates for a selection of 20 in-town couriers and delivery services. For each company, the table describes the name of the company, the flat-rate cost for a package weighing less than two pounds, the rate for the first pound of a regular (non-flat-rate) package, the rate for each pound after the first of a regular package, the number of times each company will pick up packages each day, whether the company will pick up packages on the weekend, and whether the company offers a guaranteed delivery time.

Sort By: On-time guarantee ▼

Name	Flat Rate (less than 2 pounds)	Rate 1st pound	Rate, Subsequent Pounds	Pickups per Day	Weekend Pickups	On-Time Guarantee
Parcelmouth	1.75	0.79	1.11	1	n	y
PDQ Delivery	3.15	1.99	1.43	1	n	y
Caravan Sarah	3.87	1.85	2.25	1	n	y
Box Populi	1.88	0.65	1.45	2	n	y
Letter Fly	1.98	0.71	1.37	2	n	y
Faster Masters	1.99	0.58	1.55	1	y	y
Psycho Cyclist Couriers	2.3	0.95	1.53	1	y	y
A.S.A.P.	3.23	0.75	2.55	1	y	y
Speedy Fleet	2.58	0.85	1.9	2	y	y
Courier & Drives	3.23	1.22	2.1	2	y	y
Ad Astra	3.33	1.75	1.75	2	y	y
Zip Ship	2.45	1.05	1.5	2	n	n
Car-Go Shipping	2.66	1.19	1.5	2	n	n
Rapid Riders	2.35	1.04	1.4	3	n	n
Next Day Jay	2.56	0.99	1.75	3	n	n
Git-R-Gone	2.79	0.88	2	3	n	n
Packard's Packages	2.5	1.11	1.4	1	y	n
Moto Go-To	2.43	1.15	1.42	2	y	n
Tom Swift Delivery	2.47	1.33	1.2	2	y	n
The Tony Express	3.22	2	1.3	2	y	n

5. Of the companies that offer an on-time guarantee but no weekend pickups, the company with the median flat-rate price is Box Populi.

   - O True
   - O False

Sort By [Pickups per day ▾]

Name	Flat Rate (less than 2 pounds)	Rate 1st Pound	Rate, Subsequent Pounds	Pickups per Day	Weekend Pickups	On-Time Guarantee
Parcelmouth	1.75	0.79	1.11	1	n	y
Faster Masters	1.99	0.58	1.55	1	y	y
Psycho Cyclist Couriers	2.3	0.95	1.53	1	y	y
Packard's Packages	2.5	1.11	1.4	1	y	n
PDQ Delivery	3.15	1.99	1.43	1	n	y
A.S.A.P.	3.23	0.75	2.55	1	y	y
Caravan Sarah	3.87	1.85	2.25	1	n	y
Box Populi	1.88	0.65	1.45	2	n	y
Letter Fly	1.98	0.71	1.37	2	n	y
Moto Go-To	2.43	1.15	1.42	2	y	n
Zip Ship	2.45	1.05	1.5	2	n	n
Tom Swift Delivery	2.47	1.33	1.2	2	y	n
Speedy Fleet	2.58	0.85	1.9	2	y	y
Car-Go Shipping	2.66	1.19	1.5	2	n	n
The Tony Express	3.22	2	1.3	2	y	n
Courier & Drives	3.23	1.22	2.1	2	y	y
Ad Astra	3.33	1.75	1.75	2	y	y
Rapid Riders	2.35	1.04	1.4	3	n	n
Next Day Jay	2.56	0.99	1.75	3	n	n
Git-R-Gone	2.79	0.88	2	3	n	n

6. No company with two or more pickups per day has a better flat rate than any company with one pickup per day.

   o True

   o False

Sort By [Flat rate (less than 2 pounds) ▼]

Name	Flat Rate (less than 2 pounds)	Rate 1st Pound	Rate, Subsequent Pounds	Pickups per Day	Weekend Pickups	On-Time Guarantee
Parcelmouth	1.75	0.79	1.11	1	n	y
Box Populi	1.88	0.65	1.45	2	n	y
Letter Fly	1.98	0.71	1.37	2	n	y
Faster Masters	1.99	0.58	1.55	1	y	y
Psycho Cyclist Couriers	2.3	0.95	1.53	1	y	y
Rapid Riders	2.35	1.04	1.4	3	n	n
Moto Go-To	2.43	1.15	1.42	2	y	n
Zip Ship	2.45	1.05	1.5	2	n	n
Tom Swift Delivery	2.47	1.33	1.2	2	y	n
Packard's Packages	2.5	1.11	1.4	1	y	n
Next Day Jay	2.56	0.99	1.75	3	n	n
Speedy Fleet	2.58	0.85	1.9	2	y	y
Car-Go Shipping	2.66	1.19	1.5	2	n	n
Git-R-Gone	2.79	0.88	2	3	n	n
PDQ Delivery	3.15	1.99	1.43	1	n	y
The Tony Express	3.22	2	1.3	2	y	n
A.S.A.P.	3.23	0.75	2.55	1	y	y
Courier & Drives	3.23	1.22	2.1	2	y	y
Ad Astra	3.33	1.75	1.75	2	y	y
Caravan Sarah	3.87	1.85	2.25	1	n	y

7. Parcelmouth offers the best deal on both flat-rate and 2-pound packages.

O True

O False

Sort By Select...

Book Title	Publisher	Format	Retail Price	Publisher Profit per Book	Highest Sales Ranking	Current Sales Ranking	Number of Weeks on Sales Charts	Total Retail Sales to Date
Rollicking Through Rome	Ing Travel	ebook	$13.99	$5.31	2	4	4	$83,940
Peering at the Pyramids	Ing Travel	ebook	$14.99	$4.64	10	18	8	$71,952
Walking the Great Wall	Ing Travel	ebook	$14.99	$5.20	7	16	8	$83,944
Rollicking Through Rome	Ing Travel	Hardcover	$28.00	$5.60	8	9	8	$190,400
Peering at the Pyramids	Ing Travel	Hardcover	$30.00	$7.20	5	11	12	$342,000
Walking the Great Wall	Ing Travel	Hardcover	$30.00	$7.50	3	10	12	$360,000
Rollicking Through Rome	Ing Travel	Trade paperback	$17.00	$3.06	3	3	4	$136,000
Walking the Great Wall	Ing Travel	Trade paperback	$18.00	$2.52	11	15	8	$144,000
My Blarney Stone Kiss	MacCarthy and Ray	ebook	$4.49	$0.53	50	76	3	$1,616
Irish Pubs 'Round the World	MacCarthy and Ray	ebook	$9.99	$3.60	8	11	5	$59,940
Irish Pubs 'Round the World	MacCarthy and Ray	Hardcover	$19.99	$3.39	14	20	9	$125,937
Ireland: By Land and Sea	MacCarthy and Ray	Hardcover	$23.99	$4.56	9	15	7	$151,137
My Blarney Stone Kiss	MacCarthy and Ray	Trade paperback	$6.49	$0.64	46	69	3	$1,557
Irish Pubs 'Round the World	MacCarthy and Ray	Trade paperback	$13.99	$3.33	2	6	5	$156,895
Belgium on Bicycle	Pedal Power Books	ebook	$9.99	$3.39	22	37	10	$27,970
Bike Maine's Back Roads	Pedal Power Books	ebook	$10.99	$3.84	14	29	12	$39,564
Bike Maine's Back Roads	Pedal Power Books	Hardcover	$22.99	$3.68	19	35	16	$183,920
Belgium on Bicycle	Pedal Power Books	Hardcover	$25.99	$4.16	21	33	14	$109,158
Bike Maine's Back Roads	Pedal Power Books	Trade paperback	$14.99	$2.25	15	37	13	$94,435
Belgium on Bicycle	Pedal Power Books	Trade paperback	$15.99	$1.98	20	38	11	$35,178

The table provided gives sales information about a selection of 20 travel books. For each book, the table describes the book title, the publisher, the format in which the book was released, the retail price of the book, the publisher profit from the book at that price, the highest weekly sales ranking the book received, the current sales ranking, the number of weeks the book has been on the sales charts, and the total book sales to date.

Sort By Format ▾

Book Title	Publisher	Format	Retail Price	Publisher Profit per Book	Highest Sales Ranking	Current Sales Ranking	Number of Weeks on Sales Charts	Total Retail Sales to Date
Irish Pubs 'Round the World	MacCarthy and Ray	Trade paperback	$13.99	$3.33	2	6	5	$156,895
Walking the Great Wall	Ing Travel	Trade paperback	$18.00	$2.52	11	15	8	$144,000
Rollicking Through Rome	Ing Travel	Trade paperback	$17.00	$3.06	3	3	4	$136,000
Bike Maine's Back Roads	Pedal Power Books	Trade paperback	$14.99	$2.25	15	37	13	$94,435
Belgium on Bicycle	Pedal Power Books	Trade paperback	$15.99	$1.98	20	38	11	$35,178
My Blarney Stone Kiss	MacCarthy and Ray	Trade paperback	$6.49	$0.64	46	69	3	$1,557
Walking the Great Wall	Ing Travel	Hardcover	$30.00	$7.50	3	10	12	$360,000
Peering at the Pyramids	Ing Travel	Hardcover	$30.00	$7.20	5	11	12	$342,000
Rollicking Through Rome	Ing Travel	Hardcover	$28.00	$5.60	8	9	8	$190,400
Bike Maine's Back Roads	Pedal Power Books	Hardcover	$22.99	$3.68	19	35	16	$183,920
Ireland: By Land and Sea	MacCarthy and Ray	Hardcover	$23.99	$4.56	9	15	7	$151,137
Irish Pubs 'Round the World	MacCarthy and Ray	Hardcover	$19.99	$3.39	14	20	9	$125,937
Belgium on Bicycle	Pedal Power Books	Hardcover	$25.99	$4.16	21	33	14	$109,158
Walking the Great Wall	Ing Travel	ebook	$14.99	$5.20	7	16	8	$83,944
Rollicking Through Rome	Ing Travel	ebook	$13.99	$5.31	2	4	4	$83,940
Peering at the Pyramids	Ing Travel	ebook	$14.99	$4.64	10	18	8	$71,952
Irish Pubs 'Round the World	MacCarthy and Ray	ebook	$9.99	$3.60	8	11	5	$59,940
Bike Maine's Back Roads	Pedal Power Books	ebook	$10.99	$3.84	14	29	12	$39,564
Belgium on Bicycle	Pedal Power Books	ebook	$9.99	$3.39	22	37	10	$27,970
My Blarney Stone Kiss	MacCarthy and Ray	ebook	$4.49	$0.53	50	76	3	$1,616

8. MacCarthy and Ray has books with the highest total retail sales in two formats.

   ○ True

   ○ False

Sort By [Number of Weeks on Sales Chart ▼]

Book Title	Publisher	Format	Retail Price	Publisher Profit per Book	Highest Sales Ranking	Current Sales Ranking	Number of Weeks on Sales Charts	Total Retail Sales to Date
Bike Maine's Back Roads	Pedal Power Books	Hardcover	$22.99	$3.68	19	35	16	$183,920
Belgium on Bicycle	Pedal Power Books	Hardcover	$25.99	$4.16	21	33	14	$109,158
Bike Maine's Back Roads	Pedal Power Books	Trade paperback	$14.99	$2.25	15	37	13	$94,435
Peering at the Pyramids	Ing Travel	Hardcover	$30.00	$7.20	5	11	12	$342,000
Walking the Great Wall	Ing Travel	Hardcover	$30.00	$7.50	3	10	12	$360,000
Bike Maine's Back Roads	Pedal Power Books	ebook	$10.99	$3.84	14	29	12	$39,564
Belgium on Bicycle	Pedal Power Books	Trade paperback	$15.99	$1.98	20	38	11	$35,178
Belgium on Bicycle	Pedal Power Books	ebook	$9.99	$3.39	22	37	10	$27,970
Irish Pubs 'Round the World	MacCarthy and Ray	Hardcover	$19.99	$3.39	14	20	9	$125,937
Peering at the Pyramids	Ing Travel	ebook	$14.99	$4.64	10	18	8	$71,952
Walking the Great Wall	Ing Travel	ebook	$14.99	$5.20	7	16	8	$83,944
Rollicking Through Rome	Ing Travel	Hardcover	$28.00	$5.60	8	9	8	$190,400
Walking the Great Wall	Ing Travel	Trade paperback	$18.00	$2.52	11	15	8	$144,000
Ireland: By Land and Sea	MacCarthy and Ray	Hardcover	$23.99	$4.56	9	15	7	$151,137
Irish Pubs 'Round the World	MacCarthy and Ray	ebook	$9.99	$3.60	8	11	5	$59,940
Irish Pubs 'Round the World	MacCarthy and Ray	Trade paperback	$13.99	$3.33	2	6	5	$156,895
Rollicking Through Rome	Ing Travel	ebook	$13.99	$5.31	2	4	4	$83,940
Rollicking Through Rome	Ing Travel	Trade paperback	$17.00	$3.06	3	3	4	$136,000
My Blarney Stone Kiss	MacCarthy and Ray	ebook	$4.49	$0.53	50	76	3	$1,616
My Blarney Stone Kiss	MacCarthy and Ray	Trade paperback	$6.49	$0.64	46	69	3	$1,557

9. Every book with at least 12 weeks on the sales charts has made at least $30,000 in total retail sales to date.

   O True

   O False

Sort By **Publisher** ▼

Book Title	Publisher	Format	Retail Price	Publisher Profit per Book	Highest Sales Ranking	Current Sales Ranking	Number of Weeks on Sales Charts	Total Retail Sales to Date
Rollicking Through Rome	Ing Travel	ebook	$13.99	$5.31	2	4	4	$83,940
Peering at the Pyramids	Ing Travel	ebook	$14.99	$4.64	10	18	8	$71,952
Walking the Great Wall	Ing Travel	ebook	$14.99	$5.20	7	16	8	$83,944
Rollicking Through Rome	Ing Travel	Hardcover	$28.00	$5.60	8	9	8	$190,400
Peering at the Pyramids	Ing Travel	Hardcover	$30.00	$7.20	5	11	12	$342,000
Walking the Great Wall	Ing Travel	Hardcover	$30.00	$7.50	3	10	12	$360,000
Rollicking Through Rome	Ing Travel	Trade paperback	$17.00	$3.06	3	3	4	$136,000
Walking the Great Wall	Ing Travel	Trade paperback	$18.00	$2.52	11	15	8	$144,000
My Blarney Stone Kiss	MacCarthy and Ray	ebook	$4.49	$0.53	50	76	3	$1,616
Irish Pubs 'Round the World	MacCarthy and Ray	ebook	$9.99	$3.60	8	11	5	$59,940
Irish Pubs 'Round the World	MacCarthy and Ray	Hardcover	$19.99	$3.39	14	20	9	$125,937
Ireland: By Land and Sea	MacCarthy and Ray	Hardcover	$23.99	$4.56	9	15	7	$151,137
My Blarney Stone Kiss	MacCarthy and Ray	Trade paperback	$6.49	$0.64	46	69	3	$1,557
Irish Pubs 'Round the World	MacCarthy and Ray	Trade paperback	$13.99	$3.33	2	6	5	$156,895
Belgium on Bicycle	Pedal Power Books	ebook	$9.99	$3.39	22	37	10	$27,970
Bike Maine's Back Roads	Pedal Power Books	ebook	$10.99	$3.84	14	29	12	$39,564
Bike Maine's Back Roads	Pedal Power Books	Hardcover	$22.99	$3.68	19	35	16	$183,920
Belgium on Bicycle	Pedal Power Books	Hardcover	$25.99	$4.16	21	33	14	$109,158
Bike Maine's Back Roads	Pedal Power Books	Trade paperback	$14.99	$2.25	15	37	13	$94,435
Belgium on Bicycle	Pedal Power Books	Trade paperback	$15.99	$1.98	20	38	11	$35,178

10. The total retail sales of Ing Travel's hardcover books is more than the total retail sales of MacCarthy and Ray's and Pedal Power Books' hardcovers and ebooks combined.

   o True

   o False

Answer Key

TABLE ANALYSIS PRACTICE

1. False
2. False
3. True
4. False
5. False
6. True
7. True
8. False
9. True
10. True

Answers and Explanations

TABLE ANALYSIS PRACTICE

1. False

Lone Tree Books' "Poison Was the Cure" has the highest retail profit per book ($4.63) in hardcover, Tumbler Books' "The Stocking Stalker" has the highest retail profit per book in mass-market paperback ($2.63), and J. Brint & Sons' "Text 'M' for More Murders" (at $3.51) has that rank in trade paperback.

2. False

Lone Tree Books's highest-ranked book was 14th.

3. True

Only four books have been on the charts for at least ten weeks ("'S' Is for Significant Stabbings" in trade paperback and hardcover, "The Killer Wore Killing Clothes" in mass-market paperback, and "Text 'M' for More Murders" in hardcover), and all of them have at least 30,000 sales to date.

4. False

"Text 'M' for More Murders" in hardcover sold fewer total copies, but its retail profit per book is much higher.

5. False

Here are the five companies meeting the criteria mentioned with their flat rates: Caravan Sarah (3.87), PDQ Delivery (3.15), Letter Fly (1.98), Box Populi (1.88), Parcelmouth (1.75). Of these, the median (or middle) value is Letter Fly at 1.98.

6. True

Parcelmouth (one pickup per day, flat rate 1.75) has a better rate than all other companies.

7. True

At $1.75 and $1.90, respectively, Parcelmouth offers the best rates.

8. False

MacCarthy and Ray's "Irish Pubs 'Round the World" had the highest sales in trade paperback, but Ing Travel had the highest sellers in hardcover ("Walking the Great Wall," $360,000) and in ebook ("Walking the Great Wall," $93,944).

9. True

The six books that have been on the sales charts for at least 12 weeks have all made at $30,000 to date: "Bike Maine's Back Roads" in three formats and "Peering at the Pyramids," "Walking the Great Wall," and "Belgium on Bicycle" in hardcover.

10. True

Ing Travel's total retail sales for hardcovers is $892,400. MacCarthy and Ray's and Pedal Power Books' total retail sales for both hardcovers and ebooks is $699,242.

Two-Part Analysis

Facility A and Facility B each have two machines installed, Machine 1 and Machine 2. Machine 1 can produce a shipment of goods in 4 hours on its own, and Machine 2 can produce a similar shipment in 2 hours on its own. Facility A uses both machines working separately, while Facility B has the machines working together at the same time.

1. Identify the smallest number of shipments of goods Facility A could make and the smallest number of shipments of goods Facility B could make after at least 12 hours of continuous work at each facility.

Facility A	Facility B	
O	O	8
O	O	9
O	O	12
O	O	15
O	O	16
O	O	18

2. Identify a number of shipments of goods that can be made at Facility A and a number of shipments of goods that can be made at Facility B after 16 hours of work, with any fractional shipments discarded at the end of each 8-hour shift.

Facility A	Facility B	
O	O	9
O	O	12
O	O	16
O	O	18
O	O	20
O	O	24

Company Z has two seasonal sales drives, Spring and Fall. The Spring sales drive last year sold an average of 3,000 units per week during its four-week push. The current Fall sales drive is expected to exceed Spring's sales drive by 4,000 units during its four-week push, despite only selling 1,000 units its first week, and next Spring's drive is expected to have a weekly average equal to half of the average of Fall's last three weeks.

3. Identify a number of sales that could occur during the third week of Fall's sales drive, and a number of sales that could occur during the third week of the next Spring sales drive, assuming that actual sales are close to average weekly sales.

Fall Sales Drive	Spring Sales Drive	
O	O	2,500
O	O	3,000
O	O	3,500
O	O	4,000
O	O	4,500
O	O	5,000

4. Identify the total number of sales for the Fall sales drive and the total number of sales for the next Spring sales drive.

Fall Sales Drive	Spring Sales Drive	
O	O	10,000
O	O	11,000
O	O	12,000
O	O	14,000
O	O	16,000
O	O	18,000

SmartWerks is hiring a project coordinator and is considering two candidates for the position, Petr and Ananth. Petr has a proven track record of completing projects 25% late and 30% under budget, while Ananth has a record of completing projects 10% early and 25% over budget. The company loses $1,000 for every week that its projects are late, and it saves $1,000 for every week that projects are early, with whatever fraction of a week remains counting as a full week.

5. Identify the expected final costs for Ananth and Petr, based on their previous performance, if they were each given a project that is expected to take 12 weeks and is expected to cost $50,000.

Ananth	Petr	
O	O	$25,500
O	O	$29,000
O	O	$31,500
O	O	$38,000
O	O	$45,000
O	O	$60,500

6. Identify the expected final costs for Ananth and Petr, based on their previous performance, if they were each given a project that is expected to take 2 weeks and is expected to cost $10,000.

Ananth	Petr	
O	O	$5,500
O	O	$6,333
O	O	$8,000
O	O	$10,500
O	O	$11,500
O	O	$12,333

Answers and explanations begin on the next page.

Answer Key

TWO-PART ANALYSIS

1. 9, 16
2. 12, 20
3. 5,000; 2,500
4. 16,000; 10,000
5. $60,500; $38,000
6. $11,500; $8,000

Answers and Explanations

TWO-PART ANALYSIS

1. 9, 16

Facility A has its machines producing separately, so in 4 hours, Machine 1 will produce one shipment of goods, and Machine 2 will produce two shipments of goods, so Facility A will produce 3 shipments every four hours, and 9 shipments in 12 hours.

Facility B has the machines working together, so their combined work will = (Machine 1)(Machine 2)/(Machine 1 + Machine 2) = (4 × 2)/(4 + 2) = 8/6 = 4/3 = 1⅓ shipments in an hour. Facility B will, therefore, produce 5⅓ shipments every 4 hours, or 16 shipments in 12 hours.

2. 12, 20

Facility A has its machines producing separately, so in 4 hours, Machine 1 will produce one shipment of goods, and Machine 2 will produce two shipments of goods, so Facility A will produce 3 shipments every 4 hours, and 12 shipments in 16 hours.

Facility B has the machines working together, so their combined work will = (Machine 1)(Machine 2)/(Machine 1 + Machine 2) = (4 × 2)/(4 + 2) = 8/6 = 4/3 = 1⅓ shipments in an hour. Facility B will, therefore, produce 5⅓ shipments every 4 hours, and 10⅔ shipments in 8 hours. The fractional shipment is discarded at the end of each 8-hour shift, so Facility B will produce 20 shipments in 16 hours.

3. 5,000; 2,500

During the last Spring drive, Company Z sold 3,000 units a week for 4 weeks, for a total of 12,000. Sales during the Fall drive are expected to exceed this (16,000), but during the first week, only 1,000 have been sold, so the company will need to average 5,000 per week for weeks 2–4. The next Spring drive will average half of that each week, or 2,500 per week. You may find it helpful to make a chart:

Week	Spring 1	Fall 1	Spring 2
1	3,000	1,000	2,500
2	3,000	5,000	2,500
3	3,000	5,000	2,500
4	3,000	5,000	2,500
Total	12,000	16,000	10,000

4. 16,000; 10,000

During the last Spring drive, Company Z sold 3,000 units per week for 4 weeks, totaling 12,000. The Fall drive is expected to exceed this total (16,000), but only 1,000 units have been sold so far; therefore, sales need to average 5,000 per week for weeks 2–4. The next Spring drive will average half of that each week, or 2,500. You may find it helpful to make a chart:

Week	Spring 1	Fall 1	Spring 2
1	3,000	1,000	2,500
2	3,000	5,000	2,500
3	3,000	5,000	2,500
4	3,000	5,000	2,500
Total	12,000	16,000	10,000

5. $60,500; $38,000

Petr will be 30% under budget, so his costs will start off at $35,000. He will also be 25% late on this 12-week project, so he will be done in 15 weeks, adding on $3,000 to costs for a total of $38,000.

Ananth will be 25% over budget, so his costs will start off at $62,500. He will also be 10% early, so he will be done 1.2 weeks ahead of schedule, saving $2,000 for a total of $60,500.

6. $11,500; $8,000

Petr will be 30% under budget, so his costs will start at $7,000. He will also be 25% late on this 2-week project, so he will be done in 2.5 weeks, adding $1,000 to the budget for a total of $8,000.

Ananth will be 25% over budget, so his costs will start at $12,500. He will also be 10% early, so he will be done 0.2 weeks ahead of schedule, saving $1,000 for a total of $11,500.

Chapter 5

Analytical Writing Assessment

Section Overview

ANALYTICAL WRITING ASSESSMENT PRACTICE

The Analytical Writing Assessment (AWA) is the first section of the GMAT. Once you begin the exam, you will be presented with the Analysis of an Argument essay assignment. You will have 30 minutes to read the prompt, organize your response, and complete the task.

For the essay, you will analyze a given topic and then type your essay into a simple word processing program. Spell check and grammar check functions are not available in the program, so you will have to check those things carefully yourself. One or two spelling errors or a few minor grammatical errors will not lower your score. But many spelling errors can hurt your score, as can errors that are serious enough to obscure your intended meaning.

Thirty minutes is not enough time to produce the same kind of essay you've written for college classes. Nor is it enough time to do a lot of trial and error as you type. It is, however, enough time to write a "strong first draft" if you plan carefully, and that's what the essay graders are looking for.

ESSAY FORMAT AND STRUCTURE

Your task for the Argument essay is to assess the logic and use of evidence in an argument. You need to explain the ways in which the author has failed to fully support that conclusion, regardless of whether you agree or disagree with the argument.

Let's take a look at a sample prompt:

> The following appeared in a report presented for discussion at a meeting of the directors of a company that manufactures parts for heavy machinery:
>
> > "The falling revenues that the company is experiencing coincide with delays in manufacturing. These delays, in turn, are due in large part to poor planning in purchasing metals. Consider further that the manager of the department that handles purchasing of raw materials has an excellent background in general business, psychology, and sociology but knows little about the properties of metals. The company should, therefore, move the purchasing manager to the sales department and bring in a scientist from the research division to be manager of the purchasing department."

> Consider how logical you find this argument. In your essay, be sure to discuss the line of reasoning and the use of evidence in the argument. For example, you may need to consider what questionable assumptions underlie the thinking and what alternative explanations or counterpoints might weaken the conclusion. You may also discuss what types of evidence would strengthen or refute the argument, what changes in the argument would make it more logically sound, and what, if anything, would help you better evaluate its conclusion.

Where are the holes in the argument? In what ways does it fail to be completely convincing? Why might the plan fail? Not only do you have to identify its major weaknesses, but you must also explain them.

SCORING

Unlike the total and scaled scores, Analytical Writing Assessment scores aren't available on Test Day. When you do get your score, it will take the form of a number from 1 to 6 in increments of 0.5 (you get a zero if you write off-topic or in a foreign language). Although you should strive for the best score possible, an essay graded 4 is "satisfactory," and an essay graded 3 is not.

AWA			
Percentile	**Score**	**Percentile**	**Score**
90%	6	10%	3.5
77%	5.5	6%	3
57%	5	4%	2-2.5
39%	4.5	3%	0.5-1.5
20%	4	0%	0

Percentiles vs. Scaled Scores for the AWA

Percentiles give a slightly different perspective on the AWA. To break the median, you have to score a 5 or higher. Few programs, though, seem to use the AWA score to differentiate candidate competitiveness. It's more of a reality check against the writing skills that you demonstrate in your application essays.

Analytical Writing Assessment

1. Discuss how well reasoned you find the following arguments. In your discussion be sure to analyze the line of reasoning and the use of evidence in the argument. For example, you may need to consider what questionable assumptions underlie the thinking and what alternative explanations or counterexamples might weaken the conclusion. You can also discuss what sort of evidence would strengthen or refute the argument, what changes in the argument would make it more logically sound, and what, if anything, would help you better evaluate its conclusion.

   The following appeared in a regional fitness journal:

   > "A recent survey of this journal's readers found that over 80% are or plan to be on a low-carbohydrate diet. This should serve as a warning to restaurants in our region. If they do not add low-carbohydrate meals to their menus, they could stand to lose 80% of their business."

2. Discuss how well reasoned you find the following arguments. In your discussion be sure to analyze the line of reasoning and the use of evidence in the argument. For example, you may need to consider what questionable assumptions underlie the thinking and what alternative explanations or counterexamples might weaken the conclusion. You can also discuss what sort of evidence would strengthen or refute the argument, what changes in the argument would make it more logically sound, and what, if anything, would help you better evaluate its conclusion.

   The following appeared as part of a promotional campaign to sell advertising on channels provided by the local cable television company:

   > "Advertising with Cable Communications Corp. is a great way to increase your profits. Recently the Adams Car Dealership began advertising with Cable Communications, and over the last 30 days, sales are up 15% over the previous month. Let us increase your profits, just as we did for Adams Cars!"

Answers and Explanations

ANALYTICAL WRITING ASSESSMENT

Sample Essay 1

The author of this argument suggests that restaurants need to add low-carbohydrate meals to their menus or they could lose 80% of their business. As evidence to back up this conclusion, the author notes that a recent survey of the journal's readers found that 80% are or plan to be on a low-carbohydrate diet. The conclusion is not valid, however, because the argument contains a serious flaw in logic—namely that the readers of a fitness journal are representative of all people in the region. In addition, the argument has a number of flaws in logic that need to be redressed with additional evidence.

The logical flaw in the argument revolves around the evidence used by the author. He or she cites a survey of the readers of a fitness journal in order to draw a conclusion about all restaurant patrons in the region. This is a problematic logical leap. There is no reason for restaurant owners to believe that fitness journal subscribers behave as the general population does. Just because 80% of the readers of the fitness journal are already on or are considering a low-carbohydrate diet does not mean that the same is true of the general population. Therefore, there is no reason to believe that 80% of restaurant patrons will be looking for low-carbohydrate meals. In order to correct this flaw, the author needs to show evidence that the readers of the journal do behave as the rest of the population does, or include other evidence showing that 80% of all restaurant patrons are looking for low-carbohydrate options. If the author cannot offer either of these pieces of information, he or she needs to qualify her conclusion.

The argument is also plagued by gaps in logic. Without further evidence to shore up the argument, it becomes difficult to evaluate the author's conclusion. The first such gap is the implicit belief that the low-carbohydrate diet craze has not already affected the restaurant industry.

Some portion of the 80% cited by the author is already on low-carbohydrate diets and presumably has been for some time. Restaurants may already have lost business due to this phenomenon and, therefore, do not stand to lose an additional 80% of business. In order to better evaluate the conclusion, the author should provide additional details on the breakdown of the 80% and how long people have been on the diet.

A second gap in logic is the notion that restaurants do not already have a sufficient amount of low-carbohydrate options. It could be that subscribers to the low-carbohydrate diet are proficient at finding low-carbohydrate meals on just about any menu. Alternatively, the dieters could also be happy eating only the low-carbohydrate components of any standard entrée. To support her conclusion, the author should show evidence that the dieters are not satisfied with the low-carbohydrate options now offered and that this may prevent them from eating out.

Finally, the author needs to support the implication that low-carbohydrate dieters actually stick to their diets when they eat out. It could be that the dieters use restaurant experiences as a time to cheat on the diet. If this were true, then restaurants need not worry about losing business. The author needs to offer evidence that the dieters keep to their diets while eating out.

In summary, it is difficult to accept the conclusion that restaurants in the region risk losing 80% of their business if they do not add low-carbohydrate options to their menus given the current state of the author's argument. In order to craft a better argument, the author should first eliminate her logical flaw by not drawing a conclusion regarding all restaurant patrons from evidence about only one sub-group of the population. The author also needs to provide additional evidence about the low-carbohydrate dieters and their needs in order to not leave large lapses in logic.

Sample Essay 2

The promotional campaign by Cable Communications Corporation argues that all businesses would benefit from advertising with the cable television company in the form of increased profitability. As evidence to back up this assertion, the promotional campaign notes the experience of the Adams Car Dealership, a recent advertiser with Cable Communications Corporation. Over the last 30 days, Adams Cars has seen a 15% increase in sales over the previous month. The argument as it now stands is unconvincing because it is missing evidence that would make the argument more well reasoned and also suffers from poorly defined vocabulary, which makes the argument less easy to understand.

The argument presupposes that the example of the Adams Car Dealership is relevant for other businesses. It could be that there is a particular advantage from advertising for car dealerships because car buyers are willing to travel around to buy a car. The same may not be said, for example, of a dry cleaner. In general, people will take their dry cleaning business to the closest dry cleaner because it is a commodity service and a relatively small expenditure. Thus, advertising would be much more effective for a car dealership than a dry cleaner.

In order to convince business owners that they should advertise with Cable Communications, the promotional campaign should show additional evidence from a wide variety of business that have benefited by advertising with the company. The argument presupposes that the 15% increase in sales at Adams Car Dealership is a direct result of the recent advertising campaign with Cable Communications Corporation. It could be that the dealership had announced a sale for this month or that the previous month's sales were sea- sonably low—for example sales in March might always be better than sales in February due to some exogenous factor. In order to better believe that Adams benefited from the advertising campaign with Cable Communications, business owners need evidence that there was not some other factor causing the 15% increase. Perhaps evidence could be shown comparing the last 30 days' sales with those of the same period in the previous year, or the last time the dealership was running the same promotions.

The final area of presupposition is that business owners do not have a better option for advertising. A company may get a higher increase in profits by advertising in print media or the phone book. In order for business owners to make an informed decision regarding their advertising expenditures, they need to see a comparison between Cable Communication's offering and the offerings of other advertising outlets.

The argument also suffers from poorly defined vocabulary. The first piece of such vocabulary is the word "recently." From just this word, it is impossible to tell when the advertising began. If Adam's advertising began three months ago, it would not be very impressive that sales increased 15% between month two and month three of the advertising campaign. Why would there not have been a boost before the most recent month? If the promotional campaign told business owners exactly when Adams began advertising, the owners would have a better ability to evaluate the argument's conclusion.

The author should also clarify the phrase "increase your profits." The promotional campaign's argument gives no details on the fees associated with advertising with Cable Communications. If Adams Cars had to develop an ad and pay large sums to Cable Communications to run the ad, the total cost of advertising with the cable company very well may have exceeded the additional profits derived from increased sales. Without additional information in this regard, business owners cannot possibly evaluate the argument's conclusion.

In order to craft a well-reasoned argument, the promotional campaign by Cable Communications needs to better define its vocabulary and offer more evidence. To better convince business owners of the benefits of advertising with Cable Communications, the company should provide additional details regarding the relevance of cable advertising to multiple business types, the exact nature of Adams's increase in sales, the ability of cable advertising to outperform other forms of advertising, and the true costs of advertising with Cable Communications. With this additional information, the promotional campaign would be much more convincing when it concludes that advertising with Cable Communications is a great way to increase a business's profits.

Chapter 6

Getting Ready for Test Day

GMAT Checklist

The GMAT is offered by appointment, at your convenience, almost every day of the year. You will be required to register online before making an appointment.

CHOOSE A TESTING CENTER

Before you register, find a testing center that's convenient for you and determine whether that site has available seats. Each testing center operates on its own schedule and can accommodate varying numbers of test takers. To locate a testing center near you, go to mba.com.

REGISTER AND SCHEDULE YOUR APPOINTMENT

Available time slots change continuously as people register for the test. You will find out what times are available at your chosen testing center when you register. You may be able to schedule an appointment within a few days of your desired test date, but popular dates (especially weekends) fill up quickly. Admissions deadlines for business schools vary. Check with the schools and make your test appointment early enough to allow your scores to be reported before the schools' application deadlines.

You may register and schedule your appointment online, by phone, by mail, or by fax. For more details on registration, go to mba.com.

THE DAY OF THE TEST

You should arrive at your testing center 30 minutes before the time of your scheduled appointment. You must complete a number of security measures before you will be allowed to take the exam.

A late arrival (15 minutes or more) may result in you being turned away from the testing center and forfeiting of your test fee.

PROHIBITED ITEMS

The following items cannot be brought into the testing room:

- Electronics such as cell phones, media players, personal data assistants (PDAs), cameras, radios, and photographic devices
- Any timepieces, including wristwatches, stopwatches, and watch alarms
- Notes, scratch paper, books, pamphlets, dictionaries, translators, and thesauruses
- Pens and pencils
- Measuring tools such as rulers
- Calculators and watch calculators

Essentially, you can't bring anything that may cause distractions, provide aid during testing, or be used to remove exam content from the testing room. It is possible that your testing center has storage space available, such as lockers, where you can leave possessions that are prohibited from the testing room. However, this may not be the case at all centers. Call your testing center to inquire about storage and plan accordingly.

BREAKS

The length of your appointment is approximately four hours. Two breaks are scheduled in the exam—one after the Integrated Reasoning section and another after the Quantitative section. If you exceed the allotted break time, the excess time will be deducted from the next section of your exam. For more information on administrative regulations and testing procedures, visit mba.com.

THE WEEK BEFORE TEST DAY

As Test Day approaches, you may find your anxiety is on the rise. You shouldn't worry. After the preparation you've received from this book, you're in good shape for the test. To calm any jitters you may have, though, let's go over a few strategies for the couple of days before the test. In the week or so leading up to Test Day, you should do the following:

- Visit the testing center. Sometimes seeing the actual room where your test will be administered and taking notice of little things—such as the kind of desk you'll be working on, whether the room is likely to be hot or cold, etc.—may help to calm your nerves. And if you've never been to the testing center, visiting beforehand is a good way to ensure that you don't get lost on Test Day. If you can go on the same day of the week and at the same time of day as your actual test, so much the better; you'll be able to scope out traffic

patterns and parking. Remember, on Test Day you must be on time—the computers at the testing centers are booked all day long.
- Practice working on test material, preferably a full-length test, at the same time of day that your test is scheduled for. Treat this experience as if it were the real Test Day.
- Time yourself while practicing so you don't feel as though you are rushing on Test Day.
- Evaluate thoroughly where you stand. Use the time remaining before the test to shore up your weak points. But make sure not to neglect your strong areas; after all, those are where you'll rack up most of your points.

THE DAY BEFORE TEST DAY

This advice might seem counterintuitive, but try to avoid intensive studying the day before the test. There's little you can do to improve your score at this late date, and you may just wind up exhausting yourself and burning out. Our advice is to review a few key concepts, get together everything you'll need for Test Day (acceptable photo identification, the names of schools to which you'd like to send your GMAT scores, directions to the testing center, a healthy snack for the break), and then take the night off entirely. Go to see a movie, stream a video, or watch some TV. Try not to think too much about the test; just relax and store up some energy for the big day.

ON TEST DAY

Test Day should contain no surprises. Test takers who feel in control of the events leading up to the test take that confidence with them into the testing center.

Leave early for the testing center, giving yourself plenty of time. Read something to warm up your brain; you don't want the GMAT to be the first written material your brain tries to assimilate that day. Dress in layers for maximum comfort. That way, you'll be able to adjust to the testing room's temperature. In traveling to the testing center, leave yourself enough time for traffic or mass transit delays.

Be ready for a long day. Total testing time, remember, is three and a half hours. When you add the administrative paperwork before and after, and the two eight-minute breaks, you're looking at an experience of four hours or more.

You will feel most prepared and confident if you have an understanding of how the logistics of Test Day will play out.

Here are some strategic reminders to help guide your work on Test Day:

- Read each question stem carefully and reread it before making your final selection.
- Don't get bogged down in the middle of any section. You may find later questions more to your liking. So don't panic. Eliminate answer choices, guess, and move on.
- Don't fall behind early. Even if you get most of the first 10 questions right, you'll wind up rushing yourself into enough errors that you cancel out your early success. Keep a steady pace throughout the test and finish each section strong, avoiding the penalty for not completing all the questions.

After Test Day, you should . . .

- Congratulate yourself for all the hard work you've put in. Make sure you celebrate afterward—and start thinking about all of the great times you'll be having at the business school of your choice!
- Plan your approach to business school applications, including references and essays.
- Expect to wait approximately 20 days for your Official Score Report (which includes your Analytical Writing score) to be posted online.